Rural Social Movements in Latin America

UNIVERSITY PRESS OF FLORIDA

Florida A&M University, Tallahassee
Florida Atlantic University, Boca Raton
Florida Gulf Coast University, Ft. Myers
Florida International University, Miami
Florida State University, Tallahassee
New College of Florida, Sarasota
University of Central Florida, Orlando
University of Florida, Gainesville
University of North Florida, Jacksonville
University of South Florida, Tampa
University of West Florida, Pensacola

Rural Social Movements in Latin America

Organizing for Sustainable Livelihoods

EDITED BY

CARMEN DIANA DEERE AND FREDERICK S. ROYCE

University Press of Florida
Gainesville/Tallahassee/Tampa/Boca Raton
Pensacola/Orlando/Miami/Jacksonville/Ft. Myers/Sarasota

Copyright 2009 by the University of Florida Center for Latin American Studies
Printed in the United States of America. This book is printed on Glatfelter
Natures Book, a paper certified under the standards of the Forestry Stewardship
Council (FSC). It is a recycled stock that contains 30 percent post-consumer
waste and is acid-free.

14   13   12   11   10   09   6   5   4   3   2   1

Library of Congress Cataloging-in-Publication Data
Rural social movements in Latin America : organizing for sustainable livelihoods
/ edited by Carmen Diana Deere and Frederick S. Royce.
p. cm.
Includes bibliographical references and index.
ISBN 978-0-8130-3332-7 (alk. paper)
1. Social movements—Latin America. 2. Rural development—Latin America.
3. Sustainable development—Latin America. 4. Latin America—Rural
conditions. I. Deere, Carmen Diana. II. Royce, Frederick S.
HN110.5.A8R87 2009
303.48'4098091734—dc22   2009001938

The University Press of Florida is the scholarly publishing agency for the State
University System of Florida, comprising Florida A&M University, Florida At-
lantic University, Florida Gulf Coast University, Florida International University,
Florida State University, New College of Florida, University of Central Florida,
University of Florida, University of North Florida, University of South Florida,
and University of West Florida.

University Press of Florida
15 Northwest 15th Street
Gainesville, FL 32611-2079
www.upf.com

Contents

Figures

Tables

Abbreviations and Acronyms

AICO	Autoridades Indígenas de Colombia (Movement of Indigenous Authorities of Colombia)
ALBA	Alternativa Bolivariana para América Latina y El Caribe (Bolivarian Alternative for Latin America and the Caribbean)
AMLAE	Asociación de Mujeres Nicaragüenses Luisa Amanda Espinoza (Luisa Amanda Espinoza Association of Nicaraguan Women)
ANAMURI	Asociación Nacional de Mujeres Rurales e Indígenas (National Association of Rural and Indigenous Women, Chile)
ANAP	Asociación Nacional de Agricultores Pequeños (National Association of Small Farmers, Cuba)
ANIPA	Asamblea Nacional Indígena Plural por la Autonomía (Plural National Indigenous Assembly for Autonomy, Mexico)
ANMTR	Articulação Nacional de Mulheres Trabalhadoras Rurais (National Articulation of Rural Women Workers, Brazil)
ANMUCIC	Asociación Nacional de Mujeres Campesinas e Indígenas de Colombia (National Association of Peasant and Indigenous Women of Colombia)
ANUC	Asociación Nacional de Usuarios Campesinos (National Association of Peasant Beneficiaries, Colombia)
ANUC-UR	Asociación Nacional de Usuarios Campesinos-Unidad y Reconstrucción (National Association of Peasant Beneficiaries-Unity and Reconstruction, Colombia)
APPO	Asamblea Popular de los Pueblos de Oaxaca (Popular Assembly of the Peoples of Oaxaca, Mexico)
ASAPROM	Asamblea de Productores Mixes (Assembly of Mixe Producers, Oaxaca, Mexico)

ASOCODE   Asociación Centroamericana de Organizaciones Campesinas para la Cooperación y el Desarrollo (Central American Association of Peasant Organizations for Cooperation and Development)

ATC   Asociación de Trabajadores del Campo (Association of Rural Workers, Nicaragua)

ATOs   Alternative trade organizations

AUC   Autodefensas Unidas de Colombia (United Self-defense Forces of Colombia)

CAFTA   Central American Free Trade Agreement

CAOI   Coordinación Andina de Organizaciones Indígenas (Andean Coordinator of Indigenous Organizations)

CECCAM   Centro de Estudios para el Cambio en el Campo Mexicano (Center for the Study of Change in the Mexican Countryside, Oaxaca, Mexico)

CHESF   Companhia Hidrelétrica do São Francisco (São Francisco Hydroelectric Company, Brazil)

CIDOB   Confederación de Pueblos Indígenas de Bolivia (Confederation of Indigenous Peoples of Bolivia)

CIOAC   Central Independiente de Obreros Agrícolas y Campesinos (Independent Central Union of Agricultural Workers and Peasants, Mexico)

CIW   Coalition of Immokalee Workers, Florida, United States

CLAC   Coordinadora Latinoamericana y del Caribe de Pequeños Productores de Comerico Justo (Latin American and Caribbean Network of Small Fair Trade Producers)

CLOC   Coordinadora Latinoamericana de Organizaciones del Campo (Latin American Coordinator of Rural Organizations)

CNC   Confederación Nacional Campesina (National Peasant Confederation, Mexico)

CNI   Congreso Nacional Indígena (National Indigenous Congress, Mexico)

CNPA   Coordinadora Nacional Plan de Ayala (Plan of Ayala National Coordinator, Mexico)

CNS   Conselho Nacional dos Seringueiros (National Council of Rubber Tappers, Brazil)

COB   Central Obrero Boliviano (Central Workers' Union of Bolivia)

COCAMTROP	Coordinadora Campesina de Mujeres del Trópico (Coordinator of Peasant Women of the Tropics, Bolivia)
COCEI	Coalición Obrero Campesino Estudiantil del Istmo (Coalition of Workers, Peasants, and Students of the Isthmus, Oaxaca, Mexico)
COCOCH	Consejo Coordinador de Organizaciones Campesinas de Honduras (Coordinating Council of Peasant Organizations of Honduras)
COI	Congreso de Organizaciones Indias de Centroamérica, México, y Panamá (Congress of Indian Organizations of Central America, Mexico, and Panama)
COICA	Coordinadora Indígena de la Cuenca Amazonica (Indigenous Coordinator of the Amazon Basin)
COLACOT	Confederación Latinoamericana de Cooperativas y Mutuales de Trabajadores (Latin American Confederation of Cooperatives and Mutual Societies)
COLSIBA	Coordinadora Latinoamericana de Sindicatos Bananeros (Latin American Coordinator of Banana Unions)
CONACAMI	Confederación Nacional de Comunidades Afectadas por la Minería (National Confederation of Communities Affected by Mining, Peru)
CONAIE	Confederación de Nacionalidades Indígenas del Ecuador (Confederation of Indigenous Nationalities of Ecuador)
CONAMUCA	Confederación Nacional de Mujeres del Campo (National Confederation of Rural Women, Dominican Republic)
CONASUPO	Compañía Nacional de Subsistencias Populares (National Company of Popular Consumption, Mexico)
CONFENIAE	Confederación de Nacionalidades Indígenas de la Amazonía Ecuatoriana (Confederation of Indigenous Nationalities of the Ecuadorean Amazon)
CONFEUNASSC	Confederación Unica Nacional de Afiliados al Seguro Campesino (National Unitary Confederation of Affiliates to the Peasant Social Security System, Ecuador)
CONIC	Coordinadora de Organizaciones y Naciones Indígenas del Continente (Coordinator of Indigenous Organizations and Nations of the Continent)
CONIC-Guatemala	Coordinadora Nacional Indígena y Campesina-Guatemala (National Indigenous and Peasant Coordinator, Guatemala)

CONTAG	Confederação Nacional dos Trabalhadores na Agricultura (National Confederation of Agricultural Workers, Brazil)
COPPIP	Conferencia Permanente de Pueblos Indígenas del Perú (Permanent Conference of Indigenous Peoples of Peru)
CPE	Coordination Paysanne Européenne/Coordinación Campesina Europea (European Peasant Coordinator)
CPT	Comissão Pastoral da Terra (Pastoral Land Commission, Brazil)
CRAB	Comissão Regional de Atingidos por Barragems (Regional Commission of People Affected by Dams, Brazil)
CRIC	Consejo Regional Indígena del Cauca (Regional Indigenous Council of Cauca, Colombia)
CSCB	Confederación Sindical de Colonizadores de Bolivia (Syndical Confederation of Bolivian Colonists)
CSUTCB	Confederación Sindical Única de Trabajadores Campesinos de Bolivia (Confederation of Peasant Workers of Bolivia)
CUT	Central Única dos Trabalhadores (Central Workers' Union, Brazil)
DNTR/CUT	Departamento Nacional dos Trabalhadores Rurais do CUT (National Department of Rural Workers of the CUT, Brazil)
ECUARUNARI	Ecuador Runacunapac Riccharimui. Confederación de los Pueblos de Nacionalidad Kichua del Ecuador (Confederation of Quichua Peoples of Ecuador)
ELN	Ejercito de Liberación Nacional (National Liberation Army, Colombia)
EZLN	Ejercito Zapatista de Liberación Nacional (Zapatista National Liberation Army, Mexico)
FAO	Food and Agriculture Organization of the United Nations
FARC	Fuerzas Armadas Revolucionarias Colombianas (Colombian Revolutionary Armed Forces)
FASE	Federação de Órgãos para Assistência Social e Educacional (Federation of Agencies for Social and Educational Assistance, Brazil)
FEJUVE	Federación de Juntas Vecinales (Federation of Neighborhood Committees, El Alto, Bolivia)
FEMUPROCAN	Federación Agropecuaria de Cooperativas de Mujeres

	Productoras del Campo de Nicaragua (Federation of Agricultural Cooperatives of Rural Women Producers of Nicaragua)
FENOCIN	Federación Nacional de Organizaciones Campesinas, Indígenas, y Negras del Ecuador (National Federation of Peasant, Indigenous, and Black Organizations of Ecuador)
FIOB	Frente Indígena de Organizaciones Binacionales (Binational Front of Indigenous Organizations, Mexico and United States [formerly Oaxaca Indigenous Binational Front, preceded by FM-ZB])
FLO	Fairtrade Labeling Organizations International
FLOC	Farm Labor Organizing Committee, United States
FM-ZB	Frente Mixteco-Zapoteco Binacional (Mixtec-Zapotec Binational Front, Mexico and United States)
FNMCB-BS	Federación Nacional de Mujeres Campesinas Bolivianas "Bartolina Sisa" (Bartolina Sisa National Federation of Bolivian Peasant Women)
FNO	Fondo Constitucional de Financiamento do Norte (Constitutional Fund for Financing of the North, Brazil)
FRENAPI	Frente Nacional de Pueblos Indios (Indigenous Peoples' National Front, Mexico)
FSLN	Frente Sandinista de Liberación Nacional (Sandinista National Liberation Front, Nicaragua)
FTAA	Free Trade Area of the Americas
FTF	Fair Trade Federation
GATT	General Agreement on Trade and Tariffs
GMCR	Green Mountain Coffee Roasters
GTZ	Deutsche Gesellschaft für Technische Zusammenarbelt (German Agency for Technical Cooperation)
HTA	Hometown associations
IBAMA	Instituto Brasileiro do Meio Ambiente e dos Recursos Naturais Renováveis (Brazilian Institute of the Environment and Renewable Resources)
ICT	Internet communications technologies
IDRC	International Development Research Centre, Canada
IFAT	International Federation for Alternative Trade
ILO	International Labour Organization of the United Nations
IMF	International Monetary Fund

INCORA   Instituto Colombiano de Reforma Agraria (Colombian
              Institute of Agrarian Reform)
INCRA   Instituto Nacional de Colonização e Reforma Agrária
              (National Institute for Colonization and Agrarian Reform,
              Brazil)
INRA   Instituto Nacional de Reforma Agraria (National Institute
              of Agrarian Reform, Bolivia)
IOAM   Instituto Oaxaqueño de Atención al Migrante (Oaxacan
              Institute for Attention to the Migrant, Mexico)
IPAM   Instituto de Pesquisa Ambiental da Amazônia (Amazo-
              nian Institute for Environmental Research, Brazil)
MAB   Movimento dos Atingidos por Barragens (Movement of
              People Affected by Dams, Brazil)
MAS   Movimiento al Socialismo (Movements Toward Socialism,
              Bolivia)
MDTX   Movimento para o Desenvolvimento da Transamazônica
              e do Xingu (Movement for Development of the Transam-
              azon and Xingu, Brazil)
MIP   Movimiento Indígena Pachakutec (Pachakutec Indigenous
              Movement, Bolivia)
MLP   Mujeres Luchadores Progresistas (Women Fighting for
              Progress, Oregon, United States)
MNR   Movimiento Nacional Revolucionario (National Revolu-
              tionary Movement, Bolivia)
MST   Movimento dos Trabalhadores Rurais Sem Terra (Land-
              less Rural Workers' Movement, Brazil)
MST-Bolivia   Movimiento de los Trabajadores Campesinos Indígenas
              Sin Tierra de Bolivia (Indigenous, Peasant and Landless
              Workers Movement of Bolivia)
NAFTA   North American Free Trade Agreement
NFFC   National Family Farm Coalition, United States
NFU   National Farmers Union, Canada
NGO   Non-governmental organization
ONIC   Organización Nacional Indígena de Colombia (National
              Indigenous Organization of Colombia)
PCUN   Pineros y Campesinos Unidos del Nordoeste (Northwest
              Treeplanters and Farmworkers United, Oregon, United
              States)

PRI   Partido Revolucionario Institucional (Institutionalized
                    Revolutionary Party, Mexico)
PROAMBIENTE Programa de Desenvolvimento Socioambiental da
                    Produção Familiar Rural (Program for the Socioenviron-
                    mental Development of Rural Family Production, Brazil)
PSDB   Partido da Social Democracia Brasileira (Brazilian Social
                    Democracy Party)
PT   Partido dos Trabalhadores (Workers' Party, Brazil)
RITA   Red Indígena de Turismo de México, A.C. (Indigenous
                    Tourist Network of Mexico)
RITS   Rede de Informações para o Terceiro Setor (Information
                    Network for the Third Sector, Brazil)
SECO   Staatssekretariat für Wirtschaft (State Secretariat for Eco-
                    nomic Affairs, Switzerland)
SER   Servicios del Pueblo Mixe (Services of the Mixe People
                    [NGO], Oaxaca, Mexico)
SERRV   Sales Exchange for Refugee Rehabilitation Vocation (inter-
                    national)
SFL   Sustainable Food Laboratory
SNC   Sistema Nacional de Unidades de Conservação (National
                    System of Conservation Units, Brazil)
TCP   Tratado de Comercio de los Pueblos (Trade Agreement of
                    the Peoples)
UCIZONI   Unión de Comunidades Indígenas de la Zona Norte del
                    Istmo (Union of Indigenous Communities of the Northern
                    Zone of the Isthmus, Oaxaca, Mexico)
UFW   United Farm Workers, United States
UNAG   Unión Nacional de Agricultores y Ganaderos (National
                    Union of Farmers and Ranchers, Nicaragua)
UNICEF   United Nations Children's Fund
UNORCA   Unión Nacional de Organizaciones Regionales Campesi-
                    nas Autónomas (National Union of Regional Autonomous
                    Peasant Organizations, Mexico)
USLEAP   United States Labor Education in the Americas Project
WINFA   Windward Islands Farmers' Association
WTO   World Trade Organization
WVIP   Willamette Valley Immigration Project, Oregon, United
                    States

Acknowledgments

This book grew out of a conference on the alternative visions of development of the Latin American rural social movements held at the University of Florida, February 23–25, 2006. Rural social movement leaders from Bolivia, Brazil, Guatemala, Mexico, Nicaragua, Peru, and the United States participated in the conference in addition to academics and scholar activists from Brazil, Canada, Colombia, Mexico, and the United States. Purposely invited to the conference were social movement leaders of organizations that were members of the Latin American Coordinator of Rural Organizations (CLOC) and La Vía Campesina as well as leaders of social movements, such as the continental indigenous movement, who were not members of these transnational organizations.

A highlight of the conference was learning about the alternative visions that unite these rural social movements as well as the points of disagreement and tension between them. Another was exploring the impact of hemispheric connections and linkages—specifically, international migration, the fair trade movement, and the Internet revolution—on the viability and strengthening of Latin American rural social movements. This volume is unusual in that it brings together the analyses of researchers of social movements with the voices of the leadership of many of these organizations.

We wish to thank the other members of the conference planning committee, Hanna Covert, Cristina Espinoza, Victoria Gómez de la Torre, Tony Oliver-Smith, and Anna Peterson, for their efforts in bringing together such a dynamic group of social movement leaders and scholars. We are also grateful to the other conference participants for their input, particularly Deborah Barry, David Bray, Robert Reinauer and the representatives of the Florida-based Coalition of Immokalee Workers.

The conference, which was the fifty-fifth annual conference of the University of Florida Center for Latin American Studies, was partially supported, as was the preparation of this book, by a grant from the Ford Foundation, Mexico City; by the Department of Education, Title VI grant to the

Florida Consortium of Latin American and Caribbean Studies; and by the University of Florida International Center, the Transnational and Global Studies Center, and the Office of the Vice President for Research.

Finally, we greatly acknowledge the assistance of Eleanor Lewis, Jacob Schultz, and Jessica Caicedo of the Center for Latin American Studies in preparing the manuscript for publication.

Introduction

The Rise and Impact of National and Transnational Rural Social Movements in Latin America

CARMEN DIANA DEERE AND FREDERICK S. ROYCE

There is little question but that the rural social movements are currently among the most dynamic social movements in the Americas. Whether in Seattle, Cancún, or Mar del Plata—cities now immortalized because of the large protests that took place there either against the World Trade Organization (WTO) or the Free Trade Area of the Americas (FTAA)—Latin American rural social movements have been among those in the lead in denouncing the exclusionary character of neoliberal globalization. As the essays in this volume show, the current dynamism of the rural social movements is in large measure related to the unprecedented attack on rural livelihoods unleashed by the neoliberal model of development. The repercussions of the neoliberal assault on natural resources—land, forests, water, and minerals—have been particularly severe for those whose livelihoods depend upon them.

Since the 1980s new national-level rural organizations have emerged throughout the region and represent sectors previously excluded from the main peasant organizations and rural unions of the past, such as the indigenous, landless, environmental, and rural women's movements. In the 1990s a number of new, national, rural social movements arose in opposition to large-scale development projects such as dam construction and mining. Moreover, after a period of relative decline, some of the long-standing national peasant organizations and rural unions revitalized while new peasant organizations formed. Further, since the 1990s many of these organizations have joined together to build transnational social movement organizations and associations at the subregional, hemispheric, and global levels. As a result, the rural social movements in Latin America have emerged as among the best organized as well as the most fervent critics of the neoliberal model of development in the region (Petras and Veltmeyer 2001).

Currently, the main transnational, social movement organizations are three: the Latin American Coordinator of Rural Organizations (CLOC); the Continental Coordination of Indigenous Nationalities and Peoples of Abya Yala; and La Vía Campesina, the international association that brings together organizations of small and medium farmers, agricultural workers, rural women, and indigenous peoples from four continents. The catalysts for the formation of these transnational organizations were events surrounding 1992, the quincentenary of the discovery of the Americas.

In 1989 at the First Latin American Meeting of Peasant and Indigenous Organizations in Bogotá, Colombia, activities denouncing the quincentenary took on the name "500 Years of Indigenous and Popular Resistance" campaign.[1] Subsequent meetings in support of the campaign—known as Encuentros Continentales—took place in Guatemala in 1991 and Nicaragua in 1992. The latter was the largest hemispheric meeting to date of indigenous peoples, peasants, and rural workers, with 668 delegates from 26 countries in attendance. It resulted in the decision to construct a broader continental movement, the Indigenous, Black, Popular, and Peasant Continental Movement, as well as a regional organization, CLOC, with the specific goal of confronting neoliberalism through joint actions throughout the Americas. The founding congress of CLOC was held in Peru in 1994 (CLOC 1997). In terms of scope, some 88 rural organizations from 25 Latin American countries attended CLOC's fourth congress in Guatemala in 2005 (see chapter 3).

The trajectory of the continental indigenous movement parallels that of CLOC and while membership in the two movements overlaps to a certain extent, its history is punctuated by the objective of forming its own autonomous, continental indigenous association. In July 1990, shortly after the meeting in Bogotá in 1989, the Confederation of Indigenous Nationalities of Ecuador (CONAIE) and others convoked a meeting in Quito limited to indigenous representatives. This meeting, the First Continental Meeting of Indian Peoples, was attended by representatives of some 120 indigenous nations of the Americas. In the "Declaration of Quito" these organizations affirmed the specificity of their demands in the "500 Years of Resistance" campaign and that their top priority was the demand for indigenous autonomy and self- determination ("Declaración de Quito" 1990). Soon after, they formed their own hemispheric indigenous association, the Coordinator of Indigenous Organizations and Nations of the Continent (CONIC).

While a number of indigenous organizations attended the *encuentros* of 1991 and 1992 that led to the formation of CLOC, they continued to meet separately, holding the Second Continental Meeting of Indigenous Peoples in Temoaya, Mexico in 1993. Coinciding with the UN International Year of the World's Indigenous Peoples, this meeting was organized by CONIC and attended by representatives of some twenty-six indigenous nations and organizations ("Temoaya Declaration" 1993). After a hiatus, the process of continental meetings resumed in the new millennium, with continental indigenous summits being held in 2000 (Teotihuacan, Mexico), 2004 (Quito), and 2007 (Tecpán, Guatemala). It was at this latter summit, attended by some two thousand delegates from twenty countries, that the Continental Coordination of Indigenous Nationalities and Peoples of Abya Yala was formed.[2]

The origins of La Vía Campesina also date from the early 1990s. In 1992 representatives of peasant and farmer organizations from Central America,[3] North America, and Europe attended the second congress of the Nicaraguan National Union of Farmers and Ranchers (UNAG) in Managua as observers. Discussions there led to the call for the first congress of La Vía Campesina in Mons, Belgium in 1993, where it was officially constituted as a transnational organization of rural social movements. La Vía Campesina's last congress in 2004 was attended by representatives of 143 organizations from 76 countries in the Americas, Europe, Asia, and Africa.[4] The majority of the organizations in CLOC also belong to La Vía Campesina. La Vía Campesina's membership from the Western Hemisphere is somewhat broader, since it includes a number of organizations from the English-speaking Caribbean that are not members of CLOC, as well as farmer organizations from the United States and Canada.

What unites most of the members of CLOC and La Vía Campesina is 1) their critique of neoliberal policies in agriculture in all of its dimensions, but specifically, for being anti-peasant; 2) their commitment to creating an alternative development project around the pillars of integral agrarian reform, sustainable development, and food sovereignty; and 3) their commitment to social justice, including ethnic, racial, and gender equity. This book brings together analysis and discussion of rural social movements that are part of CLOC and La Vía Campesina and/or the indigenous continental movement as well as of regional and national organizations not affiliated with any of these hemispheric social movement organizations. A central question of the book is the extent to which this alternative development project and vision of social justice is shared among these diverse rural organizations.

The first part of this book focuses on the role of CLOC and La Vía

Campesina in globalizing the struggle of the rural social movements and their visions of an alternative rural world. The second part considers a common demand of many of the organizations that constitute these transnational movements—land and territory—and the continuing need for agrarian reform. The main organizations analyzed here include the Landless Rural Workers' Movement of Brazil (MST) and the Movement of Landless Peasant and Indigenous Workers of Bolivia (MST-Bolivia), in addition to regional movements of indigenous and Afro-descendents in Colombia that have organized around the demand for territorial rights.

The third part turns to other struggles for sustainable rural livelihoods and social justice and includes analyses of the Movement of People Affected by Dams (MAB) of Brazil; the National Confederation of Communities Affected by Mining (CONACAMI) of Peru; the Federation of Agricultural Cooperatives of Rural Women Producers of Nicaragua (FEMUPROCAN); and the Bartolina Sisa National Federation of Bolivian Peasant Women (FNMCB-BS). It also considers two of the regional environmental movements in the Amazon, the rubber tappers' movement and one of Amazonian colonists, as well as an incipient movement focusing on the protection of biodiversity and indigenous culture in Mexico affiliated with the Plural National Indigenous Assembly for Autonomy (ANIPA).

The fourth part focuses on a different set of hemispheric and global connections: the impact and challenges of the Internet revolution for rural organizing; the implications of international migration on the viability of rural social movements and the role of binational rural organizations, such as the Indigenous Front of Binational Organizations (FIOB) of Mexico and the United States; and the contribution and challenges of the fair trade movement emanating in the United States and Europe in expanding the options for peasant farming and rural organizing in Latin America. In the remainder of this introduction we consider the context that has led to the rise and consolidation of rural social movements and their hemispheric associations; the points of convergence and difference among the organizations that are part of CLOC and La Vía Campesina and those that are not; the challenges of alternative globalizations; and, finally, some of the achievements to date of the rural social movements.

The Context: "The Countryside Can Endure No More"

The rise of new social movements across Latin America is generally associated with the debt-induced economic crisis of the 1980s and the impact of structural adjustment policies, the struggle for and political opening represented by the transition to democracy, and the rise of identity politics in a period marked by the relative decline in traditional forms of representation such as political parties and unions (Escobar and Alvarez 1992; Slater 1995; Foweraker 1995). Together with the growth and enabling role of NGOs and transnational advocacy networks that have facilitated contestation around the meaning of citizenship, these factors certainly provide part of the explanation for the growth of the women's and indigenous movements in many countries. But these factors alone cannot explain why by the end of the twentieth century *rural* social movements were not only among the most resilient, but also among the most dynamic in challenging neoliberal globalization. This is a salient question since Latin America's rural peoples now constitute only around one-fifth of the region's total population (CEPAL 2006).

We argue that the dynamism of the rural social movements in the current period is largely related to the unprecedented attack on rural livelihoods unleashed by neoliberal globalization—summed up by the slogan of some one hundred thousand peasants who marched to Mexico City in January 2003, claiming "the countryside can endure no more"—combined with the substantial growth in the capacity and political space for rural organizing, including transnationally. Rural Latin America has undergone a fundamental economic restructuring over the past several decades as a result of structural adjustment policies. Neoliberal policies have promoted a free market economy in all of its dimensions (free land, labor, input, and product markets) that favors export production over production for the internal market. The combination of the withdrawal of the state from the provision of services geared to the maintenance of domestic agriculture, along with the opening of the Latin American economies, has had a devastating impact on peasant economies nearly everywhere (Edelman 1999; Crabtree 2003; Kay 2004; Bartra 2004). Moreover, the opening to foreign investment in concert with the promotion of nontraditional exports and expanded lumber, livestock, and oil production has pushed the agricultural frontier nearly to its limits, with potentially devastating implications for many indigenous groups as well as colonists.

The specific timing and manner by which reform and institutional change in agriculture was fostered varied considerably across the region, with heterogeneous results.[5] Overall, growth rates for the Latin American agricultural sector were negative in the 1980s and were still much below the average of the 1970s during the 1990s (David et al. 2001, table 1). Due to the spectacular growth in nontraditional exports, however, a positive agricultural trade balance was achieved—the objective of neoliberal restructuring. Yet as a result of reduced trade barriers, between 1979 and 2001 the growth rate of the value of Latin America's agricultural imports was almost twice that of exports, leading by 2001 to a dwindling positive trade balance (García Pascual 2003). Among the main items in which the region experienced a trade deficit in that year were those crucial to food sovereignty—beans, rice, cereals, milk and dairy products—and textile fibers.

These reforms accentuated the already strong differentiation that existed in Latin America between regions, producers, and dynamic and traditional products (David et al. 2001). The most dynamic growth sectors—nontraditional exports such as oil seeds, livestock, vegetables, and fruit—are largely produced by the most modern and capitalized farmers with links to agro-industry and by multinational agribusinesses. Those in decline include traditional exports such as coffee, sugar, and cotton as well as grains, roots, and tubers, with the latter (as well as coffee) generally produced by small farmers. State support was reduced or eliminated for precisely those regions, products, and producers that are less competitive. The implementation of neoliberal policies has thus come at a very high cost, exacerbating social and economic inequalities.

During the lost decade of the 1980s the incidence of rural poverty reached 65 percent. Although the incidence of poverty began to decline during the 1990s, in 2005 59 percent of rural Latin Americans were still categorized as poor, and 32.5 percent as indigent (CEPAL 2006, Table 1.6.1). Moreover, rural poverty in Latin America has a strong ethnic dimension. Among the factors accounting for the high incidence of rural poverty in Latin America is the extremely unequal distribution of land, with Latin America exhibiting the greatest degree of inequality among all world regions. During the 1990s land became even more concentrated as the number of small farms in existence decreased in countries such as Brazil, Chile, Uruguay, Argentina, Bolivia, Colombia, and Mexico. The incidence of rural poverty in the 1990s was concentrated among own-account and unpaid family workers in agriculture (that is, peasants) and was linked among other factors to the distress of agricultural production for the internal market under neoliberalism (David et al. 2001).

The modernization of Latin American agriculture, based on increasing mechanization, the use of chemicals, and computerized production and processing, has also been accompanied by a reduction in the size of the permanent labor force and a greater reliance on temporary workers. As

Lara Flores (1998) argues, the key to productive reconversion under neo-liberalism is the adaptability of the labor force to market expansions and contractions. In Latin America this adaptability has been achieved through greater reliance on precarious employment, or what she terms "primitive or savage flexibilization." Hence, the relation between steadily increasing labor productivity in agriculture and rural immiseration (Spoor 2002). It has also been accompanied by a feminization of the agricultural labor force (Deere 2006).

What makes the current situation unprecedented is not just the assault on natural resources under neoliberalism, since such offensives have taken place under various waves of export-oriented growth in the past. Rather, it is in terms of the repercussions for those whose livelihoods depend upon such resources or whose lives are uprooted by the construction of dams or booms in timber, mining, and agro-export. For at the beginning of the twenty-first century, the two main escape routes for dispossessed peasants are coming to a close or are unappealing: migration to the agricultural frontier or to the cities. Latin America's mega cities are no longer the point of attraction that they were in the past, given the high levels of underemployment characterizing the bloated informal sector, the deterioration in the provision of urban amenities, and the high levels of crime. Hence the appeal of a rural alternative among urban shantytown dwellers that movements such as the MST have been able to capitalize upon. Moreover, whereas in the past migration to the agricultural frontier had provided the traditional alternative to landlessness in Central America, the Andes, and Brazil, the margins of the frontier are now being reached, with displaced peasants often in competition for new lands with agribusiness and oil and mining exploration interests, as well as indigenous groups fighting against such encroachment of their traditional territories. Not surprisingly, international migration both interregionally and from Latin America to the United States and Europe has increased substantially over the past two decades (Cortés Castellanos 2005; chapter 16, this volume). This raises a particular challenge for organizing by rural social movements in terms of whether their constituencies follow "exit versus voice"—analyzed by Jonathan Fox and Lynn Stephen in chapters 15 and 16, respectively.

In this generally unfavorable macro situation, rural men and women—indigenous, white, black, and mestizo—have increasingly mobilized in defense of their livelihoods, to contest their social exclusion, and to redefine the terms and content of citizenship. Following Bebbington (2004, 180), we define livelihoods in terms of how people make a living as well as the sorts of meanings people attach to *how* they make their living. Most of the chapters in this volume are concerned with the ways in which people struggle to defend their livelihoods and enhance what they value in their modes of living, illustrating Bebbington's argument that livelihoods, culture, and politics are highly interrelated.

Besides motivation, the rise and consolidation of rural social movements in this period are also related to the political opening that has favored organizing efforts and to the growing capacity of peasants, rural workers, and indigenous people to organize, or what Tarrow (1998) calls changes in political opportunity and mobilizing structures. Among the many benefits of the transition to formal democratic rule in most countries is that the political associational space has broadened. Political liberalization has created a more favorable environment for organizing in that, as Yashar (2005, 76) notes, at the very least "the state does not trample on the capacity to associate and speak out."

With respect to the capacity to organize, three factors stand out: the growing levels of rural literacy and schooling, the supportive role of transcommunity and transnational advocacy networks, and the impact of the telecommunications revolution. Rural literacy rates have always lagged significantly behind urban rates in Latin America, but in recent decades significant gains have been made in bridging this gap.[6] In addition, rural schooling levels among young people have increased as well, facilitating the emergence of a new generation of rural leaders, ready to take advantage of the capacity-building efforts of NGOs and other external actors as well as new technologies.

Yashar (2005, 72) emphasizes the role of transcommunity networks and how at various times, the state, churches, unions, and/or NGOs have all played crucial roles in supporting the growth of social movements: "networks enable people (or communities) to interact, to exchange information, to build social capital, and to mobilize for change." Keck and Sikkink (1998, 8) highlight the role of transnational advocacy networks, which they define as "forms of organization characterized by voluntary, reciprocal and horizontal patterns of communication and exchange," which form to promote causes, ideas, and norms. They highlight how these provide voice to groups that might be suppressed at home, and when projected internationally, "echo back into their own countries," bringing alternative voices and visions to inform and reframe domestic debates (Keck and Sikkink 1998, x).

Transnational advocacy networks have played a particularly important role in garnering domestic and international support for international conventions around women's and indigenous rights. The ILO Convention 169 on Indigenous Rights in 1989 played a similar role in galvanizing the indigenous movement as did the Convention on the Elimination of Discrimination Against Women in 1979 for the women's movement. The process leading up to the UN's Fourth World Conference on Women in Beijing in 2005 under the leadership of Latin American feminist NGOs was particularly important for Latin American rural women, providing the catalyst for the organization of a number of the new national rural women's networks and associations with a gender rights agenda.[7]

With respect to the indigenous movement, Yashar (2005, 71) argues that transcommunity networks "fostered the communication and cooperation that was essential for transcending geographic dispersion, language barriers, and cultural unfamiliarity" by providing "the forum for future indigenous leaders to meet, share common experiences, develop a common language, identify common problems, and articulate common goals." Both Yashar and Brysk (2000) show how these networks, including transnational ones, played important roles in generating a sense of indigenous identity, particularly in the first generation of indigenous organizations, when cultural divisions often overshadowed common problems and objectives. But all too often in the literature advocacy networks and social movements are conflated in analyses of domestic "civil society."[8] As Tarrow (1998) emphasizes and Yashar (2005) reminds us, these are analytically distinct and cannot be reduced to one another.[9]

The impact of the telecommunications revolution on the capacity to organize cannot be ignored. Most of the rural social movements that we focus upon were born during the "fax age," when communications depended on unreliable land lines. But by the late 1990s a number of these organizations had access to computers, were communicating with their membership and each other via e-mail, and had Web pages. A growing literature, for example, explores the role of the Internet in formatting a sense of cultural identity among indigenous groups as well as their ability to learn from each other's struggles and accomplishments (Becker and Delgado 1998; Monasterios 2003). Rising literacy and schooling levels served as an important precondition for the rural social movements to take advantage of the Internet, notwithstanding the fact that its potential has not been fully realized (see chapter 14). The rapid spread of cell phone usage throughout Latin America since 2000 has greatly improved the capacity of rural organizations to mobilize their membership on short notice for meetings, marches, and demonstrations. Finally, the capacity to organize has been fortified by eased mobility (both socially and in terms of infrastructure) between rural and urban areas and more adroit use of the media by the new generation of rural leaders (Kay 2004).

Among the factors that make Latin America a particularly interesting region to study at this point in time—besides the fact that rural social movements are making and breaking governments—is that most of the same factors that have led to the rise and consolidation of new regional and national rural social movements (including new and revitalized peasant organizations and rural unions)[10] have also precipitated the growth and consolidation of transnational rural social movements. This process has been mutually interactive, with the growth of a strong hemispheric movement in turn strengthening national, regional, and local rural organizations.

The struggle against the impact of neoliberal policies at home has been inextricably linked to mobilization against free-trade agreements and the conditions under which Latin American countries participate in multilateral organizations such as the WTO. As understanding has spread that it is not just particular government policies that threaten livelihoods, but a model of development of global dimensions, the Internet has facilitated the exchange of common analyses, organizational objectives, strategies for action, and the possibility for coordinated mobilizations throughout the hemisphere. Thus CLOC and La Vía Campesina have taken a leading role in the World Social Forums that have been held annually since 2001, the Hemispheric Social Forums that have been organized since 2004, and in the series of protests held in conjunction with the meetings of the WTO and other international organizations as well as the hemispheric-level summit meetings intended to build toward adoption of the FTAA.

The chapters in this volume contribute to two of the central questions of social movement theory: why social movements arise and how they are consolidated (Foweraker 1995). While some authors give greater weight to explaining the origins of particular social movement struggles and the motivation to organize (chapters 2, 3, 5, 6, and 12), others emphasize strategy (chapters 1 and 4); most do both. Similarly, while some authors place greater emphasis on the role of identity (chapters 1, 7, 12, and 13), most demonstrate that, for successful social movements, the process of constructing a social movement identity or framing goes hand in hand with material demands—securing a sustainable livelihood—and demands for inclusion as citizens, for these are often inseparable (Bartra and Otero 2006).

Shared Visions, Different Struggles

Besides being primarily rural-based movements, the organizations discussed in this volume that are part of CLOC and La Vía Campesina and those that are not (whether national or regional organizations) share a number of commonalities. These organizations represent the voices of those traditionally excluded from social, economic, and political power. They are usually autonomous in their relations with traditional political parties as well as the state. They are all dedicated to the pursuit of social justice through nonviolent means. By organizing around concrete demands, they are seeking recognition of their basic human and social rights. They are all concerned with the defense of rural livelihoods and, increasingly, with the development of sustainable livelihoods—ones that respect nature and traditional knowledge and are ecologically and environmentally sustainable. But they have followed different paths in molding their alternative visions of sustainable livelihoods.

Agrarian reform is among the central demands of most of the organizations that are part of CLOC and La Vía Campesina. Reflecting the continuing high concentration of land in the hands of few owners in Latin America and the lack of opportunities in the cities, the pursuit of agrarian reform gained a new saliency at the end of the twentieth century, fueled by the demands of the landless rather than the hacienda tenants of previous decades. As Peter Rosset argues in chapter 2, the vision of integral agrarian reform being demanded today draws upon the lessons of the past (the incomplete and unsatisfactory results of previous land reform efforts) and is substantially broader, encompassing a policy framework to make family farming and cooperatives sustainable. These points are well illustrated in the two subsequent chapters focusing on Brazil's MST. The relative success of the MST in getting land into the hands of the landless has inspired the organization of the landless throughout the region, such as the landless movement in Bolivia. Silvestre Saisari, a leader of the MST-Bolivia, describes in chapter 6 the arduous struggle of the landless to make various Bolivian governments comply with the country's existing agrarian reform legislation and, particularly, to guarantee the basic human rights of those struggling to effect agrarian reform. He also lays out the vision of agrarian reform its members aspire to, one inspired by the principles of La Vía Campesina, but with its own twists, such as the emphasis on communal enterprises.

Many of the social movements whose organizations are not part of

CLOC or La Vía Campesina were formed around specific assaults on their livelihoods, such as deforestation in the Amazon or the construction of large-scale dams and mining projects in Brazil and Peru. Composed primarily of small farmers, they initially organized to defend a way of life. Their demands soon broadened from the defense of the natural resources upon which they rely to seeking sustainable livelihoods that would improve living standards while being ecologically and environmentally sustainable.

One of the major differences between the social movements linked to CLOC and La Vía Campesina and many of the others is with respect to the scope of their demands. For CLOC and La Vía Campesina it is the model of development that is at issue, specifically neoliberal globalization. In their view there are two competing models of social and economic development: an industrial model of agriculture being fostered by neoliberalism, and a peasant model. Their primary struggle is against the "globalized, neoliberal, corporate-driven model where agriculture is seen exclusively as a profit making venture and productive resources are increasingly concentrated into the hands of agro-industry" (Desmarais 2002, 99). Having led to their impoverishment as well as the degradation of the environment, this model threatens the peasantry and rural communities with extinction. The alternative project of these organizations is to build a "more humane rural world" where agriculture is farmer-driven and based on peasant production that is economically viable and ecologically sustainable.

For CLOC and La Vía Campesina an integral agrarian reform is just one component of a broader change in national development policy, one that encompasses food sovereignty. Food sovereignty is the right of a country to produce its own food on its own territory, and it brings together four elements: food as a basic human need (and not just a tradable commodity, as in the neoliberal model); food production as a basic right and obligation of the peasantry; food security (that is, adequate food supplies) as a distribution issue; and foodstuffs as a production issue in terms of how they are produced and by and for whom (Vía Campesina 1996). As Annette Desmarais explains in chapter 1, La Vía Campesina has globalized this broad alternative vision by articulating a peasant identity and becoming a major player at international forums in defense of family farming.

Many of the other rural social movements began as one-issue movements, although it is most useful to locate them at different points on a continuum in the advocacy of social change. The anti-dam movement in Brazil and the anti-mining movement in Peru, for example, grew out of local movements organized around either the demand for compensation for damages suffered or to block further developments that compromise their livelihoods. As Carlos Vainer shows in chapter 7, and the social movement leader Miguel Palacín illustrates in chapter 8, as these movements became national in scope they began to confront national energy, mining, and environmental policies.

In the case of the Brazilian anti-dam movement, part of the process of consolidating itself as a national movement was by developing alliances with other national social movements, such as the MST and other organizations that carry the banner of the Brazilian "Popular Project," a decidedly antineoliberal coalition; in 1997 it also joined CLOC and La Vía Campesina. The Peruvian anti-mining movement, in contrast, is part of the continental indigenous movement and has not joined these other hemispheric organizations. The president of CONACAMI, Miguel Palacín, concurrently serves as the general coordinator of the Andean Coordinator of Indigenous Organizations (CAOI) and served on the organizing committee of the Third Continental Indigenous Summit in 2007.

In large measure the indigenous movements in Latin America evolved out of the peasant movements of past decades, particularly in Mexico, Bolivia, Ecuador, and Colombia, but at different paces. As Alvaro Velasco Álvarez shows in chapter 7, in Colombia the indigenous and Afro-Colombian movements were products of the 1980s and in many ways reached their zenith just as other national indigenous movements were gaining strength. The adoption of ILO Convention 169 in 1989 with its emphasis on the right to self-determination, autonomy, and recognition of indigenous territories played a major role in boosting indigenous organizations throughout the continent as did the series of events around 1992 mentioned earlier. There is little question but that the indigenous movement become a continental movement in its own right in the 1990s, pressing national governments to ratify Convention 169, while simultaneously playing an important role in the formation of the hemispheric rural social movement built around the construction of CLOC.

Even though some of the most active organizations within CLOC are primarily indigenous—such as the National Indigenous and Peasant Coordinator (CONIC-Guatemala) in Guatemala, the Plan of Ayala National Network (CNPA) in Mexico, and the Confederation of Peasant Workers of Bolivia (CSUTCB)—sustaining the participation of many of the other indigenous organizations and attracting new ones to CLOC has been a major challenge.[11] Participation in CLOC congresses has fluctuated widely, with indigenous organizations being among those less likely to participate actively and consistently.[12] Various factors explain this: on the one hand, the intensity of national-level struggles for indigenous rights, particularly in Mexico, Ecuador, and Bolivia, that absorbed the energies of indigenous organizations from the 1990s onward; and on the other, the fear among these that participation in alliances with hemispheric popular movements with a strong mestizo base, such as CLOC, would dilute their demands.

Ecuador's CONAIE, one of the strongest indigenous organizations in the region,[13] has been one of the most reluctant to build alliances with other rural social movements, both nationally and internationally, and is neither a member of CLOC nor La Vía Campesina.[14] As noted earlier, it has taken the lead in convoking many of the indigenous-only hemispheric meetings and summits. While the declarations emanating from these meetings recognize the shared aspects of the struggle against "the dominant system of oppression" with other popular movements and condemn neoliberal globalization in no uncertain terms, they continuously stress how their top priority must remain the right to autonomy and self-determination (Burguete Cal y Mayor 2007).

As Delgado (1994, 82) reflects, in the major attempts in Latin America "to mix class/popular-oriented movements with ethnic/gendered ones, there have been more failures than successes." In the meetings leading up to the formation of CLOC (the *encuentros* in Guatemala in 1991 and in Nicaragua in 1992), a number of indigenous leaders walked out after finding that there was no room for those primarily concerned with issues of indigenous identity, autonomy, and self-determination. A particular bone of contention in this period was whether the *populares* were simply including indigenous organizations in the call for unity to capitalize on the "500 Years of Resistance Campaign" (Hale 1994).

Indigenous organizations have been hesitant to join CLOC and La Vía Campesina for many of the same reasons that as national movements they have rejected alliances with multiethnic parties: the fear that in decision making their organizations will be subordinated to mestizo leadership; that unity or party loyalty will dominate over their own organization's priorities; that their own indigenous demands will become diluted; and that in public office their own leaders will become co-opted or corrupted (Van Cott 2005, 105).

Von Cott argues that a number of factors converged in the 1990s that encouraged indigenous organizations to form their own indigenous parties, including the disarray of traditional political parties, particularly the Left, with which many of these movements had been at some point associated. The process of constitutional reform in some countries sometimes also served as a catalyst to the formation of indigenous parties. In Ecuador, CONAIE formed the Pluricultural Pachakutik United Movement in 1995, which briefly formed part of a ruling junta in the military coup d'état of 2000. Later, as part of a coalition it won the presidential elections of 2002, which resulted in five indigenous leaders being appointed to the cabinet (O'Connor 2003; Van Cott 2005). In this same period, several indigenous parties formed in Bolivia, and later the coca growers federations formed the MAS, the Movement Toward Socialism, which narrowly lost the presidential elections of 2002 before finally succeeding in 2006.

Perhaps the incursion into participation in national politics and governance by indigenous organizations has been one of the reasons that the continental indigenous movement has been slow to consolidate its own hemispheric social movement organization. It was only after CONAIE lost a considerable amount of prestige domestically from its participation in Ecuadorian politics that it once again took up the banner of the continental indigenous movement, hosting the Second Indigenous Summit in Quito in 2004.

In Mexico the national indigenous movement began to form around the 500 Years of Indigenous, Black, and Popular Resistance Council, linked to the events of 1992. Throughout the 1990s indigenous organizations were part of an intense movement to construct a common indigenous proposal for autonomy, organized as the Plural National Indigenous Assembly for Autonomy (ANIPA), a movement that developed separately from but was also galvanized by the Zapatista movement (EZLN) in southern Mexico. Between 1995 and 1998 ANIPA, which brings together approximately one hundred different indigenous organizations, held seven national assemblies to develop its legislative proposal on autonomy, one based on a three-tiered system of autonomy at the regional, municipal, and community levels (Ruiz Hernández 2000). In this same period the Zapatistas convoked three national indigenous congresses (in 1996, 1997, and 2001) in support of its proposal for constitutional change, the Cocopa Law, which synthesized the San Andres Accords (signed between the EZLN and the Mexican government in 1996) with respect to indigenous autonomy rights. Neither ANIPA's nor the Zapatistas' autonomy proposals came to fruition, with the legislature passing a very watered down version of the Cocopa Law in 2001 (Bartra and Otero 2005).

As Cecilio Solís Librado, the leader of ANIPA, explains in chapter 11, while ANIPA has played a leadership role hemispherically (hosting, for example, the First Indigenous Continental Summit in 2000 along with

CONIC) over time the organization has become increasingly focused on constructing local-level development alternatives. He describes ANIPA's initiative to take advantage of the growth of tourism and the appreciation of biodiversity to develop alternative livelihood strategies for indigenous communities and to do so in such a way that fosters indigenous cultural identity. It provides an example of how the issues of the environmental and indigenous movements have oftentimes converged and fused. But this approach contrasts markedly with CLOC and La Vía Campesina's goal of changing the model of development.[15]

Many of the propositions of the continental indigenous movement, organized now as the Continental Coordination of Indigenous Nationalities and Peoples of Abya Yala, are currently very similar to those of CLOC and La Vía Campesina, suggesting a process of convergence as these organizations mature. For example, in the Declaration of Iximche that resulted from the Third Continental Summit in Guatemala in April 2007, neoliberal globalization was denounced in no uncertain terms, including free-trade agreements. Moreover, while the demands for the right to indigenous autonomy, self-determination, and territory continue to figure most prominently, the continental indigenous movement has incorporated the demand for food sovereignty as its own. This declaration also stressed the need for alliances with other social movements in the struggle against neoliberalism and oppression ("Declaración de Iximche" 2007).

Another challenge facing CLOC in building a truly unified hemispheric rural movement is the incorporation of the autonomous national rural women's organizations. The origin of many of the latter is found in the women's secretariats or commissions that were formed during the 1980s within the peasant organizations and rural unions. Given the difficulties that peasant women found in having their needs and demands recognized, many of these went on to form their own autonomous organizations in the 1990s (Deere and León 2001). The chapters by the peasant leader Martha Valle on Nicaragua's FEMUPROCAN, by George Ann Potter with the peasant leader Leonilda Zurita on the "Bartolina Sisas" of Bolivia (the FNMCB-BS), and by Lynn Stephens on the organization of indigenous Mexican women in the United States and Mexico all tell the story of why rural women found it necessary to form their own organizations, with varying degrees of autonomy.

The "Bartolina Sisas" have gone on to take a leadership role within CLOC and La Vía Campesina, and, according to Potter and Zurita, are even more strongly identified with the goals of these organizations than its mixed-sex counterpart organization, the CSUTCB.[16] The FEMUPROCAN and other strong autonomous rural women's organizations, such as the National Association of Peasant and Indigenous Women of Colombia (ANMUCIC), in contrast, are not members. In the case of FEMUPROCAN it has concentrated its efforts on building alliances with other women's organizations at the national and subregional levels.[17]

Paralleling the debates among indigenous organizations with regard to the importance of autonomy, much debated among rural women is the best manner to pursue a gender agenda and press feminist demands, whether inside or outside the mixed-sex organizations and at the national or hemispheric level. The rural women's organizations that belong to CLOC and La Vía Campesina can take credit for some advances with respect to gender equality within these organizations. For example, most documents of CLOC and La Vía Campesina are now written in gender neutral language, specifying that the protagonists are peasant men and women. This is no small accomplishment, since it represents a shift from the language of exclusion to one of inclusion, and one that helps to overcome the traditional invisibility of women. Also, gender analysis is increasingly being integrated into all themes, which is a major step forward, for it recognizes that unequal gender relations are not just a problem of women, but of the whole society and are embedded in every political, social, economic, and ideological issue. Finally, these transnational organizations now have the goal of attaining 50 percent female participation in their leadership. The Coordinating Committee of La Vía Campesina began implementing this provision in 1999 by requiring that each world region be represented by one man and one woman. Since then this requirement has been adopted by some of the participating organizations in CLOC, such as the Brazilian MST, as discussed in chapter 5 by the MST leaders Daniel Correa and Andréia Borges Ferreira.

The incorporation of gender concerns into the practice and substantive propositions of CLOC and La Vía Campesina (such as for women's land rights) is partly due to the development of autonomous national rural women's organizations in the 1990s that are not afraid to identify with feminism. This has opened up space for a gender discourse within the mixed-sex rural movements, in part because the autonomous rural women's movements and the mixed-sex movements are often competing for membership, encouraging the mixed-sex organizations to become much more accommodating to women and their demands. Another factor that has facilitated the adoption of a gender perspective within CLOC has been the very interaction between CLOC and La Vía Campesina. The strong presence of European farmer organizations in the latter, from countries where the gender equality discourse was more advanced than in Latin America, certainly had an impact on the evolution of attitudes and concerns within CLOC. At the same time, the incorporation of gender issues by CLOC and other mixed-sex organizations is also tied to the deliberations over what the alternative project is to consist of. This vision of the alternative society is necessarily built around the principles of equality, social justice, and full citizenship and has begun to produce the understanding that a transformation of gender relations is a precondition.

Alternative Globalizations and North-South Relations

Whether examining the effects of globalization on rural societies, or the cross-border organizational responses and alternatives, a transnational perspective infuses this volume. The chapters in the final part demonstrate some of the ways that the north-south dynamic goes beyond northern imposition of neoliberalism on a resistant South and elucidate the effects of movement across borders on broader social movements.

As noted earlier, it is well recognized that the rapid spread of Internet communications technologies have vastly increased the ability of social movements to mobilize on national, hemispheric, and global scales. In chapter 14 Scott Robinson argues that actors in the social movements must both improve their use of such technologies where available and increase their pressure on elites for digital inclusion of the sectors they represent. He emphasizes that, even where some level of communications technology competence has been achieved by social movements, adoption is usually limited to basic e-mail and Web consultation, with more complex and powerful manifestations of digital technology generally ignored. The resources for improving Internet communications and other digital capability for social movements are dispersed among local info-development enthusiasts, foreign NGOs and corporations, and national government programs, none of which necessarily support or even understand the goals of social movements. An interesting question is whether the Bolivarian Alternative for Latin America and the Caribbean (ALBA)[18] will extend involvement in electronic alternative media beyond TeleSur and systematically offer upgrading of skills and/or equipment to social movement organizations around the Americas.

Mexico and the United States represent the most massive and abrupt encounter between north and south in the Americas. Both Jonathan Fox and Lynn Stephen examine the migration of people between Mexico and the United States. Indeed, both authors include a particular organization, the Indigenous Front of Binational Organizations (FIOB), among their case studies to help answer a key question: is out-migration a substitute for collective action, or can it lead to new forms of collective action? Fox, in chapter 15, takes a broader sample, examining hometown associations and other migrant-led membership organizations as instances of a "migrant civil society," and their positive links to organizing in their countries of origin. In chapter 16, Stephen focuses on the experiences of two women's organizations, both primarily indigenous and with a presence in Mexico and the western United States. Again, the protagonists are largely economic refugees from rural, southern, post-NAFTA Mexico. She describes how the transborder experience itself has provided these immigrants with a "bifocal vision," a heightened ability to focus simultaneously on life in their U.S. surroundings and their places of origin in Mexico (or vice versa). Stephen, like Fox, concludes that exiting can lead to voice, both as migrants and as immigrants.

The case studies selected to demonstrate the ability of migrants to engage in collective action in their countries of origin and to retain or enhance their voices could be interpreted as "the exceptions that prove the rule" of exit-negating voice. Yet that would obscure an important point: even if exiting generally tends to diminish voice, local collective action, and pressure for positive change, it does not always and inevitably do so. These authors' examples demonstrate immigrant communities maintaining and even enhancing voice, in spite of ongoing and seemingly inevitable exiting, with potentially positive implications for the nurturing and growth of Latin American rural social movements.

Fair trade as described by Michael Conroy in chapter 17 is fundamentally a north-south transnational movement. However, the fair trade movement is largely inspired by and controlled from the North, and it requires adherence by participating farmers in the South to externally developed rules. Fair trade is therefore not itself a Latin American rural movement, although it works with, provides support to, and may even require the existence of rural social movements for its relevance and success. Thus, the organized small farmer families who receive benefits from the fair trade movement are largely distinct from the fair trade movement itself, although Conroy describes some cases of increased organization by fair trade producers, creating linkages to social movements such as the Brazilian MST and hence CLOC. Still, the fair trade movement plays a role similar to that of sympathetic foreign NGOs, whose financial and technical support is often appreciated, but who are ultimately held at arm's length by their social movement beneficiaries.

A particular strength of Conroy's chapter is his explanation of the range of approaches that exist (not always harmoniously) within the diverse fair trade movement. Yet in spite of differences within the fair trade movement and between the fair trade movement and the rural social movements, there remains considerable potential for expanded collaboration. Fair trade could, for example, be of particular benefit to countries implementing or deepening agrarian reform, and that have successfully promoted small-farmer cooperatives. More broadly, the fair trade movement, with its widespread network of student, church member, and responsible consumer advocates, could provide fertile ground in the United States and Europe for understanding and support for Latin American rural social movements. For the moment, however, Conroy shows how, as a movement in Europe and the United States, fair trade is currently struggling to navigate a course among extremely divisive issues both on the producing and consuming sides of the business.

Impact of the Rural Social Movements

Among the criteria used to measure the success of social movements is whether they emerge then "persist and create an enduring social awareness," as Brysk (2000, 246) proposes. Another certainly more substantive criterion is whether a social movement is able to gain both recognition and acceptance of its demands and bring about changes in public policies that enhance the well-being of its members. The Latin American rural social movements can take credit for a number of achievements over the past two decades, particularly with respect to raising social awareness. Collectively, they deserve much of the credit for the heightened public consciousness in contemporary Latin America regarding a broad range of issues, from environmental degradation and the importance of conserving biodiversity, to recognition of indigenous rights and those of Afro-descendents, to the continuing need to address land redistribution, including women's land rights. The concepts of sustainable development and sustainable livelihoods—neither of which are uniquely attributable to the rural social movements but which have provided a coherent conceptual framework for most of their demands—have certainly gained widespread acceptance in Latin America, at least at the rhetorical level. It is much more complicated to evaluate the extent to which social movements have brought about changes in public policies, and, particularly, whether members of social movements are better off as a result of these initiatives.

As Peter Rosset notes in chapter 2, one of the major achievements of the rural social movements is that agrarian reform is now back on the agenda of a number of Latin American governments. Partly as a result of the Global Campaign for Agrarian Reform launched by La Vía Campesina and NGO allies in 1999, and partly due to a reconsideration of the need for land redistribution among international organizations such as the World Bank, contending models of land reform are now being implemented throughout the region.[19] Thus far, the agrarian reform that most bears the stamp of its protagonist is that of Brazil. As Miguel Carter argues in chapter 4, the MST was largely responsible for the pace of the Brazilian agrarian reform under the government of Fernando Henrique Cardoso, and he provides a detailed analysis of why it was so successful in influencing state policy.

Chapter 5, by the MST leaders Daniel Correa and Andréia Borges, in contrast, considers why the pace of the agrarian reform has slowed down under the government of Luiz Inácio Lula da Silva and emphasizes the challenges facing the landless movement, including that of consolidating the agrarian reform settlements. Nonetheless, under the Lula government the MST has played a much more influential role than in the past in shaping policy toward the agrarian reform settlements with respect to credit, technical assistance, and educational policy (Deere and Medeiros 2006). Moreover, there is a growing body of evidence of the positive impact of agrarian reform settlements in the municipalities in which these are located and on the standard of living of the beneficiaries (Leite et al. 2004).

The environmental movements in the Brazilian Amazon have perhaps been even more successful than the MST in having their demands incorporated as state policy. In chapter 10, Mary Allegretti and Marianne Schmink describe the development of the rubber tappers' movement and that of Amazon colonists, and how they have been successful in having their proposals for the creation of extractive reserves and a program based on the payment for environmental services, respectively, adopted as alternative development models in the Amazon. Their insightful analysis also illustrates some of the contradictions that arise when social movements subsequently become dependent on government action and state resources. They warn that new vulnerabilities are generated that may undermine the sustainability of the social movements themselves.[20]

In the broad scope of things, the indigenous movement in Latin America has probably achieved more with respect to its demands over the past three decades than any of the other rural social movements, particularly in the Andes. Indigenous territories with varying degrees of autonomy have now been recognized in Colombia, Ecuador, and Bolivia, and these Andean countries are now constitutionally pluriethnic states. The mobilization of Colombian ethnic minorities in the 1980s resulted in approximately one-fifth of Colombian national territory being set aside as either indigenous reserves or Afro-Colombian territories. Part of its success was its ability to link together the issues of biodiversity and cultural diversity, gaining the support of environmentalists and others in the process—an example being followed by other indigenous movements. According to Alvaro Velasco Álvarez (chapter 7), however, achieving constitutional recognition is one thing; attaining relative autonomy in governance is quite another. Attenuating these achievements have been very real obstacles, such as the ongoing civil war and neoliberal state policies. On another front, considerable progress has been made with respect to bilingual education, another indigenous demand, particularly in Ecuador, where CONAIE itself controls its content (Van Cott 2005).

At another level of analysis, one of the main achievements of the rural social movements has been the broadening of democracy in at least two senses: by virtue of their organizations, these movements have achieved a voice and a level of participation in the public sphere unheard of in the past. And in various countries of the region political parties have come to power either with the support of the rural social movements or are constituted by them. Miguel Carter, in his analysis of the MST in chapter 4, makes a very strong case on how the MST, as the motor force behind the broader struggle for social justice in Brazil, has strengthened civil society and acted as a force for the reduction of inequality and the protection of human rights. The impact of the Brazilian rural social movements as a whole, through their Popular Project for Brazil, may well turn out to be of more lasting duration and historical significance than simply the election of Lula to the presidency.

The hope of the Bolivian social movement leaders writing in this volume is that the presidency of Evo Morales turns out to be different from that of Lula's. They perhaps have even more at stake, since Morales's party, the Movement Toward Socialism, is itself a coalition of social movements rather than a traditional political party. The rural women's organizations analyzed by Potter and Zurita in chapter 13 are among its main constituents. They are already worried about gender issues taking a back seat to more pressing issues in the face of the acute class and ethnic struggle that has been unleashed by Morales's election. Expectations, however, continue to run high that he will be able to respond to the aspirations of the rural social movements.

As the CLOC leader Juan Tiney argues in chapter 3, CLOC and La Vía Campesina are partially responsible for the lack of conclusion of the FTAA in addition to raising awareness of the unequal terms of neoliberal globalization embodied in the rules of the WTO.[21] While no Latin American government has yet adopted food sovereignty as national policy, disenchantment with free-trade agreements is widespread, as seen in the platforms of many recently elected governments that are part of the recent "pink tide" as well as in the platforms of opposition candidates who lost by slim margins in Mexico and Costa Rica. It is certainly to be hoped that the experience gained by several decades of fair trading will someday inform government trade policies, although regarding north-south trade, such seems a distant possibility.[22]

In sum, the essays in this volume together demonstrate that over the past three decades the rural social movements have changed the landscape of Latin American civil society, making it much more vibrant as well as inclusive. Through their collective voices and actions the rural social movements have shown that peasants and indigenous peoples are not simply going to disappear—certainly not without a struggle—and moreover, if they were to do so, such would be a social loss. Their visions of sustainable livelihoods provide concrete alternatives to neoliberalism and offer hope that, indeed, another world—a more just and inclusive world—is possible.

Notes

Authors' note: An earlier version of this chapter was presented at the Sawyer Seminar entitled "The Changing Nature(s) of Land: Locating Agrarian Publics," University of North Carolina, December 7–8, 2007. The authors are grateful to the participants as well as to Phillip Williams at the University of Florida for helpful comments.

1. The meeting in Bogotá in October 1989 that launched the 500 Years of Indigenous and Popular Resistance campaign was preceded by a meeting of the pan-indigenous network in Quito in 1987 and the First International Forum on Human Rights of the Indian Peoples, held in Oaxaca, Mexico in September 1989 (Brysk 2000; Bartra and Otero 2005). Burguete 2007 highlights the tension at the meeting in Bogotá between peasant and indigenous groups that has led indigenous organizations to date their continental political history from the 1990 Quito *encuentro*. The Bogotá declaration was signed by representatives of both groups from seventeen countries.

2. It is not clear whether CONIC is still in existence. This organization organized the Second Continental Indigenous Summit in Teotihuacan, Mexico, in 2000 but is not mentioned in the communications regarding subsequent continental summits. See Burguete 2007 and the documents at www.cubrecontinentalindigena.org, accessed January 4, 2008.

3. Peasant organizations from Central America joined together to form the Central American Association of Peasant Organizations for Cooperation and Development (ASOCODE) in December 1991 (Edelman 1998). Throughout the 1990s ASOCODE played an important role in building both CLOC and La Vía Campesina; the operational secretariat of the latter was based at ASOCODE's headquarters in Tegucigalpa, Honduras until 2004.

4. See chapter 1.

5. This section draws on Deere 2006.

6. Between the decades of the 1960s and 1990s, for example, the ratio of rural to urban literacy rates in the six largest Latin American countries fell from 159 to 116 (Astorga et al. 2005, table 4).

7. For the specific organizations that arose out of the Beijing process, see Deere and León 2001. On the general importance of Beijing for the national and international women's movements, see Alvarez 1998.

8. Several of the authors in this volume discuss the tension that often characterizes the relationship between rural social movements and NGOs. With respect to the women's movement, these tensions are well analyzed in Alvarez 1998; on the peasant movement, see Edelman 1999 for a good case study of the competition for resources between peasant organizations and NGOs.

9. With respect to the transnational advocacy networks and transnational social movements, the main difference according to Tarrow (1998, 188) is that "advocacy networks are connective structures that cross national boundaries, whereas social networks are the bases for contentious politics within domestic society"; that is, the building blocks of social movements.

10. In terms of the growth of new peasant organizations, the case of Mexico stands out. Beginning in the 1980s, a number of local and regional organizations, seeking independence and autonomy vis-à-vis the state, broke with the official National Peasant Confederation to form their own regional and national associations (Bartra and Otero 2005). Several of these are founding members of CLOC and led the march on Mexico City in 2003 under the banner "the countryside can endure no more": the Plan of Ayala National Coordinator (CNPA), the National Union of Regional Autonomous Peasant Organizations (UNORCA), and the Independent Central Union of Agricultural Workers and Peasants (CIOAC). The revitalization of traditional rural unions over the last two decades is best exemplified by the case of the National Confederation of Agricultural Workers (CONTAG) in Brazil and El Surco in Chile, both of which are also members of CLOC.

11. It is worth noting that of the twelve organizations on the organizing committee for the Third Continental Indigenous Summit in Guatemala in 2007, three also belong to CLOC: CONIC-Guatemala, CSUTCB, and the MST-Bolivia. Of the other conven-

ing organizations, those represented in this volume include ANIPA (chapter 11) and CONACAMI (chapter 9) (Declaración del Comité 2006).

12. From the eighty-four organizations participating at CLOC's first congress in Lima in 1994, the number dropped to only thirty-seven at the third congress in Mexico in 2001, before returning to eighty-eight organizations at the fourth congress in Guatemala City in 2005 (CLOC 1994, 1997, 1998, and 2001; and see chapter 3, this volume).

13. CONAIE was formed through the fusion in 1986 of the two main peasant and indigenous organizations in Ecuador: the Confederation of Indian Organizations of the Ecuadorean Andes, ECUARUNARI, representing the peasant federations of the sierra; and the Confederation of Indigenous Nationalities of the Ecuadorian Amazon (CONFENIAE). In the late 1990s it included some 220 organizations among its membership, representing on the order of 80 percent of the community-level organizations of the country (Van Cott 2005, 107).

14. The Ecuadorean members of CLOC are the National Federation of Peasant, Indigenous, and Black Organizations of Ecuador (FENOCIN), and the National Unitary Confederation of Affiliates to the Peasant Social Security System (CONFEUNASSC).

15. While the Zapatista movement is not a member of CLOC nor La Vía Campesina, there is much greater affinity among these movements than with ANIPA, and the EZLN and La Vía Campesina often exchange messages of solidarity (Hernández Navarro 2007).

16. Other autonomous national rural women's organizations that participate actively in CLOC and La Vía Campesina and that have been in the leadership of these movements are the National Articulation of Rural Women Workers (ANMTR) of Brazil, the National Confederation of Rural Women (CONAMUCA) of the Dominican Republic, and the National Association of Rural and Indigenous Women (ANAMURI) of Chile. On the difficulty that indigenous women have faced in forming their own autonomous organizations, see Deere and León 2001.

17. On the alliances of rural women's organizations in Central America, see Fundación Arias 1998.

18. The ALBA is an emerging Latin American and Caribbean integration initiative led by the Venezuelan Hugo Chávez based on social development goals shared by key Latin American rural social movements and CLOC (Bossi 2005; Harris and Azzi 2006).

19. For an overview of the debate and ongoing initiatives, see the essays in Rosset, Patel, and Courville 2006. On the Global Campaign for Agrarian Reform, also see Vía Campesina n.d.

20. The sustainability of social movements is, of course, a recurrent concern in the literature; see Hellman 1992.

21. On the broader role of social movements in the debate over free trade and anti-FTAA mobilizations, see Korzeniewicz and Smith 2001.

22. Once again, it is the ALBA, a south-south initiative supported by CLOC and La Vía Campesina, that arguably provides the most widespread fair trade benefits today—

as seen through agreements to provide petroleum products "at fair prices"—that may offer some promise for the immediate future (Bossi 2005; Padgett 2006).

References

Alvarez, Sonia. 1998. "Latin American Feminisms 'Go Global': Trends of the 1990s and Challenges for the New Millennium." In *Cultures of Politics, Politics of Cultures: Re-Visioning Latin American Social Movements*, edited by Sonia E. Alvarez, Evelina Dagnino, and Arturo Escobar, 293–324. Boulder, Colo.: Westview Press.

Astorga, Pablo, Arne R. Berges, and Valpy Fitzgerald. 2005. "The Standard of Living in Latin America during the Twentieth Century." *Economic History Review* 58 (4): 765–96.

Bartra, Armando. 2004. "Rebellious Cornfields: Towards Food and Labour Self-sufficiency." In *Mexico in Transition: Neoliberal Globalism, the State, and Civil Society*, edited by Gerardo Otero, 18–36. Black Point, Nova Scotia: Fernwood Publishing; London: Zed Books.

Bartra, Armando, and Gerardo Otero. 2005. "Indian Peasant Movements in Mexico: The Struggle for Land, Autonomy, and Democracy." In *Reclaiming the Land: The Resurgence of Rural Movements in Africa, Asia, and Latin America*, edited by Sam Moyo and Paris Yeros, 383–410. London and New York: Zed Books.

Bebbington, Anthony. 2004. "Livelihood Transitions, Place Transformations: Grounding Globalization and Modernity." In *Latin America Transformed: Globalization and Modernity*, 2nd ed., edited by Robert N. Gwynne and Cristóbal Kay, 173–92. London: Arnold.

Becker, Marc, and Guillermo Delgado-P. 1998. "Latin America: The Internet and Indigenous Texts." *Cultural Survival Quarterly* 21 (4): 23–28.

Bossi, Fernando. 2005. "10 puntos para conocer el ALBA: Construyendo el ALBA desde los pueblos." Portal ALBA. http://www.alternativabolivariana.org/modules. php?name=News&file=article&sid=470, accessed May 30, 2007.

Brysk, Alison. 2000. *From Tribal Village to Global Village: Indian Rights and International Relations in Latin America*. Stanford, Calif.: Stanford University Press.

Burguete Cal y Mayor, Araceli. 2007. "Cumbres Indígenas en América Latina." Agencia Internacional Prensa Indígena. http://www.llacta.org/notic/2007/not0411b.htm, accessed January 3, 2007.

CEPAL. 2006. *Anuario estadístico de América Latina y el Caribe: 2006*. Santiago: CEPAL.

CLOC (Coordinadora Latinoamericana de Organizaciones del Campo). 1994. "Declaración Final" from First CLOC Congress, Lima, February. <http://movimientos. org/cloc/docs, accessed August 1, 2000.

———. 1997. "Hitos históricos del proceso organizativo." September 18. http://movimientos.org/cloc/docs, accessed August 1, 2000.

———. 1998. "Declaración de Brasilia (2da. CLOC)." *Boletín de Intercambio* 1 (February). http://movimientos.org/cloc/docs, accessed August 1, 2000.

———. 2001. "Declaración Final: III Congreso de la Coordinadora Latinoamericana de Organizaciones del Campo," August 11. http://movimientos.org/cloc/docs, accessed August 15, 2002.

Cortés Castellanos, Patricia. 2005. *Mujeres Migrantes de América Latina y el Caribe: Derechos humanos, mitos, y duras realidades.* Serie Población y Desarrollo 61. Santiago: CEPAL.

Crabtree, John. 2003. "The Impact of Neo-liberal Economics on Peruvian Peasant Agriculture in the 1990s." In *Latin American Peasants,* edited by Tom Brass, 131–61. London: Frank Cass.

David, M. Beatriz de A., Cesar Morales, and Monica Rodríguez. 2001. "Modernidad y heterogeneidad: Estilo de desarrollo agrícola y rural en America Latina y el Caribe." In *Desarrollo rural en América Latina y el Caribe: La construcción de un nuevo modelo?* edited by Beatriz David, Cesar Morales, and Monica Rodríguez, 41–88. Santiago: CEPAL and Alfaomega.

"Declaración del Comité Organizador de la III Cumbre Continental Indígena." 2006. http://cumbrecontinentalindigena.org, accessed January 3, 2008.

"Declaración de Iximche." 2007. III Cumbre Continental de Pueblos y Nacionalidades Indígenas del Abya Yala, March. http://cumbrecontinentalindigena.org, accessed January 3, 2008.

"Declaración de Quito." 1990. Primer Encuentro Continental de Pueblos Indígenas, July. http://cumbrecontinentalindigena.org, accessed January 3, 2008.

Deere, Carmen Diana. 2006. "¿Feminización de la agricultura? Asalariadas, campesinas, y reestructuración económica en América Latina." *ALASRU* (Mexico) 4: 77–136.

Deere, Carmen Diana, and Magdalena León. 2001. *Empowering Women: Land and Property in Latin America.* Pittsburgh, Pa.: University of Pittsburgh Press.

Deere, Carmen Diana, and Leonilde Medeiros. 2006. "Agrarian Reform and Poverty Reduction: Lessons from Brazil." In *Land, Poverty, and Livelihoods in an Era of Globalization,* edited by A. Haroon Akram-Lodhi, Saturnino M. Borras Jr. and Cristóbal Kay, 80–118. New York: Routledge.

Delgado, Guillermo. 1994. "Ethnic Politics and the Popular Movement." In *Latin America Faces the 21st Century: Reconstructing a Social Justice Agenda,* edited by Susanne Jonas and Edward J. McCaughan, 77–88. Boulder, Colo.: Westview Press.

Desmarais, Annette-Aurelie. 2002. "The Vía Campesina: Consolidating an International Peasant and Farm Movement." *Journal of Peasant Studies* 29 (2): 91–124.

Edelman, Marc. 1998. "Transnational Peasant Politics in Central America." *Latin American Research Review* 33 (3): 49–86.

———. 1999. *Peasants against Globalization: Rural Social Movements in Costa Rica.* Stanford, Calif.: Stanford University Press.

Escobar, Arturo, and Sonia Alvarez, eds. 1992. *The Making of Social Movements in Latin America: Identity, Strategy, and Democracy.* Boulder, Colo.: Westview Press.

Foweraker, Joe. 1995. *Theorizing Social Movements.* London: Pluto Press.

Fundación Arias. 1998. *Diagnóstico sobre la organización de las mujeres rurales em Centroamérica.* San José: Fundación Arias para la Paz y el Progreso Humano.

García Pascual, Francisco. 2003. "El ajuste structural neoliberal en el sector agrario latinoamericano en la era de la globalización." *European Review of Latin American and Caribbean Studies* 75: 3–29.

Hale, Charles H. 1994. "Between Che Guevara and the Pachamama: Mestizos, Indians, and Identity Politics in the Anti-quincentenary Campaign." *Critique of Anthropology* 14 (1): 9–39.

Harris, David Evan, and Diego Azzi. 2006. "ALBA—Venezuela's Answer to "Free Trade": The Bolivarian Alternative for the Americas." Focus on the Global South, Occasional Paper 3. São Paulo, Brazil; Bangkok, Thailand. http://www.focusweb.org/pdf/alba-book.pdf, accessed May 30, 2007.

Hellman, Judith Adler. 1992. "New Social Movements and the Question of Autonomy." In *The Making of Social Movements in Latin America: Identity, Strategy, and Democracy*, edited by Arturo Escobar and Sonia E. Alvarez, 52–61. Boulder, Colo.: Westview Press.

Hernández Navarro, Luis. 2007. "El zapatismo y Vía Campesina." *La Jornada* (Mexico City), July 31. http://www.jornada.unam.mx/2007/07/31/index, accessed August 3, 2007.

Kay, Cristóbal. 2004. "Rural Livelihoods and Peasant Futures." In *Latin America Transformed: Globalization and Modernity*, , 2nd ed., edited by Robert N. Gwynne and Cristóbal Kay, 232–50. London: Arnold.

Keck, Margaret E., and Kathryn Sikkink. 1998. *Activists Beyond Borders: Advocacy Networks in International Politics*. Ithaca, N.Y.: Cornell University Press.

Korzeniewicz, Roberto Patricio, and William C. Smith. 2001. "Protest and Collaboration: Transnational Civil Society Networks and the Politics of Summitry and Free Trade in the Americas." *The North-South Agenda* 51 (September). Miami: North-South Center.

Lara Flores, Sara. 1998. *Nuevas experiencias productivas y nuevas formas de organización flexible del trabajo en la agricultura mexicana*. Mexico City: Juan Pablo Editores and Procuraduría Agraria.

Leite, Sergio, et al. 2004. *Impacto dos Assentamentos: Um estudo sobre o meio rural*. São Paulo: Edunesp and NEAD.

Monasterios, Gloria. 2003. "Abya Yala en Internet: Políticas comunicativas y representaciones de identidad de organizaciones indígenas en el ciberespacio." In *Políticas de identidades y diferencias sociales en tiempos de globalización*, edited by Daniel Mato, 303–30. Caracas: FACES and Universidad Central de Venezuela.

O'Connor, Erin. 2003. "Indians and National Salvation: Placing Ecuador's Indigenous Coup of January 2000 in Historical Perspective." In *Contemporary Indigenous Movements in Latin America*, edited by Erick D. Langer with Elena Munoz, 65–80. Wilmington: Jaguar Books.

Padgett, Tim. 2006. "Venezuela's Oil Giveaway." *Time Magazine*, Feb. 7. http://www.time.com/time/nation/article/0,8599,1157172,00.html, accessed May 30, 2007.

Petras, James, and Henry Veltmeyer. 2001. "Are Latin American Peasant Movements Still a Force for Change? Some New Paradigms Revisited." *Journal of Peasant Studies* 28 (2): 83–118.

Rosset, Peter, Raj Patel, and Michael Courville, eds. 2006. *Promised Land: Competing Visions of Agrarian Reform.* San Francisco: Food First Books.

Ruiz Hernández, Margarito. 2000. "The Plural National Indigenous Assembly for Autonomy (ANIPA): The Process of Creating a National Legislative Proposal for Autonomy." In *Indigenous Autonomy in Mexico,* edited by Aracely Burguete Cal y Mayor, 24–52. IWGIA Document No. 94. Copenhagen: International Working Group for Indigenous Affairs.

Slater, David. 1985. *New Social Movements and the State in Latin America.* Amsterdam: CEDLA.

Spoor, Max. 2002. "Policy Regimes and Performance of the Agricultural Sector in Latin America and the Caribbean during the Last Three Decades." *Journal of Agrarian Change* 2 (3): 381–400.

Tarrow, Sidney. 1998. *Power in Movement: Social Movements and Contentious Politics.* 2nd ed. Cambridge: Cambridge University Press.

"Temoaya Declaration." 1993. Second Continental Encounter of Indigenous Peoples, October. http://nativeweb.org., accessed January 3, 2008.

Van Cott, Donna Lee. 2005. *From Movements to Parties in Latin America: The Evolution of Ethnic Politics.* Cambridge: Cambridge University Press.

Vía Campesina. 1996. "Presentación: II Conferencia Internacional de Vía Campesina," April 26. http://movimientos.org/cloc/docs, accessed August 1, 2000.

———. n.d. "Pan, Tierra, y Libertad: Plataforma de la Campaña Global por la Reforma Agraria." http://www.rds.org.hn/Vía/campaign, accessed August 15, 2002.

Yashar, Deborah J. 2005. *Contesting Citizenship in Latin America: The Rise of Indigenous Movements and the Postliberal Challenge.* Cambridge: Cambridge University Press.

I

Globalizing the Struggle, Globalizing Hope

1

La Vía Campesina

Globalizing Peasants

ANNETTE AURÉLIE DESMARAIS

About seven years ago while looking for an appropriate graduate school I had an interesting discussion with an anthropologist who, after hearing about my intent to study a global peasant movement, looked at me askance and said, "But peasants no longer exist!" She then proceeded to provide me with numerous academic sources indicating just that.[1] I found this encounter quite disconcerting because I had been working for about ten years with people from around the world who called themselves peasants. In fact, for years I had heard numerous comments similar to the following one made by Marcel Carreon Mundo (2000), a Mexican peasant leader, during my interview with him: "A campesino comes from the countryside. There have always been campesinos. What did not exist before were investors, industrialists, political parties, etc. Campesinos have always existed and they will always exist. They will never be abolished." My interaction with the anthropologist reaffirmed my desire and commitment to document and analyze the formation, consolidation, and functioning of the transnational peasant movement called La Vía Campesina.[2]

My interest in researching peasants is both personal and political. I was a farmer for about fourteen years in Saskatchewan, Canada, but it was not until I was in Nicaragua, teaching preventative maintenance of farm machinery to members of agricultural cooperatives, that I began to understand the importance of farmers being organized.[3] When I returned to Canada, I was hired to work with the Canadian National Farmers Union (NFU) to facilitate the building of linkages between the NFU and its counterparts around the world. In this capacity, I have worked as technical support to La Vía Campesina since its inception in 1993. My motive in conducting research on and with La Vía Campesina is to support and accompany the movement in its efforts for social change. An important contribution in this process is to privilege the experiences, voices, and visions of peasants, rural women, and farmers themselves, which I aim to do in this chapter.

The chapter begins with a brief introduction to La Vía Campesina, followed by an examination of the factors that contributed to the rise, consolidation, and global articulation of this growing rural movement. The discussion then addresses two key elements of Vía Campesina's resistance to neoliberal globalization: the successful building of unity within diversity, and the deeply political act of articulating a peasant identity.

What Is La Vía Campesina?

Formally constituted in 1993, La Vía Campesina is a transnational movement that embraces organizations of peasants, small- and medium-scale farmers, rural women, farmworkers, and indigenous agrarian communities based in the Americas, Asia, Europe, and Africa. The movement is the most important global rural social movement to have emerged in recent times, and it continues to gain momentum.

Whenever and wherever global institutions meet to discuss agricultural and food issues, La Vía Campesina is now there. At ministerial conferences of the World Trade Organization (WTO), meetings of the World Bank and the International Monetary Fund (IMF), and gatherings of the United Nations Food and Agriculture Organization (FAO) and the World Social Forum, among others, the presence of Vía Campesina has not gone unnoticed.[4]

Since La Vía Campesina's inception, farming peoples around the world have marched together in the streets of Paris, Geneva, Seattle, Rome, Genoa, Porto Alegre, Quebec City, Jakarta, and Hong Kong, among other cities. With its members wearing dark green caps, *pañuelos* (handkerchiefs), and white t-shirts, waving green flags all decorated with its brightly colored logo, and energetically chanting slogans, La Vía Campesina has become an increasingly visible actor of radical opposition to the globalization of a neoliberal and corporate model of agriculture (Desmarais 2005).

This resistance took an extreme turn on September 10, 2003—the first day of the Fifth Ministerial Conference of the WTO, held in Cancún, Mexico—with the tragic death of the Korean farm leader, Lee Kyung Hae. Lee, along with another 120 Koreans, had joined La Vía Campesina's delegation in Cancún in efforts to get the WTO out of agriculture. Wearing a sign that said "WTO kills Farmers," Lee walked up to the high wire fence that had been built to "protect" trade negotiators from protestors and stabbed himself to death.

This ultimate and tragic act of resistance symbolized what La Vía Campesina had been saying all along: liberalization of agriculture is a war on peasants; it decimates rural communities and destroys farming families. Lee's desperate cry for change subsequently helped strengthen La Vía Campesina as it has since declared September 10 an International Day of Protest against the WTO. On that day, organizations in many countries mobilize for food sovereignty. Clearly, Lee's death has not been in vain.

The growing visibility of La Vía Campesina as a key actor, strongly rooted in local communities while at the same time increasingly engaged and more skillful on the international stage, has attracted the attention of many rural organizations in search of alternatives. Initially, when the movement was first formed in 1993 it brought together 46 organizations from 5 world regions. By 2000, when the Third International Conference was held in Bangalore, India, 101 organizations were members. During the movement's Fourth International Conference, held in Itaici, Brazil in June 2004, 42 additional organizations joined La Vía Campesina (Desmarais 2007). Nearly half of these are peasant organizations based in Asia, where the majority of the world's peasants live. Shortly after the Fourth International Conference the Central American region formally dissolved ASOCODE (the Central American Association of Peasant Organizations for Cooperation and Development, a regional organization that had existed prior to La Vía Campesina) and created a new regional entity called Vía Campesina Centroamericana, which now embraces 26 organizations. Thus in 2007 La Vía Campesina had on the order of 149 member organizations from 56 countries. As table 1.1 illustrates, the International Coordinating Committee of La Vía Campesina consists of 2 organizations from each of 8 world regions.[5]

Origins of La Vía Campesina

Clearly, La Vía Campesina is filling an important void. To better understand this rural movement let us consider why La Vía Campesina was formed and how it succeeded in consolidating itself as a transnational movement. Here, Alberto Gómez (interview, 2000), one of the regional coordinators for La Vía Campesina, highlights the driving force that pushed peasants and farmers to work together across borders:

Table 1.1. International Coordinating Committee of La Vía Campesina, 2007

Region	No. of Members	Representatives	
North America	11	UNORCA (Mexico)	Unión Nacional de Organizaciones Regionales Campesinas Autónomas
		NFFC (USA)	National Family Farm Coalition
Central America	26	COCOCH (Honduras)	Consejo Coordinador de Organizaciones Campesinas de Honduras
		ATC (Nicaragua)	Asociación de Trabajadores del Campo
Caribbean	11	ANAP (Cuba)	Asociación Nacional de Agricultores Pequeños
		CONAMUCA (Dominican Republic)	Confederación Nacional de Mujeres del Campo
South America	30	MST (Brazil)	Movimento dos Trabalhadores Rurais Sem Terra
		FNMCB-BS (Bolivia)	Federación Nacional de Mujeres Campesinas de Bolivia "Bartolina Sisa"
Europe	23	CPE (Belgium)	Coordinadora Campesina Europea
East/ Southeast Asia	23	FSPI (Indonesia)	Federation of Indonesia Peasant Union
		KWFA (Korea)	Korean Women's Peasant Association
South Asia	20	KRRS (India)	Karnataka Rajya Ryota Sangha
		BKF (Bangladesh)	Bangladesh Krishok Federation
Africa	5	UNAC (Mozambique)	União Nacional de Camponeses
		CNOP (Mali)	Coordination National de Organizations Paysannes
Total	149		

Source: Compiled by the author from a list of member organizations in the draft conference proceedings of the Fourth International Conference of La Vía Campesina held in Brazil in 2004.

Globalization is affecting us in distinct ways, our lives and our patrimony. Globalization is a global offensive against the countryside; it is a global offensive against small producers and family farmers that are not in the logic of an "efficient" countryside, an industrialized countryside. It is a global advancement against peasants' and small producers' visions for resource management, conservation of biodiversity, and all of these issues. . . . We are all facing the same enemies in this globalization. And, all of these have first and last names, they are the big companies, the transnationals. So, there are different circumstances, but we are facing the same global tendency driven by the governments of the richest countries for the benefit of the large transnationals.

By the time La Vía Campesina was formally constituted in April 1993, links had already been established among Canada's NFU, ASOCODE in Central America, the National Union of Farmers and Ranchers (UNAG) and the Women's Section of UNAG in Nicaragua, the National Union of Regional Autonomous Peasant Organizations (UNORCA) in Mexico, the Peasant Movement of the Philippines, and the Windward Islands Farmers' Association (WINFA) in the Caribbean. Similarly, European farm organizations had established ties with counterparts in South America, Asia, and Africa. Exchanges that focused on sharing knowledge of sustainable practices—such as the Peasant to Peasant project—were also vital to bringing together Central American and Mexican peasant organizations (Holt-Giménez 1996, 2006; Edelman 1998, 56–7).[6] Many other rural social movements throughout Latin America had also engaged in a similar process of organizational exchanges within (and beyond) the region, all of which eventually contributed to the formation of the Latin American Coordinator of Rural Organizations (CLOC), which held its first congress nine months after the formation of La Vía Campesina.

As the Uruguay Round of the GATT drew to a close in 1994, peasant and farm organizations clearly understood that international trade agreements would result in even more fundamental changes to the structure of agricultural economies and the social fabric of rural communities. This economic liberalization and the globalization of an industrialized model of agriculture prompted farm and peasant leaders in the North and the South to mobilize beyond national borders and to organize themselves in La Vía Campesina. As João Pedro Stédile, a leader of the Brazilian Landless Rural Workers' Movement (MST) the organization serving as the regional coordinator for South America for La Vía Campesina at the time, explained:

It is very striking that it is only now that farmers are starting to achieve a degree of worldwide coordination, after five hundred years of capitalist development. Workers have had an international day for over a century, and women for not much less, but farmers have only just agreed to mark one—17 April, a source of pride to us: a tribute to Carajás. As long as capitalism meant only industrialization, those who worked on the land limited their struggle to the local level. But as the realities of neoliberal internationalization have been imposed on us, we've begun to hear stories from farmers in the Philippines, Malaysia, South Africa, Mexico, France, all facing the same problems—and the same exploiters. The Indians are up against Monsanto, just as we are in Brazil, and Mexico, and France. It's the same handful of companies—seven groups, in total, worldwide—that monopolize agricultural trade, and control research and biotechnology, and are tightening their ownership of the planet's seeds. The new phase of capitalism has itself created the conditions for farmers to unite against the neoliberal model. (Stedile 2002, 99)

For peasants the WTO and its Agreement on Agriculture quickly became key targets of resistance. Indeed, without the WTO, it is highly doubtful that the Vía Campesina would have emerged. The women of the Vía Campesina acknowledged this in a press release at the WTO Ministerial Meeting in Seattle in 1999 when they thanked the WTO for creating the conditions that had enabled farming families to establish their common ground and begin carving new spaces for negotiation and collective action (Vía Campesina 1999).

The Vía Campesina Alternative

La Vía Campesina was created in radical opposition to a particular vision of development reflected in many national governments and global institutions like the WTO, the World Bank, and the IMF. In the countryside this type of development involved the modernization of agriculture and had led to what some call high modernist agriculture, structurally adjusted agriculture, or corporate-led agriculture (Scott 1998; Qualman and Wiebe 2000). An earlier version of this model of agriculture has ravaged the countryside in the North for nearly a century and it was this model that was rapidly globalized through structural adjustment programs and the signing of regional and global free-trade agreements. The model is based on the idea that the great majority of peasants everywhere must disappear and that those who remain are left to compete against each other in efforts to gain a greater share of the international marketplace.

La Vía Campesina completely rejects this misguided logic. It argues that the conflict is not between farmers of the North and peasants in the South. Rather, resistance to the instruments of neoliberalism—this includes the policies of national governments, transnational corporations, the WTO, the World Bank, IMF, the G8—must be seen as a struggle between two competing models of social and economic development.

On the one hand is a globalized, neoliberal, corporate-driven model where agriculture is seen exclusively as a profit-making venture and productive resources are increasingly concentrated in the hands of agro-industry. This is a model where food has become a mystery for many people. It simply appears like magic on the shelves of grocery stores. Raw crops disappear from fields and go through some magical processes that turn wheat, coconut oil, and tomatoes into frozen pizza treats. Food emerges hermetically sealed and neatly packaged in brightly colored cardboard boxes with a label that says "may contain. . . . "

La Vía Campesina, on the other hand, envisions a radically different, more humane model, one where agriculture is based on food sovereignty, a concept that the movement introduced in the international arena at the World Food Summit held in Rome in 1996. To La Vía Campesina, food is a basic human right and thus all peoples must have "the right to define their agricultural and food policy" to ensure domestic food security and the well-being of their farming populations (Vía Campesina 1996, 2000a, 2000b).[7] La Vía Campesina stresses that food sovereignty means that peoples have the "right to produce [their] own food in [their] own territory" in ways that enhance the environment and peoples' cultural values (Vía Campesina 2000a). Food sovereignty means that agriculture is farmer-driven, production of food is located close to where it is consumed, and producing food is ecologically sustainable while being economically viable. A food sovereignty approach aims to eliminate the distance between production and consumption and thus disempower the corporate interests that have inserted themselves at numerous links along the industrial food chain in efforts to garner increasing profits. Food sovereignty gives life to La Vía Campesina's firm conviction that "another agriculture is possible."[8]

Building Unity within Diversity

Resistance, for La Vía Campesina, entails much more than organizing massive protests in the streets, although for peasant organizations everywhere this certainly remains a critical resource for social change. However, for those organized in La Vía Campesina, resistance also means bringing together a great diversity of organizations from the North and the South around a particular vision. Rafael Alegría (2000), a peasant leader from Honduras who headed the Operational Secretariat of La Vía Campesina from 1996 to 2004, put it like this during our interview:

> I think that what really unites us is a fundamental commitment to humanism because the antithesis of this is individualism and ma-

terialism. . . . The common problems of land, production, technology, markets, ideological formation, training, poverty—all of these we have in common. But what also unites us are great aspirations. We are all convinced that the current structures of economic, political, and social power are unjust and exclusionary. What unites us is a spirit of transformation and struggle to change these structures all over the world. We aspire to a better world, a more just world, a more humane world, a world where real equality and social justice exist. These aspirations and solidarity in rural struggles keep us united in La Vía Campesina.

How exactly does La Vía Campesina succeed in building this unity that Alegría emphasizes? Elsewhere, I have argued that the roots of the movement stretch back to the 1980s when rural organizations in the North and the South engaged in numerous north-south, south-south, and north-north organizational exchanges and dialogue (Desmarais 2002). Through these exchanges—which lasted anywhere from one week to six weeks and sometimes longer—farm leaders would spend time in each others' countries learning about the changes taking place in the agricultural sector, analyzing how peasant organizations were responding, examining the various resistance strategies, and looking carefully at the alternatives that organizations were putting into place. The exchanges were instrumental in enabling peasants and farmers to close the north-south divide by effectively establishing much common ground. In reflecting on his visits with Canadian and American farmers, Pedro Magaña (interview, 2000), a former leader with UNORCA, explained:

An important conclusion for me was that the model and conditions in which the family farmers of the United States find themselves is not a future that we want for ourselves. Then, we turn around and see our own situation and we don't want that either. It really had an impact on me. I believed that American farmers were super producers, that they were doing really well, they had the best, an organized development superior to ours. Now I know this is not the case. . . . They have lost the quality of life. Today a farmer must work fourteen to fifteen hours a day . . . they are living on credit. Often they lose the land. Their children do not work the land; they have to leave. They've lost the community life. The quality of food is seriously questioned because of the high use of chemicals and hormones. The suicide of American and European farmers is a daily occurrence. We do not want to go there.

This was one of my first big lessons and experiences from my visit to the United States.

We also had the opportunity to host Canadian farmers. They went to Guanajuato and were shocked to see how small our land holdings are, how backward our technology is, the differences in costs of production and how high our interest rates are. . . . But, in the end . . . we face the same transnational strategy, a strategy of capital accumulation with a devastating consequence on people's economy. Our enemy is the same. The strategies may be different. But, as farmers, our objective is the same: give to society adequate and healthy food. But the governments do not recognize the social function of the production of food. And, this is the common objective of the global struggle, that the social function of agriculture be recognized, that the farmers' rights to produce . . . be recognized.

During an interview in 2001, Stuart Thiesson, a former executive director of the NFU, commented: "The thing that maybe tied you together, or the commonality of it, was the role of the multinational corporations in all of these areas. . . . Being able to bring back [the experiences] and have people understand what the role was of the multinationals was an important aspect of those exchanges because it didn't matter whether you were a peasant or whether you had a 1,600 acre farm; the multinationals had their influence in terms of your business. And now, of course, the encroachment of multinationals in terms of farmers is getting closer to home all the time."

And a Caribbean farm leader, Simon Alexander, after spending six weeks with NFU members in Saskatchewan as part of the Canadian-Caribbean Agricultural Exchange Project, found more similarities than differences between Canadian and Caribbean farmers. He summed it up: "Things are not all rosy up here . . . When I first arrived here, I saw all the big machinery and thought the farmers here must be very rich. But that's not the case. There are a lot of poor farmers in Canada . . . Everywhere it's the same thing . . . It is a struggle just to survive. The big buyers make all the money and they leave us the scraps" (quoted in Pugh 1990, 3).

Through these exchanges and ongoing dialogue, farm leaders came to understand each other's realities and define the nature of solidarity. According to Lisa Chemerika (interview, 2002), a member of the NFU who participated in an exchange with WINFA:

It is amazing how much these experiences became part of our daily lives. I still keep in touch with some of the people I met on my first exchange, I still think about the people I met, I still think about the Caribbean and I wonder how they are surviving. You are so far away from home and it is all so foreign, but it is amazing to go to a country where things are so different yet there are so many similarities because Canada and the Caribbean are export-based economies . . . These were very political exchanges. We would spend hours and hours discussing the history of agriculture, the international economy, analyzing the current situation, the role of peasant organizations and how they are organized . . . It forced us to really think about and understand better what was going on in our own countries. These exchanges were about getting to know one another and building relations of trust and respect.

Armed with this kind of social capital, a sophisticated collective analysis based on daily realities, a collective will not to be "disappeared," and a commitment to build alternatives to neoliberalism—all of these led many of the farm leaders who had participated in exchanges within and beyond their regions to give birth to the Vía Campesina.

Of course it is important to point out that the international encounters also challenged cultural preconceptions. When two Latin American peasant leaders were meeting with farmers in rural India, one of the Indian farmers asked me, "Are they really peasant leaders?" Somewhat surprised by the question, I responded, "Why yes. What made you ask this question?" He responded, "Well, they are too big to be farmers. The only big people here in this part of India are the policemen and the bureaucrats." During the same trip, we were contemplating where we could go for dinner. The Latin American leaders had had enough Indian food and insisted on going to a restaurant where they could eat "a whole chicken." Professor Nanjundaswamy, then the leader of the Karnataka State Farmers Association who was hosting the delegation visit, very politely explained that the only restaurant where this was available was Kentucky Fried Chicken. He went on to explain that this was the very restaurant that his organization, in protest, had ransacked a couple of years earlier. Consequently, getting a whole chicken was completely out of the question![9]

A different sort of frustration was experienced by a member of the Canadian NFU when he participated in the Vía Campesina delegation to the World Social Forum a few years ago.[10] His frustration was rooted in La Vía Campesina's apparent lack of interest in Robert's Rules of Order and specifically the movement's failure to understand the need for, and practice of, passing resolutions during its meetings. Actually, it was the member of the NFU who failed to appreciate that La Vía Campesina's meetings demand careful attention to numerous cultural experiences and dynamics and, consequently, require ways of working that are a far departure from European or North American practice.

These examples underscore that for most farm organizations, working internationally provides significant opportunities for building leadership capacity. As leaders accumulate experience through Vía Campesina delegations, regional meetings, and international conferences, there is greater appreciation for the diversity reflected within the movement. This diversity is seen as a significant counterforce to the homogenizing forces of globalization. Hence, for La Vía Campesina resistance also includes conscious efforts to understand and respect differences while strengthening a commitment to build unity within that diversity.

La Vía Campesina brings together a great diversity of organizations. First, the international movement brings together different types of organizations such as those for peasants, rural women, small to medium farmers, farmworkers, and the indigenous. And while most organizations in the Vía Campesina are strictly rural-based, others have developed an urban constituency and are actively working in an urban setting. For example, while the MST works primarily with the landless in the countryside it also has started work in the shanty towns to form "rurban" settlements (*assentamentos rurbanos*), which involves setting up urban-based families on small plots of land close to, or within, city limits (Stédile 2002, 92). In Puebla, Mexico, UNORCA organizes urban street vendors, and in Vera Cruz UNORCA played a significant role in organizing transport carriers (Ladron de Guevarra, interview, 2000). Meanwhile, the newly formed Union Paysanne in Quebec brings together farmers with—among others—researchers, students, consumer groups, and eco-tourism businesses who are all committed to building an alternative to *malbouffe* and industrial agriculture.[11]

Geographically, La Vía Campesina represents organizations from the Americas, Asia, Europe, and Africa, each with its own regional and local cultural particularities. Interest among Arab organizations in future collaboration surfaced when La Vía Campesina sent a four-person delegation to Palestine in 2002 to establish contacts with farmers' organizations, better understand the situation of Arab and Israeli farming peoples, and develop a long-term strategy for joint work to protect the rights of farming families.[12]

Within La Vía Campesina, there is also diversity in the political scale at which affiliated farmer and peasant organizations are constituted. Some organizations, like the Karnataka State Farmers Association, are organized only at the state level. Canada's NFU, in contrast, is a national organization, while UNORCA in Mexico is a national federation that works in twenty-three of the Mexican states. Still others, like ASOCODE (prior to its dissolution) and the European Peasant Coordination (CPE) are regional entities bringing together national organizations. Each of these different organizational structures demands particular skills, experience, and knowledge in negotiating among its defined membership. Consequently, each of these organizations has its own unique organizational culture, which may assist or hinder its ability to function well in a multicultural and diverse international movement.

In large measure, La Vía Campesina's strength derives from the way it is woven together by and from organizations embedded in their own particular political, economic, social, and cultural contexts. Just how does La Vía Campesina succeed in building unity within the diversity of organizations? To answer this question, we must return to where this chapter began, with the debate on the very existence of peasants.

The Significance of Identity

Marx predicted that with agrarian capitalism peasants would simply disappear. The masters of globalization expect them to succumb to large commercial farms. And yet, peasants are stubbornly refusing to go away. Indeed, in the face of a development model geared to ensure the near extinction of peasants and small farmers, La Vía Campesina is redefining what it means to be a peasant or a small farmer. Some, like Cliff Welch (2001), argue that what is actually occurring is a process we might call "re-peasantization" as national and international organizations proudly embrace the term peasant to describe themselves (Edelman 1999, 2001a, 2001b, 2003). This is certainly the case for many of La Vía Campesina organizations in Latin America that were formed in the late 1980s and the early 1990s. Asian organizations, too, such as the Federation of Indonesian Peasant Unions and the Peasant Movement of the Philippines, are clearly affirming their peasant identities.[13]

What does it mean that peasants and farmers belonging to La Vía Campesina proudly declare themselves peasants? In the English language literature of Europe, the term peasant is specifically linked to feudalism. In the colonial context, and especially in other languages, its meaning expanded. Thus *paysan* or campesino were always to some extent broader categories. But, even in its broadest usage—campesino in Latin America—peasants were viewed as remnants of the past. In everyday usage the term has most often been pejorative and the demise of peasants was welcomed by capitalists, national planners, and development specialists, indeed, by virtually everyone but the peasants themselves.

In this context resurrecting "peasants" is an act of resistance. Nettie Wiebe, the former president of the NFU and a former regional coordinator of La Vía Campesina, explains this very clearly:

> If you actually look at what "peasant" means, it means "people of the land." Are we Canadian farmers "people of the land"? Well, yes, of course. And it's important to take that language back . . . We too are peasants and it's the land and our relationship to the land and food production that distinguishes us . . . We're not part of the industrial machine. We're much more closely linked to the places where we grow food and how we grow food, and what the weather is there . . .
>
> The language around this matters. It begins to make us understand that "people of the land"—peasantry everywhere, the millions of small subsistence peasants with whom we think we have so little in common—identifies them and it identifies us. They're being evicted from their land, and that decimates their identity and their community. And we're also being relocated in our society—it's as undermining for us as it is for them.
>
> The language? As long as you keep us in separate categories and we're the highly industrialized farmers who are sort of quasi-business entrepreneurs and they're the subsistence peasants, then we can't see how closely we and all our issues are linked. (quoted in Edelman 2003, 187)

It is precisely this vision that the name "La Vía Campesina" itself suggests. At the conference held in Mons, Belgium, where La Vía Campesina was formally constituted, there was quite heated debate about the name and what the name represented.

Delegates from Great Britain declared that the literal translation—Peasant Road or Peasant Way—would be completely inappropriate because of the derogatory connotation attached to the term "peasant" and the fact that peasants really did not exist in the English countryside. However, as Saturnino (Jun) Borras, a former representative of the Peasant Movement of the Philippines and a founding member of the Vía Campesina, recalled in an interview in 2001, many argued in favor of using the term "peasant" because "farmer" also had connotations "that did not capture the nature and character of the farm sector we do represent." In the end, a compromise was reached; delegates opted not to translate "Vía Campesina" into English. Of course, keeping only the Spanish name also has its challenges. For example, in a number of national conventions of the NFU a couple of farmers have passionately spoken about the need to continue to belong and work with the "Vía Cappuccino!"

Reclaiming the meaning of "peasant" is perhaps one of La Vía Campesina's most important accomplishments. Whether a peasant, *paysan, paysanne*, campesino, *campesina*, small farmer, *agricultor, agricultora, productor, productora,* rural worker, or indigenous peasant—all have embraced and have been embraced by La Vía Campesina. And just as Marc Edelman (1999) found in his work on Costa Rican peasants, those involved in La Vía Campesina do not necessarily distinguish among these terms. This is best captured by Karen Pedersen, the women's president[14] of the NFU in Canada, who argued:

> The language around us is changing all the time. Historically, we were peasants. Then when that term came to mean "backward" we became "farmers." In these days "farmer" has the connotation of inefficiency and we are strongly encouraged to be more modern, to see ourselves instead as managers, business people, or entrepreneurs capable of handling increasingly larger pieces of territory.
>
> Well, I am a farmer and I am a peasant. Through my participation in the Vía Campesina I learned that I had much more in common with peasants then I did with some of my agribusiness neighbors. I am reclaiming the term peasant because I actually believe that small is more efficient, it is socially intelligent, it is community oriented. Being a peasant stands for the kind of agriculture and rural communities we are striving to build.[15]

If some people in the Canadian NFU are "rediscovering" their peasant roots, others in Mexico had never doubted them. For instance, Emiliano Cerros Nava, a member of the Executive Commission of UNORCA in Mexico, patiently explained in an interview in 2000, "This debate in the literature . . . is a fabrication at a higher level, by those who know more. In the countryside, out there, there is no such debate. We continue being peasants. That's the way it is."

This is a politicized identity.[16] It reflects people who share a deep commitment to place, people deeply attached to a particular piece of land, people who are all part of a particular rural community, and people whose mode of existence is under threat. This place-bound identity, "people of the land," reflects belief in the right to be on the land. They have the right and obligation to produce food. They have the right to be seen as fulfilling an important function in society at large. They have the right to live in viable communities and the obligation to build community. All of these form essential parts of their distinct identity as peasants. In the context of today's globalization, articulating identity across borders based on locality and tradition is a deeply political act.

La Vía Campesina has jealously guarded its peasant and farmer-led status. All Vía Campesina representatives are either farming themselves or they have been selected, appointed, or elected by farm organizations. It has successfully resisted the persistent intrusions (some well-intentioned and some not so well-intentioned) of NGOs, reformist farm organizations, and international institutions. La Vía Campesina restricts its membership to organizations of peasants, farmers, rural women, farmworkers, and indigenous communities who formally must demonstrate agreement with the positions and principles of La Vía Campesina. In the case of those rural organizations that also have urban bases La Vía Campesina strongly encourages these to send only their rural representatives to participate in Vía Campesina delegations, meetings, and conferences. Non-governmental organizations cannot be members.

In this way, La Vía Campesina has succeeded in clearly articulating and firmly placing in the international arena the needs, interests, demands, and visions of those who actually produce food.[17] Through the concept of food sovereignty La Vía Campesina has helped focus international agriculture and food deliberations on issues such as agrarian reform, genetically modified organisms (GMOs) and the control and ownership of seeds, sustainable agricultural practices, human rights and gender equality in the countryside, and the relationships between international trade, food insecurity, and poverty in rural areas. La Vía Campesina argues that the new concept of food sovereignty offers a concrete alternative to the neoliberal view of agriculture and food; it is an alternative vision that is grounded in the daily realities of those who produce food.

La Vía Campesina's peasant identity reflects a deep attachment to culture. The production, distribution, preparation, consumption, and celebration of food are all fundamental aspects of rural cultures. Seeds are perhaps peasants' most precious and, in many cases, deeply cultural and sacred resource.

La Vía Campesina regularly engages in the ritual of exchanging seeds. In virtually all international gatherings of La Vía Campesina, representatives bring seeds from their homelands to exchange with their counterparts from different parts of the world. At the first World Food Summit, which was held in Rome in 1996, La Vía Campesina distributed its declaration, "The Right to Produce and Access to Land, Food Sovereignty: A Future without Hunger," accompanied by a small package of seeds to all delegates attending the official summit. It also brought truckloads of earth into the city to form a small plot of land and peasants, rural women, indigenous peoples, and farmers engaged in a symbolic act of planting seeds. And La Vía Campesina concluded the NGO Forum on Food Sovereignty (held in Rome under the framework of the World Food Summit: Five Years Later, in June 2002) by distributing seeds collected from around the world while delegates listened to music and a poem expounding the sacredness of seeds (Wiebe, interview, 2002).

In doing this, La Vía Campesina helps ground the debates. In giving, exchanging, or symbolically planting seeds, the essence of life, La Vía Campesina takes the familiar and fundamental in peasants' daily reality to impress on "others" the profound importance of farmers' relationship to seeds and to the land. These actions leave a visual imprint of an important yet very simple message: we, the peasants and farmers of the world, take seeds, plant them, and turn them into food. This is our role in society and it is a vital contribution. We are talking about real people and real lives whose whole mode of existence is under threat. Nettie Wiebe captures a critical aspect of what is at the heart of La Vía Campesina—the "right to be": "La Vía Campesina is . . . a movement of people of the land who share a progressive agenda . . . which means we share the view that people—small farmers, peasants, people of the land—have a right to be there. . . . That it's our job to look after the earth and our people. We must defend it and we have to defend it in the global context" (quoted in Arcellana 1996, 10).

It is this shared commitment not to be "disappeared" that drives La Vía Campesina. The movement continues to gain momentum as it collectively defines the alternative vision of food sovereignty, a vision that is clearly articulated through a carefully negotiated, locally rooted yet global, peasant identity. All of this is clearly reflected in La Vía Campesina's slogan, "Let's globalize the struggle, let's globalize hope."

Notes

1. There is an extensive literature on the role of the peasantry. Key historical references include Lenin 1954; Chayanov 1966; Moore 1966; Wolf 1966, 1969; Paige 1975; and Scott 1976, 1985. For more recent debates, see, among others, Bryceson et al. 2000; Otero 1998; Kearney 1996; Bernstein and Byrer 2001; Brass 2005; and McMichael 2006a, 2006b.

2. This chapter is based on my Ph.D. dissertation (Desmarais 2003a), a revised version that has been published as Desmarais 2007.

3. One of my key mentors in this process was Martha Valle, who at the time was a regional leader of the women's section of UNAG. See chapter 12 in this volume for a historical overview of organized peasant women in Nicaragua.

4. See Desmarais 2002, 2003a, 2003b, 2007; Borras 2004; Patel 2006; and Edelman 2003.

5. Organizations that have initiated their integration into La Vía Campesina include the Japanese Family Farmers' Movement and the U.S.-based Rural Coalition. Decisions regarding membership status for these organizations and others that wish to join the movement will be finalized at the next international conference, scheduled for Africa in October 2008.

6. A number of other factors contributed to expanding peasants' perspectives beyond the local and national levels. Edelman (personal communication) has pointed out that the expansion of the fair trade movement combined with peasant and farm organizations' involvement in value-adding activities provided new opportunities for international engagement.

7. For further discussion of food sovereignty, see Montagut and Dogliotti 2006; Patel 2005; Windfuhr and Jonsén 2005; GRAIN 2005; Long 2005; Desmarais 2003a, 2003b; Rosset 2003; and Menezes 2001. Also see "The World Is Not for Sale: Priority to Peoples' Food Sovereignty," http://www.citizen.org/documents/wtooutoffood.pdf, accessed February 28, 2008.

8. See Peter Rosset's chapter in this volume for a discussion of how food sovereignty can inform the conceptualization and implementation of genuine agrarian reform.

9. For various views on this particular protest, see Assadi 1995, 1996, 1998; Shiva 1996; and Gupta 1998.

10. This information surfaced in a telephone conversation with the NFU representative.

11. *Malbouffe* (usually translated as junk food) is a concept that was developed by the Confédération Paysanne in France in its struggle against the globalization of industrial agriculture. *Malbouffe* gained worldwide recognition through José Bové, the Confédération Paysanne's charismatic leader, who was imprisoned for dismantling a McDonald's outlet still under construction in the small town of Millau in 1999. As Bové explains, *malbouffe* is "food from nowhere. . . [it has] the same taste from one end of the world to the other"; it has been stripped of "taste, health and [its] cultural and geographical identity. Junk food is the result of the intensive exploitation of the land to maximize yield and profit" (Bové and Dufour 2001, 54–55).

José Bové traveled to Quebec and met with Union Paysanne leaders in the spring of 2001 to explain French farm politics and to exchange ideas about organizing strategies. This helps explain why a rejection of *malbouffe* was integrated into the Union Paysanne's vision for change.

12. The four Vía Campesina delegates were Paul Nicholson (Euskal Herriko Nekazarien Elkartasuna and CPE), Doris Gutierrez de Hernandez (Vía Campesina Operational Secretariat), Mário Lill (MST), and José Bové (Confédération Paysanne and CPE).

13. An earlier version of this section forms part of Desmarais 2008.

14. In order to ensure gender and youth parity in the leadership of the organization, the NFU has three presidents: the NFU president, a NFU women's president, and a NFU youth president.

15. Karen Pedersen's statement was made during a meeting of women farmers involved in the Farm Families Employment Practices research project held in Saskatoon, Saskatchewan, on March 1, 2003.

16. As Miles (2001, 149) reminds us, the articulation of a shared identity must be seen as "a political achievement . . . not a given condition" and these politicized identities become "foundations to reach out from, not walls to hide behind." Many social movement theorists highlight the significance of, and complex processes involved in, the construction of collective identities within local and/or national social movements (Melucci 1988, 1989; Escobar and Alvarez 1992; Starn 1999; Radcliffe 1990; Radcliffe and Westwood 1996, among others). More recent studies confirm the power of constructing alternative identities in the context of globalization (Stammers 1999; Miles 2001; and Eschle 2001, among others).

17. La Vía Campesina, of course, is not the only social actor in the international arena representing the interests of rural peoples. See Borras 2004 for an exploration of rival movements in the context of agrarian reform, Edelman 2003 for a survey of the major transnational agrarian movements, and Desmarais 2003b for an analysis of how Vía Campesina's positions and strategies differed from that of the International Federation of Agricultural Producers and international NGOs.

References

Arcellana, Nancy Pearson. 1996. "Rural Women's Workshop Highlights: From the Fields of Home to the City of Rome." In *Proceedings of the Rural Women's Workshop, the NGO Forum, and World Food Summit Activities held in Rome, Italy, November 6–16, 1996*. Manila: ISIS.

Assadi, Muzaffar. 1995. "Dunkelism and Peasant Protest in Karnataka: A View from Within." *Social Action: A Quarterly Review of Social Trends* 45 (2): 191–204.

———. 1996. "'Chickens,' 'Greens,' and 'Ragi Balls': A Discourse on Kentucky Fried Chickens (KFC)." *Social Action: A Quarterly Review of Social Trends* 46 (2): 179–91.

———. 1998. "Attack on Multinationals: Re-enactment of Gandhian Violence." *Economic and Political Weekly*, May 18: 1184–86.

Bernstein, Henry, and Terence J. Byres. 2001. "From Peasant Studies to Agrarian Change." *Journal of Agrarian Change* 1 (1): 1–56.

Borras, Saturnino M. 2004. "La Vía Campesina: An Evolving Transnational Social Movement." *TNI Briefing Series* 2004/6. Amsterdam: Transnational Institute.

Bové, José, and Francois Dufour. 2001. *The World Is Not for Sale*. Interviews by Gilles Luneau. Translation by Anna de Casparis. London: Verso.

Brass, Tom. 2005. "The Journal of Peasant Studies: The Third Decade." *The Journal of Peasant Studies* 32 (1): 153–80.

Bryceson, Deborah, Cristóbal Kay, and Jos Mooij, eds. 2000. *Disappearing Peasantries? Rural Labour in Africa, Asia, and Latin America*. London: Intermediate Technology Publications.

Chayanov, Alexander. 1966. *The Theory of Peasant Economy*. Edited by Daniel Thorner, Basile Kerblay, and R.E.F. Smith. Homewood, Ill.: Richard D. Irwin.

Desmarais, Annette Aurélie. 2002. "The Vía Campesina: Consolidating an International Peasant and Farm Movement." *Journal of Peasant Studies* 29 (2): 91–124.

———. 2003a. "The Vía Campesina: Peasants Resisting Globalization." Ph.D. diss., Department of Geography, University of Calgary.

———. 2003b. "The WTO . . . Will Meet Somewhere, Sometime. And We Will Be There." Published as part of the project entitled *Voices: The Rise of Nongovernmental Voices in Multilateral Organizations*. Ottawa: North-South Institute. http://www.nsi-ins.ca/english/pdf/Voices_WTO_Desmarais.pdf, accessed on December 20, 2006.

———. 2005. "United in the Vía Campesina." *Food First Backgrounder* 11 (4). Oakland, Calif.: Foodfirst.

———. 2007. *La Vía Campesina: Globalization and the Power of Peasants*. Black Point, Nova Scotia: Fernwood Publishing; London: Pluto Press.

———. 2008. "The Power of Peasants: Reflections on the Meanings of the Vía Campesina." *Journal of Rural Studies* 24 (2): 138–49.

Edelman, Marc. 1998. "Transnational Peasant Politics in Central America." *Latin American Research Review* 33 (3): 49–86.

———. 1999. *Peasants against Globalization: Rural Social Movements in Costa Rica*. Stanford, Calif.: Stanford University Press.

———. 2001a. "Toward an Anthropology of Some New Internationalisms: Small Farmers in Global Resistance Movements." Paper presented at the American Ethnological Society and the Canadian Anthropology Society, May 2–6, Montreal.

———. 2001b. "Social Movements: Changing Paradigms and Forums of Politics." *Annual Review of Anthropology* 30: 285–317.

———. 2003. "Transnational Peasant and Farmer Movements and Networks." In *Global Civil Society Yearbook 2003*, edited by M. Kaldor, H. Anheier, and M. Glasius, 185–220. Oxford: Oxford University Press.

Eschle, Catherine. 2001. *Global Democracy, Social Movements, and Feminism*. Boulder, Colo.: Westview Press.

Escobar, Arturo, and Sonia E. Alvarez, eds. 1992. *The Making of Social Movements in Latin America: Identity, Strategy, and Democracy*. Boulder, Colo.: Westview Press.

GRAIN. 2005. "Food Sovereignty: Turning the Global Food System Upside Down." Editorial. http://www.grain.org/seedling/index.cfm?id=329, accessed on December 20, 2006.

Gupta, Akhil. 1998. *Postcolonial Developments: Agriculture in the Making of Modern India*. Durham, N.C.: Duke University Press.

Holt-Giménez, Eric. 1996. "The Campesino a Campesino Movement: Farmer-Led Sustainable Agriculture in Mexico and Central America." Policy Report. Oakland, Calif.: Food First Institute for Food and Development Policy.

———. 2006. *Campesino a Campesino: Voices from Latin America's Farmer to Farmer Movement for Sustainable Agriculture*. Oakland, Calif.: Food First Institute for Food and Development Policy.

Kearney, Michael. 1996. *Reconceptualizing the Peasantry: Anthropology in Global Perspective*. Boulder, Colo.: Westview Press.

Lenin, Vladimir Illyich. 1954. *The Agrarian Question and the "Critics of Marx."* Moscow: Progress Publishers.

Long, Clara. 2005. "Food Sovereignty and the Vía Campesina: The Evolution of a Counter-hegemonic Discourse." M.A. thesis, Department of Geography and Environment, London School of Economics and Political Science.

McMichael, Philip. 2006a. "Reframing Development: Global Peasant Movements and the New Agrarian Question." *Canadian Journal of Development Studies* 27 (4): 451–83.

———. 2006b. "Peasant Prospects in the Neoliberal Age." *New Political Economy* 11 (3): 407–18.

Melucci, Alberto. 1988. "Getting Involved: Identity and Mobilization in Social Movements." In *From Structure to Action: Comparing Social Movement Research Across Cultures*, edited by Bert Klandermans, Hanspeter Kriesi, and Sidney Tarrow, 329–48.International Social Movement Research 1. Greenwich, Conn.: JAI.

———. 1989. *Nomads of the Present: Social Movements and Individual Needs in Contemporary Society*. Edited by John Keane and Paul Mier. Philadelphia: Temple University Press.

Menezes, Francisco. 2001. "Food Sovereignty: A Vital Requirement for Food Security in the Context of Globalization." *Development* (Rome) 44 (4): 29–33.

Miles, Angela. 2001. "Global Feminist Theorizing and Organizing: Life-Centred and Multi-Centred Alternatives to Neoliberal Globalization." In *Globalization and Social Movements*, edited by Pierre Hamel, Henri Lustiger-Thaler, Jane Nederveen Pieterse, and Sasha Roseneil, 140–65. New York: Palgrave.

Montagut, Xavier, and Fabrizio Dogliotti. 2006. *Alimentos globalizados: Soberanía alimentaria y comercio justo*. Barcelona: Icaria.

Moore, Barrington. 1966. *Social Origins of Dictatorship and Democracy: Lord and Peasant in the Making of the Modern World*. Boston: Beacon Press.

Otero, Gerardo. 1998. *Farewell to the Peasantry? Political Class Formation in Rural Mexico*. Boulder, Colo.: Westview Press.

Paige, Jeffrey. 1975. *Agrarian Revolution: Social Movements and Export Agriculture in the Underdeveloped World*. New York: Free Press.

Patel, Rajeev. 2005. "Global Fascism, Revolutionary Humanism, and the Ethics of Food Sovereignty." *Development* 48 (2): 79–83.

———. 2006. "International Agrarian Restructuring and the Practical Ethics of Peasant Movement Solidarity." *Journal of Asian and African Studies* 41 (1–2): 71–93.

Pugh, Terry. 1990. "Life on a Canadian Farm: A New Experience for Youth." *Union Farmer* (Saskatoon), October, p. 3.

Qualman, Darrin, and Nettie Wiebe. 2000. "The Structural Adjustment of Canadian Agriculture." Paper prepared for the Canadian Centre for Policy Alternatives and the SAPRI/CASA Project, August. Ottawa: Canadian Centre for Policy Alternatives.

Radcliffe, Sarah. 1990. "Multiple Identities and Negotiation over Gender: Female Peasant Union Leaders in Peru." *Bulletin of Latin American Research* 9 (2): 229–47.

Radcliffe, Sarah, and Sallie Westwood. 1996. *Remaking the Nation: Place, Identity, and Politics in Latin America.* London: Routledge.

Rosset, Peter. 2003. "Food Sovereignty: Global Cry of Farmer Movements." *Food First Backgrounder* (Institute for Food and Development Policy) 9 (4). http://www.foodfirst.org/pubs/backgrdrs/2003/f03v9n4.html, accessed on July 26, 2004.

Scott, James. 1976. *The Moral Economy of the Peasant: Rebellion and Subsistence in Southeast Asia.* New Haven, Conn.: Yale University Press.

———. 1985. *Weapons of the Weak: Everyday Forms of Peasant Resistance.* New Haven, Conn.: Yale University Press.

———. 1998. *Seeing like a State.* New Haven, Conn.: Yale University Press.

Shiva, Vandana. 1996. "More Than a Matter of Two Flies: Why KFC Is an Ecological Issue." *Third World Resurgence* 67: 2–4.

Stammers, Neil. 1999. "Social Movements and the Challenge to Power." In *Politics and Globalisation: Knowledge, Ethics, and Agency,* edited by Martin Shaw, 73–88. London: Routledge.

Starn, Orin. 1999. *Nightwatch: The Politics of Protest in the Andes.* Durham, N.C.: Duke University Press.

Stédile, João Pedro. 2002. "Landless Battalions: The Sem Terra Movement of Brazil." Interview with João Pedro Stédile. *New Left Review* 15: 77–104.

Vía Campesina. 1996. "The Right to Produce and Access to Land." Position of the Vía Campesina on food sovereignty presented at the World Food Summit, November, 13–17, Rome.

———. 1999. "Women Farmers Say No to WTO." Press release, December 3. http://www.viacampesina.org/main_en/index.php?option=com_content&task=view&id=56&Itemid=35, accessed on March 2, 2007.

———. 2000a. "Food Sovereignty and International Trade." Position paper approved at the Third International Conference of the Vía Campesina, October 3–6, 2000, Bangalore.

———. 2000b. "Bangalore Declaration of the Vía Campesina." Declaration at the Third International Conference of the Vía Campesina, October 3–6, Bangalore. http://www.viacampesina.org/main_en/index.php?option=com_content&task=view&id=53&Itemid=55, accessed on March 2, 2007.

Welch, Cliff. 2001. "Peasants and Globalization in Latin America: A Survey of Recent Literature." Paper presented at the Twenty-third International Congress of the Latin American Studies Association, September 6–8, Washington, D.C.

Windfuhr, Michael, and Jennie Jonsén. 2005. *Food Sovereignty: Towards Democracy in Localized Food Systems*. Warwickshire, U.K.: FIAN-International, ITDG Publishing.

Wolf, Eric. 1966. *Peasants*. Englewood Cliffs, N.J.: Prentice Hall.

———. 1969. *Peasant Wars in the Twentieth Century*. New York: Harper and Row.

Interviews

Alegría, Rafael, Vía Campesina Operational Secretariat (1996–2004). Interview with author, September 10, 2000, Tegucigalpa, Honduras.

Borras, (Jun) Saturnino, former representative of the Kilusang Magbubukid ng Pilipinas (KMP) [Peasant Movement of the Philippines] and founding member of the Vía Campesina. E-mail interview with author, March 19, 2001.

Carreon Mundo, Marcelo, leader with the Organización de Ejidos de Productores Forestales de la Zona Maya. Interview with author, February 28, 2000, Felipe Carrillo Puerto, Quintana Roo, Mexico.

Cerros Nava, Emiliano, member of the Executive Commission of the UNORCA in Mexico. Interview with author, February 23, 2000, Mexico City.

Chemerika, Lisa, former participant and coordinator of the Canadian-Caribbean Agricultural Exchange Program (CCAEP). Telephone interview with author, August 25, 2002.

Gómez Flores, Alberto, former executive coordinator of UNORCA. Interview with author, April 6, 2000, Mexico City.

Ladron de Guevarra, Ernesto, former staff person with UNORCA. Interview with author, February 25, 2000, Mexico City.

Magaña Guerrero, Pedro, former regional coordinator of UNORCA for Guanajuato. Interview with author, March 13, 2000, Mexico City.

Thiesson, Stuart, former executive secretary of the NFU. Interview with author, October 4, 2001, Saskatoon, Saskatchewan.

Wiebe, Nettie, former president of the National Farmers Union and regional coordinator of the Vía Campesina. Interview with author, June 17, 2002, Saskatoon, Saskatchewan.

2

Agrarian Reform and Food Sovereignty

An Alternative Model for the Rural World

PETER ROSSET

Food sovereignty implies the implementation of radical processes of compre-
hensive agrarian reform adapted to the conditions of each country and region,
which will provide peasant and indigenous farmers—with equal opportunities
for women—with equitable access to productive resources, primarily land, water
and forests, as well as the means of production, financing, training and capacity
building for management and interlocution.
—Final Declaration, World Forum on Food Sovereignty, Havana, September 7, 2001

At the start of the new millennium, we find the rural world everywhere to
be in a state of crisis. For the nations of the South, the historical origins of
this crisis can be found in colonial land grabs and the displacement of farming peoples from fertile lands with adequate rainfall toward steep, rocky
slopes, deserts, margins, and infertile rainforest soils, and the progressive
incorporation of these displaced peoples into poorly paid seasonal labor
forces for export agriculture. As a result of this legacy, only slightly modified in the postcolonial period, the landless and near-landless have long
made up the poorest of the poor.

In recent decades, neoliberal economic policies, promoted by international financial institutions such as the World Bank, the International
Monetary Fund, and the World Trade Organization and implemented by
national governments, have typically made the conditions in rural areas
even worse. The initiatives that most directly affect rural populations consist of trade, macroeconomic, and sectoral policies that have conspired to
undercut the economic viability of peasant, small and family farmers, and
cooperative/collective agriculture. These policies include trade liberalization and the subsequent flooding of local markets with dumped, cheap food
imports, against which local farmers can scarcely compete. The policy set
typically requires the cutting of price supports and subsidies for food pro-

ducers and the privatization of credit, commercialization, and technical assistance. These policies are accompanied by excessive export promotion, the patenting of crop genetic resources, and a bias in agricultural research toward expensive technologies such as genetic engineering. Increasingly, smaller and poorer farmers find that credit is inadequate or too expensive to cover rising production costs, buyers are scarce and more monopolistic than ever, and prices are too low to cover credit and production costs (Hellinger et al. 2001; Lappé et al. 1998). The net result has been a significant and continued deterioration in the access by the poor to land, as they are forced to sell off land they own, cannot afford land rentals or similar arrangements, or lose land by defaulting on credit (European Commission 1999; Rosset 2001b; Ziegler 2002).

While aggressively applying neoliberal policy initiatives, national governments drag their feet in implementing already existing land reform and land redistribution policies, and they have by and large resisted—sometimes using force—efforts by civil society organizations, such as movements of the landless, to push for the implementation of these policies (Langevin and Rosset 1997; Agencia EFE 2000; Rosset 2001b; Ziegler 2002). They have stood by as land has increasingly been commercialized and watched passively as business interests—both agricultural (that is, plantations) and nonagricultural (that is, petroleum and mining)—and large infrastructure projects (that is, hydroelectric dams) have encroached on communal and public lands, and territories of indigenous peoples (Bryant 1998; European Commission 1999; Rosset 2001b). Finally, most national governments have done nothing as agricultural commodity chains—on both the input (that is, seeds) and output (that is, grain trading) sides—have become increasingly concentrated in the hands of a very few transnational corporations. By virtue of their near-monopoly status these corporations are increasingly setting costs and prices unfavorable to farmers, putting all, especially the poorest, in an untenable cost-price squeeze, thus further encouraging the abandonment of agriculture (ETC Group 2001; Heffernan 1999; Rosset 2001b; Ziegler 2004).

In fact, governments and multilateral institutions have essentially taken up only one policy initiative on a more or less global scale, which they have presented as a "positive" step to redress land access issues. This initiative, or series of initiatives, consists of accelerating, building upon, and "featuring" policies to title lands, facilitate land markets, and, increasingly, promote "land bank" credit for land purchases by the poor—all designed and supported by the World Bank. This is so-called market-assisted or negotiated land reform (Deininger 2001, 2003). Unfortunately, there is mounting evidence that these policies are unlikely to significantly improve access by the poor to land, or give them more secure tenure. In fact there is good reason to believe they will actually worsen the situation in many places (Borras 2003a, 2005, 2006).

Thus it should come as no surprise that it is in rural areas where the worst poverty and hunger are still to be found. The expansion of agricultural production for export, controlled by wealthier producers, who own the best lands, continually displaces the poor to ever more marginal areas for farming. They are forced to fell forests located on poor soils, to farm thin, easily eroded soils on steep slopes, and to try to eke out a living on desert margins and in rainforests (Lappé et al. 1998).

But the situation is often worse on the most favorable lands. The better soils of most countries have been concentrated into large holdings used for monocultural production for export with intensive use of mechanization, pesticides, and chemical fertilizers. Many of our planet's best soils—which had earlier been sustainably managed for millennia by precolonial traditional agriculturalists—are today being rapidly degraded, and in some cases abandoned completely, in the short term pursuit of export profits and competition. The productive capacity of these soils is dropping rapidly due to soil compaction, erosion, water logging, and fertility loss, together with growing resistance of pests to pesticides and the loss of biodiversity (Lappé et al. 1998; Pingali et al. 1997).

The products harvested from these more fertile lands flow overwhelmingly toward consumers in wealthy countries. Impoverished local majorities cannot afford to buy what is grown, and because they are not a significant market, national elites essentially see local people as a labor source—a cost of production to be minimized by keeping wages down and busting unions. The overall result is a downward spiral of land degradation and deepening poverty in rural areas. Even urban problems have rural origins, as the poor must abandon the countryside in massive numbers, migrating to cities where only a lucky few make a living wage, while the majority languishes in slums and shanty towns (Lappé et al. 1998).

If present trends toward greater land concentration and the accompanying industrialization of agriculture continue unabated, it will be impossible to achieve social or ecological sustainability. At the same time, research shows the potential that could be achieved by the redistribution of land. Small farmers are more productive, more efficient, and contribute more to broad-based regional development than do the larger corporate farmers who hold the best land (Rosset 1999). Small farmers with secure tenure can also be much better stewards of natural resources, protecting the long-term productivity of their soils and conserving functional biodiversity on and around their farms (Altieri et al. 1998).

A Clash of Models in the Rural World

Many of the world's organizations of family farmers, peasants, the landless, rural workers, indigenous people, rural youth, and rural women have joined together in a global alliance, La Vía Campesina.[1] According to La Vía Campesina, we are facing a historic clash between two models of economic, social, and cultural development for the rural world. The dominant model and its negative effects have been described above, and La Vía Campesina counterposes an alternative paradigm called food sovereignty. Food sovereignty starts with the concept of economic and social human rights, which include the right to food (Vía Campesina 2002; Vía Campesina et al. n.d.-a, n.d.-b, 2005). But it goes further, arguing, as does Jean Ziegler, the UN special rapporteur for the Right to Food that there is a corollary right to land and even that rural peoples have the "right to produce" (Ziegler 2002, 2004).

In the food sovereignty paradigm, feeding a nations' people is an issue of national security—of sovereignty, if you will. If the people of a country must depend for their next meal on the vagaries of the global economy, on the goodwill of a superpower not to use food as a weapon, on the unpredictability and high cost of long-distance shipping, then that country is not secure, neither in the sense of national security nor in the sense of food security. Food sovereignty thus goes beyond the concept of food security, which has been stripped of real meaning (Rosset 2003).

Food security means that every child, woman, and man must have the certainty of having enough to eat each day; but that concept says nothing about where that food comes from or how it is produced. Thus Washington policy makers are able to argue that importing cheap food from the United States is a better way for poor countries to achieve food security than producing it themselves. But massive imports of cheap, subsidized food undercut local farmers, driving them off their land. They swell the ranks of the hungry, and their food security is placed in the hands of the cash economy just as they migrate to urban slums where they cannot find jobs that pay a living wage. To achieve genuine food security, people in rural areas must have access to productive land and receive prices for their crops that allow them to make a decent living (Rosset 2003; Vía Campesina et al. n.d.-a, n.d.-b, 2005).

But it also means that access to land and productive resources is not enough. The current emphasis in trade negotiations on market access for exports, to the detriment of protection of domestic markets for domestic producers, is a critical problem. According to La Vía Campesina (2002), "food sovereignty gives priority of market access to local producers. Liberalized agricultural trade, which gives access to markets on the basis of market power and low—often subsidized—prices, denies local producers access to their own markets" and thus violates the right to produce while undercutting local and regional economic development. One way to promote local economic development in rural areas is to create local circuits of production and consumption, where family farmers sell their produce in local towns and villages and buy other necessities from artisans and merchants in those towns. As has been clearly demonstrated in a recent landmark study in Brazil, the presence of agrarian reform settlements boosts local economies, even when a country lacks a "real" agrarian reform policy (Leite et al. 2004).

In this way, money circulates several times in the local economy, generating town employment and enabling farmers to make a living. If instead, all that farmers produce is exported to faraway countries that pay international market (that is, low) prices, and all that they buy is also imported, then all profits from the system are extracted from the local economy and can only contribute to economic development in remote locations like Wall Street. Food sovereignty places the emphasis on local markets and local economies as the basic sine qua non of fighting hunger and poverty (Rosset 2003).

Only by changing development tracks from the export-led, free-trade-based, industrial agriculture model of large farms, land concentration, and the displacement of peoples can we stop the downward spiral of poverty, low wages, rural-urban migration, and environmental degradation. Redistributive land reform and a reversal of dominant trade policy hold the promise of change toward a smaller farm, family-based, or cooperative model, with the potential to feed the poor, lead to broad-based economic development, and conserve biodiversity and productive resources (Rosset 1999, 2001a).

This brings us back to the argument of La Vía Campesina that we are facing a clash of models for the rural world, a clash of economic development models. The contrast between the dominant model, based on agro-exports, neoliberal economic policies, and free trade, versus the food sovereignty model, could not be starker (see table 2.1).

Table 2.1. Dominant Model Versus Food Sovereignty Model

Issue	Dominant Model	Food Sovereignty
Trade	Free trade in everything	Food and agriculture exempt from trade agreements
Production priority	Agro-exports	Food for local markets
Crop prices	"What the market dictates" (leave the mechanisms that enforce low prices intact)	Fair prices that cover costs of production and allow farmers and farm workers a life with dignity
Market access	Access to foreign markets	Access to local markets; an end to the displacement of farmers from their own markets by agribusiness
Subsidies	While prohibited in the Third World, many subsidies are allowed in the U.S. and Europe, but are paid only to the largest farmers	Subsidies that do not damage other countries via dumping are okay (i.e., grant subsidies only to *family* farmers, for direct marketing, price/income support, soil conservation, conversion to sustainable farming, research, etc.).
Food	Chiefly a commodity; in practice, this means processed, contaminated food that is full of fat, sugar, high fructose corn syrup, and toxic residues	A human right: specifically, should be healthy, nutritious, affordable, culturally appropriate, and locally produced
Being able to produce	An option for the economically efficient	A right of rural peoples
Hunger	Due to low productivity	Problem of access and distribution, due to poverty and inequality
Food security	Achieved by importing food from where it is cheapest	Greatest when food production is in the hands of the hungry, or when produced locally
Control over productive resources (land, water, forests)	Privatized	Local, community controlled
Access to land	Via the market	Via genuine agrarian reform
Seeds	Patentable commodity	Common heritage of humanity, held in trust by rural communities and cultures; "no patents on life"
Rural credit and investment	From private banks and corporations	From the public sector, designed to support family agriculture

Dumping	Not an issue	Must be prohibited
Monopoly	Not an issue	The root of most problems
Overproduction	No such thing, by definition	Drives prices down and farmers into poverty; we need supply management policies in U.S. and E.U.
Farming technology	Industrial, monoculture, chemical-intensive; uses GMOs	Agro-ecological, sustainable farming methods, no GMOs
Farmers	Anachronism; the inefficient will disappear	Guardians of culture and crop germ plasm; stewards of productive resources; repositories of knowledge; internal market and building block of broad-based, inclusive economic development
Urban consumers	Workers to be paid as little as possible	Need living wages
Genetically Modified Organisms (GMOs)	The wave of the future	Bad for health and the environment; an unnecessary technology
Another world (alternatives)	Not possible/not of interest	Possible and amply demonstrated

Source: Rosset 2003.

On virtually every issue related to food, agriculture, and rural life, the positions are contrary. Where one model sees family farmers as a quaint but inefficient anachronism that should disappear with development (unless some farmers stay on as Disneyland-like attractions for bucolic rural tourism), the other sees them as the basis of local economies, as the internal market that enabled today's industrial economic powerhouses such as the United States, Japan, China, and South Korea to get off the ground in times past (Rosset 1999, 2003).

As for hunger, one model sees boosting exports from the giant plantations of the wealthy as the way to generate the foreign exchange needed to import cheap food for the hungry, while the other sees the conversion of farmland that once belonged to family farmers, peasants, and indigenous peoples to export cropping as precisely the key driving force behind the growth of hunger and immiseration in rural areas. Finally, while the dominant model is based on chemical-intensive large-scale monoculture, with genetically modified crops (GMOs), the food sovereignty model sees these industrial farming practices as eventually destroying the land for future generations, and it counterposes a mixture of traditional knowledge and sustainable, ecologically based farming practices (Rosset 2003; Vía Campesina et al. n.d.-a, n.d.-b, 2005). Overall, this is why the Landless Rural Workers' Movement (MST) of Brazil, a member of La Vía Campesina, says that "the enemy is the model," and the goal of the struggle is a transition of models. The MST argues that while agrarian reform is a critical piece in this transition, by itself it is not enough. To be successful, it must be imbedded with a larger policy emphasis on food sovereignty.[2]

Ongoing Agrarian Reforms

The "Official" Reforms

The World Bank is taking the lead in promoting, and in some cases financing, comprehensive reforms of land tenure, including titling, cadastres and land registries, land market facilitation, market-assisted or negotiated land reforms, and credit, technical assistance, and marketing support (Rosset 2004; Deininger and Binswanger 2001; Deininger 2001, 2003; Bond 2000). Here the World Bank has followed the lead of its own development economists, who have found that severe inequality in land tenure retards economic growth, poverty alleviation, and efforts to use soils sustainably (Deininger 2003; Deininger and Binswanger 2001). In this policy environment other institutions, including governments, aid agencies, and other development banks, are following the lead of the World Bank and aggressively implementing some, or in some cases, all of these reforms (de Janvry et al. 2001; Burns et al. 1996).

While one might applaud the fact that thanks to the World Bank it is no longer taboo to propose land reform as a key element in sustainable development (de Janvry et al. 2001; Rosset 2002), the World Bank's land policies are largely failing to address the underlying causes of poverty and exclusion (Borras 2003a, 2005, 2006). Land titling programs can lead to new land loss, as in Thailand (Leonard and Narintarakul Na Ayutthaya 2006), and conflicts, as in Mexico (de Ita 2006), and the cost of land banks makes their potential scope woefully inadequate when compared to the magnitude of landlessness, as in Guatemala (Garoz and Gauster 2005). Moreover, "beneficiaries" of land banks are strapped with heavy debts for expensive land of dubious quality as in Guatemala and Brazil (Garoz and Gauster 2005; Sauer 2006). Furthermore, market-based "solutions" tend to depoliticize the problem of landlessness, which by its nature can only be resolved by structural changes of a kind that can only be addressed in the sphere of politics, rather than that of the market (Rosset 2002, 2004). Finally, these "reforms" are carried out while leaving the neoliberal policy environment, so inimical to family agriculture, and the "model," intact. We can hope for little positive change, then, from these efforts (Barraclough 1999; Borras 2006).

State-led Land Reforms

"In every Latin American case where significant land redistribution benefiting the rural poor took place, the state played a decisive role," wrote the late Solon Barraclough (1999, 33). Unfortunately, he also wrote, in every case where reform was denied or deformed, the state also played a critical role. Only two contemporary governments, in Latin America or elsewhere, can truly be said to have a sincere commitment to genuine land reform, including a transition of models geared to making family-scale and cooperative agriculture more viable. These are Cuba and potentially Venezuela (Rosset et al. 2006).

While Cuba's original revolutionary land reform took place in the 1960s, Funes et al. (2001) show how a second "reform within the reform" allowed Cuba to escape from a food crisis in the 1990s, in what might be the closest example to a true transition from an agro-export model toward more of a food sovereignty-like model of the kind called for by La Vía Campesina. Among the key elements that made such a transition possible was, first of all, access to land by the rural majority. Cuba's "second" land reform to break up state farms into smaller, cooperative, and individual production units was possible because the expropriation of land from landlords had already taken place. Second, the de facto protection from dumping provided by the trade embargo provided a positive condition (albeit for a very negative reason), in that higher prices for farmers provided the economic viability and incentives needed for agriculture itself to survive the crisis. The other key factors were state support for the transition (shifts in credit, research, extension education, and so forth, to support the new model), a highly organized rural sector, which made the rapid dissemination of change possible, and the existence of autochthonous, agro-ecological technology (from both accumulated peasant knowledge and from scientific institutions) to help break dependence on no longer available imported inputs (Funes et al. 2001).

The case of Venezuela is still very much up in the air. While the government of President Hugo Chavez has made clear its commitment to genuine agrarian reform, a number of factors, including the resistance of landlords and bureaucrats, the failure (so far) to address the dumping effects of massive food imports, and the relative lack of organization of the peasantry into an actor, or at least active subject to push land reform, have so far conspired to keep progress uneven at best (Wilpert 2006).

Land Reform from Below

Barraclough (1999, 36) noted that "in every case where significant land reforms occurred, protests and demands by organized peasant producers and rural workers made crucial contributions to bringing them about." Today movements around the world are engaged in a wave of land occupations that are putting the pressure on governments to respond. The mid-to-late 1980s and 1990s saw the appearance, and in some cases, the coming of age, of a new generation of well-organized movements of landless peasants and rural workers. While the landless have always engaged in takeovers (in Spanish, *recuperación*) of idle lands, there has been a qualitative change in the organization and political savvy of contemporary groups. Landless movements are bringing land reform to national and international policy debates—even as they seize, occupy, and plant idle lands—often at a tremendous cost of lives lost and arbitrary arrests. These movements are growing rapidly around the world, from Brazil, Paraguay, Bolivia, Honduras, and Nicaragua, to South Africa, Zimbabwe, Indonesia, Thailand, India, and countless other countries.[3] Indeed, across most of the Third World, we are seeing the emergence of a new source of hope and dynamism from these largely nonviolent poor people's movements that sidestep government inaction and take matters firmly into their own hands (Rosset 2001a).

Brazil and the very successful Landless Rural Workers' Movement (MST) are a case in point. While large landowners in Brazil on the average leave more than half of their land idle, 25 million peasants struggle to survive in temporary agricultural jobs. Founded in 1985, the MST organizes landless workers to occupy idle lands, using the "social function of land" clause in Brazil's Constitution to legalize their claims, though they must defend themselves against the hired guards of the landowners and government security forces. Today more than 300,000 families—more then 1 million people—have won title to over 8 million hectares of land through actions led by the MST, a veritable reform from below (Langevin and Rosset 1997; Mançano Fernandes 2001; Wolford 2001; Wright and Wolford 2003).

Today we have a new opportunity to learn the lessons of past reforms and apply them to the practical goals of development. Land reform is no longer a taboo subject in the discourse on development, thanks in part to the World Food Summit in 1996, and to the somewhat unfortunate initiatives of the World Bank. Next we look at the important roles redistributive land reform can play in the move toward more sustainable development.

The Case for Redistributive Land Reform

The redistribution of land can fulfill a number of functions in more sustainable development (Barraclough 1999; Ziegler 2002; Rosset 1999). Dozens of land reform programs have been carried out since World War II. In looking back at the successes and failures, we can distinguish between what might be called "genuine" or "radical" land reforms and the "fake" or "non-egalitarian" reforms (Lappé et al. 1998; Sobhan 1993).

Land Reform and Poverty

Sobhan (1993) examined the outcome of virtually every land reform program carried out in the Third World since World War II. When quality land was actually distributed to the poor, and the power of the rural oligarchy to distort and "capture'" policies was broken ("radical" redistribution), real, measurable poverty reduction and improvement in human welfare has invariably been the result. Japan, South Korean, Taiwan, Cuba, and China are all good examples. In contrast, countries with reforms that gave only poor quality land to beneficiaries and/or failed to alter the rural power structures that work against the poor ("non-egalitarian") have failed to make a major dent in rural poverty (Sobhan 1993). The more successful reforms triggered relatively broad-based economic development. By including the poor in economic development, these countries built domestic markets to support national economic activity (Sachs 1987). The often tragic outcome of failed reforms was to condemn the "beneficiaries" to marginalization from national economic life, as they frequently assumed heavy debts to pay for the poor quality land they received in remote locations without credit or access to markets and in policy environments hostile to small farmers (Sobhan 1993; Thiesenhusen 1995).

While Sobhan looked at national-level statistics to derive his conclusions, Besley and Burgess (2002) recently looked at the history of land reform in sixteen individual Indian states from 1958 to 1992. While these were by and large not radical reforms in Sobhan's sense, many did abolish tenancy and reduce the importance of intermediaries. The authors found a strong relationship between land reform and the reduction of poverty. Leite et al. (2004) found that settlers in land reform settlements in Brazil earn more than they did before, and more than families that are still landless. They eat better, they have greater purchasing power, they have greater access to educational opportunities, and they are more likely to be able to unite their families in one place (rather than "lose" family members to migration). In fact, land reform holds promise as a means to stem the rural-urban migration that is causing cities in the Third World to grow beyond the capacity of urban economies to provide enough jobs. Even in Zimbabwe, where land reform was ended prematurely and is very incomplete, the evidence shows that beneficiaries are substantially better off than others (Deininger et al. 2000).

Another way of looking at the social benefits of land reform is in terms of the cost of creating a new job. Estimates of the cost of creating a job in the commercial sector of Brazil range from two to twenty times more than the cost of establishing an unemployed head of household on farm land through agrarian reform. Land reform beneficiaries in Brazil have an annual income equivalent to 3.7 minimum wages, while still landless laborers average only 0.7 of the minimum. Infant mortality among families of beneficiaries has dropped to only half of the national average (Stédile 1998). Sobhan (1993) argues that only land reform holds the potential to address chronic underemployment in most countries of the Third World. Because small farms use more labor—and often less capital—to farm a given unit of area, a small-farm model can absorb far more people into gainful activity and reverse the stream of out-migration from rural areas.

Land Reform and Productivity

In the past there was a long-standing debate concerning the likely effects of the redistribution of farm land to the poor, which almost inevitably leads to smaller production units. One concern was that that, when freed from exploitative sharecropping, rental, or labor relationships, the poor would retain a greater proportion of their own production for their own consumption (not necessarily a bad thing), thus leading to a net decrease in food availability for other consumers. However, this argument has been put to rest by the evidence (Sobhan 1993), and by the productivity gains that can be achieved by shifting to smaller-scale, more intensive styles of production. In Brazil family farm agriculture produces 24 percent of the total national value of production of beef, 24 percent of milk, 58 percent of pork, and 40 percent of poultry and eggs. It also generates 33 percent of cotton, 31 percent of rice, 72 percent of onions, 67 percent of green beans, 97 percent of tobacco, 84 percent of cassava, 49 percent of maize, 32 percent of *soya*, 46 percent of wheat, 58 percent of bananas, 27 percent of oranges, 47 percent of grapes, 25 percent of coffee, and 10 percent of sugar. In total, family farm agriculture accounts for 40 percent of the total national value of production, while occupying just 30.5 percent of the cultivated land area. Family farms generate fully 76.9 percent of the national employment in agriculture while receiving only 25.3 percent of farm credit (Pengue 2005).

In fact, data show that small farms almost always produce far more agricultural output per unit area than larger farms, and they do so more efficiently (Rosset 1999). This holds true whether we are talking about industrial countries or any country in the Third World. This is widely recognized by agricultural economists as the "inverse relationship between farm size and output" (Tomich et al. 1995; Rosset 1999). A recent report (Rosset 1999) examined the relationship between farm size and total output for fifteen countries in the Third World. In all cases, relatively smaller farm sizes were much more productive per unit area—two to ten times more productive—than larger ones. Thus redistributive land reform is not likely to run at cross-purposes with productivity issues.

Land Reform and Economic Development

As Jean Ziegler (2002), the special rapporteur of the Commission on Human Rights on the Right to Food notes, "Agrarian reform that is truly transformative and redistributive has proved to be fundamental in reducing poverty and hunger in many countries, and can be a key to generating economic growth that benefits the poorest." But surely more tons of grain is not the only goal of farm production; farm resources must also generate wealth for the overall improvement of rural life—including better housing, education, health services, transportation, local economic diversification, and more recreational and cultural opportunities.

In the United States, the question was asked more than half a century ago: what does the growth of large-scale, industrial agriculture mean for rural towns and communities? Walter Goldschmidt's (1978) classic study of California's San Joaquin Valley in the 1940s compared areas dominated by large corporate farms with those still characterized by smaller family farms. In farming communities dominated by large corporate farms, nearby towns died off. Mechanization meant that fewer local people were employed, and absentee ownership meant that farm families themselves were no longer to be found. In these corporate-farm towns, the income earned in agriculture was drained off into larger cities to support distant enterprises, while in towns surrounded by family farms, the income circulated among local business establishments, generating jobs and community prosperity. Where family farms predominated, there were more local businesses, paved streets and sidewalks, schools, parks, churches, clubs, and newspapers, and there were better services, higher employment, and more civic participation.

Studies conducted since Goldschmidt's original works confirm that his findings remain true today (see Fujimoto 1977; MacCannell 1988; Durrenberger and Thu 1996). The Amish and Mennonite farm communities found in the eastern United States provide a strong contrast to the virtual devastation described by Goldschmidt in corporate farm communities. Lancaster County in Pennsylvania, which is dominated by these small farmers who eschew much modern technology and often even bank credit, is the most productive farm county east of the Mississippi River. It has annual gross sales of agricultural products of $700 million, and it receives an additional $250 million from tourists who appreciate the beauty of traditional small farm landscapes (D'Souza and Ikerd 1996).

If we turn toward the Third World we find a similar situation. On the one hand, there is the devastation caused by land concentration and the industrialization of agriculture, while on the other there are local benefits to be derived from a small farm economy—in one case, created by "land reform from below." Leite at al. (2004) describe how local towns benefit from the commerce that is generated when estates belonging to absentee landlords are turned into productive family and cooperative farming enterprise through land reform driven from below. A study of one such municipality, Julho de Castilhos, found that while the MST settlement possessed only 0.7 percent of the land, its members paid 5 percent of the taxes, making the settlement into the municipality's second largest rural tax payer (Movimento dos Trabalhadores Rurais Sem Terra [MST] 2001).

It is clear that local and regional economic development can benefit from a small farm economy, as can the life and prosperity of rural towns. But what of national economic development? History has shown us that a relatively equitable, small farmer-based rural economy provides the basis for strong national economic development. This "farmer road to development" is part of the reason why, for example, the United States early on in its history developed more rapidly and evenly than did Latin America, with its inequitable land distribution characterized by huge haciendas and plantations interspersed with poverty-stricken subsistence farmers (de Janvry 1981). In the early decades of the United States, independent "yeoman" farmers formed a vibrant domestic market for manufactured products from urban areas, including farm implements, clothing, and other necessities. This domestic demand fueled economic growth in the urban areas, and the combination gave rise to broad-based growth (Sachs 1987).

The postwar experiences of Japan, South Korea, and Taiwan in the capitalist world, and China, Cuba, and more recently, Vietnam, in the socialist world, also demonstrate how equitable land distribution fuels economic development. At the end of the Second World War, circumstances, including devastation and foreign occupation, conspired to create the conditions for "radical" land reforms in the former countries—while revolutions did the same in the latter—breaking the economic stranglehold of the landholding class over rural economic life. Combined with trade protection to keep farm prices high and targeted investment in rural areas, farm families rapidly achieved a high level of purchasing power, which guaranteed domestic markets for fledging industries (Rosset 1999; Lappé et al. 1998; Sachs 1987; IFAD 2001).

The postwar economic "miracles" of the three capitalist countries were each fueled at the start by internal markets centered in rural areas, long before the advent of the much heralded "export orientation" policies that much later on pushed those industries to compete in the global economy. This was a real triumph for "bubble-up" economics, in which redistribution of productive assets to the poorest strata of society created the economic basis for rapid, relatively inclusive development. This analysis in no way is meant to suggest that all policies pursued by these countries were positive, or should be blindly replicated. However, their experience does stand in stark contrast to the failure of "trickle down" economics to achieve much of anything in the same time period in areas of U.S. dominance, such as much of Latin America (Sachs 1987). More generally, there is now a growing consensus among mainstream development economists, long called for by many in civil society, that inequality in asset distribution impedes economic growth (Solimano 2000).

A key distinction that Sobhan (1993) makes is between "transformative" agrarian reforms and others. In most redistributive reforms those who actually receive land are at least nominally better off than those who remain landless (unless and until policies inimical to small farm agriculture lead them to lose their land once again). However, certain agrarian reforms have been the key step in allowing entire nations to change development tracks. In these cases countries—Japan, South Korea, China, Taiwan, and others—have "jumped" from the excluding, downward spiral into poverty and environmental degradation to the upward spiral of broad-based improvements in living standards that produce strong internal markets, which in turn lead to more dynamic and inclusive economic development. Sobhan shows by comparative analysis what the transformative reforms, those that led to real social transitions, had in common. In brief, the majority of the landless and land poor benefited, the majority of the arable land was affected, the stranglehold of entrenched power structures over rural life and economy was broken, and favorable, enabling economic policies were in place. A key feature of the more successful reforms is that farm families were seen as key actors to be mobilized in national economic development—whereas in failed reforms they have typically been seen as indigents in need of charitable assistance.

Land Reform and the Environment

The benefits of small farm economies extend beyond the merely economic sphere. Whereas large, industrial-style farms impose a scorched-earth mentality on resource management—no trees, no wildlife, endless monocultures—small farmers can be very effective stewards of natural resources and the soil. To begin with, small farmers utilize a broad array of resources and have a vested interest in their sustainability. At the same time, their farming systems are diverse, incorporating and preserving significant functional biodiversity within the farm. By preserving biodiversity, open space, and trees, and by reducing land degradation, small farms provide valuable ecosystem services to the larger society. In the United States, small farmers devote 17 percent of their area to woodlands, compared to only 5 percent on large farms. Small farms maintain nearly twice as much of their land in "soil improving uses," including cover crops and green manures (D'Souza and Ikerd 1996). In the Third World, peasant farmers show a tremendous ability to prevent and even reverse land degradation, including soil erosion (Templeton and Scherr 1999). They can and/or do provide important services to society at large, including sustainable management of critical watersheds, thus preserving hydrological resources, and the in situ conservation and dynamic development and management of the basic crop and livestock genetic resources upon which the future food security of humanity depends.

Compared to the ecological wasteland of a modern export plantation, the small farm landscape contains a myriad of biodiversity. The forested areas from which wild foods and leaf litter are extracted; the wood lot; the farm itself with intercropping, agro-forestry, and large and small livestock; the fish pond; and the backyard garden, all allow for the preservation of hundreds if not thousands of wild and cultivated species. Simultaneously, the commitment of family members to maintaining soil fertility on the family farm means an active interest in long-term sustainability not found on large farms owned by absentee investors. If we are truly concerned about rural ecosystems, then the preservation and promotion of small, family farm agriculture is a crucial step we must take.

Clearly, land reform to create a small farm economy is not only good for local economic development but is also a more effective social and environmental policy than allowing business as usual to keep driving the poor out of rural areas and into burgeoning cities.

Moving Forward: Guidelines for the Future

Rather than following the World Bank's market-based approach, policy makers and social movements should learn from the successes and failures of the period after World War II and from ongoing reforms. A set of useful guidelines should include the following:

- Severe inequality in landholdings—like the *latifundia/minifundia* pattern in many parts of Latin America—is inefficient, environmentally and socially destructive, immoral, and impedes broad-based development. A range of perspectives and concerns—from economic and social human rights to economic growth—all lead to the conclusion that we must once and for all eliminate the *latifundia* (Rosset 2001a; "Histórico da campanha pela emenda constitucional" 2001; Ziegler 2002).
- When families receive land, they must not be saddled with heavy debt burdens. This can be accomplished by government expropriation of idle lands, with or without compensation for former owners (Sobhan 1993; Borras 2003b).
- Secure tenure and/or access rights are critical to ensuring long-term food security for families and communities. Without such security and/or rights it is also difficult for families and communities to invest in land improvement, means of production, and/or conservation measures (Lastarria-Cornhiel and Melmed-Sanjak 1998).
- Women must have the right to hold title to land. When titles are vested exclusively in male heads of households, domestic disputes or the premature death of a spouse inevitably lead to the destitution of women and children (Deere and León 2001; Monsalve Suárez 2006).

- The land distributed must be of good quality, rather than ecologically fragile soils that should never be farmed, and it must be free of disputed claims by other poor people (Rosset 2001a).
- The rights of indigenous and other peoples to land, forests, water, and other common property resources must be guaranteed and protected, as must their right to manage them using customary law and tradition. Provision must be made for individual and/or collective rights, depending on each sociocultural situation. No one recipe can be applied everywhere (Hall 1998; Stavenhagen 2004).
- People need more than land if they are to be successful. There must also be a supportive policy environment and essential services such as credit on reasonable terms, infrastructure, support for ecologically sound technologies, and access to markets and fair prices (Sobhan 1993; Sachs 1987; Adams 2000; IFAD 2001). Perhaps most critical is a step back from damaging free-trade policies and dumping—which drive down farm prices and undercut the economic viability of farming—to be replaced by a food sovereignty perspective that places the highest priority on national production for national markets (World Forum on Food Sovereignty 2001; Rosset 2003).
- Truly transformative reforms will also require investment in rural areas to assure such basic services as schools, health clinics, potable water, and basic infrastructure (Sobhan 1993).
- The power of rural elites to distort and capture policies, subsidies, and windfall profits in their favor must be effectively broken by the reforms (Sobhan 1993).
- The vast majority of the rural poor must be beneficiaries of the reform process (Sobhan 1993).
- Successful reforms are distinguished from failed ones by a motivation and perception that the new small family farms that are created are to be the centerpiece of economic development, as was the case in Japan, Taiwan, China, and Cuba. When land reform is seen as "welfare" or as a charitable policy for the indigent, failure has been the inevitable result (Sobhan 1993; Sachs 1987; Rosset 2001a).
- In today's conservative, neoliberal political environment, strong grassroots poor people's movements are critical to pushing the reform process, stopping government foot-dragging and, when necessary, taking matters into their own hands. Land occupations are one of the most effective, proven methods of pressuring governments to act (Wolford 2001; Langevin and Rosset 1997; Barraclough 1999; Wright and Wolford 2003).

Notes

Author's note: This chapter is a slightly revised version of Peter Rosset's conclusion in Rosset et al. 2006, chapter 16. Reprinted by permission of Food First Books/Institute for Food and Development Policy, Inc.

Epigraph: This meeting was the civil society preparatory meeting for the World Food Summit +5. http://www.fao.org/Regional/Lamerica/ong/cuba/pdf/06apoeng. pdf, accessed February 28, 2008

1. http://www.viacampesina.org, accessed February 28, 2008.

2. João Pedro Stédile, a leader of the MST, personal communication. Also see chapter 5 by Corrêa and Borges Ferreira in this volume.

3. For Zimbabwe, see Moyo and Yeros 2005; for Chiapas, see Rosset 1995; for the MST in Brazil, see Langevin and Rosset 1999; and Wolford 2001.

References

Adams, Martin. 2000. *Breaking Ground: Development Aid for Land Reform*. London: Overseas Development Institute.

Agencia EFE. 2000. "More Have Died in Brazil Land Struggle Than at Dictators' Hands." Agencia EFE wire story, September 6.

Altieri, Miguel, Peter Rosset, and Lori Ann Thrupp. 1998. "The Potential of Agroecology to Combat Hunger in the Developing World." Food First Policy Brief 2. Institute for Food and Development Policy. Barraclough, Solon L. 1999. "Land Reform in Developing Countries: The Role of State and Other Actors." UNRISD Discussion Paper 101. Geneva: United Nations.

Besley, Timothy, and Robin Burgess. 2000. "Land Reform, Poverty Reduction, and Growth: Evidence from India." *Quarterly Journal of Economics* 115 (2): 389–430.

Bond, Patrick. 2000. *Elite Transition: From Apartheid to Neoliberalism in South Africa*. London: Pluto; South Africa: University of Natal.

Borras, Saturnino M. Jr. 2003a. "Questioning Market-Led Agrarian Reform: Experiences from Brazil, Colombia, and South Africa." *Journal of Agrarian Change* 3 (3): 367–94.

———. 2003b. "Questioning the Pro-Market Critique of State-Led Agrarian Reform." *European Journal of Development Research* 15 (2): 105–28.

———. 2005. "Can Redistributive Reform Be Achieved via Market-Based Voluntary Land Transfer Schemes? Evidence and Lessons from the Philippines." *Journal of Development Studies* 41 (1): 90–134.

———. 2006. "The Underlying Assumptions, Theory, and Practice of Neoliberal Land Policies." In *Promised Land: Competing Visions of Agrarian Reform*, 99–128. Oakland, Calif.: Food First Books.

Bryant, Coralie. 1998. "Property Rights for the Rural Poor: The Challenge of Landlessness." *Journal of International Affairs* 52 (1): 181–205.

Burns, Tony, Bob Eddington, Chris Grant, and Ian Lloyd. 1996. "Land Titling Experience in Asia." Paper prepared for the International Conference on Land Tenure and Administration, Orlando, Florida, November.

Deere, Carmen Diana, and Magdalena León. 2001. *Empowering Women: Land and Property Rights in Latin America.* Pittsburgh, Pa.: University of Pittsburgh Press.

Deininger, Klaus. 2001. "Negotiated Land Reform as One Way of Land Access: Experiences from Colombia, Brazil, and South Africa." In *Access to Land: Rural Poverty and Public Action,* edited by Alain de Janvry, Gustavo Gordillo, Jean-Philippe Platteau, and Elisabeth Sadoulet, 315–48. New York: Oxford University Press.

———. 2003. *Land Policies for Growth and Poverty Reduction.* Washington, D.C.: World Bank; Oxford: Oxford University Press.

Deininger, Klaus, and Hans Binswanger. 2001. "The Evolution of the World Bank's Land Policy." In *Access to Land: Rural Poverty and Public Action,* edited by Alain de Janvry, Gustavo Gordillo, Jean-Philippe Platteau, and Elisabeth Sadoulet, 406–40. New York: Oxford University Press.

Deininger, Klaus, Roger van den Brink, Hans Hoogeveen, and Sam Moyo. 2000. "How Land Reform Can Contribute to Economic Growth and Poverty Reduction: Empirical Evidence from International and Zimbabwean Experience." SARIPS, April 26.

De Ita, Ana. 2006. "Land Concentration in Mexico after PROCEDE." In *Promised Land: Competing Visions of Agrarian Reform,* edited by Peter Rosset, Rajeev Patel, and Michael Courville, 148–64. Oakland, Calif.: Food First Books.

De Janvry, Alain. 1981. *The Agrarian Question and Reformism in Latin America.* Baltimore: John Hopkins University Press.

De Janvry, Alain, Elisabeth Sadoulet, and Wendy Wolford. 2001. "The Changing Role of the State in Latin American Land Reforms." In *Access to Land: Rural Poverty and Public Action,* edited by Alain de Janvry, Gustavo Gordillo, Jean-Philippe Platteau, and Elisabeth Sadoulet, 279–303. New York: Oxford University Press.

D'Souza, Gerard, and John Ikerd. 1996. "Small Farms and Sustainable Development: Is Small More Sustainable?" *Journal of Agricultural and Applied Economics* 28 (1): 73–83.

Durrenberger, E. Paul, and Kendall M. Thu. 1996. "The Expansion of Large-Scale Hog Farming in Iowa: The Applicability of Goldschmidt's Findings Fifty Years Later." *Human Organization* 55 (4): 409–15.

ETC Group. 2001. "Globalization, Inc. Concentration in Corporate Power: The Unmentioned Agenda." ETC Group Communique 71. http://www.etcgroup.org/en/materials/publications.html?pub_ id=247 , accessed February 28, 2008.

European Commission. 1999. "Agriculture and Rural Development Policy in Developing Countries." Phase I, Task A, Diagnostic Report. http://europa.eu.int/comm/development/outputs/diagnostic/html/.

Fujimoto, Isao. 1977. "The Communities of the San Joaquin Valley: The Relationship between Scale of Farming, Water Use, and the Quality of Life." Testimony before the House Subcommittee on Family Farms, Rural Development, and Social Studies, Sacramento, Calif., October 28.

Funes, Fernando, Luis García, Martin Bourque, Nilda Pérez, and Peter Rosset, eds. 2001. *Transformando al campo Cubano: Avances de la agricultura sostenible.* Havana and Oakland, Calif.: ACTAF, CEAS, and Food First.

Garoz, Byron, and Susana Gauster. 2005. "FONTIERRAS: Structural Adjustment and

Access to Land in Guatemala." http://www.landaction.org/display.php?article=335, accessed February 28, 2008.

Goldschmidt, Walter. 1978. *As You Sow: Three Studies in the Social Consequences of Agribusiness.* New York: Allenheld, Osmun.

Hall, Ruth. 1998. "Design for Equity: Linking Objectives with Practice in Land Reform." Proceedings of the International Conference on Land Tenure in the Developing World, University of Cape Town, South Africa, January 27–29.

Heffernan, William. 1999. "Consolidation in the Food and Agriculture System." Report to the National Farmers Union. Columbia: University of Missouri.

Hellinger, Douglas, Helen Hansen-Kuhn, and April Fehling. 2001. "Stripping Adjustment Policies of Their Poverty-Reduction Clothing: A New Convergence in the Challenge to Current Global Economic Management." Washington, D.C.: Development Group for Alternative Policies. http://www.developmentgap.org/worldbank_ imf/Stripping_Adjustment_Policies.pdf, accessed March 1, 2008.

"Histórico da campanha pela emenda constitucional." 2001. *Repartir a Terra* (Brazil) 1 (1): 3.

IFAD (International Fund for Agricultural Development). 2001. *Rural Poverty Report 2001: The Challenge of Ending Rural Poverty.* New York and Oxford: Oxford University Press.

Langevin, Mark S., and Peter Rosset. 1997. "Land Reform from Below: The Landless Worker's Movement in Brazil." *Food First Backgrounder* (Institute for Food and Development Policy) 4 (3) (Fall).

Lappé, Frances Moore, Joseph Collins, and Peter Rosset, with Luis Esparza. 1998. *World Hunger: Twelve Myths.* 2nd ed. New York: Grove; London: Earthscan.

Lastarria-Cornhiel, Susana, and Jolyne Melmed-Sanjak. 1998. *Land Tenancy in Asia, Africa, and Latin America: A Look at the Past and a View to the Future.* Madison: Land Tenure Center.

Leite, Sérgio, Beatriz Heredia, Leonilde Medeiros, Moacir Palmeira, and Rosângela Cintrão. 2004. *Impactos dos assentamentos: Um estudo sobre o meio rural Brasileiro.* Brasília: Núcleo de Estudos Agrários e Desenvolvimento Rural (NEAD).

Leonard, Rebeca, and Kingkorn Narintarakul Na Ayutthaya. 2006. "Thailand's Land Titling Program: Securing Land for the Poor?" In *Promised Land: Competing Visions of Agrarian Reform,* edited by Peter Rosset, Rajeev Patel, and Michael Courville, 129–47. Oakland, Calif.: Food First Books.

MacCannell, Dean. 1988. "Industrial Agriculture and Rural Community Degradation." In *Agriculture and Community Change in the U.S.: The Congressional Research Reports,* edited by In L. E. Swanson, 15–75. Boulder, Colo.: Westview Press.

Mançano Fernandes, Bernardo. 2001. "The Occupation as a Form of Access to Land." Paper presented at the Twenty-third Congress of the Latin American Studies Association, Washington, D.C., September 6–8.

Monsalve Suárez, Sofia. 2006. "Gender and Land." In *Promised Land: Competing Visions of Agrarian Reform,* edited by Peter Rosset, Rajeev Patel, and Michael Courville, 192–207. Oakland, Calif.: Food First Books.

Movimento dos Trabalhadores Rurais Sem Terra (MST). 2001 *Os empreendimentos sociais do MST*. Manuscript. Sao Paolo: MST.

Moyo, Sam, and Paris Yeros. 2005. "Land Occupations and Land Reform in Zimbabwe: Towards the National Democratic Revolution." In *Reclaiming the Land: The Resurgence of Rural Movements in Africa, Asia, and Latin America*, edited by Sam Moyo and Paris Yeros, 165–205. London: Zed Books.

Pengue, Walter. 2005. "Agricultura industrial y agricultura familiar en el Mercosur: El pez grande se come al chico . . . siempre?" *Le Monde Diplomatique*, Edición Cono Sur 71: 7–9.

Pingali, P. L., M. Hossain, and R.V. Gerpacio. 1997. *Asian Rice Bowls: The Returning Crisis?* Wallingford: CAB International.

Rosset, Peter. 1995. "Understanding Chiapas." In *First World, Ha Ha Ha! The Zapatista Challenge*, edited by Elaine Katzenberger, 157–67. San Francisco: City Lights Books.

———. 1999. "The Multiple Functions and Benefits of Small Farm Agriculture in the Context of Global Trade Negotiations.," Food First Policy Brief (Institute for Food and Development Policy) 4. http://www.foodfirst.org/node/246, accessed March 1, 2008.

———. 2001a. "Tides Shift on Agrarian Reform: New Movements Show the Way." *Food First Backgrounder* (Institute for Food and Development Policy) 7 (1) (Winter).

———. 2001b. "Access to Land: Land Reform and Security of Tenure." FAO World Food Summit, Five Years Later Civil Society Input, Case Study. http://www.landaction.org/display.php?article=179, accessed March 1, 2008.

———. 2002. "The Good, the Bad, and the Ugly: World Bank Land Policies." Paper presented at the seminar "The Negative Impacts of the World Bank's Policies on Market-Based Land Reform." George Washington University, Washington, D.C., April 15–17. http://www.landaction.org/display.php?article=177, accessed March 1, 2008.

———. 2003. "Food Sovereignty: Global Rallying Cry of Farmer Movements." *Food First Backgrounder* (Institute for Food and Development Policy) 9 (4): 1–4.

———. 2004. *El derecho a la Tierra: Cuatro textos sobre la reforma agraria*. Barcelona: Agora Nord-Sud.

———. 2006. "Moving Forward: Agrarian Reform as a Part of Food Sovereignty." In *Promised Land: Competing Visions of Agrarian Reform*, edited by Peter Rosset, Rajeev Patel, and Michael Courville, 301–21. Oakland, Calif.: Food First Books.

Rosset, Peter, Rajeev Patel, and Michael Courville, eds. 2006. *Promised Land: Competing Visions of Agrarian Reform*. Oakland, Calif.: Food First Books.

Sachs, Jeffrey D. 1987. "Trade and Exchange Rate Policies in Growth-Oriented Adjustment Programs." In *Growth-Oriented Adjustment Programs*, edited by Vittorio Corbo et al., 291–325. Washington, D.C.: International Monetary Fund and World Bank.

Sauer, Sérgio. 2006. "The World Bank's Market-Based Land Reform in Brazil. In *Promised Land: Competing Visions of Agrarian Reform*, edited by Peter Rosset, Rajeev Patel, and Michael Courville, 177–91. Oakland, Calif.: Food First Books.

Sobhan, Rehman. 1993. *Agrarian Reform and Social Transformation: Preconditions for Development*. London: Zed Books.

Solimano, Andrés. 2000. "Beyond Unequal Development: An Overview." In *Distributive Justice and Economic Development: The Case of Chile and Developing Countries*, edited by Andrés Solimano, Eduardo Aninat, and Nancy Birdsall, 17–36. Ann Arbor: University of Michigan Press.

Stavenhagen, Rodolfo. 2004. "Indigenous Peoples in Comparative Perspective—Problems and Policies." United Nations Development Programme, Human Development Report Office, Occasional Paper, Background Paper for HDR 2004, 2004/14.

Stédile, João Pedro. 1998. *Questão agrária no Brasil*. 6.a Edição. São Paulo: Editora Atual.

Templeton, S. R., and S. J. Scherr. 1999. "Effects of Demographic and Related Microeconomic Change on Land Quality in Hills and Mountains of Developing Countries." *World Development* 27 (6): 903–18.

Thiesenhusen, William C. 1995. *Broken Promises: Agrarian Reform and the Latin American Campesino*. Boulder, Colo.: Westview Press.

Tomich, Thomas P., Peter Kilby, and Bruce F. Johnston. 1995. *Transforming Agrarian Economies: Opportunities Seized, Opportunities Missed*. Ithaca, N.Y.: Cornell University Press.

Vía Campesina. 2002. "Food Sovereignty." Flyer distributed at the World Food Summit +5, Rome, Italy.

Vía Campesina et al. N.d.-a. "Our World Is Not for Sale: Priority to People's Food Sovereignty. WTO out of Food and Agriculture." http://www.citizen.org/documents/wtooutoffood.pdf, accessed February 28, 2008.

———. N.d.-b. "Peasants, Family Farmers, Fisherfolk, and Their Supporters Propose People's Food Sovereignty as Alternative to US/EU and G20 positions." http://www.citizen.org/documents/wtofood.pdf, accessed February 28, 2008.

———. 2005. "WTO in Crisis: Groups Offer Alternative Plan to Protect People's Food Sovereignty." http://www.nffc.net/resources/statements/WTO_GC_Stmnt_2005.pdf, accessed February 28, 2008.

Wilpert, Gregory. 2006. "Land for People Not for Profit in Venezuela." In *Promised Land: Competing Visions of Agrarian Reform*, edited by Peter Rosset, Rajeev Patel, and Michael Courville, 249–64. Oakland, Calif.: Food First Books.

Wolford, Wendy. 2001. "Case Study: Grassroots-Initiated Land Reform in Brazil; The Rural Landless Workers' Movement." In *Access to Land: Rural Poverty and Public Action*, edited by Alain de Janvry, Gustavo Gordillo, Jean-Philippe Platteau, and Elisabeth Sadoulet, 304–14. New York: Oxford University Press.

World Forum on Food Sovereignty. 2001. Final Declaration. Havana, September 7. http://www.foodfirst.org/archive/media/news/2001/havanadeclaration.html, accessed March 1, 2008.

Wright, Angus, and Wendy Wolford. 2003. *To Inherit the Earth: The Landless Movement and the Struggle for a New Brazil*. Oakland, Calif.: Food First Books.

Ziegler, Jean. 2002. "Report of the Special Rapporteur of the Commission on Human Rights on the Right to Food." New York: United Nations General Assembly, A/57/150, August 27.

———. 2004. "Economic, Social, and Cultural Rights: The Right to Food." Report submitted by the Special Rapporteur on the right to food, in accordance with Commission on Human Rights resolution 2003/25. Geneva: UN Commission on Human Rights, E/CN.4/2004/10, February 9.

3

For Life, Land, Territory, and the Sovereignty of Our People

The Latin American Coordinator of Rural Organizations

JUAN TINEY

The Latin American Coordinator of Rural Organizations (CLOC) is the regional organization of La Vía Campesina in Latin America and the Caribbean. The CLOC is made up of more than 88 national and regional rural organizations in 25 countries (see table 3.1 for a partial listing). Our membership includes women, men, and young people, the landless, small-scale producers, workers, indigenous people, mestizos, and Afro-descendants.

Through CLOC we coordinate our movements, struggles, and activities at the regional, hemispheric, and global levels. We unite our voices and thoughts; share our experiences, achievements, and difficulties; and develop proposals to transform society. Together, we are constructing alternatives to the current model of development, with the objective of developing a peasant vision of a just and egalitarian future, free from any form of discrimination.

This chapter is based on the resolutions of the CLOC's fourth congress, which took place in Guatemala, on October 9–12, 2005. It is also based on the internal and public debates held in Caracas, Venezuela, in March 2006 within the framework of the World Social Forum.

At CLOC's fourth congress, we reviewed the decade-long process of building the organization, and of the struggle led by CLOC during these years. We also analyzed the strategies of the neoliberal capitalist system in order to define and coordinate our own lines of action and resistance, as well as to generate a new model of society for our hemisphere. We are active participants in most of the popular resistance movements, such as those for the equality of women, the preservation of ecological diversity, and the defense of the collective rights of indigenous people and of those of African descent. We are committed to the struggle against imperialism.

Table 3.1. Partial Listing of Organizations that Belong to the Latin American Coordinator of Rural Organizations (CLOC)

Country	Acronym	Name
Argentina	APENOC	Asociación de Productores del Noroeste de Córdoba
	MOCASE	Movimiento Campesino de Santiago del Estero
Belize	BAPO	Belize Association of Producers Organization
Bolivia	CSCB	Confederación Sindical de Colonizadores de Bolivia
	CSUTCB	Confederación Sindical Unica de Trabajadores Campesinos de Bolivia
	FNMCB-BS	Federación Nacional de Mujeres Campesinas de Bolivia "Bartolina Sisa"
Brazil	ANMTR	Articulação Nacional de Mulheres Trabalhadoras Rurais
	CONTAG	Confederacão Nacional dos Trabalhadores na Agricultura
	CPT	Comissão Pastoral da Terra
	MAB	Movimento dos Atingidos por Barragens
	MPA	Movimento dos Pequenos Agricultores
	MST	Movimento dos Trabalhadores Rurais Sem Terra
Chile	ANAMURI	Asociación Nacional de Mujeres Rurales e Indígenas
	NEHUEN	Confederación Nacional Sindical Campesina e Indígena de Chile El Surco
Colombia	ANUC-UR	Asociación Nacional de Usuarios Campesinos - Unidad y Reconstrucción
	FENSUAGRO	Federación Nacional Sindical Unitaria Agropecuaria
Costa Rica	MNC-CR	Mesa Nacional Campesina
Cuba	ANAP	Asociación Nacional de Agricultores Pequeños
Dominican Rep.	CONAMUCA	Confederación Nacional de Mujeres del Campo
Ecuador	CONFEUNASSC	Confederación Unica Nacional de Afiliados al Seguro Campesino
	FENOCIN	Federación Nacional de Organizaciones Campesinas, Indígenas, y Negras del Ecuador
Guatemala	CONIC	Coordinadora Nacional Indígena y Campesina
Honduras	COCOCH	Consejo Coordinador de Organizaciones Campesinas de Honduras
Mexico	CCC	Central Campesina Cardenista
	CIOAC	Central Independiente de Obreros Agrícolas y Campesinos
	CNPA	Coordinadora Nacional Plan de Ayala
	UNORCA	Unión Nacional de Organizaciones Regionales CampesinasAutónomas
Nicaragua	ATC	Asociación de Trabajadores del Campo
Paraguay	MCP	Movimiento Campesino Paraguayo
Peru	CCP	Confederación Campesina del Perú

Source: http://movimientos.org/cloc/indice_miemb.php3, accessed December 2, 2007.

Today, the rural landscape of Latin America is being "restructured" through the massive intrusion of financial capital and transnational enterprises, which are taking possession of and hoarding farmland, along with indigenous territories and natural resources. They are appropriating Latin America's biodiversity as well as its cultural knowledge. They are also turning food production into a commodity regardless of the consequences. Therefore, we call on our members to be on the alert and resist. We must continue building an alternative in the countryside, an alternative based on unity and solidarity and which is in harmony with nature.

The transnational agro-export model promotes monoculture and the consolidation of *latifundios* along with large-scale commercial production.[1] It eradicates the possibilities for small-scale production to subsist, and it promotes the expulsion of peasants from the countryside, generating poverty in its wake.

The imposition of this model has gone hand in hand with the militarization of the countryside. Peasant movements have been maligned and repressed, with these actions justified as part of the fight against terrorism and drug trafficking. Foreign military bases have been established in several of our countries and they act as launching points for carrying out various imperial projects for territorial control, such as Plan Puebla-Panama, Plan Colombia, Plan Dignidad, and others.

Most Latin American countries are involved in negotiations for free-trade agreements, mainly with the United States and the European Union, the terms of which are inherently unequal. These agreements have been concluded even though they go against the explicit will of the population. In rural areas, these agreements lead directly to the sale of land and natural resources to capitalist financial interests. They also result in the imposition of policies that prioritize the market and go against the people's collective and individual rights.

The neoliberal model has resulted in the privatization of public services, the disappearance of social programs, higher unemployment, and the expulsion of peasants from the countryside, causing their subsequent migration. It has also resulted in the overexploitation of workers and the intensification of poverty.

The CLOC therefore declares its relentless opposition to neoliberal capitalism. We oppose the policies imposed by the international financial institutions, such as the World Bank, the International Monetary Fund, and the Inter-American Development Bank, among others, that prioritize the interests of transnational corporations over human and environmental rights. We oppose free trade, the rules and regulations of the World Trade Organization (WTO), and all of the instruments of economic domination imposed by the United States and the European Union. We join the Bolivarian Alternative for the Latin America and the Caribbean (ALBA) and commit ourselves to its consolidation and further development.

We reject the payment of the onerous foreign debt imposed on our countries, a debt that has already been amply repaid, and yet continues to eat away at our national budgets. Instead, our national budgets should be used to eliminate hunger, a problem that affects millions of Latin Americans.

In our vision, land, water, mineral, and energy resources and biodiversity constitute the heritage of our peoples. We therefore oppose their privatization and commoditization. It is the people who should decide how these resources are used and managed, based on human needs, rather than those of the market.

We defend peasant agriculture, which is based on productive practices that respect nature. We demand the recovery of and defend the use of native seeds, which are part of the patrimony of our people. We reject the use of transgenic or genetically engineered seeds and the patenting of living organisms. We warn small- and medium-scale producers, and those large-scale producers that are responsible members of the community and respect the environment, not to use genetically engineered seeds, particularly those that are produced with the "terminator" technology (suicide seeds). These could ultimately leave more than 1.4 billion peasants all over the world without access to seeds. We also condemn the sale of such suicide seeds.

We defend the people's right to grow their own food, according to their culture and needs, based on the principle of food sovereignty. We will continue to fight for profound agrarian reforms based on gender equality and equal rights among all people. With these reforms we aspire to the creation of a just peasant society, built in the spirit of solidarity and respect for biodiversity.

We demand the demilitarization of the countryside, the immediate closing of foreign military bases and the withdrawal of foreign troops from our countries, and a halt to the persecution of peasant movements and their leaders. We demand freedom for all political prisoners who have been imprisoned simply for fighting for their rights and those of their people. We reaffirm our solidarity with Cuba, a country harassed and condemned by an unjust and inhumane embargo by the United States and demand unconditional respect of Cuba's sovereignty and its socialist cause. We support the

Bolivarian revolution's quest for rural justice, including the agrarian reform being implemented by the government of Venezuela.

Among the international meetings in which we have played an active role in recent years are the Alternative People's Summit held in Mar del Plata, Argentina, in November 2005, and the march against the WTO's Ministerial Meeting in Hong Kong, in December 2005, organized by La Vía Campesina and other organizations. As part of La Vía Campesina, we participated in the organizing committee for the Sixth World Social Forum and Second Social Forum of the Americas, both held during January 2006, in Caracas. These international meetings serve to raise consciousness, through discussion and education, among members of CLOC, and they allow us to communicate our ideas and positions to a broader public. The CLOC also participated in the Parallel Forum to the International Conference on Agrarian Reform and Rural Development, organized by the FAO in Brazil in March 2006, and in two other important forums on natural resources held during 2006, the International Biodiversity Conference in Brazil, and the World Water Forum in Mexico.

Anywhere in the world, wherever governments and international agencies discuss agriculture, food, natural resources, biodiversity, water—that is, our future—we will be present and make our ideas known through marches and mobilizations. We must make others aware of our cause: we need them to listen to us and respect our point of view.

We will be present wherever there is a struggle or mobilization against imperialism and its effects in the countryside, such as at the Third Indigenous People's Continental Summit in Guatemala in 2007. We also participate in the Day of Indigenous, Black, and Popular Resistance in October of each year, which is celebrated in all of our member countries, with 2007 marking the eighth celebration.[2]

We are on the alert to any possible attempt to revive the negotiations for the Free Trade Area of the Americas (FTAA). I say "revive" because we buried the FTAA at Mar de Plata, Argentina, in November 2005. Now we have targeted the WTO, which survived the meetings in Hong Kong in December of 2005, but sooner or later will have to be dismantled. Agriculture and foodstuffs are not simply commodities. Their commodification means denying food to the world's disenfranchised, as well as the death of the planet's biodiversity. The role of genetically engineered seeds in the latter process is evident.

The theme of CLOC's fourth congress was the following: "A decade of struggle, united against imperialist looting. Surrender . . . Never!" We invite you to join our struggle, those of you who have the privilege of education. We hope you will use your knowledge to serve people and humanity, rather than to serve the current system—the empire, and its institutions and its instruments—all of which have caused such injury to humanity and the planet. That is why we say: "Globalize the Struggle! Globalize Hope!"

Notes

1. Editors' note: For more about the dominant agro-export system, see chapter 2 in this volume.

2. We also attend the national congresses of our member organizations, such as the MST congress and the youth congress of the Pastoral Land Commission (CPT) in Brazil.

II

Land, Territory, and Agrarian Reform

4

The Landless Rural Workers' Movement and the Struggle for Social Justice in Brazil

MIGUEL CARTER

Over the hilly savannah leading to Brasília, more than twelve thousand peasants marched to demand agrarian reform in May 2005. Carrying bright-red flags in an orderly three-mile queue, the members of the Landless Rural Workers' Movement (MST) walked for sixteen days. Nowhere was it noted that this event was the world's largest and most sophisticated long-distance protest march ever organized.[1]

The logistical set up for the 125-mile mobilization was impressive. At night, the marchers slept in large circus tents assembled along the highway. Each day they were served three meals, prepared by a cooking staff of 415 people. Food donations from land reform settlements linked to the MST and contributions from church organizations, local and state governments, and other national and international sympathizers assured necessary resources for the mobilization. Throughout the march, the MST's mobile radio station broadcasted special programs, available to participants through ten thousand small radio receivers on loan from the World Social Forum. More than sixty-five vehicles were employed to transport the circus tents, portable toilets, and personal belongings from one campsite to the next. Afternoons and evenings were reserved for study and consciousness-raising activities, as well as recreation, movie screenings, and cultural festivals, with performances by peasant musicians, dancers, and poets from all regions of the country.

As the march worked its way to the nation's capital, representatives of the MST were busy meeting with government ministers, congressional leaders, and judicial authorities. Aside from petitioning for land reform, they lobbied in support of several rural development projects and protection of their human rights. Over the course of two weeks, emissaries from the MST participated in fifty gatherings with twenty different government ministries.

On the last day of the march, the peasants led a procession of twenty thousand people to the presidential palace. On route, they demonstrated in front of the U.S. Embassy, where they repudiated American consumerism and imperialism. Shortly after, they held another rally in front of the Finance Ministry to protest its conservative fiscal policies. A large sign described the ministry as a *fazenda do FMI* (an IMF estate).

At the Palacio da Alvorada, President Luiz Inácio Lula da Silva warmly welcomed a delegation of fifty members of the MST and supporters from the church, labor, student, and human rights organizations, as well as national celebrities. Lula delighted his visitors by putting on an MST cap. The government agreed to reinstate the U.S.$850 million budget cuts for land reform and offer additional subsidized credits for land reform communities. But few other petitions made by the MST were actually met.

Here stands an illustrative portrait of Latin America's largest and most prominent social movement. Since its formation in southern Brazil in the early 1980s, the MST has developed a formidable grass-roots organization, with a nationwide presence, an estimated 1.1 million members, over 2,000 agricultural settlements, a network of 1,800 primary and secondary schools, a national university, 88 rural cooperatives, and 96 food processing plants.[2] In the last two decades, the MST has prodded the Brazilian government to distribute close to 3.7 million hectares, a territory the size of Switzerland or the state of West Virginia.[3] After the mid-1990s, the MST earned national fame as a leading critic of neoliberal policies and a forceful voice on behalf of Brazil's underprivileged majority.[4]

In recent years, the MST has become an influential voice in international advocacy networks such as the World Social Forum and La Vía Campesina. By placing agrarian reform on Brazil's public agenda, the MST has helped stimulate growing global interest in land redistribution. A noteworthy manifestation of this trend took place in early 2006, when the United Nation's Food and Agriculture Organization (FAO) convened its Second International Conference on Agrarian Reform and Rural Development. The last time the FAO had held a gathering on this topic was in 1979. The event in 2006 was hosted by the Brazilian government in Porto Alegre, Rio Grande do Sul, not far from where the MST was actually born.[5]

The MST's many accomplishments and longevity are unique for a poor people's movement. Nowadays, the MST represents more than just a vehicle for mobilizing landless people and empowering peasants. It also embodies a powerful symbol and source of inspiration in the broader struggle for social justice in Brazil and elsewhere. As with other historical mobilizations for justice around the world—Western Europe's extension of mass suffrage, India's struggle for independence, the U.S. civil rights movement, South Africa's fight against apartheid, Bolivia's indigenous revival, and the global advocacy networks for women's rights—Brazil's struggle for land and basic citizenship rights in the countryside has become a catalyst for wider social transformations and an emblem of hope among those with progressive aspirations.

Why does the MST play this role? How does it challenge Brazil's stark societal disparities? And, what are its main effects on democracy? In addressing these questions, this chapter will, firstly, set the context for the MST's struggle and briefly review the movement's history. Secondly, it seeks to explain the movement's unusual endurance and evaluate its main sources of strength. Thirdly, it probes the MST's reliance on public activism—a particular form of social conflict that combines pressure politics and bargaining with state authorities.

Influential Brazilian intellectuals have been highly critical of the MST's confrontational demeanor and maintain that such actions constitute a "threat to democracy." Contrary to these views, this chapter argues that the movement's relation to Brazil's democratic process is a substantially positive one. The chapter concludes with an appraisal of the MST's approach to furthering social justice. It does so in light of the prevailing twentieth-century positions on how to reduce social inequality, suggesting that the movement's pathway toward this provides glimpses of an alternative venue, grounded on a radical form of democracy.

The MST: Context, History, and Sources of Strength

The setting for the MST story—Brazil—is the fifth largest country in the world, both in territory and population, the ninth leading economy, and the second most unequal society in terms of income distribution. In Brazil the wealthiest 10 percent of the population hold 46 percent of the nation's income, while the poorest 50 percent possess only 13 percent (IPEA 2005, 51–61). In the countryside, asset distribution is even more unequal. Scarcely 1 percent of the landholders control 45 percent of the nation's farmland, while close to 37 percent possess only 1 percent. By all accounts, Brazil holds one of the world's highest concentrations of land (IBGE 1996).

The nation's stark social disparities are responsible for producing a disjointed, apartheid-like society.[6] In rural Brazil, a highly modernized and dynamic agricultural economy coexists with a pauperized society in which more than half of the population lives below the national poverty line. The nation is a leading global producer and exporter of major food commodities—notably sugar, coffee, oranges, soybeans, and beef—yet according to a government survey, more than 25 million Brazilians, 14 percent of the population, have suffered from hunger in recent years (World Bank 2005, 275; IPEA 2005, 56). In recent decades Brazil has become largely urbanized and currently only one-fifth of its population lives in the countryside and works in agriculture (CEPAL 2004). Still, the number of landless people is estimated between 3.3 and 6.1 million families, while Brazil's unproductive farmland comprises more than a quarter of the national territory (Del Grossi et al. 2001; MDA 2003, 43 and table 5.1.1.1). The MST's place in Brazilian society needs to be appraised amid such contrasting realities.

Existing social and agrarian inequalities have deep roots. Brazil's land tenure arrangements were forged during Brazil's colonial history, with vast land grants (*sesmaria*) to privileged Portuguese families, and sustained thereafter under different political systems: empire, oligarchic republic, military rule, and political democracy. Agrarian inequities owe much to the traditional strength of Brazil's landlord class and its highly privileged access to state protection and resources.[7] These historical legacies are still clearly discernible. As an illustration, between 1995 and 2005 each of Brazil's largest landlords had access to U.S.$1,587 from public coffers for every dollar made available to a landless family.[8]

The first stirrings for land reform in Brazil took place during the mid-1950s, in the northeast region, and gained broader impetus during the early 1960s. The country's first national agrarian reform initiative was thwarted, nevertheless, by a conservative military coup d'état in 1964, days after its promulgation. Thereafter, Brazil's burgeoning rural social movements suffered extensive state repression and corporatist controls. As a result, the debate over agrarian reform was largely removed from the public agenda. After the coup in 1964, the military government adopted Brazil's first agrarian legislation, the Land Statute, which buttressed its conservative efforts to colonize the Amazon region.

A new surge for land reform erupted with force in the early 1980s. The MST emerged in this context and was officially established in January 1984 in the grain-belt city of Cascavel, Paraná. The movement was created under the aegis of the Pastoral Land Commission (CPT), an ecumenical church organization established in 1975. Through its progressive national network, the CPT helped forge a coalition of peasant groups involved in different and widely scattered land struggles across Brazil's southern half. Undoubtedly, the most widely recognized of all these mobilizations was the landless camp at Natalino's country road crossing in Rio Grande do Sul in 1981. The Natalino episode is in many regards the Brazilian equivalent to the bus boycotts in Montgomery, Alabama in 1955–56. In effect, both struggles for social justice were propelled by religious organizations and served to catalyze impressive nationwide movements (Carter 2002, 2003).

The MST's genesis in southern Brazil was facilitated by the region's relatively high levels of rural development, state capacity, education, and social capital. The strong family farm legacy, particularly in the states of Rio Grande do Sul, Santa Catarina, and Paraná, a consequence of intense European immigration after the mid-1800s, helped foster a historically active and inventive civil society. More specifically, the movement's emergence in southern Brazil was spurred by: 1) previous land mobilizations in the late 1950s and early 1960s, which set an important historical precedent; 2) an accelerated leap toward agricultural modernization, beginning in the mid-1960s, that excluded many small farmers from participation in the land market; 3) the construction of large hydroelectric dams, starting in the early 1970s, that displaced numerous peasant families; 4) enhanced political opportunities for mobilization in the late 1970s as result of the military regime's gradual opening; and 5) the progressive engagement of religious agents, inspired by a theology of liberation and Catholic innovations ushered after the Second Vatican Council (1962–65). Indeed, nowhere in the chronicle of world religion has a leading spiritual institution played as significant a role in support of land reform as has the Brazilian Catholic Church.[9]

In 1985 the newly installed civilian government led by José Sarney announced the implementation of an ambitious land reform plan. Influential representatives of the landlord class, however, were able to thwart the initiative and forestall progressive agrarian reform measures in the Constitution of 1988. In many parts of the Brazilian countryside, landlord associations hired gunmen to assassinate peasant leaders and progressive pastoral agents.

After the mid-1980s, the MST expanded across Brazil through the work of movement activists from the south and support from the church's progressive network and several rural trade unions. A decade later, the movement had established a foothold in twenty-three of the country's twenty-seven federal units. The MST gained ample national visibility during the mid-1990s through the substantial increase of land mobilizations after 1995 and significant media coverage of dramatic developments in the countryside. The national press gave considerable attention to a series of land occupations in the Pontal do Parapanema region, in the western edge of São Paulo, Brazil's wealthiest and most populous state. Two massacres of landless peasants in the Amazon region further compounded awareness of the country's agrarian problems. In August 1995 the police executed nine members of a local landless organization, including a seven-year old child, in Corumbiara, Rondônia. The repercussions of this episode, however, paled next to the national and international dismay conveyed over the police massacre of nineteen MST peasants in Eldorado dos Carajás, Pará in April 1996. Televised footage of the event helped stir loud public condemnation of the police bloodbath and galvanized national sympathy for the landless movement.

Adding to this momentum, two months later, Brazil's television mogul O Globo aired *O Rei do Gado* (The king of cattle), a highly popular soap opera that offered a benign, albeit patronizing depiction of the landless struggle. Together, these developments enhanced the MST's public prominence and general recognition as Brazil's leading social movement. By April 1997, amid the movement's well-publicized national march to Brasília, opinion polls showed that 94 percent of the population thought the MST's struggle for land reform was just, and 85 percent indicated a support for nonviolent land occupations as a way to accelerate government reform efforts (Comparato 2003, 190–91).

Land distribution surged between 1996 and 1999. In the wake of the massacre at Eldorado dos Carajás, President Fernando Henrique Cardoso created the Agrarian Reform Ministry to accelerate land expropriations and purchases. Yet Cardoso's government felt threatened by the MST's growing mobilization, enhanced popularity, close ties with the rival Workers' Party (PT), and forceful critique of the president's neoliberal policies. Hence, Cardoso's second administration ushered in a discernable effort to undermine the MST. Among other measures, the government cut back public funding for agrarian reform and scaled back its settlement program. With the support of the World Bank, it instituted a local, market-based approach to land distribution, which severely undercut the MST's capacity for collective action.[10] Furthermore, the government began to criminalize the movement's protest activities, punishing all land occupations, while promoting a media campaign to discredit the MST's public image. The federal government's retreat on agrarian reform coincided with the devaluation of the national currency in 1999, which facilitated the exports of the agribusiness sector, enhanced land values, and reduced opportunities for government land purchases.[11]

The election of President Lula in 2002 brought a measure of respite to the MST. After all, Lula and the MST had long held friendly relations. The new PT administration no longer sought to criminalize the movement's protest activities, despite repeated demands for a *mano dura* (heavy hand) approach by right-wing politicians and the conservative media establishment. Amid ongoing pressure tactics by the MST, Lula's government has maintained an open dialogue with its leaders. During its first term, it increased funding for agricultural settlements and the MST's educational projects. Yet Lula has fallen short on his land reform promises and disappointed those within the MST who hoped his government would steer away from the neoliberal fiscal policies of his predecessor. In spite of these misgivings, the MST mobilized on Lula's behalf in the presidential vote of 2006 to ensure the defeat of his more conservative opponent, Geraldo Alckmin, of Cardoso's Brazilian Social Democracy Party (PSDB).[12]

By the early 2000s, Brazil had more than seventy peasant organizations mobilizing for land reform. The MST remains predominant in the south, where it originated. But the struggle in the northeast and the Amazonian region has been led primarily by rural trade unions, affiliated with the National Confederation of Agricultural Workers (CONTAG), and various locally organized movements, including informal groups of squatters. More than 26 percent of Brazil's agrarian settlements are connected to the MST.[13] Over 90 percent of the land distributed since 1979, however, resulted from mobilizations undertaken by peasants groups that were not linked to the MST. This is particularly the case in the Amazonian region, where close to 80 percent of Brazil's land distribution has taken place. All told, between 1979 and 2006, the Brazilian state assigned close to 46 million hectares for land distribution (Carter and Carvalho 2009). The vast majority of these allocations have resulted from peasant land struggles.

Human rights violations have been a recurrent dilemma in the Brazilian countryside, especially in the Amazonian and northeastern regions. According to the CPT, between 1985 and 2003, 1,349 people, including dozens of children, were killed in different rural conflicts. As a rule, such crimes have taken place amid striking levels of impunity.[14]

The Endurance and Strength of the MST

In Brazil, few issues are as contentious as land reform. The MST's cutting-edge role in the social struggle to advance its implementation has earned it glowing accolades on the political left and spiteful comments among those with conservative views. In recent years, the Right has gone as far to portray the MST's mass occupations of large idle farms as "acts of terrorism" (Graziano 2006). This sense of paranoia on the right finds a natural counterpart in the romanticized depictions offered by the idealist left. Both revel in the MST's revolutionary potential, albeit for opposite reasons. Each side exaggerates considerably. In doing so, they generally overplay the MST's influence on Brazilian affairs.

Though unusually long lived and complex for a social movement, the MST is essentially a poor peoples' association. It operates with limited resources and is susceptible to many of the collective action problems that can be found among grass-roots organizations.[15] In some regards, the MST's public recognition and strength stems from an important level of media aggrandizement. News coverage of the MST, though, has been mostly negative and at times blatantly hostile. The myths and misunderstandings about the MST constructed by the Brazilian press cannot be underestimated.[16]

The MST's strength, while virtual in some respects, is also grounded on real sources of power. The enveloping context has shaped many of these strengths. In particular, three different conditions in Brazil help explain the movement's present vigor: its basic political freedoms; the stark inequities in wealth and the large number of destitute people; and the state's conservative land reform policies. The MST has been able to expand its organizing efforts and make demands on the government thanks to the nation's political liberties and competitive elections. In turn, Brazil's apartheid society assures the movement a large contingent of potential recruits, given the lack of decent work opportunities for its poorest inhabitants. Restrained by the interests of landlords and agribusiness, the state's land policies have focused mainly on attenuating rural conflicts rather than transforming the nation's agrarian structure in support of family farmers. Because of the state's conservative inertia, the MST has had to boost its organizational capacities both to pressure public authorities and make up for inadequate government services. This has led the MST to establish educational centers, cooperatives, and other programs designed to support its members and train its cadres. State response to some of the MST's demands, however delayed and partial, has enhanced the movement's attractiveness among its actual and potential participants.

Amid these conditions, the MST has been able to cultivate its own mobilizing resources, which include seven basic sources of strength. These are its 1) mobilization capacity, 2) strategic creativity, 3) sophisticated organizational structure, 4) investment in education, 5) numerous allies, 6) access to material resources, and 7) ideal interest orientation.

1. Mobilization Capacity. The movement possesses a large membership and an adroit ability to mobilize masses of people. Its estimated 1.5 million members include a dedicated core group of roughly twenty thousand activists (Carter and Carvalho 2009). The movement has sponsored some of the largest demonstrations in recent Brazilian history, such as the gathering of one hundred thousand people in front of the National Congress to demand agrarian reform in April 1997. In the last two decades, much of Brazil's visible protest activity—long distance marches, sit-ins, street demonstrations, and protest camps— have either been led by the MST or included participants of the movement.

2. Strategic Creativity. Since its inception, the MST has fostered inventive means for dealing with its logistical problems. The MST's ingenuity is most clear in the way its local activists plan and carry out their land occupations, generally risky endeavors involving peaceful mass mobilizations conducted with tactical acumen. The movement has also been creative in its fundraising efforts. For instance, in Rio Grande do Sul, the MST established a labor cooperative to help sustain its landless camps. Organized in 1996, CooperTchê supplies workers to agribusiness firms. By 2000, its net profit had reached U.S.$400,000, half of which served to finance mobilizations by the MST.[17] Over the years, the movement has shown a considerable capacity for innovation and the ability to learn from past mistakes. For example, after the mid-1990s, the MST began to reappraise the movement's attachment to an industrialized, chemical dependent model of agriculture and to foster a growing enthusiasm for agro-ecology. The creation in 1997 of BioNatur, the movement's first organic seed production cooperative, established in Rio Grande do Sul, marked a turning point in this process. In 2003, after extensive lobbying by women of the MST, the movement introduced provisions to establish gender equality in its leadership structure.

3. Sophisticated Organizational Structure. The movement's national coordination, decentralized bodies, and organic leadership enable it to function in a cohesive yet flexible manner. Internally, the movement operates through a complex network of collective decision-making bodies that encompass national, state, regional, and local levels of representation, sixteen different tasks teams (dealing with matters such as finance, international relations, health, education, and culture), and a national confederation of cooperatives.[18] The MST has

recently strengthened its communication efforts by adding two news agencies and a publishing house to its long-established news journal and magazine. The movement relies extensively on volunteers. It is not a bureaucratic organization. Yet over the years it has improved its level of professionalism. Today, the MST's main national and state offices employ regular staff, albeit at minimal living stipends. Though consistent and synchronized in many of its tactics, the movement allows for regional variation and experimentation. Its leaders are essentially of peasant origin. They reside mostly in agricultural settlements, live modestly, and maintain close ties with their constituency.

4. Investment in Education. The movement has placed a uniquely strong emphasis on the education of its participants and cadres. This sets the MST apart from most other peasant movements in Latin America. Presently, the MST runs a network of 1,800 primary and secondary schools, which are attended by 160,000 children. Its 8,000 teachers use pedagogical methods inspired by Paulo Freire and teaching materials developed by the MST's own educational team (Carter and Carvalho 2009). Furthermore, the MST has established an adult literacy program, which in 2003 served close to 30,000 people (MST 2004b). The movement has devoted significant resources in preparing its activists and has created several training centers for this. During the last two decades it held hundreds of workshops on a range of issues—such as health, education, gender, political economy, and ecology—for more than 100,000 activists (Carter and Carvalho 2009). In early 2005 the movement inaugurated its first university, the Escola Nacional Florestan Fernandes, named after a renowned Brazilian intellectual, on an attractive campus near the city of São Paulo.

5. Numerous Allies. The MST has effective ties to, and relies upon, a resourceful network of supporters in Brazilian civil and political society. Moreover, the movement has become adept at capitalizing on sympathetic pockets within the Brazilian state, including those in the national land reform institute, INCRA. Civil society support for the MST involves a range of actors, most notably among liberal sectors of the Catholic Church and traditional Protestant denominations, national labor and peasant unions, progressive NGOs, and elements of the country's educational and cultural establishment. Within political society, the movement historically has enjoyed the backing of the leftist Workers' Party and other progressive forces. The MST has also benefited from global sources of funding, principally from church

agencies in Europe. Furthermore, it has received many national and international distinctions, such as Sweden's Alternative Nobel Prize, bestowed by the Right Livelihood Foundation in 1991, and the King Baudouin International Development Prize, conferred by the government of Belgium in 1996. The movement maintains ties with many organizations around the globe, including MST solidarity groups established in fourteen European and North American countries. Through its affiliation with La Vía Campesina, the MST maintains contacts with small farmers' organizations in forty-three nations. Over the years, the MST has played an active role in several Brazilian networks advocating social change, including the National Forum for Agrarian Reform and Justice in the Countryside.[19]

6. Access to Material Resources. Though an organization of poor people, the MST is endowed with a modest supply of material resources—vehicles, offices, computers, cell phones, and the like—needed to carry out its basic engagements. Its financial means come from a variety of sources. These include monies for development projects that are administered by the movement and underwritten by national and state governments, as well as international agencies. In addition, the MST receives contributions from its cooperatives and members, through informal union-like dues, usually a 2–3 percent surcharge on agricultural credits obtained from the federal government. Landless encampments normally secure their food through a combination of sources, such as donations from INCRA, state and local governments, family and friends, and assistance from an array of sympathizers within civil society.

7. Ideal Interest Orientation. Within the MST, and particularly among its activists, one often finds a strong sense of identity, forceful convictions, and intense social energy. The MST's struggles are usually driven by more than just material interests. They are also frequently infused with what Max Weber defined as an ideal interest (or value-rational) motivation toward social action. Ideal interest actors are strategically oriented toward the fulfillment of an absolute, nonnegotiable goal. The MST's struggles are often carried out through a fusion of striving and attaining, rather than a concern for optimizing. In the process, they generate strong feelings that help refuel its mobilizations. Ideal interest orientations are manifest and strengthened through the regular display of dense symbolic repertoires—flags, songs, chants, marches, theater, and other ritual gatherings—that stir

courage and vitality among its participants. Members of the MST describe these moments as comprising part of their *mística*. In conversations with activists in the movement it is not uncommon to hear them convey expressions of striking emotional attachment, such as "I love the MST," "The MST is my life."[20]

The MST's Public Activism and Impact on Democracy

The venue through which the MST challenges Brazil's stark social disparities is as noteworthy as the impetus itself. The movement's surprising success has been intimately entwined with its capacity to engage in a distinct form of social struggle: public activism. This approach to social conflict is substantially different from that of an armed insurgency, a scattered riot, or what James Scott (1985, 1990) defines as "everyday forms of resistance" to describe informal, discreet, and disguised forms of popular aggression. Unlike these other patterns of social confrontation, the MST's public activism involves an organized, politicized, visible, autonomous, periodic, and nonviolent form of social conflict.

Actions carried out through public activism are geared toward drawing public attention; influencing state policies through pressure politics, lobbying, and negotiations; and shaping societal ideas, values, and actions. Typically, mobilizations of this kind employ an array of modern repertoires of contention, such as demonstrations, marches, petitions, group meetings, hunger strikes, protest camps, and election campaigns, along with acts of civil disobedience such as sit-ins, road blockades, building takeovers, and organized land occupations. Unlike other approaches to social conflict, public activism's nonviolent thrust makes it essentially compatible with civil society and provides a legitimate democratic vehicle for propelling social change (Carter 2006).

Public activism has become deeply ingrained in the movement's ethos and self-image. The MST was born and raised amid social conflict. *A gente tem que lutar* (We must struggle) is a lesson learned since the origins of the movement. In everyday MST parlance, all of its *victorias* (victories) and *conquistas* (conquests) are the result of grass-roots struggle, not a gratuitous concession from above. Hence, the lesson learned in the last quarter of a century is a well-established one: organize at the grass roots, pressure the state through mobilization, and then negotiate the best deal possible.

The MST's pressure politics, however ingrained, are not the result of mere ideological assumptions, as critics such as Zander Navarro (2002b) insist. Navarro maintains that the MST has "canonized" collective action as a result of its "fundamentalist" view of politics, fed by what he claims are "vulgar Marxist" ideas. Given the options available, the MST's reliance on pressure politics reflects a quite rational strategy for assuring a measure of success. Among alternative means for furthering agrarian reform— electoral contestation, legislative representation, media influence, lobbying, or armed insurgency—pressure politics is clearly the most reasonable and cost-effective option.

Fielding national election candidates or acquiring a major media outlet is clearly beyond the MST's financial means. Legislative representation offers few tactical advantages given the traditional overrepresentation of conservative rural interests in Congress (Carter 2009a)[21] and the prerogatives accorded to the executive branch for carrying out land reform. Adding to this, the MST is fully aware that lobbying without pressure politics is generally a toothless instrument. Moreover, it clearly understands that a guerrilla alternative would be a suicidal gamble.

Public activism and its disruptive tactics, then, are the only reasonable course of action available to Brazil's landless peasants. Pressure politics is first and foremost a practical response, a collective problem-solving measure—not the machination of an ideological agenda. Public activism enables the MST to stir public opinion and gain direct access to policymakers in a way that most institutional mechanisms would render ineffectual or innocuous at best. Viewed in historical terms, the MST's public activism represents a bold reaction to Brazil's durable inequities in land concentration, and a realistic attempt to overcome long-standing political impediments to agrarian reform.

This perspective, however, is not shared by the MST's critics, including influential Brazilian intellectuals such as José de Souza Martins, Zander Navarro, and Francisco Graziano.[22] These authors maintain that the MST's confrontational relations with Brazil's governing institutions represent a "threat to democracy." These critics are also inclined to depict agrarian reform as an outdated policy and treat the MST as an anachronistic movement. For Martins, one of Brazil's most renowned rural sociologists, the MST is the local equivalent to the English Luddite movement, a short-lived popular uprising in the early nineteenth century famed for wrecking new factory machines. Because the MST is incited by similar "fundamentalist" beliefs, Martin insists, it "refuses to recognize the institutional legitimacy and actions of the government and the state." In fact, according to Martins, the movement's actions and demands represent a "pre-political and precarious attempt to demolish the political order" (Martins 2000, 18–19, 26).

Martins further asserts that the MST and its church ally, the CPT, are led by radicalized middle-class intermediaries—professional activists, intellectuals, and clergy members—who filter the authentic voices and usurp the real demands of the rural poor. The ideological and partisan interests of these middle-class activists, he contests, ignore the peasantry's essentially "traditional and conservative values of land, work, family, community and religion" (Martins 2000, 49). What's more, their "apparent radicalism" does not address the "real roots of the problem," but rather serves to "maintain the social inequities . . . [they] seek to change" (Martins 2000, 60). For Martins, then, the crux of Brazil's agrarian impasse resides in the land reform activists themselves, who "manipulate" and "use" the rural poor in ways that replicate the old oligarchic patterns of domination of the landlord class (Martins 2003, 27, 44).

Navarro, a fellow sociologist, considers that "the MST has lost its reason to exist, since the time for land reform has past. In fact, it ceased to be a historic and national necessity a long time ago, under any point of view" (quoted in Scolese 2003). He further describes the MST as an "anti-systemic" and "anti-state" organization, driven by a hardened Marxist disposition toward noninstitutional venues of action (Navarro 2002a, 208, 211; 2002b, 279). Navarro argues that the MST stopped being a social movement in the 1990s. Instead, it degenerated into a "semi-clandestine," "orthodox Leninist" organization, run by a small revolutionary cadre. The MST, he stresses, is sustained through "nondemocratic" practices, a "militarist ethos" and the "quasi-religious devotion" of its activists. The group's training centers reproduce the "childish Leninism" of its national leaders and instill a "pathetic ideological mystification" of the world (Navarro 2002b, 277; 2002a, 206–7). The MST, he claims, controls its land reform settlements through autocratic impositions and manipulations, including the extortion of settlers who depend on the organization for the allocation of public funds.

Graziano, a former federal deputy and head of the INCRA under President Cardoso, insists that the modernization of large landholdings has extinguished the traditional *latifundio*. Because of this, Brazil has little or no more land to redistribute in its more developed regions (Graziano 2004, 133). Most people mobilized by the MST, he argues, are undeserving claimants. In his view, "the millions of landless people" that land reform proponents put forth "simply don't exist; they are the product of a chimera, an ideological dream" (Graziano 2004, 244). Graziano depicts the MST as "an authoritarian guerrilla organization" that is "undermining democracy" by abetting acts of "agrarian terrorism" with its land occupations (Graziano 2004, 304, 72; Graziano 2006).

These three intellectuals have helped sanction recurrent media depictions of the MST as an "authoritarian, violent, manipulative, revolutionary organization that mobilizes false landless people." As such, they have endorsed a public image that treats the landless movement as a "danger" to the Brazilian state and its democratic regime. The tacit proposition, here, clearly underpins conservative calls to curtail the MST's demands and restrain its protest activities.

Such critiques of the MST shed greater light on their authors than on the phenomena they are keen to attack. The extreme character of many of their statements, their gross oversimplifications, gratuitous charges, and the dearth of empirical evidence underlying many of their appraisals, suggests that these intellectuals may be more interested in deploying a "rhetoric of intransigence," in Albert Hirschman's (1991, 7) fitting term, than in facilitating a constructive dialogue.

The restrictive and ahistorical understanding of democracy offered in these intellectual critiques is certainly worrisome. The MST cannot be comprehended properly without an adequate contextualization of its activities, ideas, and impact. Any serious effort to grasp its actions requires ongoing field experience. Given the movement's dynamic and innovative character, frozen images can become outdated over a brief lapse of time.

Contrary to the opinion of these conservative critics of the MST, I argue that the movement's embrace of public activism—and use of disruptive tactics—has actually contributed to the advancement of democracy in Brazil in seven ways.

1. *It strengthens civil society through the organization and incorporation of marginalized sectors of the population.* Historically, Brazilian civil society associations and media outlets represented mostly the interests of the upper and middle classes. The MST's efforts to recruit among the nation's poor and provide a collective venue for making demands have promoted their empowerment. By developing networks of trust and reciprocity, diffusing grass-roots organizing skills, and spawning thousands of local popular leaders, the MST has enhanced social capital formation among Brazil's underprivileged majority. Elite interests, no doubt, are still predominant in Brazilian civil society. Yet

the inclusion of subaltern actors such as the MST has contributed to the democratization of this arena. In doing so, the MST has helped break historic patterns of civil society exclusion—the long-standing result of political repression, elite co-optation, state control of labor and peasant unions, and weak organizational capacities among Brazil's popular sectors.

2. *It fosters a civilizing process in the countryside by harnessing, articulating, and disciplining social frustrations and deploying these through constructive actions at the grass-roots level.* The MST's mobilizations contrast significantly with traditional forms of everyday peasant resistance and historic patterns of rural banditry and messianic rebellion. Building on the experience of Brazil's peasant unions, first organized in the late 1950s, the MST has helped modernize collective action in the countryside. The orderly lifestyle in the movement's protest camps and training schools illustrate well its modernizing impetus. By disciplining passions and other raw impulses into more methodical forms of behavior, the MST has helped nurture what Norbert Elias (1982) describes as a "civilizing process." Thanks to enhanced self-esteem and increased self-discipline, the MST's participants are more likely to channel their contentious behavior through peaceful and constructive means. Compared to Brazil's ever more violent criminal gangs and heightened manifestations of everyday insecurity, notably in its expanding urban slums, the MST's civil disobedience tactics could hardly be considered a national security threat. To the contrary, the movement's civilizing ethos and impact has helped stem Brazil's social decay.

3. *It facilitates the extension and exercise of basic citizenship rights— civil, political ,and social rights—among the poor.* Since its origins the MST has fought for the right to mobilize freely and exercise its democratic right to influence decisions made by public authorities, independent of the electoral process. Through legal measures and publicity efforts, it has defended the basic human rights of hundreds of peasants who have been imprisoned, abused, and assassinated for their land reform activism. In addition, by improving the material conditions and cultural resources of its members, the movement has fortified the social foundations for democracy. When basic needs are met, people are unlikely to sell their votes on election day. The sense of character forged through long years of the MST's struggle has nurtured more conscientious citizens and fostered greater participation

in local affairs. By enabling people to exercise their political rights in a meaningful way, the MST has helped integrate hundreds of thousands of Brazil's poor into the democratic process. In doing so, the MST has abetted their "transition from clientelism to citizenship" (Fox 1994). As Charles Tilly (2002) reminds us, throughout world history, citizenship rights were never created through gentle concessions from the ruling elite or the gradual enlightenment of society as a whole. Rather, these rights are the historical result of years of resistance, struggle, and bargaining with national authorities.

4. *It highlights the importance of public activism as a force for inequality reduction and a catalyst for social development.* Brazil's struggle for agrarian reform suggests that public activism is a necessary instrument for inequality reduction in starkly disparate societies. Such environments, after all, tend to produce daunting obstacles to change. Their removal requires that they be tackled with concerted, forceful, and disruptive pressure from below. If coupled with a process of negotiation at the top, this societal drive can foster an auspicious momentum for state innovation. In apartheid-like environments, amiable, top-down attempts to foster reform are likely to produce empty government promises. Brazil's struggle for agrarian reform shows that it would be disingenuous, at best, to expect a major initiative for the redistribution of wealth to involve anything less than a tough touch.

Over the years, the MST's public activism has inspired many other grass-roots associations. An array of popular movements in Brazil—those of peasant women, hydroelectric dam victims, small farmers, homeless people, and other landless groups, principally those linked to CONTAG's rural trade unions—have assimilated the MST's tactics and taken courage from its actions (Rosa 2009). In this way, the MST's public activism has contributed to an unprecedented distribution of state resources among the rural poor, through land purchases, farming and housing credits, infrastructural development, technical assistance, educational programs, and the creation of scores of rural cooperatives and food-processing plants.[23]

5. *It underscores the state's vital responsibility in protecting human rights and advancing equity-enhancing reforms.* Critics of the MST regularly accuse the movement of espousing "anti-state" views and "opposing the rule of law." A review of the MST's practices, however, reveals that its occasionally bellicose rhetoric toward public policies and agents masks a relationship that also includes many elements of

close cooperation with the state. Indeed, over the years, the movement has proven adept at working with governments at the federal, state, and local levels.[24]

The idea of a fundamental opposition between the MST and the law omits the fact that social movements around the world have also served as architects of an alternative legal order. The movement's difficulties with Brazil's legal institutions cannot ignore the judiciary's traditional pliancy to landlord interests; its cripplingly bureaucratic and class-biased procedures; and it gross impunity regarding human rights violations in the countryside. Along with these predictable legal clashes, the MST has also taken an active part in the nation's debates over the interpretation of existing laws. Through its dedicated and expanding network of lawyers, the movement is frequently involved in running legal cases and lobbying higher echelons of the judiciary. In one of its major victories, a decision in 1996 by one of Brazil's highest courts ruled that land occupations designed to hasten reform were "substantially distinct" from criminal acts against property.

Far from simply disdaining the state and its judicial apparatus, the MST and its allies actively underscore the state's central role in defending human rights and rebalancing the nation's social order (Meszaros 2000a, 2000b, 2009; Hammond 1999). The MST's recognition of the state's decisive role in effecting progressive social change explains its determined opposition to neoliberalism and its policies of public retrenchment. Indeed, in Brazil and elsewhere, neoliberal practices have undermined the state capacity to further wealth redistribution.

6. *It places an emphasis on the value of education, consciousness raising, self-dignity, and personal responsibility among its participants.* Since its first stirrings, the MST has invested extensive efforts toward raising consciousness among Brazil's poor. Its initial impetus under liberation theology led the movement to develop an early appreciation for the importance of literacy skills and nurture a sense of mystique among its participants. An active network of MST teachers and pedagogical advisors has helped affirm the movement's unique commitment to education. Its teaching resources underscore the MST's values regarding the importance of collective struggle, organization, participation, citizenship rights, solidarity, education, cultural diversity, land, and nature. With the assistance of progressive intellectuals, the movement has advanced an alternative interpretation of Brazilian history from a poor people's perspective.

The MST's mobilizations offer an especially powerful learning experience. Land struggles are regularly cited among its members as a pivotal moment in their education.[25] Through public activism, participants are encouraged to shed fatalistic views while nurturing a strong sense of agency and conviction that the world can be changed through collective struggle (Caldart 2000). In doing so, the MST's mobilizations cultivate an enhanced feeling of dignity and greater sense of responsibility among its members. This ethos produces more conscious and self-confident citizens, who are able to contribute more to the enrichment of Brazil's democratic process (Quirk 2008).

7. *It engenders a sense of utopia, hope, and affirmation of ideals imbued in Brazil's long-term and open-ended democratization process.* The MST's dynamism and demands for greater social justice in a nation afflicted by remarkable inequities represent a vital democratizing force in Brazil. From its early days, the movement has helped inspire new horizons and heartened visions of a more just society. In recent years, the belief that "another world is possible" has found a congenial setting at the assemblies of the World Social Forum. The MST has been very much involved in these gatherings since the first encounter in Porto Alegre, in 2001. In many regards, the movement's struggle for social change has upheld the dreams and desires for liberty, equality, and participation that have shaped the historic development of democracy. Democracy, after all, cannot be divorced from its ideals. By keeping a sense of utopia alive, the MST galvanizes hope and contributes a positive impetus toward Brazil's long-term, multifaceted, and ongoing democratization process.[26] Ideals and a quest for utopia can play an essential role in this process. As Max Weber (1958, 128) perceptively wrote, humans "would not have attained the possible if time and again [they] had not reached out for the impossible."

Challenging Brazil's Social Apartheid: The MST's Impetus Towards a Radical Democracy

The MST's experience provides a telling lesson for the prospects of inequality reduction in the twenty-first century. During the twentieth century, the three leading formulas for dealing with the problems of wealth disparity were market economics, social revolution, and political democracy. Market economics assumed that consistent economic growth would eventually reduce both poverty and inequality. Social revolutions, relying largely on

Marxian inspiration, upheld the need for a violent takeover of the state and drastic impositions of equalizing measures. Political democracies offered a constitutional framework allowing basic civil liberties, political competition, and mass participation in the election of governing representatives. The regime's own incentive structure, it was argued, would lead to the redistribution of wealth over the long run, namely through the development of state welfare policies.

In practice, however, each approach presented serious drawbacks. Market economics generally ignored power asymmetries and their effects on the development process. Economic growth in highly unequal societies is more likely to fuel income disparity than bridge its gap, as Brazil's "economic miracle" in the 1970s visibly showed (Paes de Barros et al. 2000). Social revolutions often ushered traumatic episodes of violence and dreadful human rights violations. In their wake, revolutionary elites often instituted draconian policies with devastating social costs, as witnessed during the Soviet Union's industrialization process and China's "Great Leap Forward." Political democracy, in contrast, has not offered clear solutions to the inequality problem either. In the 1990s, most of Latin America experienced economic growth and democratic regimes. Yet income disparity, though remaining stable in Brazil, actually increased in most other Latin American countries (Karl 2003). In Latin America, unlike the Western European and North American experiences, democracy's positive long-term impact appears to be quite uncertain and obviously of no consolation to those in dire need.

Brazil's struggle for agrarian reform provides glimpses of an alternative pathway to reducing durable inequalities in developing societies based on an impetus toward a form of *radical democracy*. This approach draws on political democracy's "enabling institutional milieu" (O'Donnell 2004, 11) but argues that this framework alone is not enough. Radical democracy stresses the importance of autonomous popular organizations, specifically their mobilization and participation in development efforts. Popular engagement can be strengthened through the creation of state partnerships with grass-roots groups and their representation in public agencies responsible for executing social policies. A radical democracy incorporates many elements of what Philippe C. Schmitter (1974) defined as a societal corporatist model for interest representation based on horizontal state-society linkages. While valuing economic growth, this approach to inequality reduction insists that the poor be included in a productive process that is ecologically sustainable and provides access to basic consumer goods and social services.

The radical democratic course, then, combines four basic elements: 1) public activism; 2) institutional mechanisms for developing state-society partnerships and effective societal accountability (Smulovitz and Peruzzotti 2000); 3) a responsive government leadership that is sympathetic to grass-roots demands; and 4) a functioning state that is capable of investing public resources for social welfare and the economic development of the poorest strata in society. The first three features presuppose a political democracy. The latter two explain the MST's support for the political left and its defense of a national development model led by a robust state rather than powerful economic actors.

The radical democratic approach to inequality reduction is certainly not devoid of problems and practical limitations. Its relevance, however, cannot be easily dismissed. Underlying this formula is a cumulus of experience and ideas that warrant closer attention. The MST's contributions to this debate are likely to stir passionate arguments and fuel creative solutions in the years to come.

The MST has made great strides since its precarious origins in the early 1980s. Nowadays, the movement is a recognized player in the global back-lash against neoliberalism and a leading Brazilian voice in the demand for greater social and environmental justice. For many people around the world, the MST has become a sign of hope that "another world is possible." "Hope," as William Sloan Coffin (2004, 19) elegantly writes, "criticizes what is, hopelessness rationalizes it. Hope resists, hopelessness adapts." In to-day's Brazil, as in other Latin American countries, the beacon of hope is held by peasant and indigenous groups. In a curious reversal of modern expectations, the continent's raw social energy, political vitality, and pro-gressive imagination are exuding greater vigor in the countryside than in its large urban metropolises. The MST, no doubt, is an emblematic expression of this audacious trend. Here, too, the wretched of the earth inspire hope by defying injustice.

Notes

Author's note: The author would like to thank Kristina Svensson for her thoughtful editorial comments.

1. This account of the MST's national march in 2005 is based on an extensive review of all leading media sources. A detailed description of this event can be found in Carter 2009b.

2. The estimate of the number of the MST's members presented here is admittedly precarious. The MST has no formal roster and no surveys have ever been taken to

quantify the movement's actual membership. By the end of 2006, the MST is estimated to have helped settle close to 135,000 families, while mobilizing an additional 150,000 families in its encampments throughout Brazil. Based on these numbers, a conservative calculus of three members per family would estimate a membership of more than 1.1 million people. The number of MST settlements is Carter and Carvalho 2009. All other figures are from MST 2004a, 2004b.

3. The area occupied by the MST's settlements is from Carter and Carvalho 2009.

4. Key sources on the MST's history and evolution include Carter 2009a; Ondetti 2008; Wright and Wolford 2003; Branford and Rocha 2002.

5. The FAO's land reform conference in Porto Alegre in 2006 came on the heels of the World Forum on Agrarian Reform, held in Valencia, Spain in 2004. Both events, in turn, were shaped by the growing number of Asian, African, and Latin American countries that have been experiencing struggles for land reform. See Carta Maior 2006; Rosset et al. 2006; and Moyo and Yeros 2005.

6. The economist Edmar Bacha (1974) coined the concept of "Belindia" to describe Brazil's dualistic pattern of development: a small, rich, first-world Belgium coexisting with a large, poor, third-world India. See Buarque 1994 on Brazil's social apartheid and the concept of "apartation."

7. On Brazil's agrarian history and structure, see Costa Delgado 2009; Medeiros 1989, 2009; Stédile 1997, 1999; and Martins 1990, 1991, 1994, 1997.

8. This figure was derived by comparing expenditures made by the Ministry of Rural Development, for landless peasants and family farmers, and public allocations made available to large landholders through the Ministry of Agriculture and Brazil's National Development Bank. Further details on the impact of social inequality on rural public expenditures can be found in Carter 2009b, table 5.

9. On the church's involvement in support of the MST, see Poletto 2009; Poletto and Canuto 2002; Adriance 1996.

10. On the World Bank's market-based approach to land redistribution, see chapter 2.

11. During the mid-1990s, sectors of the agrarian elite profited handsomely by selling land to the federal government, thanks to generous values offered by INCRA. The stabilization of inflation in 1994 and low agricultural prices decreased incentives to invest in rural properties. This surge, however, ended with the currency devaluation of 1999. On President Cardoso's agrarian reform policies and relations with the MST, see Branford 2009); Fernandes 2009; Deere and Medeiros 2007; Ondetti 2004; and Comparato 2003.

12. Early assessments of President Lula's land reform program can be found in Branford 2009; Fernandes 2009; INESC 2006; Coletivo Petista 2006; Umbelino de Oliveira 2006; and Deere and Medeiros 2007.

13. This figure covers settlements with both loose and dense ties to the MST; see Fernandes 2009. The MST's relations with other peasant groups have varied over time and space, and oscillate between close collaboration and steep competition. The MST and CONTAG, the umbrella organization for Brazil's rural trade unions established in 1963, share common goals concerning land reform and rural development policies,

but they have differed at times on tactical issues. Some of CONTAG's twenty-six state federations disagreed with the MST's land occupations, although other federations, particularly in the Amazon, were very much involved in supporting squatter land struggles. After the mid-1990s, however, CONTAG as a whole began to promote its own land mobilizations, borrowing several tactics learned from the MST. See Ondetti et al. 2009; and Rosa 2009;, and on the history and politics of CONTAG, see Maybury-Lewis 1994.

14. In only 5.6 percent of these rural killings has anyone been brought to trial, and barely fifteen landlords who ordered such crimes have been condemned by the courts; see CPT 2004. Brazil's social apartheid fuels, no doubt, an ethos of disregard for human rights. On Brazil's rural violence, see Melo 2006, 57–100.

15. For thoughtful examinations of some of the MST's recurring collective action problems, see Calvo-Sotelo 2009; Wolford 2009; and Branford and Rocha 2002.

16. Informative accounts of the Brazilian media's portrayal of the MST can be found in Lerrer 2005; Comparato 2003; and Berger 1998.

17. Interview by the author with CooperTché's original mentor, Antoninho Juscelino Mattes, tape recording, Porto Alegre, November 25, 2000; and, Viamão, Rio Grande do Sul, July 9, 2003.

18. On the MST's internal organization, see Fernandes 2009; Carter and Carvalho 2009; and Branford and Rocha 2002.

19. The MST has been active in other progressive Brazilian networks and organizations, such as the Brazilian Association for Agrarian Reform, Consulta Popular, the National Network of Popular Independent Lawyers, the Coordination of Social Movements (CMS), and more recently, the church-sponsored Popular Assembly.

20. Max Weber's ideal interest concept is treated extensively in Carter 2002 2003. The concept of "fusion of striving and attaining" is taken from Hirschman 1982, 85. Other social movement analyses that underscore the importance of passionate commitments are Goodwin, Jasper, and Poletta 2001; and Aminzade and McAdam 2001. On the MST's own descriptions of this *mística,* see Bogo 2002.

21. Brazil's problem of political overrepresentation of landlords and conservative rural districts is discussed in Carter 2009a; Snyder and Samuels 2004; and Stepan 2001. On the nation's influential *bancada ruralista,* a congressional caucus that champions agribusiness and large landholding interests, see Vigna 2001 2003. For a closer review of the MST's multiple forms of interaction with Brazilian political institutions, see Carter 2005.

22. The ideas espoused by all three analysts have received ample attention in Brazil's mainstream media. Martins, a professor emeritus of the Universidade de São Paulo, is Brazil's most prolific rural sociologist. Navarro is a sociology professor at the Universidade Federal do Rio Grande do Sul. Both are former advisors to the MST and the CPT. After the mid-1990s, Martins and Navarro had personal fallouts with these organizations and served as consultants to the Cardoso government. Graziano was the head of INCRA under President Cardoso and is a former PSDB federal deputy. He writes a regular column for three of the nation's leading newspapers and directs an NGO dedicated to the promotion of agribusiness interests.

23. Surveys of land reform settlements have found that the overwhelming majority of settlers feel their lives have improved substantially, despite serious deficiencies in the state provision of infrastructure and agricultural credits. The main recent studies of Brazilian land reform settlements are by Heredia et al. 2004; and Sparovek 2003.

24. Useful discussions and illustrations on the MST's constructive interactions with the state and government officials can be found in Sigaud 2009; Branford 2009; Wolford 2009; Ondetti et al. 2009; and Carter 2005, 2009c, 2009d.

25. In the words of dozens of MST members I have interviewed over the years, "O tempo de acampamento foi a minha faculdade" (The time spent at the landless encampment was my college degree).

26. This approach to democratization draws on Whitehead 2002.

References

Adriance, Madeleine R. 1996. *Terra prometida: As comunidades eclesiais de base e os conflitos rurais*. São Paulo: Edições Paulinas.

Aminzade, Ronald R., and Doug McAdam. 2001. "Emotions and Contentious Politics." In *Silence and Voice in the Study of Contentious Politics*, edited by Ronald R. Aminzade, et al., 14–50. Cambridge: Cambridge University Press, pp. 14-50.

Bacha, Edmar Lisboa. 1974. "O economista e o rei da Belindia: Uma fábula para tecnocratas." *Jornal Opinião* (São Paulo). Available at http://en.scientificcommons.org/22165421, accessed October 1, 2005

Berger, Christa. 1998. *Campos em confronto: A terra e o texto*. Porto Alegre: Editora da Universidade/UFRGS.

Bogo, Ademar. 2002. *O Vigor da Mística*. Caderno de Cultura 2. São Paulo: ANCA.

Branford, Sue. 2009. "Working with Governments: The MST's Experience with the Cardoso and Lula Administrations." In *Challenging Social Inequality: The Landless Rural Workers' Movement and Agrarian Reform in Brazil*, edited by Miguel Carter. Durham, N.C.: Duke University Press.

Branford, Sue, and Jan Rocha. 2002. *Cutting the Wire: The Story of the Landless Movement in Brazil*. London: Latin American Bureau.

Buarque, Cristovam. 1994. *O que é Apartação? O apartheid social no Brasil*. São Paulo: Editora Brasiliense.

Caldart, Roseli Salete. 2000. *Pedagogía do Movimento Sem Terra: Escola é mais do que escola*. 2nd ed. Petrópolis: Vozes.

Calvo-Sotelo, Elena. 2009. "Community Building in an MST Settlement in Northeast Brazil." In *Challenging Social Inequality: The Landless Rural Workers' Movement and Agrarian Reform in Brazil*, edited by Miguel Carter. Durham, N.C.: Duke University Press, forthcoming.

Carta Maior (2006). *El Foro Mundial sobre la Reforma Agraria* Available at http://www.fma.org/memoria_CartaMaio.pdf, accessed August 24, 2008.

Carter, Miguel. 2002. "Ideal Interest Mobilization: The Origins of Brazil's Landless Social Movement." Ph.D. diss., Columbia University.

————. 2003. "The Origins of Brazil's Landless Rural Workers' Movement (MST): The Natalino Episode in Rio Grande do Sul (1981–84); A Case of Ideal Interest Mobilization." Working Paper Number CBS-43–03. Centre for Brazilian Studies, University of Oxford.

————. 2005. "The Landless Rural Workers' Movement (MST) and Democracy in Brazil." Working Paper Number CBS-60–05. Centre for Brazilian Studies, University of Oxford.

————. 2006. "Shaping Civil Society: Land Reform Struggles in Brazil and Paraguay." Unpublished manuscript.

————, ed. 2009a. *Challenging Social Inequality: The Landless Rural Workers' Movement and Agrarian Reform in Brazil*. Durham, N.C.: Duke University Press.

————. 2009b. "Social Inequality, Democracy, and Agrarian Reform in Brazil." In *Challenging Social Inequality: The Landless Rural Workers' Movement and Agrarian Reform in Brazil*, edited by Miguel Carter. Durham, N.C.: Duke University Press.

————. 2009c. "The Origins and Consolidation of the MST in Rio Grande do Sul." In *Challenging Social Inequality: The Landless Rural Workers' Movement and Agrarian Reform in Brazil*, edited by Miguel Carter. Durham: N.C.: Duke University Press.

————. 2009d. "Challenging Social Inequality: Contention, Context, and Consequence." In *Challenging Social Inequality: The Landless Rural Workers' Movement (MST) and Agrarian Reform in Brazil*, edited by Miguel Carter. Durham, N.C.: Duke University Press.

Carter, Miguel, and Horacio Martins de Carvalho. 2009. "The Struggle on the Land: Source of Innovation, Strength, and Permanent Challenge to the MST." In *Challenging Social Inequality: The Landless Rural Workers' Movement and Agrarian Reform in Brazil*, edited by Miguel Carter. Durham, N.C.: Duke University Press.

CEPAL (Comisión Económica Para América Latina). 2004. *Anuario Estadístico de America Latina y el Caribe*, 2004. http://www.eclac.cl/, accessed May 19, 2006.

Coffin, William Sloan. 2004. *Credo*. Louisville, Ky.: Westminster John Knox Press.

Coletivo Petista para Reflexões sobre as Políticas Agrícola e Agrária. 2006. "Um balanço do programa de reforma agrária no governo Lula: Subsídios para o debate interno no PT." Unpublished manuscript.

Comparato, Bruno Konder. 2003. *A ação política do MST*. São Paulo: Editora Expressão Popular.

Costa Delgado, Guilherme. 2009. "The Agrarian Question and Agribusiness in Brazil." In *Challenging Social Inequality: The Landless Rural Workers' Movement and Agrarian Reform in Brazil*, edited by Miguel Carter. Durham: N.C.: Duke University Press.

CPT (Comissão Pastoral da Terra). 2004. "Assassinatos e julgamentos 1985–2003." Setor de Documentação. Unpublished report.

Deere, Carmen Diana, and Leonilde Servolo de Medeiros. 2007. "Agrarian Reform and Poverty Reduction: Lessons from Brazil." In *Land, Poverty, and Livelihoods in an Era of Globalization*, edited by A. Haroon Akram-Lodhi, Saturnino M. Borras Jr., and Cristóbal Kay, 80–118. London: Routledge.

Del Grossi, Mauro Eduardo, José Garcia Gasques, José Graziano da Sila, and Júnia Cristina P. R. da Conceição. 2001. "Estimativas das famílias potenciais beneficiárias de programas de assentamentos rurais no Brasil." In *Transformações da agricultura e políticas públicas*, edited by José Garcia Gasques and Júnia Cristina P. R. da Conceição, 457–78. Brasília: IPEA.

Elias, Norbert. 1982. *Power and Civility*. New York: Pantheon.

Fernandes, Bernardo Mançano. 2009. "The Formation and Territorialization of the MST in Brazil." In *Challenging Social Inequality: The Rural Workers' Landless Movement and Agrarian Reform in Brazil*, edited by Miguel Carter. Durham, N.C.: Duke University Press.

Fox, Jonathan. 1994. "The Difficult Transition from Clientelism to Citizenship: Lessons from Mexico." *World Politics* 46 (2): 151–84.

Goodwin, Jeff, James M. Jasper, and Francesca Poletta, eds. 2001. *Passionate Politics: Emotions and Social Movements*. Chicago: University of Chicago Press.

Graziano, Xico. 2004. *O carma da terra*. São Paulo: A Girafa.

———. 2006. "Terrorismo Agrário." *Estado de São Paulo*, May 23. http://www.estado. com.br/editorias/2006/05/23/opi-1.93.29.20060523.1.1.xml, accessed May 24, 2006.

Hammond, John L. 1999. "Law and Disorder: The Brazilian Landless Farmworkers' Movement." *Bulletin of Latin American Research* 18 (4): 469–89.

Heredia, Beatriz, Leonilde Sérvolo de Medeiros, Moacir Palmeira, Rosângela Cintrão, and Sergio Leite. 2004. *Impactos dos assentamentos: Um estudo sobre o meio rural brasileiro*. Brasília: Núcleo de Estudos Agrários e Desenvolvimento Rural.

Hirschman, Albert O. 1982. *Shifting Involvements: Private Interest and Public Action*. Princeton, N.J.: Princeton University Press.

———. 1991. *The Rhetoric of Reaction: Perversity, Futility, and Jeopardy*. Cambridge, Mass.: Harvard University Press, Belknap Press.

IBGE (Instituto Brasileiro de Geografía e Estatística). 1996. *Censo Agropecuário 1996*. Vol. 1. Rio de Janeiro: IBGE.

INCRA (Instituto Nacional de Colonização e Reforma Agrária). 2003. "Projetos de Reforma Ágrária Conforme Fases de Implementação: Período da Criação do Projeto, 01/01/1900 Até 24/07/2003." Unpublished database.

INESC (Instituto de Estudos Socioeconômicos). 2006. "Reforma Agrária no Governo Lula: Residual e Periférica." Nota Técnica 105 (March). Available at www.inesc.org. br/bibliogteca/publicacoes/notas-tecnicas/NT, accessed January 19, 2007.

IPEA (Instituto de Pesquisa Econômica Aplicada). 2005. *Radar Social*. Brasília: IPEA.

Karl, Terry Lynn. 2003. "The Vicious Cycle of Inequality in Latin America." In *What Justice? Whose Justice? Fighting for Fairness in Latin America*, edited by Susan Eva Eckstein and Timothy P. Wickham-Crowley, 133–57. Berkeley: University of California Press.

Lerrer, Débora Franco. 2005. *De como a mídia fabrica e impõe uma imagem: A degola do PM pelos sem-terra em Porto Alegre*. Rio de Janeiro: Editora Revan.

Martins, José de Souza. 1990. *Os camponeses e a política no Brasil*. 4th ed. Petrópolis: Vozes.

————. 1991. *Expropriação e violência: A questão política no campo*. 3rd rev. ed. São Paulo: HUCITEC

————. 1994. *O poder do atraso: Ensaios de sociologia da história lenta*. São Paulo: Editora HUCITEC.

————. 1997. "A questão agrária brasileira e o papel do MST." In *A reforma agrária e a luta do MST*, edited by João Pedro Stédile. Petrópolis: Vozes, 11–76.

————. 2000. *Reforma agrária: O impossível diálogo*. São Paulo: Editora da Universidade de São Paulo.

————. 2003. *O sujeito oculto: Ordem e transgressão na reforma agrária*. Porto Alegre: Editora da Universidade/UFRGS.

Maybury-Lewis, Biorn. 1994. *The Politics of the Possible: The Brazilian Rural Workers' Trade Union Movement, 1964–1985*. Philadelphia: Temple University Press.

MDA (Ministério de Desenvolvimento Agrário), Equipe Técnica. 2003. "Proposta de plano de reforma agrária." Unpublished manuscript. Brasília: MDA (October).

Medeiros, Leonilde Sérvolo de. 1989. *História dos movimentos sociais no campo*. Rio de Janeiro: FASE.

————. 2009. "Rural Social Movements in Contemporary Brazilian History: Struggles for Rights and Land Reform." In *Challenging Social Inequality: The Rural Workers' Landless Movement and Agrarian Reform in Brazil*, edited by Miguel Carter. Durham, N.C.: Duke University Press.

Melo, Joao Alfredo Telles, ed. 2006. *Reforma agrária quando? CPI mostra as causas da luta pela terra no Brasil*. Brasília: Senado Federal.

Meszaros, George. 2000a. "No Ordinary Revolution: Brazil's Landless Workers' Movement." *Race and Class* 42 (2): 1–18.

————. 2000b. "Taking the Land into Their Hands: The Landless Workers' Movement and the Brazilian State." *Journal of Law and Society* 27 (4): 517–41.

————. 2009. "The MST and the Rule of Law in Brazil." In *Challenging Social Inequality: The Rural Workers' Landless Movement and Agrarian Reform in Brazil*, edited by Miguel Carter. Durham, N.C.: Duke University Press.

Moyo, Sam, and Paris Yeros, eds. 2005. *Reclaiming the Land: The Resurgence of Rural Movements in Africa, Asia, and Latin America*. London: Zed Books.

MST. 2004a. "Quem Somos, 1984–2004: 20 Anos de Lutas, Conquistas, e Dignidade!" http://www.mst.org.br/historico/historia.htm, accessed October 2, 2004.

————. 2004b. "O MST e a Educação." http://www.mst.org.br/setores/educacao/educar.html, accessed October 2, 2004.

Navarro, Zander. 2002a. "Mobilização sem emancipação—as lutas sociais dos Sem Terra no Brasil." In *Produzir para viver: Os caminhos da produção não capitalista*, edited by Boaventura de Sousa Santos, 189–232. Rio de Janeiro: Civilização Brasileira.

————. 2002b. "O MST e a canonização da ação coletiva (reposta a Horacio Martins Carvalho)." In *Produzir para viver: Os caminhos da produção não capitalista*, edited by Boaventura de Sousa Santos, 261–82. Rio de Janeiro: Civilização Brasileira.

O'Donnell, Guillermo. 2004. "Human Development, Human Rights, and Democracy." In *The Quality of Democracy: Theory and Applications*, edited by Guillermo

O'Donnell, Jorge Vargas Cullell, and Osvaldo M. Iazzetta, 9–92. Notre Dame, Ind.: University of Notre Dame Press.

Ondetti, Gabriel. 2004. "Revolution or Palliative? Assessing the Cardoso Era Reform." Paper delivered at the Meeting of the Latin American Studies Association, Las Vegas, October 7–9.

———. 2008. *Land, Protest, and Politics: The Landless Movement and the Struggle for Agrarian Reform in Brazil.* University Park: Pennsylvania State University Press.

Ondetti, Gabriel, Emmanuel Wambergue, and José Batista Afonso Gonçalves. 2009. "From Posseiro to Sem Terra: The Impact of the MST Land Struggle in Pará." In *Challenging Social Inequality: The Rural Workers' Landless Movement and Agrarian Reform in Brazil,* edited by Miguel Carter. Durham, N.C.: Duke University Press.

Paes de Barros, Ricardo, Ricardo Henriques, and Rosane Mendonça. 2000. "A estabilidade inaceitável: Desigualdade e pobreza no Brasil." In *Desigualdade e pobreza no Brasil,* edited by Ricardo Henriques, 21–48. Rio de Janeiro: IPEA, 2000.

Poletto, Ivo. 2009. "Churches, the Pastoral Land Commission, and the Mobilization for Agrarian Reform." In *Challenging Social Inequality: The Rural Workers' Landless Movement and Agrarian Reform in Brazil,* edited by Miguel Carter. Durham, N.C.: Duke University Press.

Poletto, Ivo, and Antônio Canuto, eds. 2002. *Nas pegadas do povo da terra: 25 anos da comissão pastoral da terra.* Sao Paulo: Edições Loyola.

Quirk, Patrick W. 2008. *Emotions and the Struggle of Brazil's Landless Social Movement (MST).* Saarbrucken, Germany: VDM Publishing.

Rosa, Marcelo. 2009. "Beyond the MST: The Impact on Contemporary Brazilian Social Movements." In *Challenging Social Inequality: The Rural Workers' Landless Movement and Agrarian Reform in Brazil,* edited by Miguel Carter. Durham, N.C.: Duke University Press.

Rosset, Peter, Raja Patel, and Michael Courville. 2006. *Promised Land: Competing Visions of Agrarian Reform.* Oakland, Calif.: Food First Books.

Schmitter, Philippe C. 1974. "Still the Century of Corporatism?" *Review of Politics* 36 (January): 86–131.

Scolese, Eduardo. 2003. "Revogar MP é 'tiro no pé,' diz especialista." *Folha de São Paulo,* March 23. http://www1.folha.uol.com.br/folha/brasil/ult96u47279.shtml, accessed March 24, 2003.

Scott, James C. 1985. *Weapons of the Weak: Everyday Forms of Peasant Resistance.* New Haven, Conn.: Yale University Press.

———. 1990. *Domination and the Arts of Resistance: Hidden Transcripts.* New Haven, Conn.: Yale University Press

Sigaud, Lygia Maria. 2009. "Debaixo da Lona Preta: Legitimidade e Dinâmica das Ocupações de Terra na Mata Pernambucana." In *Challenging Social Inequality: The Landless Rural Workers' Movement and Agrarian Reform in Brazil,* edited by Miguel Carter. Durham, N.C.: Duke University Press.

Smulovitz, Catalina, and Enrique Peruzzotti. 2000. "Societal Accountability in Latin America." *Journal of Democracy* 11 (4): 147–58.

Snyder, Richard, and David J. Samuels. 2004. "Legislative Malapportionment in Latin America: Historical and Comparative Perspectives." In *Federalism and Democracy in Latin America*, edited by Edward L. Gibson. Baltimore: Johns Hopkins University Press, 131–172.

Sparovek, Gerd. 2003. *A qualidade dos assentamentos da reforma agrária brasileira.* São Paulo: Páginas e Letras Editora e Gráfica.

Stédile, João Pedro, ed. 1997. *A reforma agrária e a luta do MST.* Petrópolis: Vozes.

———. 1999. *A questão agrária no Brasil.* 7th ed. São Paulo: Editora Atual.

Stepan, Alfred. 2001. *Arguing Comparative Politics.* Oxford: Oxford University Press.

Tilly, Charles. 2002. *Stories, Identities, Political Change.* Oxford: Rowman and Littlefield.

Umbelino de Oliveira, Ariovaldo. 2006. *A não reforma agrária do MDA/INCRA no governo Lula.* Unpublished manuscript.

Vigna, Edélcio. 2001. *Bancada ruralista: Um grupo de interesse.* Argumento 8. Brasília: Instituto de Estudos Socioeconômicos (INESC).

———. 2003. "Mediação de Sementes." In *Reforma agrária: Os caminhos do impasse*, interview by Débora Lerrer. São Paulo: Editora Garçoni.

Weber, Max. 1958. *From Max Weber: Essays in Sociology.* Edited by H. H. Gerth and C. Wright Mills. New York: Oxford University Press.

Whitehead, Laurence. 2002. *Democratization: Theory and Experience.* Oxford: Oxford University Press.

Wolford, Wendy. 2009. "MST Settlements in Pernambuco: Identity and the Politics of Resistance." In *Challenging Social Inequality: The Landless Rural Workers' Movement (MST) and Agrarian Reform in Brazil*, edited by Miguel Carter. Durham, N.C.: Duke University Press.

World Bank. 2005. *World Development Report 2006: Equity and Development.* Washington, D.C.: World Bank.

Wright, Angus, and Wendy Wolford. 2003. *To Inherit the Earth: The Landless Movement and the Struggle for a New Brazil.* Oakland, Calif.: Food First Books.

5

Agrarian Reform as a Precondition for Development

The View of Brazil's Landless Rural Workers' Movement

DANIEL CORRÊA AND ANDRÉIA BORGES FERREIRA

In Brazil the concept of development is equated with progress, which is inscribed in our flag. It is not by chance that our national motto reads "Order and Progress." For progress to occur, in the vision of the Brazilian elite, there can be no debate or differences of opinion regarding their hegemonic view. Should challenges to this vision occur, they must be eliminated and destroyed by whatever means necessary—by co-optation, or by persecution and imprisonment. Thus, order can be reestablished and the progress of the elites assured.

Over the course of the twentieth century Brazil implemented a model of dependent industrialization that transformed the productive structure of the country from an agricultural one to an industrial one. The country went from being predominantly rural to urban, especially after the 1960s. Today slightly more than 80 percent of the population lives in cities, although most of the urban population resides in small cities and towns, where livelihoods are still linked to the agricultural sector. During the period of military rule (1964–84), the economy grew rapidly, but inequality grew as well, in a pattern of exclusionary development.

After two decades of military rule, Brazilian society finally faced a clear choice between two opposing views in the first direct, presidential elections, held in 1989: the neoliberal project of the dominant classes, or a democratic and popular alternative. The latter alternative was the result of the steady growth in social mobilization and popular struggles during the 1980s, which led both to the end of the military dictatorship in 1985 and the formation of the Workers' Party (PT), the Central Workers' Union

(CUT), the Landless Rural Workers' Movement (MST), and the Pastoral Land Commission (CPT).

The neoliberal project represents a new model of capital accumulation, one that is subordinated to international financial capital. Under the governments of Fernando Collor de Mello, Itamar Franco, and Fernando Henrique Cardoso, the state withdrew from the economy; that is, state enterprises were sold to private investors and many state functions were taken over by private companies. As a result of the inflation-deterring policy of high interest rates, during the government of Cardoso the internal public debt increased tenfold, while the annual average growth rate of the economy was only 2.5 percent (CEPAL 2005).

In the view of our movement, the MST, the neoliberal model does not represent a national development strategy. Rather, it is a set of economic policies that favor capital accumulation in the financial sphere (the banking sector) and businesses linked to the export sector. Moreover, these enterprises tend to invest their profits abroad, to the detriment of Brazilian development.

Lula (Luiz Inácio Lula da Silva) of the PT was elected president in 2002 with a mandate to change this situation. Nonetheless, to govern, the PT had to enter into alliances with a broad range of political parties. Representatives of the neoliberal sectors, for example, assumed the lead positions of the Central Bank and the Ministry of Agriculture. While the Lula government represented progress in terms of democratic inclusiveness—particularly when compared with the Cardoso government—it was unable to escape the neoliberal debt trap. While the government repaid its external debt on time, it neglected to pay its social debt to the Brazilian people; that is, improving the standard of living of the majority or distributing income more equally. Thus, the social crisis in Brazil continues. The MST insists on the need to build a national project that is anti-neoliberal and anti-imperialist and which responds to the demands of the people.

The Situation in the Countryside

What are the implications of this national, neoliberal project for the agricultural sector? In agriculture, the neoliberal model is represented by agribusiness, which is the new name given to capitalist agricultural development in this period. The model is actually not new, having its origin in the plantation system of large, export-oriented properties, or *latifundio*. In Brazil, the term agribusiness (*agro-negocio*) emerged in the 1990s as an ideological projection that tries to change the image of the capitalist *latifundio*. The *latifundio* is associated with exploitation, slave labor, land concentration, clientelism, and political and economic backwardness. The *latifundio* occupies the space that should be, but is not, available for the development of the country, for it is associated with unproductive land. It is this land that the MST insists should be designated for agrarian reform purposes.

The concept of agribusiness was constructed to renovate and modernize the image of capitalist agriculture in the neoliberal period. This image tries to obscure its predatory and exclusionary nature, and emphasize its productivity, its ability to incorporate new technologies, and its contribution to growth. As Bernardo Mançano (2005) says: "The latifundio excludes through unproductiveness while agribusiness promotes exclusion through intense productivity."

However it tries to hide it, agribusiness will always be associated with the concentration of land and income and the exploitation of labor. When agribusiness highlights its productivity and contribution to growth, it is attempting to establish itself as the only productive space, a sacred space where land occupations should not occur. It is in the interests of agribusiness to concentrate land and technology while monopolizing agricultural development policies. At the same time, continual increases in productivity exacerbate its main contradiction as a system of agriculture, for agribusiness generates inequality and landlessness.

Another ideological construction of the agribusiness sector is the image that it is responsible for all agricultural and livestock production in the country—that is, it is the anchor of the economy—and thus its interests are equivalent to the national interest. The mass media play an important role in reproducing this distortion. With the exception of soy, sugar cane, and orange production, the small farm or peasant sector is responsible for approximately half of the nation's agricultural production.[1] Nonetheless, the agribusiness sector receives the bulk of the agricultural credit.[2] The media totally ignore the crucial role of the small farm sector in production, employment generation, and in the attendant rural income distribution.

In smallholder agriculture the logic of production is different. Production is not simply dictated by the market, leading to monoculture; neither does it rely exclusively on external inputs. Rather, smallholder agriculture is oriented toward diversified food production and the sustainable use of natural resources. In regions of smallholder agriculture the degree of income inequality is less and human development indices (income, education, and health) are higher.[3]

It is in the interest of the agribusiness sector to integrate the small farm sector into the market, for it controls the market. In the market, small farmers end up being intensely exploited, being able to keep only a small share of the value of what they produce, while the greater part is appropriated by companies such as Cargill, Bunge, Monsanto, Sadia, and Nestle. This is the context in which the resistance of small farmers emerges, as well as where alternative development proposals are generated, such as those of La Vía Campesina—the international organization of peasants, rural workers, women's organizations, and indigenous groups, of which the MST is a part.[4]

La Vía Campesina's Principles for Rural Development

Among the key values defended by La Vía Campesina as principles for rural development are the following:

1. *Nature.* We must respect the biodiversity of the planet, including its natural resources and varied ecosystems. We also must respect traditional knowledge and cultures. We must conserve, restore, and protect the land, water, flora, fauna, and mineral resources, utilizing agriculture technologies that produce healthy food and protect the environment.
2. *Land.* Land should support life and benefit the whole society. We demand the deconcentration of land ownership and its use. Priority should be given to family or smallholder agriculture and the formation of cooperatives. We demand a comprehensive agrarian reform that includes adequate state support through favorable price policies, appropriate technical assistance, and sufficient protection to the internal market.
3. *Food Sovereignty.* Food sovereignty is the right of people and nations to define their own agricultural and food policies. It includes giving priority to local agricultural production and guaranteeing small farmers' access to land, water, seeds, and credit. It also includes the right of small farmers to sell their products at fair prices that cover their costs of production, and the right of consumers to decide what to eat, and how and for whom the food is produced.

4. *Seeds*. Small farmers have the right and obligation to produce their own seeds and to preserve biodiversity. We are against the use of transgenic seeds and the monopoly of trade, seed patents, and knowledge. Seeds are part of the heritage of all peoples and should serve humankind.

5. *Production and agricultural marketing*. Production and agro-industrial processing should be based on cooperatives or other organizations of peasants and smallholders. The commercialization of agriculture needs to be based on the principles of equality, cooperation, and fair trade. The marketing of food should not be based on profit criteria, but rather, should take into account people's needs and cultures.

The MST aims to implement the development policies of La Vía Campesina in Brazil. This requires organization, political development, and social struggle. These policies must also be articulated with the construction of a new and broader national development strategy for our country and require new means of articulation with the broader society.

The MST's Plan for Agrarian Reform

To implement agrarian reform in Brazil requires a strategy that includes resistance and the accumulation of forces. By resistance we are referring to the need for the existing agrarian reform settlements to survive and prosper. The settlements need to remain well-organized on the lands that have been gained through such struggle. These also need to be self-sufficient, producing sufficient quantities of food of good quality and diversity. The incomes generated on the agrarian reform settlements also need to be sufficient to guarantee the well-being of all.

To accumulate forces means generating experiences that contribute to the development of a new agricultural model, one based on cooperation, a change in technology, and appropriate agro-industrial processing activities. We must increase the level of knowledge and awareness among families in the settlements about Brazilian agrarian problems. This requires eliminating illiteracy and training our own technicians in all areas. Accumulating forces also requires that we connect the struggle in the countryside with that of the cities—rural with urban areas, peasants and small farmers with urban society.

In the short run a number of concrete actions are necessary to better the social conditions in the land reform settlements. Housing and sanitation systems must be improved and expanded. The lack of water and/or its poor quality is a major problem and many settlements do not yet have access to electricity. Schools must be built and their quality improved. Libraries need to be constructed and equipped and access to the Internet expanded. Provisions must be made for sports facilities and the social and housing areas of the settlements made more attractive. Cultural activities need to be developed and expanded as well.

A major challenge in the settlements is to enhance the level of cooperative activities, such as agricultural-processing activities. Access to credit for cooperative production, however, remains a significant problem. The MST needs to continue to emphasize training in cooperative development, particularly in the encampments of those waiting to receive land.

Internally, the MST is working to restructure its base units in the settlements and to strengthen local-level leadership. One of the ways that we are doing this is by promoting the participation of women and gender equality. We aim for women to be half of those participating in all of our activities, from mobilizations to training courses. Moreover, our goal is that each of our local-level base groups in the settlements and encampments be led by one female and one male coordinator. This is mirrored in the MST's national structure. The national direction of the MST is now made up of two representatives—one man and one woman—from each of the twenty-three states where the MST is organized.

Among the specific policies that we promote is that membership in the land settlements includes both the man and the woman of a couple, so that the land is registered in both of their names. This is needed so that women remain active members of the settlements and contribute to their development. Another is that child-care be provided for all of MST's activities, so that women are able to participate. All these gender-progressive policies must take place in the context of the permanent struggle for better public policies and a comprehensive agrarian reform. It is primarily in this way that we will contribute to the development of a new popular project for Brazilian society.

Nowadays, many academics and politicians say that agrarian reform is unnecessary; that agrarian reform is no longer required for the development of capitalism as it was in the past when it was viewed as a means of expanding the internal market for the industrialization effort. In fact, within the capitalist logic of maximizing profits and exploiting people and nature, this is probably true. The logic compelling agrarian reform today is based on the logic of another social system: a new project based on social participation, a more just distribution of income, and human integration with nature.

Notes

1. Of the total agricultural GDP in 2004, the family farm sector contributed 32 percent and the agribusiness sector 68 percent (DIEESE and NEAD/MDA 2006, graph 55).

2. Of the total rural credit distributed by the public sector in 2005, 96 percent of the loans were small loans of less than $R60,000 each and amounted to 39 percent of the total credit disbursed. Large loans, which represented 4 percent of the total, accounted for 61 percent of the total credit (DIESSE and NEAD/MDA 2006, table 70).

3. Editors' note: See Leite et al. 2004 for the data behind this analysis.

4. Editors' note: See chapter 1 in this volume for background on La Vía Campesina.

References

CEPAL (Comisión Económica para América Latina y el Caribe). 2005. *Anuario Estadístico de América Latina y el Caribe.* Santiago: CEPAL.

DIEESE and NEAD/MDA (Departamento Intersindical de Estadística e Estudos Socioeconomicos and Núcleo de Estudos Agrários e Desenvolvimento Rural/Ministério do Desenvolvimento Agrário). 2006. *Estatísticas do Meio Rural.* São Paulo: DIEESE and NEAD/MDA.

Leite, Sergio, et al. 2004. *Impacto dos Assentamentos: Um Estudo Sobre o Meio Rural Brasileiro.* São Paulo: EDUNESP and NEAD.

Mançano, Bernardo. 2005. "Cercas Do Latifúndio." In *Movimento Dos Trabalhadores Rurais Sem Terra.* May 25. http://www.mst.org.br/biblioteca/textos/reformagr/mancano_agronegocio.htm, accessed September 28, 2006.

6

Toward a Real Agrarian Reform in Bolivia

The Perspective of the Landless Movement

SILVESTRE SAISARI

Bolivia is experiencing an unprecedented period in the nation's history. For the first time a popular leader representing the interests of the traditionally marginalized segments of society has been elected president. Moreover, Evo Morales of the Movement Toward Socialism (MAS), who took office in January 2006, was elected by an overwhelming majority of the vote. As a result, expectations among the popular sectors that real change is possible are very high. The Landless Movement of Peasants and Indigenous Workers of Bolivia (MST-Bolivia) has great faith in our new government. It is in this context that we are developing strategies for a democratic, participatory, and pluralistic Bolivia and present our proposed initiatives.

The basic premise of the MST-Bolivia is that an alternative strategy for rural development requires respect for and guarantees of human rights—economic, social, and cultural—and an integral and participatory agrarian reform. In this chapter we first locate the struggle for land historically, explaining why there are landless peasants in Bolivia even after the country carried out a wide-scale agrarian reform. We then turn to how the human rights of those involved in the struggle for land have been continually violated. Finally, we describe the goals and proposals of the MST-Bolivia for a real agrarian reform, one that is both integral and participatory.

Why Are There Landless Peasants in Bolivia?

The situation of landlessness among the indigenous and peasant population of Bolivia goes back to the formation of the traditional hacienda, itself related to the inherited feudal structure of the Spanish colonies in the Americas. The structure of land tenancy and the accumulation of economic power and unequal social and cultural/ethnic relations are all closely related. Furthermore, control over the state apparatus in Bolivia has always been held by those groups who have traditionally hoarded political and economic power—a small white, Hispanic elite. Their position was first challenged by the social revolution of 1952, led by the National Revolutionary Movement party.

The Agrarian Reform Law of 1953 was based on the prevailing views regarding economic development of the time and had the following objectives: the redistribution of the land encompassed in haciendas or *latifundios* based on the principle that "land belongs to those who work it"; the elimination of forced servitude in order to free labor for participation in the labor market; increased production and productivity levels; and a more rational geographic redistribution of Bolivia's population (CEJIS 2005, 1). The expropriation of the *latifundios* was, for the most part, limited to the country's Andean region. Moreover, the progressive subdivision of land through inheritance reduced most parcels over time to *minifundios*, encouraging migration in subsequent decades to the eastern lowlands of the country, which comprise some two-thirds of Bolivia's territory.

During the 1970s and 1980s tens of millions of hectares and substantial credit were ceded by various governments to "new" agro-industrial entrepreneurs in the eastern lowlands in pursuit of the modernization of agriculture. Cattlemen and agribusinesses encroached with impunity on the ancestral lands of lowland indigenous communities. This process furthered capitalist development and allowed the consolidation of the neo-*latifundio* system, which concentrated economic, political, and social power even further in the hands of a small regional elite (Almaraz 2002; Romero Bonifaz n.d.). The concentration of land in the lowlands was abetted by a new phenomenon in the 1980s and 1990s, the illegal drug trade. The latter has evolved and flourished with the assistance and complicity of the political elite. As a result, land tenancy, production, and marketing have become distorted, and violence in the lowlands has become endemic.

Four decades after the original agrarian reform, land reform was back on the country's agenda. As a result of the mobilization and demands of a large segment of the rural population, a new agrarian reform law (Law 1715), known as the Ley INRA, was passed in October 1996. This law established the National Institute for Agrarian Reform (INRA) and a process for determining the legality of existing land titles—known as *saneamiento*[1]—as well as a land-titling program. The expectation was that large tracts of land would revert to the state as public lands and be available for redistribution to the landless or those with insufficient land. The law also provided for the return of ancestral lands to indigenous communities in both the highlands and the lowlands. However, the expectations of the peasant and indigenous movement concerning land redistribution, social justice, and access to economic, social, and cultural rights were again greatly frustrated.

During the first ten years of the Ley INRA (the period initially contemplated for cleaning up land titles), the agrarian reform process proved to be an almost total disappointment. Of the land area where land rights needed to be clarified, only 17 percent was titled (CEJIS 2005, table 3). Contributing to these poor results was the bureaucratic corruption within INRA and the National Agrarian Tribunal. These institutions failed to comply with and misapplied their own required procedures to the detriment of indigenous and peasant rights. Rather than providing access to land to the marginalized segments of the population, the agrarian reform process ended up furthering the concentration of land.

In addition to the problem of the agrarian structure, there are grave environmental problems, compounded by state neglect. The *latifundistas*, agro-entrepreneurs, and logging companies have used land and natural resources inappropriately. Ignoring national and international environmental norms, they have indiscriminately devastated natural resources, provoked soil erosion, and contaminated and damaged native ecosystems.

The Bolivian landless movement was born in 2000 in response to the state's inefficiency in meeting agrarian reform goals and as a result of the negative consequences of neoliberal policies, which placed the country in perpetual economic crises. The movement is composed of indigenous families, peasant migrants from the highlands, and agricultural wage workers who are landless or have access to insufficient land. Under the leadership and guidance of the MST-Bolivia, numerous families have occupied public lands and *latifundios* that do not meet an economic or social function. The occupied properties generally lack legal titles (either because they have been acquired in a fraudulent manner or have false titles), and they are not even occupied by their purported owners; most are abandoned and unproductive.

The actions of the MST-Bolivia—combined with the growing strength of the popular movements as witnessed in their ability to depose two governments (that of Sánchez de Lozada and Mesa)—galvanized the traditional power groups in the eastern part of the country. Demonstrations during January 2005 by so called civic committees[2] pressed demands for departmental autonomy, especially in Santa Cruz. One of their main goals is the decentralization of political and agrarian institutions. However, their proposed "autonomy," far from involving a strengthening of the state's democratic institutions, would modify constitutional principles dealing with possession, use, and access to natural resources to safeguard "private property" and "foreign investment." In essence, they want to preserve the status of *latifundios* as well as the surrender of natural resources (gas and petroleum) to international capital that was carried out in the 1990s.

The new government of Evo Morales now faces at least two major challenges. It must stop those forces that support undoing the agrarian reform while developing the legal framework to implement a genuine agrarian reform. This also requires restructuring the bureaucracy that, being in the hands of the elite, has so arbitrarily dealt with agrarian reform, largely explaining its meager results.

The Struggle for Land and Violations of Human Rights

The origins of the MST-Bolivia in Bolivia are linked to some eight land occupations that took place in the municipality of Yacuiba, in the province of the Gran Chaco, in the department of Tarija in 1999 and 2000. That region is characterized by a large number of abandoned and unproductive lands that during the late 1990s had attracted land-hungry peasants from the departments of Tarija and neighboring Chuquisaca. In June 2000, under the leadership of the Peasant Federation of the Province of the Gran Chaco, those occupying these estates, accompanied by various peasant and indigenous organizations in the region, marched to the city of Tarija to demand the *saneamiento* of these estates and that INRA officially adjudicate them to the landless peasants occupying them.[3]

The national government responded with Supreme Decree 25848, which declared the province of the Gran Chaco an area of emergency action for INRA's process of *saneamiento*. The institute was given one year to determine which lands might revert to the state for not meeting an economic and social function and hence be available for redistribution. This decree, however, was never implemented, partly because INRA was not given a budget sufficient to do so, among other reasons. Over the next year, those occupying the estates organized under the banner of the MST-Bolivia, with Angel Durán (the former president of the provincial Peasant Federation) becoming the first president.

The repression of the MST-Bolivia began shortly after. On October 25, 2001, an armed group dressed in army uniforms (but in actuality gunmen hired by land speculators) attacked those on the Pananti estate in Yacuiba, attempting to evict them. The army and police then moved in, assuming control of the area supposedly in order to avoid further confrontations. Nonetheless, they did nothing to stop the continual harassment of those MST-Bolivia community members who remained.

Angel Durán informed the national government of the situation at the Pananti estate and was successful in negotiating a memorandum of understanding with INRA to legalize the situation of this community. An INRA commission arrived to begin surveying the estate, seeking to identify eighty arable hectares to be turned over to these families. However, in a clear demonstration of bad faith, the commission sought to include housing sites and sterile, nonarable areas among the eight hectares selected, and the community rejected the results.

On November 9, 2001, at 5:30 in the morning, a group of approximately thirty armed men attacked those occupying the Pananti estate, killing seven people and wounding some eighteen more. Despite being at the scene, law enforcement officials did nothing to capture those involved in the attack. In fact, the subprefect refused to provide any assistance to the wounded. When hours later the wounded were removed, some died due to lack of timely medical assistance.

Subsequently, some of the community members were jailed and denied the right of counsel. During the criminal investigation, two of the Pananti community members were accused of the crime of "manslaughter resulting from a brawl" (*homicidio en riña*) and forced to testify against themselves under threats of long prison terms and possible actions against their families. Under the circumstances and without access to counsel, they had no choice but to accept the short, symbolic prison terms offered.

It took the massacre at Pananti to once again draw national attention to the land issue, the inefficiency of INRA, and the general lack of implementation of the redistributive aspects of the Ley INRA. The government convened a national dialogue, known as the Land Summit (Cumbre por la Tierra) but not much was accomplished, leading to a fourth national indigenous march in May and June of 2002. The march resulted in an accord on June 10 between the MST-Bolivia and INRA to proceed with *saneamiento* in the regions of conflict, but again, not much happened (Miranda 2002).

Several of the MST-Bolivia leaders involved in the Pananti occupation continue to stand accused as criminals. Those truly guilty of causing the violence have not been punished and the members of the MST-Bolivia, unjustly accused of being the perpetrators, have been denied a fair and impartial trial in violation of constitutional rights and guarantees. More than four years after the Pananti tragedy, the evicted families have no access to land, housing, public services, or adequate means of support. In the intervening years, the MST-Bolivia has become a national movement, occupying lands throughout eastern Bolivia, particularly in the department of Santa Cruz, but also in the western part of the country.[4] The struggle for land continues to be associated with the violation of the human rights of the members of the MST-Bolivia.

Another example is that of the United Peoples community in the province of Guarayos in northern Santa Cruz. Since the beginning of 2004 the MST-Bolivia in Santa Cruz had been discussing with the government the transfer of vacant lands in the northern part of the department to landless families, and INRA had identified 131,000 hectares of public land available for redistribution. But given the delays in the transfer, in August of that year 776 families occupied the vacant area known as Los Yuquises and founded the community of United Peoples, demanding that this land be adjudicated in their favor.

On May 7, 2005, a group of more than two hundred armed men attacked the community, setting fire to the rice crop. During the confrontation, community members managed to detain a number of the attackers and contacted the local authorities to whom they turned these people over; they also requested the intervention of the state, the church, and the International Commission for Human Rights to prevent the community from being evicted. Nonetheless, on May 25 some six hundred military and police operatives arrived and, rather than protecting the community, burned down their houses and infrastructure, destroyed their subsistence crops, and evicted the community members.

The persecution of community members and leaders of the MST-Bolivia then began. Leaders of the MST-Bolivia who had been present during the eviction of the community or who had participated in its defense have been jailed. In the process, the leaders have been denied procedural guarantees, such as the right to due process and a fair defense. The MST-Bolivia was also defamed in the press, which is controlled by the traditional elite of Santa Cruz. The MST-Bolivia was branded as a terrorist group, legitimizing the use of violence against organized peasants.[5]

Among those subsequently arrested was Luis Alberto Aguilera Salvatierra, an eighteen-year-old member of the community. Aguilera was jailed and pressured to testify against himself and the community's leadership. Without permitting him to consult a defense attorney, the government prosecutor forced him to sign a confession under duress. Several days later the prosecutor had to annul the confession since it had become known that it had been obtained through the use of torture[6] and that the purported confessor was illiterate and thus could never have written it.

Shortly after, Ponciano Sulka Chunqui, a former national director of the movement and a member of the United Peoples community, was arrested at his home only because he had been a leader when the community was founded. Based on false testimony, he was found guilty of participating in the defense of the United Peoples community during the period of the eviction and was held in detention for more than six months. He needed continuous medical attention for a urinary infection caused by bladder cancer, but this treatment was never provided. Nineteen leaders and community members of the MST-Bolivia were arrested or ordered to be arrested. In clear violation of the principle of presumed innocence, those arrested were advised that they would not be released unless they could prove that they would not escape, commit any new crimes, or disturb or impede the investigation.

As president of the MST-Bolivia of Santa Cruz, I vigorously denounced the eviction of the community of Pueblos Unidos and these detentions in the press. Shortly thereafter I was viciously attacked in downtown Santa Cruz by thugs of the Unión Juvenil Cruceñista. When the authorities arrived, instead of pursuing my attackers, they immediately took me to the Santa Cruz sentencing court, where I was presented with a complaint supposedly lodged against me in mid-2004. I had never been provided notice of this action or given the opportunity to defend myself against the allegations. My purported accusers had not presented any evidence or initiated any judicial procedures against me. I complied with all the court-imposed requirements, reporting to the designated court during more than six months, demonstrating that it was not my intention to flee or to evade justice. There has been practically no progress in the investigation of my assault, even though my attorneys and I filed a complaint. In Bolivia the judiciary is controlled by the traditional power blocs, who see to it that their agents are treated with impunity. Consequently, it is likely that the crime against me will go unpunished.

On September 7, 2005, President Eduardo Rodriguez and members of his cabinet met with a number of indigenous and peasant organizations, including the MST-Bolivia. The dialogue concluded with the signing of a memorandum of understanding, which, among other points, provided for the adjudication of lands to the Pueblos Unidos community. But after several delays, INRA inexplicably sent the file to the departmental agrarian commission in Santa Cruz for its opinion. This commission should have no jurisdiction over the matter; moreover, it is controlled by the department's prefect, who is known to serve the interests of the business sector. Not surprisingly, this commission rejected the petition. The families of the community of Pueblos Unidos, meanwhile, have been left in a most precarious position, forced to pitch tents by the side of a bridge.

The previous government, rather than respecting the fundamental human rights of the families affected by the eviction, set out to eliminate the MST-Bolivia by denying its right to represent the community of Pueblos Unidos and through the persecution of its leaders. The investigation into the confrontations surrounding the eviction of the United Peoples community has been practically dormant since the arrests described above. This leads to the conclusion that the judicial authorities are not really interested in who provoked the incident or in providing justice to the evicted families; rather, the whole matter was orchestrated to remove the MST-Bolivia as an actor on the agrarian scene. It is clear that there are powerful interests in Bolivia who want to prevent real agrarian reform at all costs.

Toward an Integral and Participatory Agrarian Reform

What do we mean by real agrarian reform in Bolivia? To start with it must be integral and participatory. It must include the immediate and equitable distribution of land suitable for cultivation and in sufficient quantity for sustainable livelihoods and the sustainable management of natural resources. By participatory we mean that all must participate in the use and enjoyment of the land and natural resources. A participatory agrarian reform also requires participation by the peasant and indigenous sectors in agrarian policymaking and social control of the agrarian processes.

In order to attain real agrarian reform, the national government must be directly involved in the recuperation of public lands. Uncultivated lands, *latifundios*, and illegally usurped lands should be subject to mandatory expropriation without compensation. Social control should be exercised through the creation of onsite field verification commissions composed of representatives of both civil society and government to make sure land serves an economic and social function. The state and the organizations demanding agrarian reform should together intercede in unproductive *latifundios* and timber and other concessions that fail to comply with their management plans or fail to pay their fees or taxes.

The creation of new agrarian reform settlements should be a top priority for the state. Beneficiary families should be able to settle on these irrespective of their place of origin and without discrimination as to their ethnic group. All bureaucratic obstacles to endowing indigenous peasant families with land should be removed.

Land, whether for agricultural use or working forests, should be ceded in a collective manner, with a collective title issued to each community in the name of all of the families that claim it. Through collective land titles, land trafficking will be eliminated and the subdivision of land into unviable *minifundios* will be prevented. The adjudication of land must be equitable, integral, and participatory, without regard to race, culture, language, gender, skin color, or political ideology or belief. Men and women must have equitable participation in land tenure or in access to collective property rights. Not only should communal property be given legal security, but collective forms of organizing—on the basis of solidarity, reciprocity, and complementarity—should be protected as well. Community development processes must be strengthened so that they guarantee the equitable use and sharing of natural resources and the protection of economic, social, and cultural rights.

An integral agrarian reform must include access to credit and state subsidies to promote food sovereignty, community production, and an ecologically based agriculture. The state should provide direct technical assistance and guarantee access to productive and clean technologies. An integral agrarian reform also requires access to markets, at the local, departmental, national, and international levels, with the state providing due protection to producers when necessary. Direct state participation in integral human development is also necessary, including the promotion of alternative education and health policies and programs that are in accord with our aspirations.

Under the direction of INRA, the state and landless peasant and indigenous families must work together in an integral and participatory manner on plans for human settlements. The principles of ILO Convention 169 must be recognized; these require respect for "uses and customs" and the communal and collective organizations of men and women from landless peasant and indigenous families. Social control of the process must be shared by the state, the organizations of landless peasant and indigenous people, and those that serve as public defenders and protectors of human rights.

One of the principal reasons for the failure of agrarian reform in Bolivia over the last fifty years, as in much of Latin America, has been its failure to properly plan or implement rural development policies. These policies must take into account basic human needs as well as the potential of new agrarian reform communities to engage in nontraditional production. It is urgent that alternative communal and collective development structures be envisioned. Individual, family-based production has not allowed the peasant economy to overcome poverty. This form of production requires peasant households to compete against large-scale agricultural producers in the market, without success. This is why we consider it necessary to promote communal and collective forms of production. Community production units, based on an equitable distribution of responsibilities and benefits, would be one way to strengthen the economy of peasant families.

For example, ecologically associated productive units could be created that would be responsible for safeguarding community production and internal consumption. These could foster ecologically responsible production and manufacturing activities based on the promotion of traditional, natural foods. Communal economic production cooperatives could be created as the technical branch of these associated productive units, responsible for providing technical assistance to improve production by family enterprises and for obtaining credits for productive projects. The transfer of technology must be aimed at improving an ecologically sustainable agricultural production. The cooperatives could also be responsible for the storage and sale of surplus production and be charged with marketing research

Finally, peasant and indigenous participation in the definition and implementation of agrarian reform is absolutely necessary. In order to assure that the reforms are democratic, a national agrarian system must be established with adequate mechanisms for citizen participation in defining agrarian policy, in directing and making decisions concerning implementation of agrarian policy, and to guarantee citizen social control. In order to assure the effectiveness of the policy and the operational transparency of the national agrarian system, the state must establish several important positions, such as an agrarian advocate general, to control and oversee the public bureaucracy in charge of the sector; and an agrarian public defender, to protect the economic, social, and cultural rights of the indigenous and peasant population.

Epilogue by the Editors

In May 2006 the Bolivian president Evo Morales announced his specific goals with respect to land policy, which included finishing the *saneamiento* process in five years and redistributing 20 million hectares of land. The proposed reform to INRA Law 1715, known as the Community-based Reorientation of the Agrarian Reform (Reconducción Comunitaria de la Reforma Agraria) was approved by the National Agrarian Commission in July and forwarded to the National Congress for approval. After months of debate in the Congress (including a boycott by legislators opposed to the reform,[7] and a fifth national march by the peasant and indigenous movement to La Paz), Law 3545, modifying the INRA Law, was approved in November 2006.

The intent of the new law is to correct the main problems in the INRA Law with respect to the *saneamiento* process in order to speed up its application. Under the original legislation, lands that had been illegally obtained or had fraudulent titles as well as those that did not meet a socioeconomic function could revert to the state as public lands. The main criterion for land not meeting its socioeconomic function was the nonpayment of taxes for two consecutive years; now failure to meet the socioeconomic function is delinked from the payment of land taxes. In addition, in the new law lands found to be idle or unproductive may also revert to the state for redistribution. Moreover, there are provisions for the social movements to participate in the process of verification. To speed up implementation, the director of INRA is given direct authority to decide if land meets the socioeconomic function criterion (Urioste 2006; Colque 2006).

A second major change involves a broadening in the criteria for expropriation of land with compensation. Previously land could only be expropriated in the interest of public utility. Now land can also be expropriated for purposes of redistribution to the landless or to consolidate indigenous communities. In a concession to the opposition, land expropriated for such purposes is to be compensated at market prices. Finally, a third major change is that public land is only to be adjudicated collectively, rather than to individuals (Morales 2006).

Critics on the right opposed any change at all in the INRA law, considering the existing legislation to have already been the result of a compromise reached in the 1990s. They thus opposed Morales's reform each step of the way and considered it an attack on the right of private property. Critics on the left, in contrast, considered the reform to be quite minimalist in that while it targets unproductive *latifundios*, it does not deal with the problem of the degree of land concentration in Bolivia, which is considerable. They advocated a maximum size limit of ten thousand hectares for cattle ranching and two thousand hectares for agricultural properties. Currently, the maximum size limit (based on the agrarian reform law of 1953) allows cattle ranches to consist of up to fifty thousand hectares. Moreover, critics on the left wanted land above the maximum size limit to be subject to expropriation without compensation or, at the very least if compensation were to be paid, for it to be valued at the declared tax rate rather than market value (Fundación Tierra 2006a, 2006b).[8]

While recognizing that the reform law of 2006 is not perfect, peasant and indigenous leaders considered the approval of this law to be a significant victory, one that would never have been achieved without their mobilization and unity. Twenty-three organizations participated in the Indigeneous Peasant March for Modification of the INRA Law, in which members marched from Santa Cruz to La Paz over thirty-one days, which once again allied the Confederation of Indigenous Peoples of Bolivia (CIDOB) and its affiliated organizations of the Amazonian lowlands with the main national peasant organizations (CSUTCB, FNMCB-BS, and the MST-Bolivia, among others) (CEJIS et al. [2007]).

According to Silvestre Saisari, what is most important about this law is its broadening of the provisions for land to revert to the state if the land is not being used for a socioeconomic function.[9] And even though the implementing legislation has yet to be approved by the National Congress, he considers the agrarian reform process finally to be moving forward.[10] For example, in October 2006 the community Pueblos Unidos was formally adjudicated the land that it had struggled to obtain. And in June 2007 the five MST-Bolivia-led communities in Yacuiba received their provisional land titles. On this occasion, the Morales government donated tractors, a truck, and seed in support of their productive efforts.

How profound this new phase of Bolivia's agrarian reform process will turn out to be depends in large measure on whether the MAS government is successful in securing approval of the country's new constitution without incurring the dismemberment of the country.[11] The MAS delegates to the Constituent Assembly approved (without the participation of the opposition) and presented a draft to the government in December 2007. Proposed Article 398, which prohibits *latifundia*, establishes a maximum farm size of either five thousand or ten thousand hectares, with the precise limit to be determined by a referendum to be held in April or May 2008.[12] Opponents of the new constitution continue to oppose any further redistribution of land at all.

Notes

Author's note: The transcript of this conference presentation was translated by Guillermo Alfonso Calvo-Mahe. The editors have incorporated material from the author's PowerPoint presentation.

1. Editors' note: *Saneamiento* is a term used in Bolivia to determine the legality of existing land titles and to define borders in the case of overlapping titles or land conflicts. *Saneamiento* is expected to lead to either the reversion of land to the state as public land (and thus available for redistribution) or the receiving of a "clear" land title by the owner.

2. The civic committees are legal entities formed by social and business organizations with the objective of protecting regional interests. In eastern Bolivia they are now, in large part, a refuge for the traditional elite that since October 2003 has found itself under siege by the social movements.

3. Editors' note: The first two paragraphs of this section on the origins of the MST-Bolivia and the land struggle in Yacuiba have been drawn from Miranda 2002 and Arnold and Spedding 2005, 90.

4. See Arnold and Spedding 2005, 92–94.

5. For a press report blaming the MST-Bolivia and the community of Pueblos Unidos for the violent events of May 2005, see Heredia García 2005.

6. He was hung by his feet with a cord and his head was covered with a nylon bag that had been soaked in insecticide. He was then repeatedly beaten and threatened with death unless he confessed.

7. On how the reforms were passed in the Senate without the opposition being present, see Burbach 2006.

8. Critics on the left were also disappointed that the Morales government did not take advantage of this opportunity to clarify the existing legal confusion regarding the property rights of small individual property holders and the communities to which they often pertain. The INRA law had abolished previous tenure arrangements in the highlands known as *pro indiviso* property, which guaranteed individual rights within communal land holdings, an apparently more satisfactory arrangement than what currently prevails (Fundación Tierra 2006b; Colque 2006).

9. Interview with Silvestre Saisari by Carmen Diana Deere, July 21, 2007, Santa Cruz.

10. Saisari is much more optimistic than some of the agrarian scholars, such as Colque (2007, 2), who argues that "there is no agrarian reform underway," and that the issue must be solved by the Constituent Assembly.

11. During 2007 the country was polarized over the drafting of the new constitution, leading to calls for regional autonomy and even secession by the lowland departments controlled by the opposition to the MAS government in what is known as "the Half Moon" (*media luna*): Santa Cruz, Beni, Pando, and Tarija. These departments formed provisional autonomy commissions that declared their relative autonomy from the state in December 2007. Motivating the call for autonomy is the desire to control land and natural resource policy (including the benefits from their exploitation) at the departmental level (*La Razón* 2007a).

12. It is estimated that only around twenty families hold extensions of land greater than ten thousand hectares; the lower limit of five thousand hectares could potentially affect four thousand families (*La Razón* 2007b). Whether land above the new legal limit would be expropriated with compensation or subject to reversion to the state was not specified in the Constitution; thus this would have to be clarified by subsequent legislation (*La Prensa* 2007).

References

Almaraz, Alejandro, ed. 2002. *Tierras Comunitarias de Origen: Saneamiento y Titulación; Guía para el patrocinio jurídico.* Santa Cruz: CEJIS-IWGIA.

Arnold, Denise Y., and Alison Spedding. 2005. *Mujeres en los movimientos sociales en Bolivia 2000–2003.* La Paz: CIDEM and ILCA.

Burbach, Roger. 2006. "Confrontation in Bolivia over Agrarian Reform." November 30. http://www.ftierra.org/ftierra1104/docstrabajo/burbach.pdf, accessed January 1, 2007.

CEJIS (Centro de Estudios Jurídicos e Investigación Social). 2005. *Reforma Agraria, frustración y destino 52 años después.* Separata, July 31, Santa Cruz de la Sierra.

CEJIS et al. [2007]. *Ley 2545 de Modificación a la Ley 1715 de Reconducción Comunitaria de la Reforma Agraria: V March Indígena y Campesina "Macabeo Choque— Betzabeth Flores" por la modificación a la Ley INRA, Octubre—Noviembre 2006.* Santa Cruz: CEJIS, IWGIA, and Oxfam.

Colque, Gonzalo. 2006. "Una nueva ley de tierras sin debate." http://www.ftierra.org/ftierra1104/docstrabajo/goni3.pdf, accessed January 1, 2007.

———. 2007. "Tenemos una reforma agraria en marcha?" http://www.ftierra.org/ftierra1204/docstrabajo/, accessed July 1, 2007.

Fundación Tierra. 2006a. "Para que la Revolución Agraria sea realidad." Memo dated October 22. In *Poca tierra para muchos, mucha tierra para pocos*, appendix 3, by Fundación Tierra. http://www.ftierra.org/ftierra1104/publicaciones/080.pdf, accessed January 1, 2007.

———. 2006b. "Para una reconducción efectiva de la Reforma Agraria: Ocho nuevas modificaciones a la Ley INRA." Memo dated October 29. In *Poca tierra para muchos, mucha tierra para pocos*, appendix 3, by Fundación Tierra,. http://www.ftierra.org/ftierra1104/publicaciones/080.pdf, accessed January 1, 2007.

Heredia García, Milton. 2005. "Pueblos Unidos, un fortín del MST impenetrable." *El Deber* (Santa Cruz de la Sierra), May 13. www.eldeber.com.bo/anteriores/20050513/economia_4.html, accessed October 20, 2006.

La Prensa. 2007. "Una ley definirá si se revierten o expropian los latifundios." December 12. http://www.laprensa.com.bo, accessed January 20, 2008.

La Razón. 2007a. "Con los estatutos, prefectos controlan tierra y tributos." December 17. http://www.la-razon.com, accessed January 20, 2008.

———. 2007b. "Unas cuatro mil familias podrían perder sus tierras." December 17. http://www.la-razon.com, accessed January 20, 2008.

Miranda, Hugo Alberto. 2002. *Informe del Estudio sobre la violación de los derechos económicos, sociales, y culturales.* Santa Cruz: Fundación Tierra. http://www.ftierra. org/ftierra1104/publicaciones/031.pdf, accessed January 2, 2007.

Morales, Evo, Presidente Constitucional de la República. 2006. *Modificación de la Ley 1715, Reconducción de la Reforma Agraria: Ley No. 3545 de 28 de noviembre de 2006.* http://www.ftierra.org/ftierra1104/docstrabajo/ley3545.pdf, accessed January 1, 2007.

Romero Bonifaz, Carlos. N.d. *50 años de reforma agraria en las tierras bajas de Bolivia.* http://www.ftierra.org/ftierra1104/docstrabajo/cromero50.pdf, accessed January 1, 2007.

Urioste F., Miguel. 2006. "La Revolución Agraria de Evo Morales." *Cuarto Intermedio* 80. http://www.ftierra.org/ftierra1104/publicaciones/077.pdf, accessed January 1, 2007.

7

The Mobilization of Colombian Ethnic Minorities

ALVARO VELASCO ÁLVAREZ

This chapter analyzes how Colombian ethnic minorities have mobilized to overcome the legacy of Spanish colonialism that had obliterated their past. It focuses on the efforts of indigenous and Afro-Colombian communities to recover their heritage and traditions, and to protect their communities from the impact of both Colombia's internal armed conflict and neoliberal policies. Their success has fundamentally transformed Colombia's political-administrative organization. Today approximately 30 percent of the country's mainland territory is designated as part of official indigenous reserves or Afro-Colombian territories. Constitutionally protected since 1991, these reserves and territories are now recognized as strategic ecological, cultural, and social assets.

Colombia is characterized by its great diversity of cultures and environments. More than sixty languages, including English (the language of the Afro-Antillean community in the archipelago of San Andrés and Providencia), are spoken, although approximately 90 percent of the population speaks only Spanish. Many of the territories inhabited by indigenous and Afro-Colombian communities extend beyond national boundaries,[1] and in fact, almost all of Colombia's borders are set in territories belonging to native populations.

Despite its rich and unique indigenous cultural heritage, Colombia has historically placed excessive emphasis on its evolution as a European colony. That which is different, "native" to the country has been devalued, along with the richness that diversity offers. However, since the beginning of the 1970s, socially excluded and ignored indigenous and Afro-Colombian communities have begun to organize and forge relationships with institutions and sectors in the country's different regions. In the process, they have generated awareness of, as well as appreciation for, the country's great cultural and biological diversity.

These accomplishments have taken place in the midst of a war to which the ethnic minorities are not a party but by which they, like all Colombians, are materially affected. They have earned everyone's respect, including that of the armed protagonists, by demonstrating that rights are not negotiable or obtained by force but rather must first be perceived and recognized by those who demand them, then constructed and earned through patient and persistent nonviolent action. Colombia's ethnic minorities have gained recognition and respect through collective actions emphasizing their lost heritage, culture, and traditions.

Rights That Flow from the Land and the Community: The Indigenous Movement, 1970–91

The mobilization of the indigenous and Afro-Colombian communities can be traced back to the peasant movement organized around the National Association of Peasant Beneficiaries (ANUC), an organization created by the government of Carlos Lleras Restrepo (1966–70) as a political base for its program of agrarian reform. The government's objective was to encourage peasants to become agricultural entrepreneurs by training them to use credit and technical assistance made available by the Colombian Institute of Agrarian Reform (INCORA). The rising expectations unleashed by the agrarian reform contributed to the development of a formidable peasant movement in the 1970s under the ideological leadership of the radical left. The movement gradually assumed characteristics of a political movement, principally Maoist in orientation but also influenced by nationalist leftist movements such as the M-19 movement and the National Liberation Army (ELN). Such radicalism, influenced by too many conflicting political ideologies, contributed to the movement's eventual fragmentation and demise.

The indigenous movement with the largest impact on contemporary Colombia, the Regional Indigenous Council of Cauca (CRIC), emerged as part of the peasant movement in the department of Cauca, a southwestern department with the country's largest concentration of indigenous communities.[2] These had a long and successful history of resistance to oppression, evidenced by the preservation of their own languages, customs, knowledge, and beliefs. But they were also familiar with the Spanish language, Colombian law, and the dominant power centers—the resources needed to participate meaningfully in the ascendant *campesino* movement.

The CRIC adopted the slogan "unity, land, and culture" to emphasize that while its members were peasants because they worked the land, they were also indigenous peoples whose identity had been forged through their historic struggle to maintain their ancestral territories. The latter was subsequently emphasized by the Movement of Indigenous Authorities of the Southwest (which later became the Movement of Indigenous Authorities of Colombia, AICO), which arose from 1977 on in opposition to the sector of the indigenous movement that had drifted toward the orthodox left.[3]

In one of the CRIC's declarations it notes that thirty years ago peasants throughout Colombia began fighting for land, wresting important areas from landlords. The CRIC was attracted by this movement because its members shared the need to struggle for land. "In the course of that struggle we realized that land was a repository of ancestral memories and that our struggle involved more than a mere quest for land; that what we needed to recover were those territories that gave birth to our distinct, original cultures" ("Declaración de las Autoridades Indígenas" 2006, 1).

Although the indigenous movement evolved in the wake of the *campesino* movement, it soon found its own path, transforming the struggle for land into one seeking affirmation of indigenous identity through the recovery and restoration of specific ancestral territories. The movement was guided by *taitas* (elders or the traditional authorities) who gave meaning to the struggle: "Guided by our elders and supported by those in the solidarity movement, we recovered the memory of our land and unearthed the mirror that reflects our reality. We rediscovered our law of origin, left to us by our ancestors in the form of myths, calendars, symbols, and rites, and came to understand our links with the sun, the earth, the air, and the water, the sources of all life. After years in hiding during the dark age that fell upon us when the colonialists arrived, the eight-pointed star, the 'Sun of the Pastos' rose again" ("Declaración de las Autoridades Indígenas" 2006, 1).

Traditional authorities in different regions organized indigenous people internally, encouraging pilgrimages to explore the history of ancestral lands from different perspectives. They infused life into native languages, reviving memory, customs, and traditions that gave new meaning to ancestral myths, celebrations, and oral traditions. Also involved in this process was the solidarity movement with indigenous peoples.[4] Composed of academics and activists, their activities incorporated the principles of participatory action research[5] and in time coalesced into various NGOs.[6] The relationship between the indigenous movements and the solidarity movement had a special significance if one accepts the view that identity is affirmed in relation to others: "As the movement evolved it became clear that our rights were not derived from royal proclamations or mestizo codes but from the land. Our rights were intimately linked to nature . . . and like everything born of the earth are continuously renewed, and deeper and better when cultivated from the heart, following the advice and traditions of our elders" ("Declaración de las Autoridades Indígenas" 1996, 1).

Indigenous communities relearned a different perception of time, non-linear, cyclical, incorporating change and constancy simultaneously. To their ancestors and elders, time was like the double helix, a symbol engraved in myriad territories that illustrates that one has to maintain a delicate balance between change and permanence in order to participate in life. Indigenous communities rediscovered their ancestral reality, a living world organically tied to the sun, the moon, and the universe, a sensitive and mutable world first felt and then seen. They discovered that their native languages had named everything around them and, through rituals and the use of sacred plants, they could communicate with all living things. They wove inter-ambient territorial webs, frameworks for relationships on which their system of life and social order were based, providing them with a foundation for proclaiming their "higher law" to the Colombian nation: "We call this law the Higher Law, not just because it is the original law, but because it is tied to the law of creation, which teaches us to maintain the delicate balance between the four vital elements and between humans and the different forms of life that comprise nature. If we learn it well, it will be effective forever, allowing the earth, our mother, to continue providing us sustenance. Our law is also higher because its structure is sufficiently flexible to protect the diversity of all living things, without excluding any communities or cultures" ("Declaración de las Autoridades Indígenas" 1996, 1–2).

In exploring and coming to understand the elements of their higher law, a process took place through which the indigenous communities were reconfigured as collective subjects with their own specific project: the re-creation of their original, autonomous cultures and a collective identity. Nonetheless, there was also a critical awareness of the need to establish relations of exchange and solidarity with others.

The "higher law" was proclaimed in 1980, on Guambiano territory close to Popayan, a city symbolic of colonial power and the capital of the department of Cauca. It was proclaimed at a solemn ceremony attended by large numbers of indigenous people from the Colombian southwest and their supporters. The media provided extensive coverage, referring to the event as an admirable civic action, recognizing the legitimacy of the indigenous demand "not to be erased from the Earth."

A few days later four thousand members of the Guambiano community (including women, children, and the elderly), led by their traditional authorities, occupied the Hacienda de las Mercedes, an important property economically that was of symbolic value as well to the traditional elite. This property was owned by the González-Caicedos, a politically well-connected family that raised one of the most famous herds of fighting bulls in the country on this hacienda. Each year the economic and political elite of the region attended a celebrated bullfight on the hacienda, which drew some of the world's most renowned bullfighters.

This property was also of great symbolic, historical, cultural, and material value to indigenous peoples, who considered it part of their ancestral territory. Because of the power of its purported owners and because it had been characterized as "adequately exploited" land under the agrarian reform law, it was outside the bounds of any agrarian reform initiative. With the proclamation of the "higher law," the estate in question became both an immediate challenge and an opportunity: the higher law had to be enforced and the ancestral lands recovered or the indigenous proclamation would be a mere "voice in the wind," hence the decision to take over the estate's one thousand hectares shortly after the issuance of the proclamation. Massive participation in the recuperation served to affirm the commitment of indigenous people to continue to exist as original peoples with their own identities and cultures.

The occupation was an unpleasant surprise for the government and the González-Caicedo family, especially since the region's most important newspaper—Cali's *El País*, a publication with close ties to the family—had only days earlier praised the indigenous community's proclamation of "higher law" and its goal of maintaining a unique cultural and community identity. Moreover, news of the indigenous occupation had been greeted sympathetically among diverse sectors of Colombian society, making it difficult to repress the occupiers without paying a high political price in terms of national and international prestige. Consequently, the family decided to negotiate the sale of the hacienda with INCORA, a tacit acknowledgment of the "higher law" claimed by the indigenous communities.

Thus, INCORA acquired the estate, planning to convey it to the Guambianos through the agrarian reform program. However, the traditional authorities and their *cabildos* (local indigenous governments) argued that INCORA had no authority in the matter because decisions as to the use, tenancy, and management of Guambiano lands were matters for the indigenous community to resolve through its own traditional structures. They argued that the estate was located on an ancient indigenous reserve (*res-guardo*) and that it was subject to the provisions of Law 89 of 1890, which recognized the right of the indigenous *cabildos* to administer their own lands and exercise police powers within the reserve. In essence, they sought to apply the basic statute governing indigenous reserves that had remained virtually unchanged since the colonial era.

Responding to the argument based on Law 89 and ignoring those based on "higher law," the central government, through the Ministry of the Interior, submitted the issue to the Tribunal of Justice (the tribunal then charged with resolving controversies between the state and individuals), requesting that it study the situation and advise it on how to resolve the dispute in compliance with applicable law. The tribunal promptly ruled that the government should turn the estate over to the local government of the Indigenous Reserve of Guambia. It ruled that local indigenous governments were institutions of public law and part of the state's administrative organization with authority over matters within the jurisdiction of their reserve. The decision marked the first time property was returned directly to a local indigenous government to manage as it deemed appropriate without participation by INCORA, an unprecedented triumph for the country's entire indigenous population. The victory made "higher law" a reality, converting Law 89 from a tool for "submitting indigenous communities to civilized life" (as provided for in its Article 3), into a vehicle to legitimize their struggle and affirm their rights.

Having succeeded in this initial confrontation, the indigenous communities moved to consolidate their victory through a two-step plan: first, by obtaining recognition of their "higher law" directly from the Colombian people; and then presenting it to the government for affirmation, demanding that it recognize that which Colombian society had already acknowledged. They put their plan into effect with the national protest march of 1981, which was headed by the indigenous authorities of the Colombian southwest. As the marchers traversed a major part of the country, they introduced Colombian society to the indigenous movement, its members, history, struggle, and demands.[7] The march included visits to many social organizations, among these universities, unions, neighborhoods, schools, factories, and cooperatives. Participants discussed their lives and customs, personally explaining what they were struggling to attain. Importantly, they also stressed that the march was a learning experience to get to know and understand the concerns of others. Marching under the slogan, "Our rights are strengthened by recognizing the rights of others," they drafted declarations of mutual support and recognition from unions, community groups, peasant organizations, intellectuals, students, and housewives.

The march concluded at the seat of the national government in Bogotá, where its leaders addressed the Colombian president in more or less the following terms: "The Colombian people have recognized our rights. The state, the government, and the nation's chief magistrate must now recognize them as well."[8] The success and popular acceptance of the march made it politically impractical to reject.[9] The government and Colombian civil society both recognized that the rights demanded by the indigenous communities to their own identity as Colombia's original inhabitants could not be ignored.

The march was not an isolated event. Land occupations by indigenous communities multiplied throughout the country. Indigenous leaders were careful to distinguish these occupations from common land invasions or crimes against property; rather, they explained that the recuperation of ancestral lands was required by their higher law in order to recover their heritage, identity, and territory, and to attain self-governance. This argument was acceptable under the Colombian legal system pursuant to penal code provisions specifying that conduct involving the exercise of a fundamental right involving an inescapable duty could not constitute a crime. As a result, numerous judicial decisions were made in favor of the positions espoused by the indigenous movement, especially involving Law 89 of 1890. The agrarian reform norms as applied to indigenous communities were substantially transformed, with local indigenous governments being recognized as institutions of public law and traditional authorities as components of governmental administration.[10]

It took the indigenous movement approximately fifteen years to bring about meaningful changes in the constitutive framework for the allocation of authority and responsibility among central, departmental, territorial, and community governments. The resulting change in perspective regarding Colombia's indigenous population had a concrete and significant effect on the country itself, especially regarding the treatment of natural resources and native cultures. In the first place, the role of the indigenous reserves were transformed from a colonialist tool for reducing "indigenous communities to a civilized life"[11] into territorial collectives administered by local indigenous governments or traditional authorities charged with protecting Colombia's natural and cultural diversity. Second, the transformation of the reserves produced a quantitative and qualitative change in Colombia's political-administrative map. The designated territories were now identified as protectorates for natural resources and cultural diversity, in contrast to former maps where they were identified as *baldíos* (uninhabited and uncultivated) and thus available for colonization and pillaging, or as dangerous jungles inhabited by savages who required conversion to "civilization" through reason or force.

Under the presidency of Virgilio Barco (1986–90) the government assimilated this transformation in the status of the indigenous reserves. Aware of his responsibility to incorporate and protect the Colombian Amazon, the president acknowledged that the time had come to recognize the indigenous communities of the Amazon as an integral part of Colombia. The establishment of the large indigenous reserves of the Amazon was the greatest practical acknowledgment of the success of the indigenous struggle. With that governmental action, the rights of the Amazonian indigenous communities to their ancestral lands were finally recognized and the indigenous were assured of their status as independent communities, part of Colombia, but with the freedom to re-create their ancestral cultures and territories. And the Amazonian territories were finally seen to be of value, not only because of the biodiversity that they offer or their environmental services, but as part and parcel of the fundamental rights of Colombia's indigenous peoples.

Despite comprising only 2.5 percent of the Colombian population, the indigenous peoples managed to earn national respect and recognition in a relatively short time. Their struggle, guided by their own ideas and concepts, was a brave, audacious, and creative struggle, but above all, one that was nonviolent. It was so successful that two representatives of the indigenous movements were elected to the Constitutional Assembly of 1990 (one representing AICO and the other the National Indigenous Organization of Colombia, ONIC) and when the assembly convened, these organizations—not withstanding their differences—had the experience and knowledge necessary to work together successfully so that their "higher law" would be elevated to the status of a constitutional right.[12]

Afro-Colombian Communities: A Continuing Quest for Freedom and Respect

The indigenous communities were not the only ones that went through a process of reaffirmation and rediscovery during this period. Afro-Colombian communities also began to tread the paths that their ancestors had sown, when, with both courage and intelligence, the escaped slaves built a culture of freedom in territories deep in the Pacific coast jungle, far from established areas.[13] Historically known as *palenques*, in these territories Afro-descendants lived in close proximity to native indigenous peoples from whom they learned how best to adapt to their exuberant natural surroundings.

The current organizational process in the Afro-Colombian communities dates from the mid-1970s[14] but was spurred during the 1980s as a result of the expansion of commercial sugar cane production throughout the southern Cauca Valley. Sugar cane production had begun in the mid-nineteenth century and as it expanded it had led to violent dispossession of many Afro-Colombian smallholders, descendents of the *palenques*. By the mid-1980s, the sugar mills were encroaching on the lands surrounding the small Afro-Colombian towns that had been formed by those previously dispossessed of their traditional lands. Small cities such as Puerto Tejada, which had mushroomed in size as migrants arrived seeking jobs in the sugar industry, began experiencing severe housing shortages because little land was available for urban expansion. As the housing situation grew steadily more difficult, there was increasing pressure to take action. The refrains of a popular song well reflect the mood of the region's Afro-Colombian population at that time:

> The sugar companies took
> our ancestral lands
> in trade for hunger wages
> and with hunger they've left us.
> Blacks produce the sweet
> but their lives are bitter.[15]

Among the factors that contributed to growing public awareness and led to affirmation of Afro-Colombian identity and the demand for justice was a participatory action research project focused on the sugar companies. During weekly public hearings presided over by community leaders in Puerto Tejada, it sought to determine whether the sugar companies were complying with Article 30 of the Constitution of 1886, which established the social function of land. Attendance and participation were overwhelming.

The decision, amply supported by the evidence, determined that the sugar companies had not only failed to meet the constitutionally mandated social function of land, but that they had expropriated the hereditary *palenque* farms from the region's Afro-Colombian peasants without due process and through deceit and violence. Shortly after the decision, on March 22,

1981, almost one thousand families took possession of forty land parcels belonging to the Ingenio Cauca in order to build housing. Subsequently, at a government-sponsored meeting to address the takeover attended by the owner of the sugar company and commanders of the local armed forces, community leaders successfully defended their actions, submitting the entire participatory action research docket in support of their claims. The owner of Ingenio Cauca, overwhelmed by the evidence, decided to donate the contested parcels to the housing project.

Subsequently, the Northern Cauca Network of Base Organizations was formed; it may have been the first network-type of organization in Colombia. Those in the network are committed to the concept of community autonomy and they initiated participatory planning processes through which "integral plans for recovery of life" were developed. Their strategic goals included the revival of traditional farms as well as of Afro-Colombian music and art. The process, including annual art and music festivals, continues in various towns and districts in the departments of Valle and Cauca.

Constitutional Recognition

The indigenous and Afro-Colombian communities' struggle to affirm their identities, recover their territories and cultures, preserve their natural environment, and strengthen community autonomy were important inputs into the Constitution of 1991. This is illustrated in its preamble and first ten articles. Three articles pertain directly to the indigenous and Afro-Colombian communities: Article 7 recognizes the ethnic and cultural diversity of the Colombian nation; Article 8 provides for the protection of natural and cultural resources; and Article 10 grants official status to native languages within their territories. The magnitude of what was achieved by indigenous and Afro-Colombian communities is appreciated by taking into account not only these but also two general articles: Article 1, which defines the general principles of territorial entity autonomy; and Article 3, which defines popular sovereignty.

Title 1 of the Constitution contains rules of interpretation applicable to the Constitution as a whole, as well as specific provisions applicable to indigenous communities. Articles 63 and 329 characterize the indigenous reserves as inalienable institutions—whose lands can not be rented or sold to outsiders or be used as collateral—and which are designed for the protection of natural and cultural diversity, that is, the reserves are placed outside the bounds of the market. Indigenous territories are implicitly recognized in that Articles 329 and 330 provide—in the context of a new territorial reorganization—for the establishment of autonomous political-administrative units governed by indigenous peoples according to their own traditions, uses, and customs. However, to date the implementing legislation required to create indigenous territories has not been passed. Article 330 also contains a paragraph that requires community consultation on projects that might result in "cultural detriment."[16]

With respect to the Afro-Colombian communities, in compliance with the requirements of Transitory Article 55 of the Constitution, Law 70 of 1993 recognizes Territories of Black Communities with characteristics similar to those of the indigenous reserves. As a result of these dispositions, approximately one-fifth of the total Colombian land area is today composed of indigenous reserves and Afro-Colombian territories, accounting for nearly four hundred thousand square kilometers.

The Constitutional Court has interpreted these provisions in numerous rulings and a well-developed jurisprudence has evolved. The following excerpts from major decisions illustrate current judicial philosophy regarding Colombia's ethnic minorities:

> . . . Recognition of cultural diversity . . . harmonizes the Constitution's rules pertaining to conservation, preservation, and restoration of the environment and the natural resources that comprise it, especially taking into account that indigenous communities are an integral part of that environment. That is even truer when indigenous communities inhabit ecosystems with exceptional characteristics and ecological value requiring protection as integral parts of the nation's natural and cultural patrimony. *Therefore, the indigenous population and its natural surroundings comprise a single system or universe, worthy of the state's complete protection.*[17]
>
> Recognition of diversity is integral to indigenous communities' fundamental rights. . . . Protection and recognition of ethnic and cultural diversity is impossible unless the various indigenous communities are granted constitutional status sufficient to permit them to . . . enjoy the benefits of their fundamental rights, as well as legal standing sufficient to protect such rights whenever they are infringed.[18]
>
> Constitutional recognition of ethnic and cultural diversity presupposes acceptance of different ways of life and ways of understanding the world, different from those of western culture.[19]

Due to indigenous and Afro-Colombian movements, Colombia currently enjoys a constitutional and legal foundation and jurisprudence that, if socially validated, will guarantee the conservation and integral protection of biodiversity, native and Afro-Colombian culture, indigenous knowledge, ecosystems, and the environment. The conservation and protection of nature are now recognized as having an undeniable sociocultural dimension and as inseparable aspects of life.

It is worth highlighting that these achievements took place in the midst of the broader continental indigenous mobilization around the quincentennial of the so-called discovery of the Americas, known as the "500 Years of Resistance Campaign." In Colombia this movement went far beyond the denunciation of the atrocities committed and of the oppressive systems implanted in the Americas. As we have seen, the aim was to recuperate territories and to re-create a way of life. What was achieved with the Constitution of 1991 was no less than an attempt to consolidate a new model of state and nation.

Neoliberal Policies and the Civil War: 1990–2006

The Constitution of 1991 opened a new way to understand and value cultural and natural diversity. However, the global political economy was moving in a different direction. An aggressive expansion of world capitalism was taking place, which sought to consolidate a new hegemonic project around neoliberal globalization. This entailed not only control of world markets but also control of territory and natural resources. This tendency ran directly counter to the quest of indigenous and Afro-Colombian communities to achieve autonomy, in addition to safeguards for human rights as well as "second generation" economic, social, collective, and environmental rights.

Colombia's sociopolitical situation since 1991 has been characterized by marked contrasts and contradictions. The government of President Cesar Gaviria (1990–94), supported by both the political elite and the leadership of organized labor, opted to promote the neoliberal agenda, minimizing the reformed political environment that the new constitution was designed to create. As a result of the ensuing tensions, there was a renewal of the civil war, consolidation and expansion of the illegal drug trade, a degradation of political standards, and increased levels of corruption, poverty, and dependence on (and intervention by) the United States.

Among the actions taken by the Gaviria government in apparent disregard for the spirit of the Constitution of 1991 was an implicit declaration of war on the Colombian Revolutionary Armed Forces (FARC), the nation's oldest insurgent movement and the only political force that remained on the sidelines of the process of the Constituent Assembly. The day the Constitution was promulgated the armed forces attacked the FARC's symbolic headquarters in La Uribe (Department of Meta), reflecting the government's commitment to an all-out war. Recent history would perhaps have been different if a political solution to the conflict had been sought at that time. The M-19 movement, originally an insurgent movement, for example, participated actively in the Constituent Assembly as a legitimate political party and might have proved a valuable intermediary.

At the same time as it renewed military operations, the government accelerated its neoliberal economic policies through external liberalization and privatization measures. In addition, it began reforms of the social security system as well as of housing and labor policies. It inaugurated a new system of contracting and natural resource concessions that provided significant tariff and tax benefits to the private sector and multinational companies. These measures resulted in growing unemployment, the exclusion of the poor from health, education, and housing, and a crisis in small- and medium-scale agriculture. The agricultural crisis, in turn, led to the acquisition of large tracts of the best lands in the country by the drug lords. The end result was an agrarian counterreform that created a new class of landlords that would end up supporting the right-wing paramilitary groups.

An unfortunate political decision during this period ended up excluding those forces that had participated in the Constituent Assembly from running for the new Congress. The Constituent Assembly had proposed that the existing Congress be dissolved and replaced by a newly elected one, in the expectation that it would be more disposed to implementing the new constitution. The traditional political elite managed this in their favor, demanding that no member of the Constituent Assembly be permitted to run for election to the new Congress. Perhaps because they had presidential aspirations and did not want to antagonize the traditional political classes, the leadership of the Constituent Assembly accepted this condition. As a result, the traditional political establishment—with its exclusionary bias—continued to maintain legislative control. Not surprisingly, few of the measures required to implement the rights and social guarantees achieved in the Constitution of 1991 have been passed.

The main recourse open to the citizenry has been to appeal to the judiciary to implement the constitutional mandates, but these actions have been insufficient in the face of the government's neoliberal model. Such litigation has led to numerous decisions against the government and its supporters, and to a well-developed constitutional jurisprudence. However, due to bureaucratic intransigence, implementation of such decisions has been slow and ineffective, frequently requiring follow-up litigation. Because neither of the other two branches of government favors an effective judiciary, the national court system has not been provided with the resources necessary to keep up with the resulting caseload. In fact, the judiciary is on the verge of collapse. Traditionalists blame the judicial system's crisis on what they perceive of as a litigious citizenry. As in other parts of the world, those who promote judicial "reform" seek to limit citizen actions and reduce the authority of the Constitutional Court.

The executive branch is firmly under the control of neoliberal technocrats and has used its control over the media to spread the message that all societal malaise, injustice, and insecurity is due to the actions of terrorist groups (a term now used for the insurgency that has battled the Colombian government for more than half a century). This assertion is given credence by the barbarous acts regularly committed by the insurgents. Thus some believe that the election of Colombia's last two neoliberal presidents (and hence the consolidation of neoliberalism as well as U.S. economic, political, and military intervention in the country) is largely due to the FARC's erratic and inhumane behavior rather than the appeal of these specific policies.

Many Colombians believe that the goal of U.S. intervention in Colombia involves a deepening of the civil war in order to attain control of Colombia's economy, and most of all its strategically valuable territories with their wealth of minerals and biodiversity. This intervention has been justified under the guise of fighting the illegal drug trade and international terrorism. Admittedly, drug trafficking is the economic foundation for both the FARC and the paramilitary forces. But peace negotiations seem a farce[20] designed to permit combatants to fortify their strongholds, benefiting only those who profit from war, while Colombia falls further and further into confusion and poverty.

Military and political intervention is not the only Colombian concern regarding the United States. According to analysts from differing ideological perspectives (including backers of the current government), the proposed free-trade agreement that the government of Álvaro Uribe (2002–6) is negotiating with the United States will harm Colombian agriculture, damage natural and cultural diversity, generate conditions favorable to the armed conflict and the illicit drug trade, and accelerate the degradation in the quality of life and the environment. Prior to his departure from office, Carlos Gustavo Cano, Uribe's minister of agriculture, noted that the U.S. government considers its free-trade agreement with Chile as the model for the one for Colombia. However, "one must take into account the roots of Colombia's social conflict and the tight relation between the state of the agricultural sector and terrorism. . . . Every time agriculture is weakened, illegal crops and the violent groups that derive profits from their cultivation and trade are strengthened" (MinAg 2004, 15–16). Thus he concluded that in the war against terrorism the defense of agriculture and the employment that it generates is fundamental.

Jorge Garay, a highly respected economic analyst, summarized the impact of recent government policies: "Poverty rates have reached 60 percent among Colombia's population and indigence is at 25 percent. The current coefficient of wealth and income concentration is higher than at any time since the 1970s. More than 60 percent of the economically active population is involved in the gray market [informal economy]. The level of human displacement due to violence and expulsion from the countryside constitutes one of the world's greatest humanitarian tragedies. With per capita income decreasing, it has to be acknowledged that living conditions for large segments of the population have deteriorated to levels not experienced for more than ten or fifteen years" (Garay 2003, 15–16).

On the political field, the power of the paramilitary groups has grown significantly.[21] The United Self-defense Forces of Colombia (AUC), as the political-military organization is known, has considerable influence in local and regional electoral debates. In fact, one of its leaders, Salvatore Mancuso, noted that as a result of the 2002 congressional elections, AUC sympathizers now held over one-third of the seats in the Colombian Congress. An investigation conducted by the Colombian weekly, *El Espectador*, disclosed that the AUC was appropriating considerable state resources: "Progressively, on a national scale, the self-defense groups are assuming control of incalculable state resources allocated to social investment, security, and official government operations . . ." (Molano Bravo 2004, 20–21). This report also pointed to growing corruption.

The Ethnic Minorities in This Scenario of Conflict

In the midst of this dark panorama, it is heartening to consider the activities of the indigenous communities. In 2002, the well-known philosopher and linguist Noam Chomsky visited the community of Tierradentro in the Department of Cauca when it was being bombarded by both the FARC and government forces. He noted, "This territory is the cradle of an exemplary example for the hemisphere of resistance to neoliberalism and of the construction of autonomous alternatives. And needless to say, these communities are demonstrating incredible courage in their nonviolent struggle to attain peace" (quoted in Podur 2002).

In September 2004, the local indigenous governments of the Department of Cauca organized an eighty-one-mile march by sixty thousand people from Popayan to Cali. The march celebrated the triumph of peaceful activism in securing the release of an indigenous leader from captivity by the FARC. Its broader goal was to secure the demilitarization of indigenous and *campesino* territories as well as respect for community autonomy and their own development plans. The "Indigenous Minga," as the march came to be called, arrived in Cali on September 17, escorted by thousands of "civic guards" appointed by the indigenous local governments. There, it was hailed as a demonstration of civil organization and valor. The marchers' slogan of "Minga for life and against death" emphasized that it did not focus on economic or political demands but was principally concerned with peace and mutual respect. As noted in a chronicle of the event: "The Minga is a shout from the depths of the country, beyond conventional notions. It has to do with the soul of the indigenous communities, with the ruin of the peasantry, with the dispossession of Afro-Colombian communities from el Atrato, with the drama that city life has become for the middle class" (Molano Bravo 2004).

President Uribe's government did all that it could to prevent the march, including hackneyed scare tactics involving alleged threats by the guerillas against its leaders. Unconcerned, they thanked the president for his "useful information," which would help them successfully conclude the Minga. The president had valid political reasons for his concern, but they did not involve the safety of those marching. During the course of the march and especially at its conclusion in Cali's sports coliseum, numerous complaints were raised against the government. Many involved the anticipated impact of the proposed free-trade agreement with the United States, demanding that it be put to a referendum and arguing that it was incumbent on all Colombians to participate in the decision because of its effects on fundamental individual and collective rights. The government's development plan was also denounced as totally contrary to community life plans. But more than anything, the participants marched to assert their dignity and the respect due their identities, traditions, territories, and own traditional authorities; to protest the assassinations of labor and indigenous leaders; and to condemn the war and all of its participants. They proclaimed to the country, "We, the indigenous communities, organized and unarmed, can defeat the war," thus emboldening other sectors of the population. As a result, other marches took place throughout Colombia, seemingly rousing Colombia's civil society from its apparent lethargy.

In addition to organizing marches and other public demonstrations, the indigenous communities began to make concrete proposals through their organizations, associations of traditional authorities, and congressmen. For example, they demanded enactment of enabling legislation to further the process of decentralization and community autonomy required to implement the constitutionally mandated territorial restructuring and formation of indigenous territorial entities. They emphasized the need to gradually build the state's politico-administrative organization, with societal participation, in order to guarantee and protect diversity. They sought an alternative to the government's tendency (inspired by the World Bank) toward decentralization from above, which serves only to strengthen the control of the old and corrupt political elite. Instead, they proposed reconfiguration of Colombia on the basis of community autonomy, characterized by active community participation within the framework of the Constitution of 1991. Indigenous leaders are quite clear that the organic law for the restructuring of territories must include recognition of the rights of nonindigenous people and the active participation of all of the citizenry in the founding, administration, and governance of the indigenous territorial entities.

At the same time, the indigenous communities have continued their own process of recovering and re-creating their ancestral histories, cultures, and traditions and of developing and implementing their own strategies for the conservation of natural resources and food security. Their activities have inspired Afro-Colombian and peasant communities to do the same and one sees examples of this throughout the country

The indigenous communities have also sought to develop stronger social, economic, and cultural ties at the regional level. Worth mentioning is the initiative of the indigenous people of Pastos, who live on the Ecuadorian frontier, as described by Efrén Tarapues Cuaical, who was a senator at the time:

On Colombia's southern Andean frontier with Ecuador rises a massive mountain known as the Knot of the Pastos, a place where the Pastos peoples have lived since time immemorial. They currently comprise twenty-two communities with a population of approximately eighty-five thousand, not including those in Ecuadorian communities. During the last thirty years, the Pastos, under the guidance of our traditional authorities, have begun a process of recovery of our ancestral memory and wisdom. This process unleashed a long struggle to recover our ancestral territory, affirm our identity, and economically, socially, and culturally rebuild our communities. A great deal remains to be done in terms of restoring the natural landscape of this territory that sustains our culture. Now, our communities have come together to start a new stage in our long struggle, addressing the various threats that hang over us while developing a new, cooperative relationship with our brethren in Ecuador and the other communities that inhabit our region.

We want to build a binational region where life and prosperity are assured for all who live here. Our proposal is the result of intense consultations, meetings, and workshops held to analyze our major problems and needs and to determine how to deal with them within the context of our higher law, our law of origin. The law that guides us requires us to reacquaint ourselves with our territory and its vital elements: the water, the earth, the light, and the wind, those elements that give life to our people and our region.

The objective of this proposal is to make our indigenous communities less vulnerable to attacks from the civil war, from drug trafficking, and from the economic and political forces that endanger our lives, culture, and territory. At the same time we seek to guarantee to our region the environmental services, especially water, without which the future of the region would be seriously in doubt. (Tarapues Cuaical 2005, n.p.)

The dual character of this proposal, both binational and regional, makes it particularly interesting and demonstrates how the process of indigenous community autonomy could prove compatible with regional interests while concurrently respecting territorial sovereignty.

Another noteworthy initiative is being implemented in the Department of the Amazon, where the Permanent Inter-administrative Coordination Board has been created through an inter-administrative agreement between the departmental government and ten associations of indigenous authorities (the latter being public entities recognized by the Constitution). The

agreement seeks to "coordinate the development, execution, and development of plans, projects, and programs that promote the integral development of the associated communities" (Amazonas 2002, n.p.). By combining
efforts, members of the board seek to develop sustainable models for governing the Department of the Amazon and in so doing provide the entire
country with an example worth emulating.

Conclusions

The history and accomplishments of Colombia's ethnic minority movements have contributed significantly to the process of recovery of Colombia, particularly in terms of respect for life and diversity. These creative,
nonviolent organizational processes are helping to repair the damage from
war, neglect, and degradation, restoring both nature and local culture. They
provide Colombians with a dignified and intelligent example of how to recover what war and neoliberal policies have taken away. Despite continuing adversity and resistance, indigenous and Afro-Colombian communities
continue to develop territories dedicated to the pursuit of life and the living,
products of patient hard work. Slowly but steadily, they are adding their
footprints to those of their ancestors. Understanding these emergent and
evolving communities also provides a means of self-discovery for Colombians as a whole.

As we have seen, the concept of territory involves much more than mere
mountains, rivers, valleys, towns, crops, and landscapes. Territory is a space
inhabited by communal memories and experiences. That is why learning to
understand it can teach so much about satisfying human needs in a manner
consistent with life's themes; about solving problems and resolving conflicts, doubts, and uncertainties; about recreating ties to the community.
Territory is the product of the relationships that are woven daily, almost
without realizing it, between human beings and their environment. The
experience of Colombia's ethnic communities demonstrates that territory
is fluid but remains permanent in space and time, even as it changes. Societies build territories in keeping with their traditions, thoughts, dreams,
and needs. Communities and their characteristics, words, beliefs, knowledge systems, and conscience spring from their territory. A way of being,
of feeling, of flowing is derived from the relationship of a specific people to
a specific territory, resulting in a collective entity. Territory is text and context that both forms a people and allows them to be understood. The lesson
that the small communities of Colombia have to teach us is that processes

of self-recognition and self-articulation of what we are shape authentic individual and collective entities.

Notes

Author's note: The original conference paper was translated from Spanish by Guillermo Alfonso Calvo-Mahe.

1. For example, the Wayu of the peninsula of La Guajira inhabit territory that extends into Venezuela. The Bari-Motilones and the Uwa, southern neighbors of the Wayu, also reside on the border with Venezuela. The Kuna and the Embera-Chami reside on the border with Panama. The Tukano reside on the eastern border with Brazil. The Amazonian Tikuna reside on the borders with Brazil and Peru. The Siona and the Kofan from the Amazonian foothills reside on the border with Ecuador. The Awa reside on the Pacific coast, on the border with Ecuador; and the Pastos reside in the Andean Ecuadorian frontier.

2. Southwestern Colombia is home to approximately 230,000 indigenous people, making up 25 percent of Colombia's indigenous population.

3. In 1979 the executive committee of the CRIC formed an alliance with the M-19 movement, thus subordinating the indigenous struggle in favor of class struggle and revolution.

4. Many of those in the solidarity movement had participated in the Colombian student movement during the 1970s. Because of their work with peasant communities, they came to understand that many of these communities were also indigenous and had other specific grievances. Researchers, principally those associated with the Fundación la Rosca, played an important role in fostering this sense of indigenous identity and in helping to differentiate the indigenous and peasant struggle.

5. Participatory action research is a methodology for intervention, development, and change within communities and groups and is most closely associated with the work of Fals Borda (1979) and Fals Borda and Rodrigues Brandão (1986).

6. Among the NGOs important to this process were the Fundación Colombia Nuestra, Fundación Centro de Estudios Andinos, and Fundaminga.

7. One of the culminating moments of the march was the meeting with the Afro-Colombian communities in Puerto Tejada, in the department of Cauca, and the subsequent meeting with the main Colombian workers' unions in Zipaquira, in the department of Cundinamarca. The march was all the more remarkable as it occurred during the state of siege imposed by the government of President Turbay Ayala (1978–82) in reaction to armed conflict involving the M-19 movement.

8. Author's field notes, November 1981.

9. Among the factors that led the public to embrace the movement was its unambiguous and unequivocal condemnation of violence, whatever its source or justification. The march and its objectives were seen as being unrelated to the insurgents' political and military goals. In fact, the armed insurgents viewed the indigenous communities' higher law as reactionary and contrary to the course of history.

10. One of the most important decisions was issued by Magistrate Humberto Mora

Osejo on behalf of the Council of State, which concluded that the local governments on the indigenous reserves were public entities of a special nature charged with the protection of indigenous peoples. See Request for Declaratory Judgment Number 1978, issued November 16, 1983, cited at *In the Indigenous Reservations*, Radicación 175 of 1988 Consejo de Estado—Sala de Consulta y Servicio Civil, http://www.alcaldiabogota. gov.co/sisjur/normas/Normal.jsp?i=388, accessed February 17, 2008.

11. See Article 3, Law 89 of 1890.

12. The indigenous movements also secured two reserved seats in the Senate and one in the lower chamber.

13. The first *palenques* were in the mountains and jungles bordering the Cauca Valley, where colonial mines and plantations using slave labor were primarily located. Later, free Afro-Colombian communities expanded throughout the region now known as the bio-geographic Choco, which includes territories within the departments of Choco, Valle, Cauca, and Nariño, from the Darien Plug on the border with Panama to the Mira River, which marks the border with Ecuador.

14. See Mina 1975 for the results of one of the first participatory action research projects among Afro-Colombians.

15. Author unknown.

16. This paragraph originated in a proposal for recognition of the right of "cultural objection" presented to the Constituent Assembly by one of the two indigenous delegates.

17. Constitutional Court of Colombia, Decision T-652, 1968 (the "Urra Case"), emphasis added.

18. The court cites constitutional Articles 1, 7, and 4 for this decision. See Constitutional Court of Colombia, Decision T-380, 1993 and T-652, 1998.

19. Constitutional Court of Colombia, Decision SU-039, 1997.

20. For example, while purportedly negotiating peace with the insurgents, the Pastrana government (1998–2002) developed Plan Colombia with the United States. For their part, during such negotiations the FARC were building unassailable fortifications to imprison their thousands of kidnap victims.

21. The paramilitary militias were organized to combat the leftist insurgency by allies of the traditional elite, especially the large landowners. They have frequently acted as informal (and illegal) adjuncts to government forces.

References

Amazonas, Department of. 2002. "Convenio Marco Interadministrativo suscrito entre la gobernación del Departamento de Amazonas y las asociaciones de Autoridades Tradicionales Indígenas para la conformación de una mesa permanente de coordinación interadministrativa." Mimeo. June 20.
"Declaración de las Autoridades Indígenas del pueblo de los Pastos al Pueblo Colombiano: Por una Colombia sin exclusiones." 2006. Pamphlet. Indigenous Reserve of Panam, Los Pastos Territory, February.

Fals Borda, Orlando. 1979. *El problema de cómo investigar la realidad para transformarla por la praxis.* 2nd ed. Bogotá: Editorial Tercer Mundo.

Fals Borda, Orlando, and Carlos Rodrigues Brandão. 1986. *Investigación participativa.* Montevideo: Instituto del Hombre and Editorial de la Banda Oriental.

Garay, Jorge. 2003. *El embrujo autoritario, primer año de gobierno de Álvaro Uribe Vélez.* Bogotá: Plataforma Colombiana de Derechos Humanos, Democracia y Desarrollo.

Mina, Mateo. 1975. *Esclavitud y libertad en el valle del río Cauca.* Bogotá: Fundación Rosca de Investigación y Acción Social.

MinAg (Ministerio de Agricultura y Desarrollo Rural). 2004. *El agro colombiano frente al TLC con los Estados Unidos.* With an introduction by Minister Carlos Gustavo Cano. Bogotá: Ministerio de Agricultura y Desarrollo Rural.

Molano Bravo, Alfredo. 2004. "Minga por la vida y contra la muerte." *El Espectador* (Cali, Colombia), September 26.

Podur, Justin. 2002. "Cauca: Su destino queda en nuestras manos." Interview with Noam Chomsky, July 12. http://www.zmag.org/content/showarticle.cfm?ItemID=2104, accessed February 17, 2008.

Tarapues Cuaical, Efrén. 2005. Introduction to "Plan de Vida del Pueblo de los Pastos." In *Plan Binacional para el fortalecimiento cultural, natural y ambiental del Nudo de los Pastos.* Bogotá: Departamento Nacional de Planeación.

III

Sustainable Livelihoods, Social Justice

8

Water for Life, Not for Death

The Brazilian Social Movement
of People Affected by Dams

CARLOS B. VAINER

Studies on the impact of large dams, such as those required either by Brazilian environmental laws for approval of large-scale projects or by multilateral agencies as a precondition for their financial support, usually include a chapter on social aspects or on the so-called socioeconomic environment. Reading through these chapters is extremely tedious, for no matter how different the context, the resulting studies are all too similar. The main concern is in detecting regularities and generalizing effects (Sigaud 1986), rather than in trying to understand how interventions from above may generate different social processes. This literature does not question the political and economic forces that are at the root of such developments. Instead, this "anthropology of dams" (Sigaud 1986) adopts a complacent realism that sees the projects as inexorable and/or beneficial[1] and focuses on minimizing or repairing their negative effects. Employing their vocabulary, these studies seek to "reduce the risks" that threaten to overwhelm the communities in question (Cernea and McDowell 2000).

What ultimately underscores the ideological bias, the technical failure, and the operational inconsistencies of these impact reports is that not one of them thus far has been capable of predicting the upsurge of resistance movements to large-scale dam construction. Even now, as social conflicts accumulate, and these struggles increasingly appear in the news, with members of these movements denouncing these projects in international forums, the experts still fail to predict the struggles, resistance, and related organization of the affected populations. Old matrices of environmental impact that inspired reports of the 1980s and 1990s as well as more recent assessments resulting from the pretentiously innovative "reconstruction and risk model" developed by the senior experts on involuntary resettlements[2] at the World Bank not only miss the mark with respect to existing social movements but are silent regarding the possibility of organized resistance.

These deficiencies can be explained by the existence of a theoretical-conceptual "blind spot" in the methods themselves, which portray the population as neither capable of acting appropriately nor of conceiving themselves as possessing rights and having interests of their own. Within this framework, the inhabitants are incapable of operating autonomously to transform the specific dam environment into a social and political arena. Here we note "a strange inversion: the human population (the 'socioeconomic environment'), forced by the engineering project, now becomes a part of the natural environment" (de Castro and de Andrade 1988, 8).

Naturalized, reified, destitute of subjectivity and, hence, unable to constitute themselves as subject, the people affected by dams cannot be thought of as collective social agents, that is, as political claimants. The silence surrounding the people affected by dams and the inability to foresee the upsurge of resistance[3] demonstrate the limits of practical anthropology and sociology, here reduced to the category of environmental consultancy, or "impactology," whose principal aim is the legitimization of large-scale projects.

This technically produced and ideologically based silence cannot, however, conceal the historical processes that herald the rise, spread, and consolidation of resistance movements against the establishment of large dams. In Brazil this process began at the end of the 1970s and gave birth in the 1990s to a national organization with ever increasing international ties, the Movement of People Affected by Dams (MAB).

Reconstructing a detailed history of this movement offers challenges that far exceed the possibilities of this chapter. While there are abundant case studies of the social and environmental effects and conflicts that have arisen as a result of the construction of specific dams (many of them theses and dissertations in addition to the reports mentioned above), no one has yet produced a detailed study of the social movement of people affected by dams on a national scale. Of course this is a relatively young movement. The First National Meeting of Workers Affected by Dams was held in Goiânia in 1989, and the First National Congress of People Affected by Dams took place in 1991, at which time MAB was constituted as a national organization.

There is one further conceptual and methodological challenge: To what extent can the opposition of people affected by dam construction be considered a single social movement? Is it possible to speak of just *one* history, since the process was marked by such different experiences arising out of the most diverse economic, social, and political contexts? Might the attempt to construct a national history obscure the multiplicity of cultural and political values that constitute unique aspects of these social movements? Recall our critique of official impactologists, who ignore different contexts in their attempt to create a universal theory of impact. Would we not commit the same error by producing one general history of the movement of people affected by dams?

The elaboration of a narrative history would ideally take into account, in a parallel, simultaneous, and relational manner, the multiple trajectories of specific movements, as well as the trajectory of the national movement of people affected by dams. A list produced by the national board of MAB includes sixty-three dams around which MAB has been actively engaged at one time or another. Documenting the history of this movement would require recovering and connecting the trajectories of these sixty-three local movements and linking them to the development of the movement on a national level. In addition, this would require describing the complex processes, not always harmonious, through which local and regional movements ultimately converged into MAB. Such a study would require examining the perceptions of the local and regional grass-roots movements of the national organization, and vice versa.

The aims of this chapter are more modest: providing a general vision of the struggles and organizations of people affected by dams in Brazil. The focus here is predominantly national, although this in no way reflects a preference for national organizations, as opposed to local or regional ones. The following section presents a summary of the origins of the national movement. The third section describes the major struggles and demands of the movement both on the local and regional level and on the national level, together with some points of conflict between the two levels of the movement. The fourth section focuses on the international relationships of the MAB. The final section highlights some specific characteristics of the movement and suggests ideas for future research.

The Origins: Itaipu

There are references to the existence of movements resisting the construction of dams in Brazil in the 1940s and 1950s (Soares 1998), but the first consistent signs of collective action occurred at the end of the 1970s. According to Germani (1982, 24), on October 16, 1978, fifteen hundred small farmers, who had been summoned by the Pastoral Land Commission (CPT), met in the courtyard of the Santa Helena church in Santa Helena, Paraná to discuss the impact of the Itaipu dam—to host the largest hydroelectric power station in the world—that would soon flood their lands.[4] They drew up a petition to President General Geisel listing twenty-three problems. Among these were lack of information about the project, including advance notice when plans for the dam were conceived that they were going to be affected; the ecological impact; the desperate situation of towns and villages affected by the construction of the dam but not scheduled to receive compensation; and, above all, the trivial amounts offered as compensation for lost farmlands and homes.

Members of the Catholic Church and the Brazilian Lutheran Evangelist Church together worked as part of the CPT and would serve on various occasions as mediators between farmers and government officials as was common during that bleak time of military dictatorship. The CPT and shortly thereafter the National Conference of Brazilian Bishops began petitioning the government, often through the press, in favor of better terms of compensation. Independent of the CPT's efforts, farmers in the municipality of Marechal Candido Rondon hired three lawyers to challenge the compensation levels offered by the Itaipu Binational Corporation, which was building the dam.[5] At the same time, rural workers' unions mobilized to support the São Miguel de Itaipu Rural Workers' Union, which fought to defend the right to compensation for tenants who were settled in the Integrated Colonization Project at Ocoí (PIC-Ocoí). The local and regional press recorded in a series of articles the grievances of the local populations regarding the environmental impact and especially, in the Guaira Municipality, the destruction of the Seven Falls (Soares 2001).[6]

The growing mobilization led to a second assembly at Santa Helena on April 7, 1979. In attendance were representatives of the unions, the state-level Federation of Rural Workers' Unions and the National Confederation of Agricultural Workers (CONTAG), the CPT, the Pontifical Commission for Justice and Peace, bishops and priests of various archdioceses in Paraná (including some from Curitiba), politicians from the state and federal legislatures, and over two thousand farmers. This assembly created the Representative Coordinating Commission, which was made up of union representatives, members of the CPT, and two farmers from each of the affected municipalities. This commission appears to be the first organized resistance by the people affected by dams.

The organization of this movement was similar to those of many other civil rights movements of the time: members relied on manifestos, petitions, the strong presence of church leaders,[7] and multiple meetings and assemblies that made an ever growing number of farmers aware of their rights and of the need to organize to fight for those rights. If for some time the Itaipu Binational Corporation had been successful at pressuring some farmers into accepting minimal compensation, as the movement became organized the very intransigence of the Binational Corporation in dealing with the movement began to provoke the opposite effect: indignation, growth, and radicalization of the resistance.

In the face of the despair of the seven thousand families whose situation remained unresolved on the eve of the flooding of the reservoir area, the movement leaders secretly plotted a course of action. On July 14, 1980, farmers surrounded the Santa Helena office, singing the national anthem and reading the manifesto "Address to the People, the Government, and the Itaipu Corporation." The manifesto demanded immediate compensation with 100 percent readjustment; resettlement of those affected by the dam in the state of Paraná; and compensation for people affected by power transmission lines. During subsequent days, those displaced by Itaipu received the solidarity of religious and lay agencies, of politicians and political parties, and of numerous social movements, all done with broad media coverage. These were the final moments of the military dictatorship, and the struggle for direct elections to choose the next president was in progress. The Movement for Justice and Land was born, and with it the organization of people affected by dams in Brazil. Itaipu is important not only because it is the largest hydroelectric power station in the world; a symbol of the national engineering sector and of state power; and the pride of the Brazilian energy sector. Itaipu is also important because it was the place where the struggle of people affected by dams began, a place where the official disdain shown toward the affected people and their rights became known and those affected took action.

The Uruguay River Basin: The Regional Commission of People Affected by Dams

In 1979 news spread that there were plans for the construction of twenty-five hydroelectric plants in the Upper Uruguay River Basin.[8] Three of these plants would affect people in two states, Rio Grande do Sul and Santa Catarina, and displace some two hundred thousand to three hundred thousand people. The dramatic example of the "expropriated of Itaipu" was evoked by those who took the initiative to inform, organize, and mobilize farmers against construction of these dams.[9] The organization and resistance that ensued in the Upper Uruguay River Basin in many respects followed a path similar to that of Itaipu: mobilization by religious and CPT activists, the presence of militant rural workers' unions, and the organization of those affected in the communities and municipalities. As in the Itaipu struggle, the dissemination of information played a fundamental role. There was, however, a decisive new factor: the communities threatened with displacement began to mobilize and organize *before* the actual construction work began.[10] On April 24, 1979, 350 farmers met in Concordia, Santa Catarina, to create the Regional Commission of Dams, which included representatives of religious groups, union members, and others. They decided to gather more information about the project from Eletrosul, the federal public utility proposing the construction of these dams, and to share this information with those who were threatened by the project.

The Regional Commission of People Affected by Dams in the Upper Uruguay River Basin (CRAB) eventually grew into an organization that covered the entire area to be affected, organized in five regional branches. A growing number of local commissions formed the basis of a structure that included municipal as well as regional commissions, the latter sending representatives to a general commission, whose executive committee provided leadership for the movement's general assemblies, which met every three years, or as circumstances required.

As the dimensions of the project became apparent—the large geographic area encompassed, the human population affected, and the economic importance of the area to be flooded—other local and regional actors become involved. From mayors to cooperatives, these actors not only mobilized but also, in some cases, tried to assume the role of regional representatives at the negotiating table with Eletrosul. In February 1983 in Carlos Gomes, one of the most active districts in the fight against the Machadinho dam, twenty thousand people took part in the March for Land, whose theme was "Water for life, not for death."[11] As pressure by those resisting the dams grew, the legislature of the state of Rio Grande do Sul created the Special Commission for Dams, which recommended that Eletrosul redesign the project.

The national political climate was very favorable for the development of these popular struggles. Beginning in the late 1970s, the urban middle classes in Brazil became increasingly disenchanted with the military dictatorship, in part due to economic stagnation, and began questioning its legitimacy. Urban neighborhood associations and popular movements simultaneously arose from and drove this process, with rural struggles and organizations playing an important role as well (de Medeiros 1989).

In this context, in 1985 CRAB collected over one million signatures for the petition entitled "No Dams," which was delivered to the agrarian reform ministry. Although at first only requesting "fair indemnification" (as expressed by the Justice and Land Movement), now CRAB began to portray the struggle as one of "land for land," emphasizing the need to resettle people affected by dams. The stage was set for open confrontation in the struggle against the construction of dams: "Yes to Land, No to Dams."

The radicalization of the movement had contradictory political results. On the one hand, it created concrete obstacles for the execution of the dam projects through a variety of direct actions. For example, survey markers placed by the construction firm were uprooted, and Eletrosul and other technical field staff were subject to lightning-strike abductions. On the other hand, a significant portion of the people affected by the dams doubted the ability of CRAB to actually stop the project. Moreover, they often believed the official propaganda that claimed that it was CRAB that was holding back negotiations between the company and the affected people. Under these circumstances, quite a few farmers accepted individual deals with the company, a decision that many would come to regret.[12]

This stalemate contributed to the agreement in 1987 between Eletrosul and CRAB. The agreement resulted in the tacit acceptance by CRAB's leaders of the construction of dams in the Uruguay River Basin, at least of the Ita and Machadinho dams. At the same time, the agreement stipulated that Eletrosul and the Brazilian electric energy sector recognize CRAB as the official representative of people affected by dams. Furthermore, the agreement formalized procedures for implementing the project. The most important of these was an end to individual negotiations and the agreement that all negotiations would be held, in each and every community, in the presence of representatives of CRAB; the linking of the construction timetable to that of negotiations for solutions to social problems; and a standing offer to all the affected people, including non-landowners, of collective resettlement.[13]

The history of the struggle since then has focused on the implementation of this agreement. The deepening national economic crisis at this time affected the electrical energy sector, and Eletrosul had to suspend activities related to the construction of new dams. Even in the case of Machadinho, which had been at the top of the list of new dams to be constructed, work stopped; in the case of Ita, construction proceeded slowly, interrupted by periods of inactivity. The movement reacted to these changing conditions by focusing its efforts on mobilizing people affected by Ita to force implementation of the agreement of 1987 and, specifically, to organize the resettlements. There are still conflicts in the area of the Ita and Machadinho dams, which are now owned by private corporations.

Itaparica: The Rural Workers' Union Takes the Leadership

In the São Francisco Valley in the Northeast, a similar role was played by the construction of the Moxoto and Sobradinho dams in the early 1970s, where no consideration whatsoever was given to social issues, as was the case in the South by Itaipu for those who potentially could be affected by dam construction in the Uruguay River Basin.

The case of Sobradinho was especially tragic.[14] That project required the flooding of 4,214 square kilometers, the expropriation of 26,000 properties, and the forced displacement of approximately 72,000 people. The dam was approved without any provisions for resettlement, enabling the government-owned São Francisco Hydroelectric Company (CHESF) to begin construction at the height of the military dictatorship in 1973; the reservoir began to fill in 1977. Although initially planned as a means to regulate the outflow of the São Francisco River, one year into construction it was decided that the Sobradinho dam would produce electrical power as well. The population was informed of its impending relocation in 1975 and was forced to choose between two alternatives: a bus ticket to São Paulo or resettlement in the drought-prone Ramalho Serra Project, 700 kilometers from their homes (MAB 1989).

Although it is generally accepted that there was no organized resistance movement of affected people in Sobradinho, there are references to the activities of unions and of the CPT in defense of displaced farmers. The main form of resistance, however, seems to have been the struggle of the displaced to obtain access to water since this is a draught-prone region. As has occurred elsewhere, people who had been resettled far from their homes returned there on their own volition to live close to the reservoir. The struggle for access to water became the organized, collective demand for irrigation systems (Sigaud et al. 1987).

As CHESF closed the Sobradinho floodgates, construction work began on the Itaparica dam. It would flood an area of 834 square kilometers and displace 40,000 people. It was not until 1979 that rural union leaders began to organize. Invoking the tragic situation at Sobradinho, where many of the affected people were relocated to semi-arid lands, the burgeoning movement focused on the following demands: land to be traded for land along the lakeshore, access to water in the homes and in the fields, and fair compensation for land improvements.

In August 1979 the first meeting of rural workers took place in Petrolândia, Pernambuco, and in that same year rural unions in several of the affected municipalities formed a union coalition, the Federation of Rural Workers' Unions of the Middle São Francisco River Basin (Pólo Sindical de Trabalhadores Rurais do Submédio São Francisco). In contrast to events in the south (Itaipu and the Uruguay River Basin), where there was a specific organization of people affected by dams, the organizational effort here took the form of inter-union linkages.[15]

The second meeting, in January 1980, brought together more than five thousand people in Petrolândia. The meetings and demonstrations were sometimes met with police violence. In 1984 the unions, with the support of experts, produced a document, "Basic Guidelines for Resettlement," in which they reiterated old demands and introduced new ones. For example, they now demanded plots of twenty-five hectares, six hectares of which would be provided with sprinkler irrigation; administration of the resettlement projects by the workers themselves; better choice of lands; and the need for roads.

But "CHESF only used to talk, nothing else," the activists remember. The lack of response to claims and the delays in implementing the social plan compared to the progress being made in construction of the dam increased tensions and provoked an accelerated radicalization of the movement. Meetings with ministers in Brasília and with the governors of Bahia and Pernambuco did not produce any solutions. In October 1985 during a mass rally six thousand demonstrators occupied the dam construction site. Yet CHESF continued rejecting the major claims and in 1986 announced that it would begin filling the reservoir the next year.

On December 1, 1986, those affected once again occupied the construction site. This time the occupation had significant regional and even national repercussions. The solidarity of members of religious groups, unions, popular organizations, NGOs, and state and federal congressmen made a difference. Work came to a standstill until an agreement was reached: land for land, the equivalent of 2.5 minimum salaries to be paid to those resettled until their new lands were in production, and participation of the displaced in the selection of the lands for resettlement and in resettlement administration.

However, as was the case in Ita and Machadinho, securing an agreement did not end the conflict: "Rural workers won a round, but many problems remain and CHESF is not complying with the terms of the agreement. Thus the struggle continues in order to assure compliance with the agreement, which was a conquest of the workers affected by the Itaparica Hydroelectric Plant" (MAB 1989, 19).[16]

Tucurui

Begun in 1975, the Tucurui hydroelectric plant on the Tocantins River created a reservoir of 2,830 square kilometers, flooded several villages, and displaced more than 5,000 families. Having received no prior information about the project, the families to be displaced were asked to register in 1978 for indemnities from Eletronorte, the state company responsible for the construction work. They were warned that from that date forward they would not be compensated for any improvements on their land or for new crops. Farmers were also assured that they would be resettled in good homes and receive fair compensation.

In 1981 the company declared that the indemnity period was over and offered only minimal compensation to those people affected who chose to leave the area on their own volition rather than be resettled. Those few who were resettled in the Moju River site faced a reality quite different from that promised: fifty hectares of extremely low-quality land (below the regional minimum land area stipulated by land reform legislation for a family farm), without access to water; moreover, the displaced were required to construct their own homes. To make matters worse, the move had been made during the rainy season, at a time when fields could not be prepared for cultivation. Following the pattern set at other sites, the compensation for permanent crops and other land improvements was negligible, based on criteria that had not even been discussed, much less negotiated. As noted by MAB (1989, 10), "The despair of small farmers and settlers increased as they realized that no resources would be provided by Eletronorte to leave the lands that would soon be flooded. They became landless, homeless, and penniless to begin life again in some other place."

At the end of 1981 the Movement of Expropriated People of Tucurui was formally created with the support of the rural workers' unions. They submitted their denunciations and claims to Eletronorte and to other government officials. In September 1982, four hundred people camped for three days outside the company's offices in the city of Tucurui. Their demands included land for land (minimum lots of one hundred hectares), village for village, house for house, and fair compensation for losses. In April 1983, two thousand people gathered at a new campsite and Eletronorte agreed to negotiations. A commission from the movement traveled to Brasília for discussions with the company's CEO. The campsite was maintained until the commission returned bearing news that Eletronorte had agreed to the one-hundred- hectare lots and promised to pay fair compensation for losses due to the delays in being able to cultivate the new lands.

As with other cases, the struggle to enforce the implementation of the agreement was as arduous as that to initiate negotiations. The construction work progressed while fulfillment of pledges to compensate and resettle those displaced languished. The floodgates were closed in September 1984 while the greater part of those affected in the municipalities of Jacunda and Itupiranga had yet to receive their lots. To make matters worse, a large number of those who had received their land plots were surprised to find that their new lands were inside the Parakanã Indian reservation, a territory that had been partially flooded as well. Under such dire conditions and faced with imminent confrontation with the indigenous people of the area, many families abandoned their lots. New demonstrations and occupations led to another round of negotiations to resolve the problem of the Parakanã reserve lands, the level of compensation, financial assistance to help clear lands for new fields, and the demarcation of lots, among other demands.

The problems become even more complicated, since six hundred of the families already resettled were again flooded out of their lands by the rising lake. Eletronorte had made a mistake in the demarcation of lands that would be flooded! Finally, in yet another tragic demonstration of irresponsibility, in which the social dimension of ecological degradation takes on an entirely new dimension, the bank of the reservoir where the majority of the displaced were resettled became infested with hordes of mosquitoes, the magnitude of which was unheard of in the region.

At Tucurui, in contrast to what occurred at other dam sites, the population *downstream* from the dam began to mobilize in opposition to the dam, especially from 1986 onward. The dam was causing degradation in water quality, which in turn affected public health, and led to a drastically reduced fish catch (an important commercial activity in the region as well as source of protein in the diet of the population). The alterations in the flow of the river were also prejudicial to those riverbank inhabitants who farmed along the low watermark. The rural unions from the various municipalities surrounding Tucurui eventually played a major role in the mobilization of these groups.[17] In 1989, five years after the inauguration of the power plant, the Commission of the People Affected by Tucurui Dam was formed, uniting those displaced by the dam as well as those affected along the low watermark of the river.

One might ask why these electric companies not only fail to take social considerations into account but also continually fail to comply with the agreements that they enter into. In their view, the end justifies the means: development requires cheap and abundant energy and thus environment and social issues are simply an obstacle to development, to be dealt with instrumentally. They are so powerful because the dam industry (here including public utilities, contractors, heavy electric equipment suppliers, and so forth) and other vested interests occupy strategic positions in the decision-making process.

The Birth of the National Movement of People Affected by Dams

It was in the mid-1980s, as we have seen, that the organization and combativeness of people affected by dams grew in various regions. The mid-1980s were also a period of growth of the rural movements in general throughout Brazil. In 1985 the Landless Rural Workers' Movement (MST) held its first congress, with fifteen hundred delegates representing twenty of Brazil's twenty-six states. In May, following the example set by the sugarcane cutters in the Zona da Mata in Pernambuco, approximately eighty thousand seasonal rural laborers, principally sugarcane cutters and orange pickers, went on strike in the state of São Paulo during the CONTAG's fourth congress. The sharpening of these conflicts in the countryside brought, little by little, changes in the governance of many rural unions. Union bureaucrats, sometimes controlled by the government or even large rural landowners, began to be replaced by more militant members. Allegiances of rural workers also began to shift, as the Central Workers' Union (CUT) and its National Department of Rural Workers grew in importance, competing with the traditional CONTAG for hegemony in rural syndicalism.

The three cases described above are important not only for their contributions to the birth of the national movement of people affected by dams, but also because they illustrate the interaction that developed in each case between the local movements of people affected by dams and the local-level rural workers' unions. In some cases, as in the Uruguay River Basin, the leaders of the more militant unions were actively involved in the movement of those displaced by dams and, indeed, it was common for a union president to sit on the municipal or regional commission of people affected by dams. In the case of the São Francisco Valley, though, it was the rural unions that directly created the organization and took up the struggle of people affected by dams. With these precedents, it is not surprising that in 1988 CRAB approached the National Department of Rural Workers of the CUT (DNTR/CUT) with a national-level proposal for the advancement of the cause of communities affected by dams.

Drawing on its national presence, DNTR/CUT helped promote several regional meetings during February and March of 1989 that would set the stage for a nationwide event. The First Regional Meeting of Workers Affected by the Xingu Hydroelectric Power Station was held in Altamira, Pará, and delegates were chosen for the national event. The State-wide Meeting on Dams in the State of Amazonas and the Inter-municipal Meeting on Dams, promoted by CPT and by CUT-Rondônia, were also held in March. In the Northeast, the Regional Meeting of People Affected by Dams was held in Igarassu, Pernambuco, and, in addition to NGOs and rural workers' unions, representatives from communities affected by the following dams attended: Castanhão (Ceará), Xingó (Alagoas and Sergipe), Pão-de-Açúcar (Alagoas and Sergipe), Pedra do Cavalo (Bahia), Sobradinho (Bahia), and Itaparica (Pernambuco and Bahia). In the Southeast, there was a meeting of representatives of people affected by dams in the Jequitinhonha Valley (Minas Gerais) and in the Rio Paraíba do Sul Valley (Minas Gerais and Rio de Janeiro). In the south, CRAB called a meeting of representatives from the Regional Commission of People Affected by Dams from the Iguaçu River (CRABI) and from the Dona Francisca dam (Rio Grande do Sul) and Itaipu (Parana), as well as of leaders from the native communities of Kaigang de Itai (Rio Grande do Sul) and Chapecozinho (Santa Catarina).

The First National Meeting of Workers Affected by Dams was held April 19–21, 1989 in Goiânia. In addition to the reports of the experiences at each dam site in each region, the meeting furthered the collective analysis of national electrical power policy and particularly the government's 2010 Plan (Eletrobrás 1987). The latter came to be seen as the principal enemy of all of the communities affected and threatened by the construction of large dams. Moreover, the declaration (the Carta de Goiânia) that emerged from the event embodied the rise of a national movement that would unite local demands by a variety of social groups affected by dams in different regions with proposals that transcended local and specific struggles. These led to a strategy of common action to challenge national electrical power policy.

The demands were several and included the elaboration of a new policy for the electrical power sector with the participation of the working class. Three demands are worth highlighting: first, an immediate solution to the social and environmental problems created by those hydroelectric power plants already constructed, with the requirement that these problems be solved before any new projects were initiated; second, compliance with the existing agreements between affected people and the power companies; third, an immediate end to subsidies for industries favored by the electrical power sector. Other demands included a call for an immediate agrarian reform controlled by workers, the demarcation of lands for native peoples and Afro-Brazilian communities who were descendants of the *quilombos* (fugitive slave communities), as well as a moratorium on the payment of the foreign debt (MAB 1989, 37).

The proceedings of this meeting, including the final statement, allow a closer examination of the issues. Beyond denouncing the situation of affected people and the negative effects of hydroelectric plants, participants at the meeting raised several topics that deserve special mention, including the discussions regarding who the affected are, and the question of tactics, strategies, and forms of organization.

The consensus at the congress broke with the conventional definition used by the electrical power sector, and indeed by some local movements, that *the affected* were only those who had been *flooded out*. Thus, the national movement, though recognizing that "historically those flooded off their lands have been the first to mobilize and, in general, the ones to stay at the front lines . . . the affected are all those who experience direct degradation of their living conditions" (MAB 1989, 34).

In terms of strategies, the movement faced a paradox. On the one hand, it wanted a new energy policy that excluded large dams as an option. On the other, it demanded better compensation and resettlement conditions for the affected people it represented. There was relative consensus that "negotiations and agreements about compensation, resettlement, etc., remedy a consummated fact, but are not the due reparation, as has been the case so far, for the social and environmental costs inflicted" (MAB 1989, 34).

Central to the discussion on strategies and tactics was the affirmation of the grass-roots, community-based nature of the organization; at the same time, the need to build the movement of those affected by dams into a broad mass movement was recognized. The main form of struggle and expression of this movement was to be direct action: mass demonstrations, occupation of sites and offices of government agencies or companies, marches on the highways and in the towns, pickets of dam sites, sit-ins, and so forth.

The consensus reached—to prioritize the grass-roots or community base in each particular local or regional anti-dam movement—recognized that there are different ways of organizing the movement. Fundamentally, either new organizations that focused on this issue were created, such as CRAB, or federations of existing organizations, such as the Central Union of the Middle San Francisco River, were formed. "Each type of organization reflects distinct social and political realities. The discussions at the national meeting did not prioritize either form, but pointed to the need for respecting different realities. Examples were made of CRAB and the Union Coalition [Pólo Sindical]" (MAB 1989, 35).

Finally, responding to the need for national coordination of local and regional movements, the Temporary National Commission of Workers Affected by Dams was formed. This commission was composed of one representative from CUT, one from the indigenous peoples, and a representative from each one of the regions: North, Northeast, Southeast, and South. This commission was put in charge of coordinating the movement and preparing for the next national meeting, during which a constitution would be elaborated for MAB as a national movement.[18]

The Evolution of MAB and Major Policy Issues

The creation of a national movement constituted the recognition that struggles of local and regional movements are incapable of laying the foundation for a comprehensive understanding of the confrontation with the electrical power model and, in a wider sense, the development model within which the hydroelectric power plants are but one element. Indigenous peoples of the Amazon and the great-grandchildren of Italian or German immigrants from the southern part of the country recognized their own struggle in each other's struggle, their own enemies on seeing each other's enemies, and so have come to the conclusion that they should somehow band together and act jointly.

But rhetoric on solidarity is insufficient to create a national movement. Such requires resources, both financial and human, to carry out the many tasks, which are significant in a country as large as Brazil. Furthermore, there was considerable sentiment against developing bureaucratic forms of centralized control, while local and regional movements were wary that a national movement might limit their autonomy. This discussion began to some degree at the national meeting in 1989, as confirmed by a recommendation in the proceedings "to respect different realities."

There were many discussions on how to organize the national movement. In general, the preference was for a federal model, in which each local or regional movement would maintain absolute political, organizational, and financial autonomy. The National Coordinating Body, with an egalitarian representation of each of the regions, would be charged with the task of linking it all together, and a small secretariat, based in São Paulo with just one or two full-time members, would give support to the work of the National Executive and National Coordinating Body.

Throughout the 1990s, MAB has faced the issue of the relationship between the political and organizational needs of the national movement and those of local and regional movements. On the one hand, there was the consensus that the basic support and raison d'être of MAB were the local movements, the affected communities, and their struggles. This is stated repeatedly at meetings and in documents: "There is no national movement without the struggles on the riverbanks and in the valleys, without organizing at the community and regional levels."[19]

On the other hand, the progress of the movement and its growing national and even international recognition require confronting broader issues of energy policy, management of water resources, and the environment, among others. These issues largely transcend not only local concerns but also the traditionally important themes of agrarian reform and national sovereignty. The challenge is all the greater since other popular movements have done little with regard to issues related to energy policy, the environment, and water resources, which are nearly always the object of studies by experts or the concern of environmentalists.

The usefulness of the National Coordinating Body was perceived in different ways by the various regional movements that invested in strengthening it. Aside from assuming the leadership in articulating the first national linkages, CRAB has been the regional organization with the most invested on a national scale,[20] even taking on a new designation over the last few years as MAB-Sul. Nevertheless, throughout the 1990s important differences of opinion emerged regarding the material and human resources that had been devoted to the national organization, while the regional movement was having great difficulty mobilizing and organizing at the base.

During its initial years, the national organization was limited to issuing guidelines for demands and putting limited pressure on the federal government. The existence of the national organization also proved useful in its dealings with other popular movements, particularly in negotiating broad guidelines, as was the case in the national demonstration called the Grito da Terra (the Cry for Land).[21] In its training program, the national leadership placed great stress on promoting mutual learning and the exchange of experiences, for example, organizing trips by local militants from one dam site to another.

More recently, there seems to be a joint effort on the part of local and regional movements to coalesce around a national agenda, strongly focused on national political issues and around the Popular Project for Brazil. Remarkable, too, is the increasing investment of militants from the National Coordinating Body in various regions, including their taking the initiative in promoting local organizations. In this way, the national front is gradually inverting the former local-national paradigm, becoming the base from which local movements—or at least some of them—are being organized. The growing national presence of MAB has also been consolidated through the promotion of courses and training programs that bring together activists from various regions and favor the creation of a national identity as strong as, or even stronger than, the identities of the local movement.

Values and Central Elements of a Political Culture in the Making

The MAB sees itself as part of a larger, broad-based, popular movement on a national scale. The defense of the interests of affected people and the fight against the prevailing environmental and energy policies are conceived as part of a broader struggle of all Brazilian people against an unfair development model that concentrates wealth and land. If partial victories against this model are considered fundamental, equally fundamental is the conviction that such victories must be rooted in local, community-based organizations.

The political culture is structured around a complex combination of elements inherited from the Latin American revolutionary Marxism of the 1960s, the theology of liberation, the democratic movement against the military dictatorship of the 1970s and 1980s, and more recently from ecological and post-Marxist libertarian and identity movements.[22] It is being permanently updated and confronted by ongoing action and debate. The following points attempt to summarize MAB's rich and varied political culture:

- Priority of grass-roots organizations and mobilization over centralized organizations;
- Democratic local organizations, where local activists and members of the movement define organizational guidelines and elect their own leaders and representatives;
- Preference for direct action by the masses, leading to negotiation, over other forms of struggle;[23]
- Autonomy of the movement with regard to the state and political parties;
- Priority to developing a collective political consciousness rather than obtaining favors or concessions;
- Total identification with the wider popular movement and its national organizations, and priority to the unity of the popular movement over alliances with other classes.

The following passage from a recent MAB manual entitled "Who We Are," provides some definitions approved in successive national congresses of the movement.

The National Movement of People Affected by Dams—MAB—is a popular mass movement dedicated to organizing the entire population affected or threatened by dams for the fight against the construction of large dams and in support of their rights, contributing in this way toward the formulation and implementation of a new energy model. We are a popular autonomous movement that arose to challenge the electrical energy sector [and we are] focused on educating and organizing workers affected by dams regardless of state or national borders. We do not discriminate based on a person's color, gender, creed, or political orientation.

The members of the movement are mostly small farmers, landless rural workers (sharecroppers, tenants, day-laborers, squatters, etc. . . .), indigenous peoples, descendents of fugitive slaves, fishermen, and miners (MAB n.d., 5).

The preceding excerpts affirm that the predominant social base of the movement is composed of rural workers, and that the movement is committed to organizing all people affected by dams. At some dams, the movement has also incorporated small businessmen, professionals from small villages, and even medium-sized landowners into its ranks. Nevertheless, the strong identification with rural workers is present throughout its history. It is no wonder then that the alliances with combative rural unions and with the Landless Rural Workers' Movement (MST) in particular have been prioritized. The similarity between the political projects of the MAB and the MST has grown in recent years. The MAB participated in the so-called Popular Project for Brazil and in the Popular Consultation, a linking of popular movements led by the MST. The MAB is also a member of La Vía Campesina, a national and international network of peasants, farmers, and indigenous movements.

Within these coalitions, MAB has had difficulties in making its points of view heard with regard to energy and environmental issues. For example, many leading activists of the MST view the construction of large-scale hydroelectric power plants as necessary for the country's development. Indeed, MAB sometimes plays the difficult role of critic of a developmentalist ideology that still predominates in large segments of Brazilian popular movements. The MAB has faced the same difficulties in its dealings with progressive parties, especially the Workers' Party (PT), whose energy program is dominated by traditional developmentalist ideology, including support for national industry through supposedly low-cost hydroelectric power.[24]

But if as a movement marked by environmental concerns MAB faces difficulties with respect to the popular movement, its relationship to the environmental movement is not always so harmonious either. MAB often confronts predominantly urban, middle-class environmental organizations that are not always sensitive to or capable of understanding the social aspects wrapped up in the energy issue.

International Relations of MAB

For the purpose of this analysis, the international relations of MAB can be broadly classified into financial and political activities. The organization needs to raise funds and other material resources internationally in order to maintain the activities of the movement. It also seeks political support in order to enhance its leverage in the struggle, including pressuring companies and international agencies engaged in the construction of dams in Brazil.

With respect to the first type of international activities, it has long been common practice among popular movements to establish regular contact

with NGOs in key countries in order to obtain financial support. It is beyond the scope of this chapter to discuss the meaning and consequences
of this type of relationship, especially with respect to the risks that may be
incurred for the autonomy of the movement. The various regional and local movements have traditionally sought financial resources through these
mechanisms, each in their own way and following their particular historical
connections.[25] Within the national organization, the same financing mo-
dality and relationships with foreign NGOs has been projected to a national
scale.

With respect to political dealings, there is also a certain tradition of autonomous actions by local or regional movements. For example, the Organization of Rural Workers' Unions of the Middle São Francisco River Basin
was successful in obtaining a hearing before the World Bank's review panel
(a mechanism whereby civil society can challenge the impact of projects financed by the World Bank). This access was achieved in part through direct
organizational relationships with NGOs and others, without having gone
through the National Coordinating Body or its Executive Board. There have
been, however, a growing number of international political initiatives undertaken by the National Coordinating Body and National Executive Board.
The most common activity is participation by organizational representatives in international events on power generation, water resources, the environment, and other topics in order to denounce what has been occurring
with dams in Brazil. Equally important have been relations with NGOs in
key countries that specialize in developing lobbying strategies that target
multilateral agencies or national governments.

Among the more important international political initiatives are affiliation with the Latin American Coordinator of Rural Organizations (CLOC)
and La Vía Campesina; promotion of the First International Meeting of the
People Affected by Dams, in Curitiba in March 1997; participation in the
Consultation Forum of the World Commission on Dams and in the International Committee on Dams, Rivers, and People; and participation in the
Second International Meeting of People Affected by Dams and Their Allies,
in Rasi Salai, Thailand, in 2003.

On various occasions these activities have been questioned, especially
when they do not seem to generate immediate returns, whether of resources
or direct political benefits. Some consider such international activities to be
more appropriate for an NGO rather than a popular movement committed to organizing and direct action. There are also concerns whether such
activities lead to a decline in militancy and are a drain on time and political

energy. A detailed analysis of these varied international relationships at the local, regional, and national levels and their potential contradictions for the movement has yet to be undertaken.[26]

Concluding Thoughts

Almost thirty years after the first action of the people affected by the Itaipu dam, MAB is facing new realities and challenges. After nearly a decade of relative stagnation in the construction of large-scale hydroelectric energy projects, the present decade seems to bode a return to the rhythm of the 1970s, with increasing investment in Brazil's two hydroelectric frontiers: the Amazon and the Uruguay River Basin. It is likely that there will be a new push for small and medium dams, whose effects are not necessarily as small as their electricity production. Unlike the 1970s, however, this new wave of dams and related hydroelectric plants will be built and operated mainly by private companies.[27] How will MAB deal with this new reality?

Having taken root primarily among small family-based farmers, MAB today is probably the popular movement with the greatest awareness of environmental issues. Indeed, it is one of the few popular movements that has been able to articulate the connection between environment and development concerns. Its analysis links the ways wealth is produced and distributed with the ways environmental resources are appropriated and controlled. Will MAB be able to influence the broader popular movement toward a reexamination of the environmental issue?[28] Furthermore, will MAB be prepared to serve as a bridge between the popular movements and progressive environmentalism?

Over the last five years, and particularly since the national meeting at Curitiba in March 2006, MAB has intensified its international initiatives, becoming in the process a well-known movement widely recognized by NGOs and multilateral agencies. However, as some from within the movement itself ask, has this international experience been transmitted to the core of the movement or has it remained an exclusive domain of the leaders who attend international events and sit at the negotiating tables of multilateral agencies? After having struggled for years to find an adequate balance between actions at the local or regional level and the national level, will MAB be capable of further projecting its role on a global scale? Conversely, can MAB afford to abdicate a consistent and systematic international role at a time when investment decisions are so tightly linked to financing by agencies such as the Inter-American Development Bank, the World Bank, the International Financial Corporation, and others? Will the movement, should it move decisively onto the global stage, be limited to representation by external mediators, mainly NGOs and activists who are not in direct contact with the people fighting in the valleys? Will the emerging networks and coalitions among grass-roots movements, such as La Vía Campesina, be able to offer an alternative to NGO networks that ignore class issues and that lack direct connection to the struggles taking place on the ground?

Some fifteen years after the inception of the nationally organized movement for the affected by dams in Brazil, MAB is facing processes of privatization and globalization. To what extent will it be capable of finding partners and forming alliances capable of meeting these challenges? These are among the political questions confronting MAB today.

Notes

Author's note: An earlier version of this chapter was presented at the workshop entitled "Social Movements in the South" at the Center for International Affairs, Harvard University, May 2002. The author is grateful to the discussants as well as to his graduate students and researchers in the Laboratory on State, Labor, Territory, and Nature at the Institute of Urban and Regional Planning and Research, Federal University of Rio de Janeiro.

1. For example, "Involuntary resettlement has been the travel companion of development throughout history and has been indelibly inscribed not only in the evolution of industrialized but also of developing nations" (World Bank Environment Department 1994, i). Or "Forced displacements arise from the need to construct infrastructure for new industries, irrigation, freeways or power supply, or from urban development with hospitals, schools and airports. These projects are undoubtedly necessary. They better the lives of many people, generate employment and better services" (Cernea and McDowell 2000, 11).

2. The World Bank, the Inter-American Development Bank, and other international agencies, as well as national organizations, use the euphemism "involuntary resettlement" to designate the processes of compulsory relocation that constitute the first and main social effect of the creation of large artificial lakes. The symbolic struggle that is now being fought around the language of social processes related to the imposition of large-scale dams offers, in itself, sufficient material for a specific analysis, but it is outside the scope of this chapter. See de Castro and de Andrade 1988; and Sigaud 1986, 1988.

3. At best, the authors of official studies present the resistance as cultural resistance to change, in the tradition of functionalistic development sociology, which was very much in vogue in the 1950s and 1960s, and which, in effect, dismisses the population of developing countries as being irrationally opposed to the eminent rationality of capitalist accumulation.

4. The Itaipu Hydroelectric Plant, with 12,600 megawatts of installed capacity, is the property of the Itaipu Binational Corporation, created through a treaty signed by Brazil and Paraguay. The reservoir covers an area of approximately 1,350 square kilometers, and its construction required the relocation of 42,444 people, of whom 38,445 lived in rural areas.

5. According to Germani 1982, this group was not very strong and was under the leadership of politicians linked to the National Renewal Alliance, the political party of the military then in power.

6. Because of its unique landscape, Seven Falls was a very important tourist site. Despite the name, there were 18 falls, and with a drop of 114 meters; the sound of the falls could be heard from miles away. Seven Falls holds the unenviable record of being the world's largest flooded cascade.

7. Pastor Werner Guchs, the general secretary of the CPT, provided an exemplary statement of the position of many progressive religious leaders who, in the second half of the 1970s and early 1980s, played a central role in the organization of popular movements all across Brazil, especially in the countryside: "Our interest is not in controlling a movement of farmworkers, though we do encourage them. Our aim is to awaken them to the solution of their own problems. It is only at the end of this awakening process that we engage in a physical sense by giving voice to their claims. . . . We do not lead the group, nor do we pull the oars; nor are we heroes who fight in place of the people. We feel everyone must work together as it is collective work, teamwork. And we are here to offer encouragement to the farmer so that he himself can make his own claims, but peacefully. We are prepared for the long journey ahead" (*Rondon-Hoje*, December 5, 1978; cited in Germani 1982, 27).

8. This account draws on the author's personal knowledge of this case, as well as Moraes 1996; Sigaud 1986; de Medeiras 1989; Grzybowski 1987; and Vainer 1990.

9. Along with the sad example at Itaipu, the dramatic experience of the flooding at Passo Real, a smaller dam constructed in the same region, was often mentioned.

10. Professors from a regional college participated alongside progressive members of the Catholic and Lutheran churches in the initial organizational work. According to Moraes 1996, this was the reason that the movement was organized even before the official announcement of the project was made.

11. Fifteen years later, this would become the slogan of the International Day of Action against Dams, for Rivers, and for Life.

12. Such accommodations were more frequent among the people affected by the Ita dam as opposed to the Machadinho dam. For more details on the collective negotiating strategies of the movement and Eletrosul's individual strategy, see Vainer 1990, 1997.

13. This detailed agreement guarantees affected people the right to participate in the valuation process of their lands and of land improvements, and to choose the lands for resettlement, among other rights.

14. The literature on Sobradinho includes Duqué 1984; Sigaud 1986; Sigaud et al. 1987; and Takfagi 1994.

15. This experience is innovative in that it overcame the jurisdictional definitions that separate union organizations in general. Here, the coalition of municipal and lo-

cal unions was constituted not only by rural unions of various municipalities but also by those of two different states, Pernambuco and Bahia. The political culture and the traditional militancy of rural unions in the state of Pernambuco probably explain this unusual situation.

16. The disregard for agreements, especially with respect to creating the conditions for agricultural activities, due to the delay in implementing irrigation projects, led to conditions of genuine anomie in some of the settlements: hopelessness, familial dismemberment, alcoholism. Despite such a scandalous situation, attempts to seek redress through the World Bank, which had supported the project, came to no avail.

17. Not until 2004 were the downstream communities recognized by Eletronorte as affected people. There is now a plan to address their losses.

18. Initially planned for 1990, the national meeting was not held until March 1992.

19. Far from being the manifestation of an extremist militant particularism (Harvey 1997), emphasis on the local and regional movements reflects the concern of avoiding the formation of centralized and centralizing bureaucracies, disconnected from the reality of the communities, local movements, and actual struggles. It also expresses the misgiving that the social movement might be excessively controlled by the wealthier and more structured among the regional and local organizations.

20. This greater investment reflects, at least in part, the superior resources available to CRAB. Many other local and regional movements were leery of CRAB's dominant influence. Gradually, forms of organization and struggle tested in the Uruguay River Basin have been to some extent exported to and adopted by other regions.

21. The Grito da Terra is an annual, nationwide demonstration that involves nearly all of the popular organizations active in the demand for agrarian reform. It is focused on a national agenda of demands that are delivered to the government and to the political parties and announced in public demonstrations. The existence of MAB as a national organization has permitted the inclusion of affected people's claims in this agenda.

22. Differing political cultures can be detected from one local or regional organization to another by examining the priority given to each of the guiding principles in specific situations. Further, as is generally the case, the sophistication of political and ideological discourse varies.

23. Negotiation is seen as the result and as an integral part of the struggle. The struggle and grass-roots mobilization are viewed as the only way to secure fair negotiations.

24. A considerable number of the leaders of MAB are affiliated with the PT. Some have taken part in electoral campaigns, and there are successful cases of elected MAB officials. Thus there are now councilmen, mayors of small towns, and even congressmen whose political militancy began with the fight against the construction of large-scale dams. Even so, MAB has not been successful in its efforts to participate in the elaboration of PT's energy program, which is controlled by experts strongly linked to the electrical energy sector and clearly committed to the construction of large-scale hydroelectric power plants. During the two presidential terms of Luiz Inácio Lula da Silva, which began in 2002, a coalition led by PT has continued with the policy of priva-

tization of the electric sector begun by Fernando Henrique Cardoso. More than forty large dams are under construction or planned, including in Amazonia.

25. Here again MAB-Sul demonstrates its uniqueness. In addition to seeking financial support from foreign NGOs, it relies heavily on its own resources, which are derived from the resettlements themselves and from payment for its service activities for which it is remunerated by the companies.

26. But see Vieira 2001; and Vainer 2001.

27. Privatization of the electric sector in Brazil, following the World Bank model, created opportunities for national and international corporations to build new hydroelectric plants in the Uruguay River Basin. Since 2002, even as conflicts between affected communities and dam builders increased, the government approved numerous new projects: Barra Grande, Campos Novos, Foz do Chapeco, and Pai Quere, among others. On the effects of privatization, see Vainer 1999.

28. In the national meeting held in Curitiba in March 2006, MAB decided to challenge the privatization of the electrical sector by launching a campaign denouncing the increase of the price of electricity and demanding lower rates for consumers. It hopes in this way to involve the urban poor in the energy issue and build alliances with urban social movements.

References

Cernea, Michael M., and Christopher McDowell. 2000. *Risks and Reconstruction: Experiences of Resettlers and Refugees*. Washington, D.C.: World Bank.

de Castro, Eduardo Viveiros, and Lúcia M. M. de Andrade. 1988. "Hidrelétricas do Xingu: O estado contra as sociedades indígenas." In *As hidrelétricas do Xingu e os povos indígenas*, edited by Leinad Ayer O. Santos and Lúcia M. M. de Andrade, 7–24. São Paulo: Comissão Pró-Índio de São Paulo.

de Medeiros, Leonilde Sérvolo. 1989. *História dos movimentos sociais no campo*. Rio de Janeiro: FASE.

Duqué, G. 1984. "Experiência de Sobradinho: Problemas fundiários colocados pelas grandes barragens." *Cadernos do CEAS* (Salvador) 91.

Eletrobrás. 1987. "Plano Nacional de Energia Elétrica 1987/2010: Relatório geral." Rio de Janeiro: Ministério das Minas e Energia/Centrais Elétricas Brasileiras S.A.

Germani, Guiomar. 1982. *Os Expropriados de Itaipu: O conflito; Itaipu x colonos*. Working Papers 3. Porto Alegre: PROPUR, Universidade Federal do Rio Grande do Sul.

Grzybowski, Cândido. 1987. *Caminhos e descaminhos dos movimentos sociais no campo*. Petrópolis: Vozes.

Harvey, David. 1997. *Justice, Nature, and Geography of Difference*. Oxford: Blackwell Publishers.

MAB (Movimento dos Atingidos por Barragens). N.d. *MAB: Uma história de lutas, desafios e conquistas*.

———. 1989. "Yes to Land, No to Dams." Publication from the First National Meeting of Workers Affected by Dams.

Moraes, Maria Stela. 1996. "No rastro das águas: Organização, liderança e represen-tatividade dos atingidos por barragens." In *Política, protesto e cidadania no campo: As lutas sociais dos colonos e dos trabalhadores rurais no Rio Grande do Sul*, edited by Zander Navarro, 62–105. Porto Alegre: Editora da Universidade/Universidade Federal do Rio Grande do Sul.

Sigaud, Lygia. 1986. *Efeitos sociais de grandes projetos hidrelétricos: As barragens de Sobradinho e Machadinho.* Rio de Janeiro: Programa de Pós-Graduação em An-tropologia Social, Museu Nacional, Universidade Federal do Rio de Janeiro (Comu-nicação 9). Mimeo.

Sigaud, Lygia, Ana Luiza Martins-Costa, and Ana Maria Daou. 1987. "Expropriação do campesinato e concentração de terras em Sobradinho: Uma contribuição à análise dos efeitos da política energética do Estado." In *Ciências Sociais Hoje.* São Paulo: ANPOCS/Vértice/Editoria Revista dos Tribunais.

Soares, Daniella Feteira. 1998. *A cidade do lago: São João Marcos e o Reservatório de Ribeirão da Lages.* Rio de Janeiro: IGEO/Universidade Federal do Rio de Janeiro.

———. 2001. *Paisagem e Memória: Dos Saltos de Sete Quedas ao lago de Itaipu.* Rio de Janeiro: Instituto de Pesquisa e Planejamento Urbano e Regional/Universidade Federal do Rio de Janeiro.

Takfagi, Maria Cristina. 1994. *Grandes projetos hidrelétricos e território: Um estudo comparativo de Paulo Afonso e Sobradinho.* Rio de Janeiro: Instituto de Pesquisa e Planejamento Urbano e Regional/Universidade Federal do Rio de Janeiro.

Vainer, Carlos B. 1990. "Implantación de grandes represas hidroelétricas, movimien-tos forzados y conflictos sociales: Nota sobre la experiencia brasileña." In *Efectos demográficos de grandes proyectos de desarrollo*, edited by J. Canales, 103–22. San Jose, Costa Rica: Centro Latinoamericana de Demografía/Fondo de Población de las Naciones Unidas.

———. 1997. "Como temos lutado e como continuaremos lutando contra as barragens." Paper presented at the Encontro Internacional de Povos Atingidos por Barragens, Curitiba, Brazil, March.

———. 1999. "Processos de Decisão, Controle Social e Privatização do Setor Elétrico (Os impactos sociais e ambientais da reestruturação setorial)." Paper presented to the Second World Commission on Dams entitled "Regional Consultation, Large Dams, and Their Alternatives in Latin America: Experiences and Lessons Learned," São Paulo, August 12–13.

———. 2001. "Building Transnational Civil Society: Notes from the Periphery." Paper presented to the Building Transnational Civil Society conference, Harvard Univer-sity.

Vieira, Flávia Braga. 2001. *Do Confronto nos Vales aos Fóruns Globais: Um estudo de caso sobre a participação MAB na Comissão Mundial de Barragens.* Rio de Janeiro: Instituto de Filosofia e Ciências Sociais/Universidade Federal do Rio de Janeiro.

World Bank Environment Department. 1994. *Resettlement and Development: The Bankwide Review of Projects Involving Involuntary Resettlement 1986–1993.* Wash-ington D.C.: World Bank.

9

The Impact of Mining
on Peruvian Peasant Communities

The Role of CONACAMI

MIGUEL PALACÍN

The National Confederation of Communities Affected by Mining of Peru (CONACAMI) is a very young organization, but it has already become quite influential. Founded in 2000, it is organized in 1,650 communities in 18 of Peru's 25 regions and it has mobilized up to one million people at a time. This social movement is the product of the huge protests that have accompanied the so-called mining boom since the 1990s. This chapter focuses on the impact of mining on Peru's people and communities and the reasons why CONACAMI resists a model of development based principally on the exploitation of mining resources.

Peru is one of the most "megadiverse" countries in the world in terms of biology, culture, and natural resource endowments. Peru's 11 ecological regions, which include 84 of the 117 globally recognized ecological zones, are inhabited by 72 ethnic groups, each with its own language and form of organization, spirituality, and economy. These tend to share, however, a similar worldview—one that conceives of man as living in harmony with nature. To sustain this harmonic relation, we draw on our collective knowledge of the flora and fauna to protect nature, not pillage her, for our livelihoods depend upon nature and biodiversity. In this way, Peru's 25,000 species of flora, including its thousands of potato and yam varieties, its 106 hydrographic basins, its fertile soils, and its forest reserves are inextricably linked to the welfare of its Amazonian and Andean indigenous communities.[1]

Peru's indigenous population of 9 million comprises 30 percent of the total population of the country, organized into 5,670 officially recognized Andean communities and 1,710 Amazonian ones. We have a long tradition of living with nature and struggling to defend her. The Andean mountains are the ancestral home for much of Peru's indigenous Quechua and Aymara as well as its mestizo population. The *pacha mama* (Mother Earth) and Apu (god of the Andes) also dwelt there until the mining companies arrived and destroyed the mountains, leaving only immense open pits, for beneath this ecological and cultural diversity the Andes contain vast, nonrenewable, mineral resources.

Cerro de Pasco, my home region in central highland Peru, has been a mining center since the colonial period and it is here that the popular struggle against mining was born several decades ago. This region was subject to pollution and environmental damage for many years attributable to the Cerro de Pasco Corporation. In 1974 this corporation was acquired by the government and now operates as Centromin. The open pit of this mine measures one kilometer wide by one-and-a-half kilometers long, and it is one kilometer deep. It yields 10,000 metric tons of ore daily, but there are now much larger mining operations.

In 2004, the Antamina mine extracted an average of 340,000 metric tons of material daily (BHP Biliton 2006), while the largest gold producer in South America, the Yanacocha complex, had a mining rate (ore and waste) of 530,000 metric tons per day (InfoMine 2006). The new rich veins are located there, in the northern department of Cajamarca. Fifteen of Peru's twenty-four regions have active mines: 148 major metal mines and 207 nonmetallic mines. In addition, there are 165 plants engaged in metallic and nonmetallic ore processing. Sixteen of the world's twenty largest mining corporations operate in Peru and their greed for profit is responsible for the consequences described below.

The year 1993 was a critical one for Peru: the mining boom started; a new constitution was adopted; a new government took office; and the government of Alberto Fujimori adopted a number of structural adjustment economic policies. By that year, four million hectares of land had been ceded to mining concessions. Seven years later, in 2000, that figure had grown to more than 25 million hectares. That is when CONACAMI was founded.

This organization, which is opposed to the government's policy of indiscriminately granting mining concessions, was initially successful in pressuring for a reduction in the total area covered by mining concessions, reducing the total to 8 million hectares. However, under the subsequent government of Alejandro Toledo, the area in mining concessions increased again to 10 million hectares in December 2005 and 13 million hectares by early 2006. Supposedly, that figure represents just 10 percent of the available mining reserves. Can you imagine what Peru would look like if all the land containing available reserves were turned into open pits like those I previously described?

In Peru mining exploitation equates with environmental destruction. Some 3,200 communities have suffered the consequences of investments in mining. Entire towns, national parks, nature reserves, and the headwaters of river basins have been affected by the development of large-scale mining. This is because mining concessions are granted by bureaucrats, who deal these out across their desks as though the country were a gaming table and the concessions were cards to be divvied up and passed out. The smallest concessions comprise 100 hectares and the largest, 30,000 hectares. And how many of these 30,000 hectare concessions can a company acquire? As many as it can afford to buy.

Mining companies have always needed fairly large tracks of land as concessions for exploration and exploitation. Today, with the new open-pit mining technology, they need even more space to store excavated deposits, to create encampments and washing fields, and to build access roads and processing installations. Consequently, mining companies occupy extensive areas of Peru, displacing communities and contaminating the earth. Livestock has been poisoned, farming damaged, biodiversity threatened, and above all, the identity and culture of the people are being harmed.[2]

The expansion of mining in Peru took place in concert with the implementation of structural adjustment policies, which changed the national development model. National development was subsequently to be based on the extraction of natural resources, and the country's principal source of income was to be derived from mineral exploitation. Those "structural adjustments" are the direct cause of the current problems of the country's communities.

Mining currently accounts for 56 percent of Peru's $17 billion in total annual exports (Banco Central 2005). Those who sell the minerals are not Peruvian, and moreover, mining concessionaires do not pay for the minerals they extract. They are only required to pay taxes that at most amount to less than 1 percent of their export income. These privileged concessionaires who have valid contracts (albeit entered into with corrupt governments) pay nothing for the minerals themselves except the cost of their extraction.

Those of us who oppose this process are considered anti-development, subversives, and even terrorists. Protest in Peru has been criminalized. For example, if more than ten people gather on the street it is considered an obstruction of roads and highways, with those involved subject to arrest and imprisonment. We face a very hard and difficult task. Four of our brethren have already been assassinated, 740 of our leaders have been tried for "crimes," and 150, including myself, have been sentenced. But such persecution has not diminished the will of our communities to fight for our rights or else I would not be here to tell you our story. People continue to protest because their livelihoods are threatened, along with the natural environment, including water supplies, the most basic requirement for life itself.

Mining requires huge quantities of water, 3 cubic meters to process 1 ton of ore. If the Antamina yields 340,000 tons of ore per day and the Yanacocha yields almost 600,000 tons, how many cubic meters of water are wasted daily? Entire watersheds have been disappearing. The transport of mined minerals to the seaport is accomplished via a slurry pipeline 300 kilometers long; it uses 70 cubic meters of water per second as a transport fluid. Water is being diverted from other watersheds into the transport pipeline, where it is mixed with high concentrations of minerals and chemicals (including cyanide) used to process the minerals. All of this contaminated water, including that draining from trucks capable of carrying more than 200 tons of ore, is eventually flushed into the environment, contaminating the aquifer. The mining companies also need to construct hydroelectric plants for their operations, which also require massive volumes of water. Hence mining activity needs to be located near water sources, and the major conflicts now are over the use and conservation of water.

The organization known as CONACAMI has had some successes in saying "no" to mining, for example, the successful struggle of the people of Tambogrande, in northern Peru near the border with Ecuador. Tambogrande is well known for producing 40 percent of the limes consumed in Peru. When gold was discovered, the community launched a successful campaign to curtail its exploitation under the slogan "Without limes there is no ceviche." In June 2002 the population of Tambogrande voted on a proposed mining concession to a division of the Canadian company Manhattan Minerals Corporation, and a resounding 98 percent of the voters rejected the proposed mining operations. However, the state's reaction to the referendum was that "it was not a legal mechanism provided for under the applicable legislative framework for approval or rejection of a mining project" (Rousseau and Meloche 2002). Nonetheless, there is no mining in Tambogrande today and there will be no mining.

The success of CONACAMI in Tambogrande has been replicated elsewhere. In Huancabamba, in the north of the country, the struggle was with the Majaz Company, a U.S. and British joint venture.[3] This concession was located on a high plateau that is the source of two important watersheds that provide irrigation for the entire Piura Valley. The company's operations were destroying the watersheds and local agriculture, and polluting the environment. With the help of CONACAMI, peasants in the region successfully organized to demand the company's departure from the region.

There are also the cases of Yanacocha and Cerro Quilish in the department of Cajamarca. Yanacocha, the largest gold mine in South America, is operated by the Denver-based Newmont Mining Company, the world's largest gold mining firm. On June 2, 2000, a mercury spill contaminated Choropampa and two neighboring towns. The incident resulted in major litigation on behalf of the numerous peasant families affected by this dangerous contamination of their environment. The litigation was initiated not in Peru, but in the United States.

The Newmont Mining Company had plans at the time to expand its operations to the Cerro Quilish region adjacent to Yanacocha. It was said that Cerro Quilish could yield anywhere between 3.7 million and 10 million ounces of gold.[4] To the mining companies that meant it had to be dug up; but to the Cajamarquinos, Cerro Quilish is a sacred place, one that has to be protected. It is also the source of all of the water consumed by the population of the city of Cajamarca. A struggle ensued over the water rights, but nonetheless, the state authorized the use of Cerro Quilish for mineral exploitation. A fifteen-day demonstration that paralyzed the city of Cajamarca succeeded in reversing this decision, and in November 2004 the Newmont Company abandoned its plans for expansion.

We are currently prosecuting a case before the Inter-American Human Rights Commission on behalf of the population of San Mateo de Huanchor in the department of Lima. The issue here is related to problems attributable to tailing deposits. Mining residues have contaminated some three hundred thousand residents with high levels of lead. In our legal case, we charge that the government of Peru "is responsible for the violation of the fundamental individual and collective rights of the members of the Community of San Mateo de Huanchor for the effects sustained by the members of the community as a result of the environmental pollution produced by a field of toxic waste sludge next to the community."[5] We have succeeded in overcoming procedural issues raised by the government and are awaiting a trial and decision on the merits. Populations in many other regions are also suffering from lead contamination.

Over twenty years ago, BHP Billiton, a large Australian mining company, displaced five communities from ten thousand hectares. After a long struggle, CONACAMI won several legal battles that finally produced tangible results. The communities obtained compensation and some land was returned to them as well. The company now contributes 3 percent of its annual income for the benefit of the people, providing the provinces where it operates with U.S. $1.4 million and local communities with U.S. $300,000 in compensation annually. However, the BHP's concessions are being sold and it is unclear what will happen in the future.

With our help, other communities have also succeeded in obtaining compensation for damages or in expelling the mining companies. Kintae, owned by Anglo-American PLC, was the first mining company with whom we managed to reach an agreement and it has suspended operations. These are some of the many projects with which we have been involved where mining is detrimental to public health and the environment.

The state has authorized the extension of many mining contracts, but the people are mobilized and the struggle is widespread. We are now facing a political confrontation with the state. The state not only seeks to make all types of protests illegal but has also designated CONACAMI as an illegal association. As of December 2005, six hundred of CONACAMI's activists have been imprisoned. The organization has also been the subject of a terrible disinformation campaign. It is currently fighting against these measures and emphatically denouncing the violation of its members' human rights.

Nonetheless, the organization continues to grow and mature. It has started to deal with issues that go beyond just compensation to those affected by mining operations. It is offering new proposals with respect to legal due process in the allocation of new mining concessions and creating new visions of development based on guaranteeing peasant and indigenous communities' access to their natural resources.

CONACAMI does not simply want a new water resource or mining law. Rather, it wants to strengthen communities as envisioned in the International Labor Organization's Convention 169, according to which indigenous communities have the right to select their own development models, models frequently based on activities other than exploitation of natural resources. It wants guaranteed access to our natural resources and to strengthen the capacities of local communities for improved resource use and the maintenance of biodiversity. It wants water to be respected as the source of life. Finally, more than anything else, it wants our communities to be treated with respect.

Notes

Author's note: The transcript of this conference presentation was translated by Guillermo Alfonso Calvo-Mahe. The editors have also incorporated material from the author's PowerPoint presentation.

1. See "Megadiversidad del Perú," www.peruecologico.com.pe, accessed June 9, 2007.

2. Editors' note: For more detail on the environmental effects of open-pit mining, see http://www.minesandcommunities.org./index.htm, accessed January 21, 2008.

3. Translator's note: On this case, see Nicaragua Solidarity Network 2005.

4. Translator's note: See Hecht 2005.

5. Translator's note: *Community of San Mateo de Huanchor and Its members v. Peru*, Case 504/03, Report No. 69/04, Inter-Am. C.H.R., OEA/Ser.L/V/II.122 Doc. 5 rev. 1 at 487 (2004).

References

Banco Central de Reserva del Perú. 2005. *Series Estadísticas 2005.* http://www.bcrp. gob.pe/bcr/index.php, accessed September 20, 2006.

BHP Biliton. 2006. *Production Report for the Quarter Ended 30 June 2006.* http:// www.bhpbilliton.com/bbContentRepository/Reports/060725BHPBProdRptQE30 Jun06.pdf, accessed September 22, 2006.

Hecht, Peter. 2005. "Peasants in Peru Near Showdown on Mercury Spill." *Miami Herald*, March 5. http://www.newsdesk.org/archives/003306.html, accessed June 13, 2007.

InfoMine. 2006. http://www.infomine.com/minesite/minesite.asp?site=yanacocha, accessed September 22, 2006.

Nicaragua Solidarity Network of Greater New York. 2005. "Two Dead at Mining Camp." *Weekly News Update on the Americas* 810, August 7. http://tania.blythe-systems.com/pipermail/nytr/Week-of-Mon-20050808/021266.html, accessed September 20, 2006.

Rousseau, Stéphanie, and François Meloche 2002. *Gold and Land: Democratic Development at Stake; Report of the Observation Mission of the Tambogrande Municipal Consultation Process in Peru.* Montreal: International Centre for Human Rights and Democratic Development. http://www.dd-rd.ca/site/publications/index.php?lang= en&subsection=catalogue&id=1345, accessed September 22, 2006.

10

When Social Movement Proposals Become Policy

Experiments in Sustainable Development in the Brazilian Amazon

MARY ALLEGRETTI AND MARIANNE SCHMINK

Thirty years ago, at the height of Brazil's military government's ambitious development policies for the Amazon, few people could have imagined the current advances in control over illegal logging and deforestation, creation of extensive protected areas, and numerous sustainable development projects focused on indigenous peoples and other rural communities. This new landscape can be credited largely to the pressures of grass-roots social movements, NGOs, and the alliances they constructed with researchers, political parties, international organizations, and the government.

This chapter analyzes two examples of innovative social movement development proposals that were adopted as public policy in Brazilian Amazonia. In the late 1980s and early 1990s, the rubber tappers movement that originated in the western state of Acre successfully pressured the government to create a new land tenure category, the extractive reserves, a public area oriented to the sustainable use of natural resources under the management of traditional populations (Allegretti 2002). In 1999–2000, a movement of agricultural colonists on the Transamazon highway developed the Proambiente, a program of land use planning and environmental services compensation for small producers, which was adopted as official government policy in 2003.

However, the social movements have faced an uphill battle for effective implementation of these programs. Despite continued participation in decision making, the programs now depend upon government action and resources, which have been slow to come due to vested interests and resistance to change. The "scaling up" of these innovative, place-based alternative development proposals also has created new vulnerabilities and new political and technical challenges for the social movements themselves.

During the past two decades, a multitude of grass-roots initiatives have challenged the dominant paradigm, constituting a "quiet revolution" in Amazonian development and providing a framework for the development of "productive conservation" practices that support resident livelihoods while promoting conservation of the natural resource base on which they depend (Hall 1997). This is a radical departure from the top-down government-sponsored Amazonian development strategies of the 1960s and 1970s that focused on mining, ranching, and colonization, and that equated progress with deforestation (Hall 1997; Hecht and Cockburn 1989; Schmink and Wood 1992). By the mid-1980s, both domestic and global environmental criticism of these development schemes converged with condemnation from human rights activists who noted that in addition to the negative ecological effects of these planned projects, such projects also blatantly disregarded the rights of indigenous and traditional peoples living in the Amazon Basin. This convergence of environmental and social concerns, along with growing resistance movements among local Amazonian groups, resulted in a search for development alternatives and placed checks on the developmentalist model linked to deforestation and social conflict (Allegretti 2002; Anderson 1990; Arnt 1994; Clusener-Godt and Sachs 1995; Hall 1997; Keck 1995; Campos and Nepstad 2006; Schmink and Wood 1992; Schneider et al. 2000).

Despite a long history of rebellion, Amazonian rural communities remained largely invisible until the expansion of government-sponsored development projects into the region in the 1970s. This chapter analyzes the factors that led to the emergence of these successful bottom-up policy proposals, linking environmental concerns, social justice, and land rights. It also addresses the dilemmas and limitations of scaling up alternative grass-roots development policies within a state power structure that is resistant to change and dominated by agro-business interests.

The Extractive Reserves

The rubber tappers' movement emerged in the western Amazonian state of Acre in the 1970s, as these previously isolated forest workers faced expulsion from their traditional areas by investors from southern Brazil, attracted by government-sponsored programs to expand the national economy into the relatively "empty" spaces of the Amazon region. The non-indigenous residents dispersed throughout Amazonia's forests can be attributed to two massive migrations from northeastern Brazil from 1870 to 1920 to supply rubber for the expanding global automobile industry (Bakx 1988; Weinstein 1983), and again from 1942 to 1945 to extract rubber in support of the allied war efforts (Martinello 1988). After the war, the Brazilian government continued to provide some support for natural rubber extraction in response to pressures from Amazonian economic elites and large industrial interests in southern Brazil. However, later policies subsidized synthetic rubber production and reduced barriers to lower-priced Asian plantation imports, undermining the Amazonian rubber industry (Costa Sobrinho 1992; Dean 1987, 108–27; Martinello 1988, 285–312; Rêgo 2002, 369–73). Some tappers abandoned the forest, and others continued their extractive activities alongside expanded subsistence production. Over several decades, these autonomous forest producers—invisible to the larger society and to the state—developed a distinct cultural identity, tied to the forest and to the rubber tapper culture, which would later provide the basis for their alternative policy proposals (Allegretti 2002; Schwartzman 1991).

The isolation and more personalized, though not necessarily friendly, relations between tappers and the local rubber concessionaire "patron" gave way in the 1970s to difficult, violent struggles against outside investors, primarily ranchers, with no appreciation for the forest and its people. Tappers, now facing an enemy who represented the polar opposite of their traditional culture, learned to defend themselves using nonviolent confrontations to stop forest clearing (Allegretti 2002; Esteves 1999). They also formed broad political alliances, and with initial support of the Catholic Church, rural labor unions, and the National Confederation of Agricultural Workers (CONTAG) in the 1970s, they began to organize and articulate their rights to land and to their own cultural heritage (Allegretti 2002; Bakx 1988; Barbosa 2000; Barp and Barp 2002; Costa Sobrinho 1992; Esteves 1999).

During the 1980s, Brazil's gradual political democratization coincided with growing mobilization of resistance movements across Amazonia (Schmink and Wood 1992, 95–135). The rubber tappers' movement emerged as the most innovative force among these movements. One part of the rubber tappers' strategy was to invert the modernist, *paulista* discourse about "empty lands" and "technological backwardness" by promoting themselves as "forest people" whose valuable forest knowledge made the standing forest a viable development alternative (Allegretti 2002; Almeida 2004; Esteves 1999, 130–79). One of their main tactics was *empates*—in which they would collectively stand in the way of workers clearing forested areas for ranches. This strategy generated growing sympathy from national and international environmental groups that began to support the movement with resources and information. These alliances also helped project innovative tapper proposals to a broader audience (Allegretti 2002; Hall 1997, 91–133; Keck 1995; Schmink and Wood 1992; Schwartzman 1991) to the extent that the tapper leader Chico Mendes gained international fame when he was awarded several global environmental prizes and gave depositions in hearings before the World Bank and the Inter-American Development Bank.

The National Council of Rubber Tappers (CNS), which was formed in 1985, with the help and support of key allies in Brazil and elsewhere, served as the means to articulate the rubber tappers' proposal for land reform measures appropriate to the needs and interests of forest people. Incrementally, the rubber tappers' need to preserve the forest in order to ensure their own survival led the CNS to fight for the creation of extractive reserves (Allegretti 2002). Their first great difficulty was to explain the particular characteristics of their livelihoods and cultures to a society and state that believed that the rubber tappers had faded away when Brazil's natural rubber production lost the world market to Asian producers at the beginning of the twentieth century. They had to convince the land reform agencies that individual family agricultural plots were too small for forest production, and environmental agencies that, rather than being expelled from rural areas, forest people could be resident stewards in protected areas. The proposal for extractive reserves—publicly owned areas conceded for use by communities with a tradition of forest-based livelihoods—was inspired by the model of indigenous territories and sought both to protect forest resources and to provide for the well-being of these "traditional" peoples.

In 1987, the National Institute for Colonization and Agrarian Reform (INCRA) created the first Agro-Extractive Settlement Project in the locale where the well-known leader Chico Mendes and his family lived. The measure, intended to halt pressures from land speculators, generated a violent reaction on the part of cattle ranchers, who assassinated Chico Mendes in December 1988. The widespread international outrage at his death increased the pressures on the Brazilian government to respond to the rubber tappers' claims. In 1990 a presidential decree created the extractive reserves as a special category of land reform and environmental protection under the institutional responsibility of the Brazilian Institute of the Environment and Renewable Resources (IBAMA).

The concept of extractive reserves was a significant victory for the rubber tappers' movement, providing an alternative form of land tenure that, for the first time, recognized the rights of traditional populations, their forms of land use and settlement patterns, their traditional knowledge of forest resources, and their potential role in conservation strategies. Unlike other land reform programs that divided up blocks of land into small family properties, the extractive reserves remained intact state lands but were conceded for thirty years to the residents. Families held use rights over large areas (250–300 hectares) and continued to exploit their dispersed forest resources in sustainable ways, as well as agreeing to limits on hunting, fishing, logging, and forest clearing. The contractual limitations on resource use by residents made the extractive reserves a new component of the mosaic of conservation strategies in Brazil's new socioenvironmental environment, later codified in new legislation that created the National System of Conservation Units in 2000.

These hybrid "sustainable use conservation" or "ecological agrarian reform" units expanded the lexicon of agrarian reform in Brazilian Amazonia, significantly affecting the region's rural landscape (Cardoso 2002; Ruiz-Pérez et al. 2005). As the CNS expanded its organizing efforts around the Amazon region, workers who were engaged in forest extraction (such as babassu nuts in Maranhão, palm fruits in Pará) and were supported by various allies, pressured for new extractive reserve areas. In 1992 the Ministry of the Environment created the National Center for the Sustainable Development of Traditional Populations inside IBAMA to administer the extractive reserves, and the CNS was able to raise financial and technical support from international organizations and, more recently, from states governments in Acre, Amapa, and Amazonas for innovative community-based development initiatives inside the reserves (Allegretti 2002; IAG 2002). From 1990 to 2007 eighty-one federal and state extractive reserves and sustainable development reserves were created, covering 21 million hectares (4.3 percent of the Brazilian Amazon) and benefiting around two hundred thousand people (ISA 2007; CNS 2005). Variations on the concept of extractive reserves were adopted around the globe, such as in the Maya Biosphere Reserve in the Guatemalan region of Petén, for example. During the 1990s, there was a short-lived boom in the literature on extractive reserves (Ehringhaus 2005).

In Acre, the rubber tappers' movement also was successful in creating a favorable state-level policy environment for its alternative development proposals (Kainer et al. 2003). Emerging from a broad base of social movements, including the organized rubber tappers' movement, the Workers' Party (PT) was formed in 1980 (Fernandes 1999, 64, 86). Beginning with modest local wins, by 1992 the PT had consolidated a political niche with the election of the charismatic Marina Silva—whose parents were rubber tappers—to the Senate, and of Jorge Viana, a young forester, as prefect of the capital, Rio Branco. In 1998, he was elected governor of Acre and his brother, Tião Viana, was elected to the Senate. Both brothers were successfully reelected for second terms, through 2006, and Marina Silva was named the Brazilian minister of the environment in 2003.

Proambiente

The Proambiente program arose fifteen years after the genesis of the proposal for extractive reserves, originating among groups of colonist farmers settled along the Transamazon highway in the eastern Amazonian state of Pará (Campos 2006; Campos and Nepstad 2006; Mattos et al. 2001). Unlike the rubber tappers of Acre, these farmers did not fit the profile of traditional, forest-dwelling peoples who had cemented their reputation as conservation allies in the 1980s and 1990s. On the contrary, they were typically viewed as environmental villains due to their practice of slash-and-burn agriculture. However, their strategies evolved within the growing convergence in Brazil on a "socioenvironmental" approach that united local populations, international and national environmental groups, and human rights advocates, an approach for which the struggle for the extractive reserves had helped pave the way (Becker 1990). The movement of the colonist farmers benefited from the experience of the CNS before it, as well as the favorable international climate fostered by the Rio Conference on Environment and Development in 1992, and the resources of the Pilot Program for the Protection of the Brazilian Rain Forest, which emerged from that meeting and which provided crucial funds to support experimentation with innovative resource use by local Amazonian communities.

In 1999, a group of colonists representing the Movement for Development of the Transamazon and Xingu (MDTX) visited Brazil's Ministry of the Environment and presented a surprising proposal: they wanted to protect one of the last large forest reserves in the Amazon, the so-called Middle Lands (Terra do Meio), and requested support for projects that would help them to develop more environmentally sound agricultural practices without the use of fire. These proposals led to the creation of a mosaic of protected areas of more than 5 million hectares, initially proposed in 2001 but implemented only in 2005 after another assassination—of Dorothy Stang, a nun who had lived for decades in the region, supporting rural communities—again led to international pressure on the Brazilian government.

The Transamazon farmers had migrated to the region in the 1970s, attracted by the military government's colonization schemes to defuse land reform tensions in southern Brazil. They were largely abandoned soon after, as government policies quickly shifted to support for large corporate investors (Wood and Schmink 1978; Schmink and Wood 1992). A long history of failed government programs tied to specific crops, supported by the credit program of the Constitutional Fund for Financing of the North (FNO), had induced expansion of cattle, increased deforestation, and left many small producers deeply in debt (Toni 1999). A generation after INCRA's initial settlement of colonists on the Transamazon, the rural workers' organizations were concerned with strategies to address their long-term production needs through more appropriate credit, tied to effective technical assistance suited to their conditions. As in other parts of the region, the movement initially emerged with support from the Catholic Church, and later from the rural labor unions. Colonists later formed the MDTX, which now represents twenty thousand farm families grouped in 113 rural and urban organizations (Campos and Nepstad 2006).

These unprecedented demands by a social movement for the creation of the mosaic of protected areas, and for new forms of credit, led to even more ambitious proposals. In alliance with other social groups, the farmers proposed an innovative new public policy to compensate small farmers in the Amazon for environmental services, called Proambiente, the Program for the Socioenvironmental Development of Family Production.

The first Proambiente proposal emerged from discussions among the state-level rural workers' federations at the first "Cry of the Amazon" (Grito da Amazônia) mobilization in May of 2000 (Proambiente 2003). The farmers focused primarily on the failures of the FNO rural credit program of the 1990s, which had been a significant driver of deforestation and inappropriate land use (Toni 1999). Over the next two years, they mobilized to pressure state and federal governments to create special credit lines (FNO Special). This success led to more complex analyses of agricultural practices, their environmental effects, and the difficulty of shifting to more appropriate production systems without a specific set of policies to support this goal.

The state-level federations of agricultural workers' unions worked with the Brazilian NGOs, the Amazonian Institute for Environmental Research (IPAM), and the Federation of Agencies for Social and Educational Assistance (FASE), which provided technical support to the process of developing a formal structure to oversee the Proambiente program and helped to seek funding. Other allies included the CNS, the National Fishermen's Movement, the Brazilian Indigenous Peoples Coordinating Organization, and the Amazonian Work Group, the latter a network of more than four hundred Amazonian grass-roots and non-governmental organizations. They created a formal Management Council to oversee ten pilot "poles" and held meetings in every state to discuss the proposal. In 2001 they signed the first formal agreement with the Ministry of the Environment to support the program, which expanded through 2002 until it was institutionalized as part of the Brazilian federal government program in 2003 and incorporated formally into the federal budget for the period 2004–7.

Proambiente was an innovative program that proposed to combine participatory land use planning at regional, local, community, and household levels; farmer-led technical assistance; implementation, testing, certification, and monitoring of alternative agro-ecological practices; and compensation for environmental services (Mattos et al. 2001; Tura and Mattos 2002). This holistic approach was a response to the frustration of farmers with previous government programs that tended to focus on single commodities, with technical support limited to filling out necessary paperwork for farm loans.

The Proambiente proposal recognized both the additional costs that would be incurred by farmers in shifting to more sustainable production systems and the society-wide benefits that this shift would generate. The value of these environmental services was understood to be equivalent to the additional costs of reducing the risks and environmental effects, which would not be internalized in the final price of products sold: that is, the opportunity cost for providing environmental services. Somewhat arbitrarily, the initial payment was set at one-half a minimum salary per month (approximately U.S.$170 in 2007). Proambiente included six environmental services: reduced or avoided deforestation; absorption or sequestration of carbon; recuperation of hydrological functions; soil conservation; conservation of biodiversity; and reduction of flammability and of fire risk (Proambiente 2003). Specific indicators were developed for each type of environmental service, and a certification system was developed to annually assess direct collective indicators for deforestation and carbon sequestration. Other indicators would be verified through a mixture of individual and collective indirect criteria via community agreements and field audits to be carried out each year.

The approach called for the creation of twelve regional Proambiente poles of approximately four hundred farm families each. At the national level and in each pole, Proambiente management councils brought together government, workers, NGOs, and other representatives of civil society. A Proambiente directorate was appointed in the Ministry of the Environment to coordinate the overall program and provide technical and political support. Usually the local rural workers' unions and their federations selected the families to participate in each pole, nominated community members to work as community agents, and selected the local NGO to serve as the technical assistance coordinator. Technical teams and community agents worked with each family to map and analyze its property and land use, develop individual plans for specific changes in practices, and sign agreements with groups of twenty to thirty families for collective monitoring. The regional council created comprehensive sustainable development plans and provided oversight for activities in the pole and linkages to other programs. According to the original proposal, farmers participating in Proambiente would receive support to develop productive activities that promoted social benefits and were compatible with natural resource conservation. Credit repayment periods were extended, and part of the credit would be paid through a socioenvironmental fund to cover costs of maintenance of permanent production systems and of environmental services to society, while technical assistance, rural extension, and social organization would be financed by the Support Fund (Mattos et al. 2001).

The Proambiente program was innovative in its grass-roots origins, in the articulation of different policy instruments for rural development, and in the establishment of environmental services payments for rural family production (Hirata 2006). Unlike the proposal for extractive reserves, Proambiente came from a social group (migrant farmers) not previously associated with environmental protection in Amazonia. This evolution demonstrated that innovative policy alternatives for rural communities could arise from new cultural identities and concepts, such as agro-ecology, not only from long-standing indigenous traditions regarding the use of resources.

The policy also innovated through an approach that recognized the diversity of systems and the complexity of cross-scale dynamics (farm, landscape, region, and global levels), using an adaptive management framework. The participatory methods adopted with community agents, local organizations, technical teams, and representative organizations provided the potential for linkages between the program and other policy initiatives. Proambiente also innovated in incorporating new environmental mechanisms such as community certification and participation in monitoring of environmental services.

Successes . . .

The successes of these social movement proposals were due to a combination of factors, at different scales, that interacted with the particular historical circumstances of different regions of the heterogeneous Amazon. In Acre, isolation favored the maintenance of an intact forest and forest-dwelling peoples during a period of transition to autonomous producers who later organized to protect their land from outsiders. On the Transamazon, it was farmers' strong connection to the market that led them to organize to address their productive needs through new proposals for alternative credit and technical assistance.

Despite these differences, the two experiences shared certain key characteristics, including the construction of movement identities closely tied to livelihoods and local cultures. Both of these social movements focused on the defense of their natural resource base for future generations and were rooted in local knowledge and livelihood practices (Hall 1997). Both cases illustrate the dynamic nature of socially constructed notions of "traditional people" (Carneiro da Cunha and Almeida 2000). The rubber tappers originally were migrants from northeastern Brazil who developed a form of rubber production adapted to the natural forest. The same appears to be happening among migrants from southern Brazil to the Transamazon highway, who are seeking to shift from agricultural to agro-forestry systems more adapted to the Amazon region.

Both took advantage of important cross-sector alliances and strategic political opportunities to pursue their struggles over several decades. Rubber tappers parlayed their identity as traditional forest dwellers into an enduring alliance with church activists, union leaders, conservationists, researchers, and politicians during a fervent period of political democratization in Brazil when environmental issues entered politics at all levels. Eventually this alliance led to penetration of the social movement into political power at the state and federal levels.

Farmers on the Transamazon benefited from the socioenvironmental discourse that originated in the alliance between environmentalists and traditional peoples and expanded to a multitude of grass-roots initiatives that challenged the dominant paradigm (Hall 1997, xxiv). They were able to incorporate sustainable land use planning and environmental services compensation into their innovative proposals for programs to support agroecological production systems at a time when a union leader, Luiz Inácio Lula da Silva, took over as Brazil's president, emphasizing social justice.

One of the most innovative ideas in the proposal for extractive reserves was the separation between property rights and use rights, already present with respect to national forests but never applied as a social policy solution. This model is distinct from the classic agrarian reform based on family private property and from classic conservation because it recognizes the right of traditional populations to protected territories. The extractive reserves rely on a new form of relationship between state and society, in which the state retains the responsibility for and ownership of the territory, while the residents adhere to rules defined and agreed upon by both parties. Similarly, Proambiente relies on an innovative agreement between producers and the state, in which the state agrees to compensate producers for environmental benefits they provide to the wider society. The service is remunerated based on proof that the producer is providing it, and this depends fundamentally on a technological change that the state must facilitate.

Another innovation common to the two cases analyzed here is their questioning of the role of scientists and scientific knowledge in the formulation of a new development model. Since the state has proven incapable of mobilizing science in the interest of the majority of the population, the social movements have been responsible for this shift. Both extractive reserves and Proambiente benefited from a high conceptual and institutional investment by research centers and NGOs. The model of shared management requires that the state internalize these public policies and provide continual scientific and technical support.

These enlightened policies at the state and national levels, reflecting the penetration of grass-roots social movements into the political mainstream, began to address the institutional and policy failures that had been the main problem for many community-based enterprises in Latin America (Richards 1997). There is little doubt that the rubber tappers' movement, NGO networks, experimental environmental projects with Transamazon colonists, and international cooperation introduced a new face to Amazon development. These socioenvironmental projects assured land and natural resources and created new opportunities for thousands of people, reduced land conflicts, provided social and economic benefits, and constituted a counterweight in regional and national power struggles. The end result was a reversal of the historical trajectory of disappearance or marginality for these Amazonian social groups.

...and Challenges

Despite these surprising and encouraging successes of grass-roots social movements in promoting innovative socioenvironmental policies, their future implementation faces formidable challenges. For one thing, a daunting array of technical and economic problems still remains to be solved (CNS 2005; Proambiente 2005). The historical lack of research devoted to forest management, and to small-scale production systems in general, means that there is relatively little technical, economic, ecological, and social data to support alternative production systems for small producers in the Amazon (Amaral 2000). Controversies therefore surround many of the social movements' proposals, including the extractive reserve model (Arnt 1994; Browder 1992; Homma 1992). The elimination in the 1990s of federal subsidies that had maintained rubber prices up to three times above the international price drastically undermined the economic base of the extractive reserves in Acre just at the time they were created. Most "tappers" abandoned rubber production as a result (Campbell 1996; Gomes 2001; Hall 1997; Salisbury 2002; Wallace 2004).

This rubber crisis is seriously testing the entire extractive production system, as tapping has been at the core of social, economic, and cultural activities within Acrean forests for over a century. With a few exceptions such as Brazil nuts, non-timber forest products, seen in the 1990s as the potential alternative livelihood basis for extractive reserves, still are in the experimental stages of processing and marketing (Ehringhaus 2005), and proposals for sustainable timber extraction are the subject of intense debate (Barreto et al. 1998; Pearce et al. 2002; Rice and Gullison 1997). Meanwhile, rubber tappers have little choice but to fall back on agriculture and ranching to make a living, further expanding deforestation even inside the reserves (Gomes 2001; Ehringhaus 2005; Wallace 2004). Even in extractive areas less dependent on rubber than in Acre, the absence of markets for non-timber forest products has made survival difficult for rural communities.

Proambiente, meanwhile, is pioneering a comprehensive new approach to participatory cross-sector land use planning and monitoring, management of diverse production systems and conservation landscapes, and measurement and compensation of environmental services provided by hundreds of small farmers dispersed across the region. There is no blueprint for this approach, and since the program was not adequately tested as a pilot program before being transformed into national policy, the demands have multiplied to cover huge settlement areas. More time is needed before the results can be adequately assessed. Although the program was designed to incorporate four hundred families in each of twelve poles, most of the poles lagged behind in the timetable for presenting results that would qualify them to receive community certification and actual payments to farmers (Agência Brasil 2005). This delay contributed to distrust and disinterest among many participants.

The principal obstacles currently facing Proambiente are legal and conceptual. For example, the lack of an organizational structure legally charged with making environmental service payments has made the payments, in practice, more like social subsidies. The lack of government experience in implementing policies with public participation has led to inappropriate and overly bureaucratic tools. The chronic lack of articulation among governmental actions for the Amazon region has led to delays in freeing funds, with these often arriving too late for the agricultural tasks they are meant to support. For Proambiente to succeed, more appropriate operational mechanisms will be needed, along with a legal framework for environmental service payments and expansion of the program beyond pilot areas to reach the whole region as well as other parts of Brazil (Hirata 2006).

Both policies—extractive reserves and Proambiente—depend strongly on state intervention to succeed because of their shared management design, which requires strong institutional relationships and constant adjustments. This is one of the most fragile aspects of the proposals, given the difficulty the Brazilian government has had in implementing effectively its environmental policies and excellent environmental laws. The other weakness is the overwhelming demands placed on rural communities. Because of the historic deficit of social investments in Amazonian communities, families have to divide their energies between problems of day-to-day survival and the shared management of extensive territories, requiring interminable meetings and responses to complex accounting questionnaires, if they are fortunate enough to be literate.

These new development models being implemented in Amazonia, based on balancing conservation and sustainable use, have established a permanent tension with pro-development groups in the government but have not significantly altered the predominant development policies. On the one hand, the social movements formulated, tested, and implemented pilot programs of all types, with varied methodologies. The state, on the other hand, which was responsible for transforming these pilot programs into public policies to benefit the whole society, has not been up to this task, even under the popular government of President Luiz Inácio Lula da Silva. As a result, the programs have fallen far short of their potential to benefit the smallholder populations of the region.

Alongside the ongoing "quiet revolution" of experiments with a grass-roots focus, the main thrust of Amazonian development policies continues to reflect the vested interests of agribusiness in the region: road construction; market penetration; expansion of logging and ranching; and conflicts over land and resource tenure. Environmental agencies such as Brazil's Ministry of the Environment (and IBAMA) are relatively weak compared to the development-focused agencies such as the Ministry of Agriculture and INCRA, the main function of the latter being land titling and resolution of rural social tensions. It is no surprise that the extractive reserves and Proambiente have suffered from a lack of government follow-through with policy implementation, technical support, and financial resources.

In Acre, a state government closely allied with the rubber tappers is facing the challenge of supporting the extractive reserves while also implementing a broader vision of alternative development for all of the regions and social groups of the state of Acre, including support for cattle ranchers, commercial timber operations, industrialization, and road paving. The success of the government's experiment in sustainable development will depend on its ability to successfully address these issues concurrently while maintaining the political support to pursue its vision through its many uncertain paths.

At the grass roots, the often precarious nature of implementation of the policies translates into less than effective local governance and community participation (Hall 1997). In the process of "scaling up" to a regional level, extractive reserves and Proambiente, proposals that emerged in particular historical moments and locations, have been introduced throughout the region, including in communities lacking a prior articulation to strong social movements. In effect, these successes have transformed a bottom-up proposal by grass-roots leaders and their allies into more top-down projects expanded to less organized groups. Ironically, the successful shift to policy advocacy at regional and national levels has often come at the expense of local organizing, leaving the social movement weaker at its base and overly dependent on support from projects by NGOs and the government (Ehringhaus 2005). Finally, the proposals face the challenge of addressing changing needs and perspectives in rural communities, particularly among new generations of workers who did not participate in the political mobilizations, and who may have different perspectives on the forest and on farming than their parents (Esteves 1999; Ehringhaus 2005; Wallace 2004).

Long-term success of these innovative grass-roots policies hinges on the ability of local groups, often with substantial support from national and international allies, to negotiate the changing and often conflictive development policy arena in the region (Hall 1997; Schmink and Wood 1992; Silva 1994). The extractive reserves, Proambiente, and other "productive conservation" initiatives cannot thrive without compatible planning for the broader landscape of which they are a part. This means continued pressure to balance the need for cross-sector strategic political alliances with investments in technical research and grass-roots organizing. Political pressure is required to keep policies on track, while buying time for the necessary learning, adaptation, and expansion of promising alternative approaches to grass-roots Amazonian development.

Notes

Authors' note: An earlier version of this paper was presented at the International Congress of the Latin American Studies Association in San Juan, Puerto Rico, in 2006.

References

Agência Brasil. 2005. "Programa Proambiente está suspenso em quatro pólos pioneiros." http://www.agenciabrasil.gov.br, accessed July 25, 2005.

Allegretti, Mary. H. 1992. "Reservas Extrativistas: Parâmetros para uma Política de Desenvolvimento Sustentável na Amazônia." *Revista Brasileira de Geografia* 54 (1): 5–23.

———. 2002. "A Construção Social de Políticas Ambientais: Chico Mendes e o Movimento dos Seringueiros." Ph.D. diss., University of Brasília.

Almeida, Mauro W. B. 2004. "Rights to the Forest and Environmentalism: Rubber-Tappers and Their Rights." *Revista Brasileira de Ciências Sociais* 19 (55) (June).

Amaral, Paulo. 2000. *Manejo Florestal Comunitário na Amazônia Brasileira: Situação Atual, Desafios e Perspectivas*. Brasília: Instituto Internacional de Educação do Brasil (IIEB).

Anderson, Anthony B., ed. 1990. *Alternatives to Deforestation: Steps toward Sustainable Use of the Amazon Rain Forest*. New York: Columbia University Press.

Arnt, Ricardo, ed. 1994. *O Destino da Floresta: Reservas Extrativistas e Desenvolvimento Sustentável na Amazônia*. Rio de Janeiro: Relume-Dumará.

Bakx, Keith S. 1988. "From Proletarian to Peasant: Rural Transformation in the State of Acre, 1870–1986." *Journal of Development Studies* 24 (2): 141–60.

Barbosa, Luiz C. 2000. *The Brazilian Amazon Rainforest: Global Ecopolitics, Development, and Democracy*. Lanham, Md.: University Press of America.

Barp, Wilson J., and Ana R. B. Barp. 2002. "Crisis and Mediation in Social and Agrarian Relations: The Case of Acre." In *Globalization and Sustainable Development in Latin America: Perspectives on the New Economic Order*, edited by S. K. Saha and David Parker, 250–75. Cheltenham, U.K. and Northampton, Mass.: Edward Elgar.

Barreto, Paulo, Paulo Amaral, Edson Vidal, and Chris Uhl. 1998. "Costs and Benefits of Forest Management for Timber Production in Eastern Amazonia." *Forest Ecology and Management* 108: 9.

Becker, Bertha. 1990. *Amazônia*. São Paulo: Ática.

Browder, John. 1992. "Extractive Reserves and the Future of the Amazon's Rainforest: Some Cautionary Observations." In *The Rainforest Harvest*, 224–35. London: Friends of the Earth.

Campbell, Constance E. 1996. "Forest, Field, and Factory: Changing Livelihood Strategies in Two Extractive Reserves in the Brazilian Amazon." Ph.D. diss., University of Florida.

Campos, Marina. T. 2006. "New Footprints in the Forest: Environmental Knowledge, Management Practices, and Social Mobilization among Colonos from the Transamazon Region." Ph.D. diss., Yale University.

Campos, Marina T., and Daniel C. Nepstad. 2006. "Smallholders, the Amazon's New Conservationists." *Conservation Biology* 20 (5): 1553–56.

Cardoso, Catarina A. S. 2002. *Extractive Reserves in Brazilian Amazonia: Local Resource Management and the Global Political Economy*. Aldershot, Hampshire, U.K. and Burlington, Vt.: Ashgate.

Carneiro da Cunha, Manuela M., and Mauro W. B. Almeida. 2000. "Indigenous People, Traditional People, and Conservation in the Amazon." *Daedalus/Journal of the American Academy of Arts and Sciences* 129 (2): 315–38.

Clusener-Godt, Miguel, and Ignacy Sachs. 1995. *Brazilian Perspectives on Sustainable Development of the Amazon Region*. Paris and New York: UNESCO/Parthenon Publishing Group.

CNS (Conselho Nacional de Seringueiros). 2005. "Unidades de Produção e Gestão Sustentável da Floresta Amazônica." Unpublished report from the Congress of Extractivist Populations and Sustainable Development in the Amazon Region, Manaus, November 29–December 2.

Costa Sobrinho, Pedro V. 1992. *Capital e Trabalho na Amazônia Ocidental*. São Paulo: Cortez.

Dean, Warren. 1987. *Brazil and the Struggle for Rubber*. Cambridge: Cambridge University Press.

Ehringhaus, Christiane. 2005. "Post-victory Dilemmas: Land Use, Development, and Social Movement in Amazonian Extractive Reserves." Ph.D. diss., Yale University.

Esteves, Benedita M. G. 1999. "Do 'Manso' ao Guardião da Floresta." Ph.D. diss., Federal University of Rio de Janeiro.

Gomes, Carlos Valério A. 2001. "Dynamics of Land Use in an Amazonian Extractive Reserve: The Case of the Chico Mendes Extractive Reserve in Acre, Brazil." Master's thesis, University of Florida.

Fernandes, Marcos I. 1999. "O PT no Acre: A Construção de uma Terceira Via." Master's thesis, Federal University of Rio Grande do Norte.

Hall, Anthony. 1997. *Sustaining Amazonia: Grassroots Action for Productive Conservation*. Manchester and New York: Manchester University Press.

Hecht, Susanna, and Alexander Cockburn. 1989. *The Fate of the Forest: Developers, Destroyers, and Defenders of the Amazon*. London: Verso.

Hirata, Marcio Fontes. 2006. "Proambiente: Um Programa Inovador de Desenvolvimento Rural." *Agriculturas* (Secretaria de Agricultura Familiar/Ministério do Desenvolvimento Agrário) 3 (1) (April): 15–17.

Homma, Alfredo K. O. 1992. "The Dynamics of Extraction in Amazonia: A Historical Perspective." In *Non-Timber Products from Tropical Forests: Evaluation of a Conservation and Development Strategy*, edited by Daniel C. Nepstad and Stephan Schwartzman, 23–31. New York: New York Botanical Garden.

IAG (International Advisory Group). 2002. "Pilot Programme to Protect the Brazilian Rain Forest." Unpublished report of the International Advisory Group, Seventeenth Meeting, Brazil, July 15–26.

ISA (Instituto Socioambiental). 2007. "Amazônia Brasileira 2007." Edição Especial. Programa Áreas Protegidas da Amazônia/MMA. http://www.socioambiental.org, accessed Feb 22, 2008.

Kainer, Karen, Marianne Schmink, Arthur C. P. Leite, and Mario J. S. Fadell. 2003. "Experiments in Forest-Based Development in Western Amazonia." *Society and Natural Resources* 16 (10): 869–86.

Keck, Margaret E. 1995. "Social Equity and Environmental Politics in Brazil: Lessons from the Rubber Tappers of Acre." *Comparative Politics* 27 (4): 409–24.

Martinello, Pedro. 1988. *A "Batalha da Borracha" na Segunda Guerra Mundial e suas Consequências para o Vale Amazônico*. Cadernos UFAC Série "C," no. 1. Rio Branco: Universidade Federal do Acre.

Mattos, Luciano, Airton Faleiro, and Cassio Pereira. 2001. "Uma Proposta Alternativa para o Desenvolvimento da Produção Familiar Rural da Amazônia: O caso do Proambiente." Presented at the fourth Encontro Nacional da Sociedade de Economia Ecológica.

Pearce, D., F. E. Putz, and J. Vanday. 2002. "Sustainable Forestry in the Tropic: Panacea or Folly?" *Forest Ecology and Management* 172: 229–247.

Proambiente. 2003. "Proambiente: Programa de Desenvolvimento Socioambiental da Produção Familiar Rural; Proposta Definitiva da Sociedade Civil Organizada Entregue ao Governo Federal em julho de 2003." http://www.gta.org.br, accessed February 22, 2008.

———. 2005. "Relatórios de Avaliação do Programa Proambiente." Unpublished reports from Proambiente Poles in Acre, Mato Grosso, Pará, Rondônia, and Tocantins states.

Rêgo, José F. do. 2002. *Estado e Políticas Públicas: A Recuperação Econômica da Amazônia durante o Regime Militar*. Rio Branco: Federal University of Acre.

Rice, Richard E., and Raymond E. Gullison. 1997. "Can Sustainable Management Save Tropical Forests?" *Scientific American* 276 (4): 44–49.

Richards, Michael. 1997. "Common Property Resource Institutions and Forest Management in Latin America." *Development and Change* 28: 95–117.

Ruiz-Pérez, Manuel, Mauro Almeida, Sonya Dewi, Eliza M. L. Costa, Mariana C. Pantoja, Atie Puntodewo, Augusto A. Postigo, and Alexandre G. de Andrade. 2005. "Conservation and Development in Amazonian Extractive Reserves: The Case of Alto Juruá." *Ambio* 34 (3): 218–23.

Salisbury, David S. 2002. "Geography in the Jungle: Investigating the Utility of Local Knowledge for Natural Resource Management in the Western Amazon." Master's thesis, University of Florida.

Schmink, Marianne, and Charles H. Wood. 1992. *Contested Frontiers in Amazonia*. New York: Columbia University Press.

Schneider, Robert, Eugênio Arima, Adalberto Veríssimo, Paulo Barreto, Carlos Souza Jr. 2000. *Amazônia Sustentável: Limitantes e Oportunidades para o Desenvolvimento Rural*. Brasília and Belém: World Bank/IMAZON.

Schwartzman, Stephen. 1991. "Deforestation and Popular Resistance in Acre: From Local Movement to Global Network." *Centennial Review* 25 (2): 397–422.

Silva, Eduardo. 1994. "Thinking Politically about Sustainable Development in the Tropical Forests of Latin America." *Development and Change* 25 (4): 697–721.

Toni, Fabiano. 1999. "State-Society Relations on the Agricultural Frontier: The Struggle for Credit in the Transamazon Region." Ph.D. diss., University of Florida.

Tura, Letícia Rangel, and Luciano Mattos. 2002. "Financiamento da Transição para a Agroecologia: A Proposta do Proambiente." Paper presented at the Encontro Nacional de Agroecologia.

Wallace, Richard. 2004. "The Effects of Wealth and Markets on Rubber Tapper Use and Knowledge of Forest Resources in Acre, Brazil." Ph.D. diss., University of Florida.

Weinstein, Barbara. 1983. *The Amazon Rubber Boom 1850–1920*. Stanford, Calf.: Stanford University Press.

Wood, Charles H., and Marianne Schmink. 1978. "Blaming the Victim: Small Farmer Production in an Amazon Colonization Program." *Studies in Third World Societies* 7: 77–98.

11

Biodiversity and Tourism as Development Alternatives for Indigenous Peoples

CECILIO SOLÍS LIBRADO

The Plural National Indigenous Assembly for Autonomy (ANIPA) is a national organization that includes fifty-four of the fifty-six officially recognized indigenous peoples in Mexico. Although the group was only formally organized approximately ten years ago, it has acted as an indigenous movement for over thirty years.[1] Mexico's indigenous movement is more accurately characterized as a group of movements, as they are various and none represents all of the country's indigenous peoples. I am among ANIPA's third generation of leaders who give continuity to the struggle bequeathed to us by our ancestors.

Through the years, we at ANIPA have worked for a series of reforms to Mexico's federal constitution, always aimed toward reclaiming autonomy and the right of self-determination for our peoples. We struggle for recognition of indigenous territories, areas that are defined by the traditions and customs of our communities and which represent geographic areas that were taken from us. But while we continue our quest of the right to self-determination and recognition of our territories, we cannot just sit and wait for these rights to be recognized. We must press forward with other measures so that we continue to progress as indigenous peoples. This brings me to my main theme, biodiversity and tourism as a development strategy.

A number of years ago a group of us, representing thirty-six different indigenous peoples, were at a meeting where we considered the meaning of biodiversity. The word did not exist in any of our languages. The closest approximation among indigenous people that we came up with was the concept of a "storage area." It is a very special storage area, for we must protect it with our lives. To despoil it would be to commit an outrage against one's own life, people, and culture.

It has been approximately twenty years since the issue of ecological conservation and protection of the environment began to attract attention in
Mexico, primarily due to the efforts of NGOs and intellectuals. And slowly
there has been growing ecological awareness among members of the urban
middle class, who feel they are beginning to suffocate from environmental
problems. For the most part, the ecological movement was constituted by
them and they were the ones who drew the attention of the press, and hence
the public, to this issue.

At the same time, there was another ecological movement, one that was
quieter and largely ignored because it did not engage in public demonstrations or organize marches in defense of natural resources, although
it always preserved them. That silent movement consisted of indigenous
peoples who in their own communities and territories assumed the role of
nature's guardians, guardians of biodiversity.

Despite the fact that indigenous people are the heirs to vast areas where
biodiversity has been preserved, various Mexican governments have incorporated indigenous territories into designated "protected areas." Some 70
percent of protected areas in Mexico are in fact located within traditional
indigenous territories. These protected areas are regulated in a sometimes
outrageous manner, so that we indigenous peoples now have to ask permission to enjoy the natural bounty of our land. We are denied our historical
right to the usufruct of the forest, of the jungle, of deserts and semi-arid
lands, and we are steadily being displaced from our ancestral homelands.

Such displacement has not been the product of a consultative process,
but rather, has been forced upon us. Our peoples have been moved elsewhere, sometimes to places that have no resemblance ecologically to our
original territories. This process has lead to a loss of knowledge regarding
biodiversity as well as an attendant cultural loss, and even the loss of indigenous identity. We have incurred pain and suffering in defense of our
indigenous territories, which for so many years provided sustenance to our
people. Sadly, we have seen our territories steadily reduced and plundered
while we have been left in abject poverty.

We indigenous people are not poor naturally; rather, we have been impoverished. We have been increasingly forsaken to processes inevitably
leading to our impoverishment. Although we reside in the midst of territories rich in biodiversity, mineral resources, and so forth, we are the poorest
of the poor. Statistics show that in Mexico we are at the bottom of the poverty ladder, and I believe the same is true for indigenous people throughout

Latin America.[2] Such impoverishment inevitably leads to high emigration from rural areas.

Over time, we have had to learn from reality and develop new strategies. We have learned how to demand our rights and when to take what is offered and seize opportunities. We have also learned that we must reassess our cultures and consider what is valued and valuable both inside and outside our communities. We have come to appreciate our languages, our identities, and our knowledge, and we have learned how to plan the use of our space and natural resources.

The case of tourism provides an example. We have observed how the foreign tourists who come to Mexico want to visit indigenous communities and protected areas. Indigenous peoples have always lived amid the region's biodiversity, thriving amid its natural bounty. It is these same attributes and the diversity of the scenery that now attract tourists. Tourists are not interested in seeing areas that have been heavily affected by modernization and environmental degradation. They come to see a region's cultural and natural wealth, its biological and scenic diversity. What we need are protected areas that are also maintained as indigenous areas, for indigenous knowledge is closely associated with the management of biodiversity.

While tourism represents the country's third most important source of foreign exchange, very little of it benefits local indigenous communities. The economic benefits of tourism are diminished en route so that when a tourist arrives in an indigenous region he or she only buys some trivial souvenir. But in addition, the tourist industry has invaded and often despoiled indigenous lands and territories, and sometimes it has had a significantly negative effect upon indigenous cultures as well.

Consequently ANIPA and my fellow leaders and I have been studying the situation of tourism, trying to develop alternatives and appropriate plans, programs, and projects, so that tourism can represent a real development opportunity for our indigenous communities. These efforts have now born fruit and we have organized the Indigenous Tourist Network of Mexico (RITA), an indigenous tourist enterprise dedicated to alternative ways of preserving natural and cultural resources and encouraging responsible tourism that would benefit our indigenous communities.[3] The network is made up of thirty-two associated micro-enterprises in sixteen different indigenous communities in fifteen of the country's states. Its mission is to promote and strengthen sustainable indigenous tourist services as a means of conserving the cultural and ecological heritage of indigenous peoples. The network will be a basis for community development by giving indigenous people access to information and strengthening their capabilities (including the transfer of appropriate technology), all in the context of active participation by the members.

The network's fundamental principles include respect for diversity, equitable participation in all activities by men and women, and the sustainable use of natural resources. It is also committed to a revalorization of our indigenous culture in the belief that our culture is as valid as Western culture, as we both have something to teach and to contribute to the world. Equally important is the commitment to work together in solidarity as well as to collaborate with governmental and non-governmental agencies on terms of equality and mutual respect, including respect for the full rights of indigenous peoples.

The network's strategic objectives include the following: to offer tourist and ecological services; to promote and support the participation of indigenous women; to generate plans, programs, and projects; to develop new enterprises in specific market niches; to initiate processes of self-development and cultural revalorization; to influence public policies; and to design and develop sustainable means of financing the work of the organization.

Each of the micro-enterprises associated with RITA has a cultural component as its base, linked to indigenous identity. Most focus on conservation and alternative uses of natural resources. The network is not like private enterprises that take without giving back. To end the widespread practice of irrational and unsustainable pillaging of natural resources, RITA is developing the means for local community members to gain sustainable control of local plant and wildlife resources through genetic reserves.[4] This requires identification of species with economic importance and the reproduction of those plants and animals by establishing local, semi-natural plant nurseries or animal breeding stock collections.[5] Ultimately, these systems for the care, management, and reproduction of flora and fauna allow indigenous peoples to maintain and increase the value of these natural resources, to create local jobs for local people, and to preserve the species in their natural habitats. Although this may sound simple, in fact it has required a process of sensitizing people to the importance of these genetic resources and training individuals to manage the plant nurseries and animal breeding facilities.

Here it is useful to give some examples of RITA's micro-enterprises and the different kinds of activities in which they engage. The group Atekokoli in the municipality of Tepoztlán in Morelos was started in 1991 by a group of young people interested in learning and passing on traditional forms of healing as a way of preserving their culture and identity. They decided to start an alternative health clinic in their community, Amatlán de Quetzal-cóatl, to serve both as a training center in traditional medicinal practices and to meet the health needs of their people. They secured a grant to buy a piece land and later to build the clinic and develop a botanical garden to grow traditional medicinal plants. In addition, to support the clinic finan-cially, the twelve members have developed an alternative tourism project where they receive tourists in their homes or in an adjoining campground and offer guided tours of the area's natural and cultural attractions.[6]

Another recent tourism project started by young people is the Xyaát cooperative in the community of Señor in Quitana Roo. They were moti-vated by the negative economic impact of tourism that they witnessed on the ecology of the Laguna Azul, and they were determined to preserve the area's ascetic beauty as well as its biological diversity. Composed of eleven members, this cooperative offers two different kinds of tours. The nature tour includes a canoe ride through the lagoon and an explanation of its fauna and wildlife, while the cultural tour focuses on traditional medicine, artisan production, typical foods, and Mayan music and folklore. Tourists may stay in homes in the community. The cooperative is also heavily in-volved in community development projects ranging from environmental education among school children to a reforestation and a recycling proj-ect.[7]

The Tazelotzin cooperative in the Sierra Norte of Puebla is an all-woman cooperative with forty-five Nahua members. With its own hotel it has taken indigenous tourism to new levels. Originally organized in 1985 as part of a women's organization of artisan producers, the women of the community of Cuetzalán del Progreso realized that if they were to attract tourists to purchase their work at prices higher than were offered by middle-men, then they would need to provide tourists with a place to stay. They secured the financing to build the ten-room hotel, with all local materials and decor, where they also display their own artisan production. The hotel has a res-taurant that offers traditional Nahua cooking.[8]

The Indigenous Tourist Network of Mexico (RITA) is the first enterprise in the tourist sector planned and managed by indigenous people.[9] The net-work has outside consultants, but they are advisors only. Their technical assistance is welcome, but only within the bounds of respect for equality and with the understanding that decisions will be made by the indigenous directorate.

The network has analyzed its strengths and weaknesses and among its major strengths is the very high biological and cultural diversity found within its territories. The members of RITA also have a shared goal, the socioeconomic and cultural development of their communities. But RITA also has its weaknesses. It still faces inadequate financing and has insufficient capabilities in the legal, accounting, and administrative realms. It needs access to state-of-the-art technology for conservation and environmental management, waste management, and related matters.

But RITA also has some accomplishments to show for its efforts. It has created a business enterprise dedicated to tourism without the assistance of political parties or religious organizations. Some doubted that this could be accomplished, but RITA succeeded. The network has its own Internet Web page and advertising materials. Its training programs are up and running and its members are being trained in everything from indigenous rights to how to formulate conservation programs. It now has the infrastructure to receive up to fifteen hundred people at a time and it has its own vehicles to transport them. With all due respect, RITA has accomplished more in three years than many other organizations.

The network is a concrete example of what ANIPA has accomplished. Sister organizations, RITA and ANIPA proceed hand in hand, one in the political process dealing with recruitment, social mobilization, and so forth; the other dedicated to the path that avails itself of the indigenous people's natural resources. The program of indigenous tourism developed by RITA should never become ANIPA's only alternative. Many other options exist within our indigenous territories. But the flow of tourists is a fact of life. The aim of ANIPA and RITA is to take advantage of this opportunity, to obtain that to which we indigenous are entitled and which serves our own ends of protecting our territories and our identities.

Notes

Author's note: This chapter is based on the translation by Guillermo Alfonso Calvo-Mahe of the transcript of the conference presentation, combined with material in a PowerPoint presentation by the author and incorporated by the editors.

1. On the organization of ANIPA, see http://www.laneta.apc.org/rci/organinteg/anippla.htm, accessed December 3, 2006.

2. Editors' note: In indigenous municipalities in Mexico (defined as where over 70 percent of the population is indigenous) in 2002, 89.7 percent of individuals were categorized as moderately poor and 68.5 percent as extremely poor. In contrast, in non-

indigenous municipalities (where less than 10 percent of the population is indigenous) 46.7 percent of individuals were moderately poor and only 14.9 percent extremely poor (Ramírez 2006, table 6.4).

3. See http://www.rita.com.mx, accessed January 2, 2007.

4. Editors' note: See Heywood and Dulloo 2005 for evidence of these practices.

5. The experiences of RITA are based on a program established by the government of Mexico known as the System of Management Units for Wildlife Conservation. See Garpow 2001.

6. See http://www.rita.com.mx/atekcult.html, accessed January 20, 2007.

7. See http://www.rita.com.mx/xyaacapa.html, accessed January 20, 2007.

8. See http://www.rita.com.mx/tazecult.html, accessed January 20, 2007.

9. The network has received some government funding by responding to grant competitions of various kinds, such as by the Secretary of Social Development, the Secretary of the Environment and Natural Resources, and the National Commission for the Development of Indigenous Peoples, among others. Its main international funding has come from the Spanish Agency for International Cooperation.

References

Garpow, Wendy J. 2001. "A New Option for Protected Areas in Mexico's Riviera?" In *Carolina Papers in International Development* 1. Chapel Hill: University Center for International Studies, University of North Carolina. http://gi.unc.edu/research/pdf/garpow.pdf, accessed May 22, 2007.

Heywood, V. H., and M. E. Dulloo. 2005. "In Situ Conservation of Wild Plant Species: A Critical Global View of Best Practices." In *IPGRI Technical Bulletin* 11. Rome: IPGRI. http://www.bioversityinternational.org/Publications/Pdf/1092.pdf, accessed May 22, 2007.

Ramírez, Alejandro. 2006. "Mexico." In *Indigenous Peoples, Poverty, and Human Development in Latin America*, edited by Gillette Hall and Harry Anthony Patrinos, 150–98. New York: Palgrave Macmillan.

12

Women Cooperative Members in Nicaragua

The Struggle for Autonomy

MARTHA HERIBERTA VALLE

The organization of rural women in Nicaragua began with the Sandinista revolution of 1979. During the 1980s peasant women became members of the National Union of Farmers and Ranchers (UNAG) while female wage workers came to be represented by the Association of Rural Workers (ATC). In addition, many rural women participated in another Sandinista mass organization, the Luisa Amanda Espinoza Association of Nicaraguan Women (AMLAE).

My organization, the Federation of Agricultural Cooperatives of Rural Women Producers of Nicaragua (FEMUPROCAN), grew out of the Women's Section of UNAG. Many of us were trained and achieved leadership positions within this mixed-sex organization. However, in the 1990s it became evident that we needed our own organization, which we achieved in 1997 when FEMUPROCAN was constituted as an autonomous organization of female farmers.

In this chapter, I summarize the highlights of three decades of organizing rural women, culminating in the organization of FEMUPROCAN. I then turn to the objectives and current activities of our organization and our view of the main problems affecting rural Nicaragua.

"If We Keep Walking We Will Always Forge a Path"

In the 1970s in Nicaragua, women of the countryside were discriminated against for being peasants, for being poor, and for being women. Men, of course, were also discriminated against for being peasants and poor, but the situation of women was always more difficult. For example, there were few schools in rural areas and these were located far from home, so it was difficult, particularly for women, to learn to read and write. For women, the only school was the home.

Most peasant families had access to only small plots of land, so they were forced to work as temporary wage workers on the large coffee or cotton plantations during the harvest season. These only hired the head of the family, in other words, the man, as the worker, but he was expected to bring his wife and children to work alongside him. What did this mean? Well, it meant that women had no rights. The wages earned by the whole family were paid to the man because he was the registered worker on the hacienda. Many of these haciendas had company stores and *cantinas* where they sold foodstuffs and liquor. All too often when the husband received the paycheck, he would drink it away, and his wife could do nothing to stop him, for she had no rights over the paycheck even though she and the children had worked hard to earn it.

Peasant women also did not have any rights as farmers. The husband was always considered the boss. For example, he was the only one who could undertake legal transactions and sell the family's crop.

Because of lack of access to sufficient land in the central areas of Nicaragua, many peasant families in the 1970s migrated to the agrarian frontier, toward the Atlantic coastal region of the country. There peasants opened up new agricultural lands, clearing the dense forest. Often, after they had cleared the forest, they would be forcefully displaced by large-scale cattle ranchers and coffee producers, who would claim property rights, forcing peasants deeper and deeper into the forest to start the process all over again. Of course, in this eastward movement, peasants were moving even further away from access to any semblance of health or educational services.

That was the situation at the moment of the triumph of the Sandinista popular revolution of 1979. The revolution brought about a radical change in the political, economic, and social structure of the country. The Sandinista National Liberation Front (FSLN) initiated new policies that signaled a complete break with the past. First of all, the countryside was given top priority. Grass-roots organizations were promoted that responded to the needs of the peasantry. A major literacy campaign was undertaken and health brigades were organized nationwide, along with the creation of health centers in rural areas. For the first time, assistance was provided to small-scale farmers for agricultural production. An agrarian reform was promulgated that expropriated land from large landowners, and an effort was begun to put land into the hands of the peasantry and rural workers. Hundreds of cooperatives of different kinds were also organized.[1]

Women played a very important role in the process. They were mobilized as technicians, as members of the health and literacy brigades, and as participants in all of these activities. However, there were limitations for women, for they were not part of the leadership. At the top, the FSLN National Directorate was composed of nine men (the commanders of the revolution), but not a single woman. Nonetheless, there were women with great capabilities, with impressive trajectories of revolutionary activity during the struggle that defeated Somoza. A few women held positions in different areas of the government, but few had high-level posts. Similarly, in the popular organizations most of the leaders were men.

The National Union of Farmers and Ranchers (UNAG) was founded in 1981 as the main national organization for peasants. Its membership came to include not only small- and medium-scale farmers, but also most of the members of the production cooperatives of various types that were promoted under the agrarian reform. According to the National Cooperative Census of 1982, there were 2,846 cooperatives in existence, including production cooperatives and credit and service cooperatives; only 44 percent of these had at least one female member and women represented only 6 percent of the total membership of 68,434 (CIERA 1983, 26)

This survey served as a wake-up call for those of us women who had been active in UNAG.[2] We saw that while it was readily accepted for women to be heads of education and health brigades, it was a whole other matter when it came to the management of economic resources such as land. At that point we decided we needed a women's division within the peasant organization in order to promote the interests of women producers and cooperative members. When we presented this idea to the male leaders of UNAG, they stared at each other and said something on the order of, "Women are already represented in UNAG; there are thousands of women who participate in our activities." They did not understand that women were not being taken seriously as agricultural producers and that their needs were not being met. This had to be addressed for women to participate with dignity within the peasant organization.

In 1986 we decided to organize a women's brigade to the coffee harvest, the María Castil Blanco Brigade, made up of some sixty female farmers and family members in the cooperatives, as a way of drawing attention to the role of women within UNAG. This experience served us well in terms of learning how to organize ourselves and providing many of us with leadership experience, and it led to the First National Meeting of Peasant Women in July 1987. A major result of this meeting was that the male leaders of UNAG agreed to the creation of the Women's Section within the organization. There were several factors that facilitated the creation of the Women's Section at that time, among them the fact that the FSLN's leadership had just adopted the position that women should be integrated in all aspects of the revolution; that AMLAE had begun encouraging the formation of women's secretariats within the various unions and organizations; and that the women's movement was pushing for "absolute equality between men and women" in the discussions over the country's new constitution (FEMU-PROCAN 2006, 7).

One of the main objectives of the Women's Section was to increase the participation of women within the cooperatives and particularly within the cooperatives' executive committees. We members of the Women's Section pressed for greater representation of women within UNAG's leadership structure at the local, departmental, and national levels, and for women's needs and concerns to be taken into account in all of the activities of the national organization. Among our main demands in this period was that women be included in all of UNAG's training programs. We started a rotating credit fund for women, so that women farmers would have access to credit for the first time. We also began to address women's practical concerns. On the production cooperatives, for example, day care centers were created so that the women could work without having to worry about their children. But addressing such concerns led to further problems with the UNAG leadership: "The struggle for gender-specific demands led members of the Women's Section to question 'women's subordination' and the 'machista positions' that prevailed in the leadership of the cooperatives and of the association. This led to tensions in the relations between the [Women's] Section and UNAG, and the topic of 'women's liberation' was demonized, considered as 'a deviation in the role of a union,' and attributed to the penetration of 'foreign feminist currents'" (FEMUPROCAN 2006, 33).

In 1989 we held the First Meeting of Peasant Women Leaders to evaluate the work of the Women's Section and to develop our plan of action for the future.[3] Given the depth of the economic crisis in the countryside at that time, one of the main goals that came out of that meeting was increasing women's access to land. One of our proposals was that women be given land that was not in use so that they could work it in collectives; also, that they be given access to inputs, machinery, credit, and technical assistance so that they could work it productively. We also insisted that when the production cooperatives had insufficient members women be encouraged to join. Likewise, when land in the agrarian reform was distributed to individual families, we demanded that it be titled in the name of the couple, so that the whole family would benefit. We also began to denounce domestic violence against women (CIERA 1989; FEMUPROCAN 2006).

In 1992, after a national consultation among the female membership, we developed a five-year strategy for the Women's Section. Part of the strategy was to reorganize ourselves into legally recognized first, second, and third-level women's organizations, which in Nicaragua take the form of cooperatives, unions, and federations, and we began doing so successfully.[4] In fact, we were so successful in increasing our membership and in obtaining funding for our projects that some of UNAG's male leaders became increasingly hostile about our activities. Moreover, they resisted increasing the participation of women within the association's leadership, particularly at the departmental and national levels. Women began to be removed from leadership positions in the organization for one reason or another; eventually, many of us within the Women's Section were replaced. Other women who were willing to follow the male leadership of UNAG were given our posts. After trying to negotiate with UNAG's male leadership for greater representation and autonomy within the mixed-sex organization for several years, in 1997 we created FEMUPROCAN as an autonomous organization of rural women farmers, and I was elected its first president.

FEMUPROCAN

As an organization of female farmers, the mission of FEMUPROCAN is to develop the capabilities of its membership to develop and promote policies that benefit them. Its vision is to promote a rural women's perspective in the economic and social affairs of the country. Among its main concerns are developing a gender analysis, fomenting cooperative development and an awareness of environmental concerns, and promoting entrepreneurship among women.

Today FEMUPROCAN has 2,100 members organized in seventy-six base-level cooperatives, two associations, one department-level cooperative, and eight unions of cooperatives. The organization is active in a large portion of the country, with a presence in six departments and one autonomous region.

Of the 2,100 direct members who are farmers, 74 percent have access to land, with an average 8.2 *manzanas*[5] per member. But of the total area, women themselves own only 18.5 percent, with the remainder being either joint property with family members or land obtained by borrowing or renting from them or others (FEMUPROCAN 2005).

We in FEMUPROCAN are conscious of the importance of land ownership for women and assist our members in purchasing it. For example, beginning in 1993 many men who had been beneficiaries of the agrarian reform began to sell their land because they thought that it was going to be taken away by the new government. We have provided the financing for some of our members to purchase this land.[6] Within the cooperatives, our aim is to develop women's leadership and management capabilities. We have what we call the "system of planning, monitoring, and evaluation" operating in fifty-three of the cooperatives. Our members are involved in the production of basic grain, organic coffee, vegetables, and cattle. Among our main activities is developing and promoting crop diversification and other alternative production techniques. One of our projects involves drip irrigation, which enables the better use of ground water and allows our members to plant a greater variety of crops and also increase crop yields. In addition, we work to improve marketing channels, and among our efforts has been the setting up of produce stands along the Pan American Highway for members to market their products directly to consumers.

We have a permanent literacy program and sponsor adult education classes for our members. We offer training in a number of specializations, such as in accounting, conducting feasibility studies, and agronomy. We also offer a short course in gender and human development. In addition, we encourage members to complete their formal schooling, including high school as well as university-level studies. This does not mean that we disparage the great practical knowledge we have as peasant women, but rather that we recognize that the lack of formal education is a limitation that we need to overcome. It is through education that we empower ourselves, although we also pursue other methods of empowerment, such as land ownership, mentioned above.

As a federation we also link up with other like-minded organizations in Nicaragua and in the region, such as the Rural Women's Roundtable and the Cooperative Roundtable. The federation is the national coordinator for Nicaragua of the Central American regional project on Women, Property of Land, and Organized Incidence, organized by the Arias Foundation. As part of that project we advocate for women's land ownership rights to figure prominently in the agenda of all the rural organizations. We are also part of the Agrarian Bloc, which includes most of the rural organizations (such as UNAG and the ATC) and NGOs in the country; the Agrarian Bloc presses the government to comply with its promises. In addition, we are members of the Latin American Confederation of Cooperatives and Mutual Societies (COLACOT).

Among our main challenges is assuring that women farmers be efficient producers who can generate incomes sufficiently high to maintain their families. We thus promote "entrepreneurial networks" and cooperation in all forms among our members. We must make peasant farming viable in all of its dimensions so that farmers are not forced to sell their land out of desperation. However, the free-trade agreement that Nicaragua has signed with the United States is a great concern, for we fear that small producers will suffer from cheap food imports.[7]

Another concern is how to stabilize the economic situation in the countryside in order to reduce rural-urban migration, for we are losing the younger generation. There are so few opportunities in rural areas that young people migrate to the city; there they often turn to prostitution and crime, given the lack of viable alternatives. We must contribute to a solution, which we believe must be a rural solution, one based on the principles of solidarity and cooperativism as well as equality between men and women.

Notes

1. Editors' note: By 1988 48 percent of Nicaragua's farmland was considered part of the reformed sector: 12 percent was in state farms, 14 percent in cooperatives of various kinds, and 21 percent assigned and/or titled individually (CIERA 1989, appendix, table 1).

2. Editors' note: The author was one of the few female leaders of UNAG at the time, serving as the vice president of UNAG for the sixth region (the departments of Matagalpa and Jinotega).

3. Editors' note: In 1989 women represented 12 percent of UNAG's membership of 125,000 (CIERA 1989, 77). They continued to be underrepresented among the cooperative membership, however. In 1988, women made up 7 percent of cooperative membership, with just about the same share of women belonging to credit and service cooperatives as production cooperatives (CIERA 1989, 125).

4. Editors' note: See FEMUPROCAN (2006, table 6) on the success of the Women's Section in organizing cooperatives out of the loosely structured women's collectives and women's projects. Membership in the UNAG Women's Section increased by one-third between 1992 and 1997, to 12,323 members.

5. Editors' note: One *manzana* is equal to 0.70 hectares or 1.73 acres.

6. We financed the purchase of 3,800 *manzanas* in just one region, providing the loans that will result in women ending up with clear title to this land.

7. Editors' note: Nicaragua is part of the Central American Free Trade Agreement (CAFTA) signed with the United States in 2004.

References

CIERA (Centro de Investigación e Estudio de la Reforma Agraria). 1983. *La mujer en las cooperativas agropecuarias en Nicaragua.* Managua: CIERA.

———. 1989. *La reforma agraria en Nicaragua, 1979–1989: Mujer y transformación de la vida rural.* Vol. 7. Managua: CIERA.

FEMUPROCAN (Federación Agropecuaria de Cooperativas de Mujeres Productoras del Campo de Nicaragua). 2005. *Memoria VIII aniversario.* Managua: Ed. "El Cooperativista."

———. 2006. *FEMUPROCAN: Una Vida de Historias, Luchas y Retos.* Managua: FEMUPROCAN and OXFAM-Canada.

13

The Peasant Women's Movement in Bolivia

"Bartolina Sisa" and COCAMTROP

GEORGE ANN POTTER WITH LEONIDA ZURITA

The lives of Bolivia's indigenous rural women have always been marked by discrimination and social exclusion. Those who participate actively in the rural social movement confront an even higher level of aggression. The marches in which they participate to press their demands and defend their rights have historically been met with repression in the form of detentions, law suits, incarceration, and even death. But the history of social movements in Bolivia has always been marked by bloodshed. The policies of most previous Bolivian governments have been characterized by great injustices. When the social movements have resisted these policies, the confrontations have been bloody and caused great suffering. Nonetheless, the peasant women's movement inspires rural women and others, and gives them hope that another Bolivia is possible, one with greater equity and social justice.

In this chapter we describe the development, demands, and current role of the peasant women's movement in Bolivia. We focus on the two major organizations, the Bartolina Sisa National Federation of Bolivian Peasant Women (FNMCB-BS) and the Coordinator of Peasant Women of the Tropics (COCAMTROP). After a brief history of each of these organizations, we turn to the demands and proposals that the FNMCB-BS and CO-CAMTROP share. In the subsequent sections we consider the initiatives of the Movement Toward Socialism (MAS) government, headed by Evo Morales, which took office in January 2006 and the extent to which his government has addressed the concerns of the rural women's movement. We conclude with an analysis of some of the challenges faced by the Bartolinas and COCAMTROP in the new MAS political landscape.

The Organization of Peasant Women Was Born on the Roads and in the Blockades

The Bartolina Sisa National Federation of Bolivian Peasant Women, also known as the Bartolinas, gets it name from the indigenous Aymara woman peasant leader who led the insurrection that liberated La Paz from the Spanish in 1781. Sisa's husband, the leader Tupak Katari, and his followers were otherwise engaged in similar battles.

The FNMCB-BS was founded in January 1980 as the female counterpart to the male-dominated Confederation of Peasant Workers of Bolivia (CSUTCB). The precursor to the Bartolinas is to be found in the rural mother's clubs, organized by the Catholic Church in the departments of Oruro and La Paz during the previous decade. The CSUTCB came to recognize that peasant women also needed to play a protagonistic role in the struggle for social justice and defense of human rights.

The Bartolinas were founded in a period of hopeful anticipation of the end to military dictatorship, and they contributed to the movement that restored Bolivian democracy in 1982. The promulgation in 1985 of Supreme Decree 21060 introduced the neoliberal structural adjustment economic model imposed by the international financial institutions and their member states, most notably the United States. It had a serious deleterious impact on the Bolivian labor movement, including the newly organized Bartolinas, due to the high unemployment and severe contraction in living standards that it brought about.[1] From 1984 to 1992 the FNMCB-BS participated in the same struggles against structural adjustment policies as the other progressive social movements. But in addition, it was caught in an internal debate within the CSUTCB regarding the "true role of women peasants and the mission of their organization," as it was known.

On the one side were the few radical separatist feminists; on the other were those who wanted the full integration of the Bartolinas within the CSUTCB. In the end, a middle position won out, one that recognized the need to coordinate with the men but also rejected the rigid structures of traditional male-dominated unionism and sought space for female alternatives. These eight years of internal debate (1984–92), while causing instability in the organization, also ended up having positive results. The Bartolinas ended up with a stronger identity as a women's organization.

In 2002 the Bartolinas defined themselves as not simply an affiliate of the CSUTCB, but rather, as an affiliated *autonomous* organization. Among their objectives is to train and promote new female union cadres; to take an ever more protagonistic role in social movements and conflicts; and to assume a growing leadership role as the men were imprisoned, in hiding, or otherwise engaged. After several more years of institutional strengthening, in 2004 the FNMCB-BS was legally recognized by the Ministry of Indigenous Affairs and the next year it was awarded status as a legal entity (*personería jurídica*), which gives it some legal protection and allows it to receive external grants, among other benefits.

Historically there have been several cross-cutting issues within the Bartolinas that have undermined unity. The first, already mentioned, has been the split between separatist feminists and "accommodating" integrationists, with the latter always seeming to win or dominate in the end. Second, there have been several regional splits: highland versus lowland, west versus east, with the added internal western highland/valley divide between Aymaras and Quechuas. A third important split has been with respect to political party sympathies. These, that more often than not follow the regional divisions, include loyalty to the more revolutionary Katarism of the Aymara highlands (represented by the Tupak Katari Revolutionary Movement and Felipe Quispe's Pachakutec Indigenous Movement) versus Evo Morales's more Quechua and accommodating MAS. While the Bartolinas, unlike the CSUTCB, were able to avoid an actual split along party lines, in May 2006 there were strains in the Bartolinas that sadly bode toward a similar potential fracture. However, now that the MAS is the governing national political entity and Quispe's party has dissipated, the Bartolinas are very publicly pro-MAS.

Fundamental to the Bartolinas is their commitment to ending the double (or triple) discrimination of being indigenous, peasant, and women. There is a saying that their peasant component is strong while their gender identity is weak. But within this framework, they advocate for peasant women's increased access to education and land. They also promote an ecologically sustainable peasant economy. Toward these ends the Bartolinas encourage their members to participate in the Ministry of Education's centers for adult education;[2] they have organized local peasant women's groups to work in their own communities with ecologically appropriate agricultural techniques; and they have led the national campaign against genetically modified organisms (GMOs).

At the international level, in the early 1990s the FNMCB-BS joined the Latin American Coordinator of Rural Organizations (CLOC) and La Vía

Campesina. Together, in 2003 they organized the first International Seminar on Agrarian Reform and Gender, hosting sixty participants from twenty-four countries. In 2004, Leonida Zurita, who was then the president of the FNMCB-BS, was named to La Vía Campesina's International Coordinating Commission. Under the auspices of CLOC and La Vía Campesina, the Bartolinas have participated in the World Social Forum every year under these organizations' banner of "Another World Is Possible." This relationship with CLOC and La Vía Campesina has given the Bartolinas international recognition and prestige not enjoyed by the male-dominated and divided CSUTCB. Finally, in 2004 the accomplishments of the FNMCB-BS in the defense of peasant women's rights were recognized by the United Nations Fund for Women with its award for education.

The History of COCAMTROP

Within the Bolivian peasant women's movement one group stands out, both in its own right and among the Bartolinas—the *cocalera* women of the coca-growing Chapare region of the department of Cochabamba. The Chapare, the region where the highlands give way to the Amazon Basin, is an area of relatively recent colonization, which began in the 1960s, and many of the colonizers are from the same Oruro/La Paz region as the founders of the Bartolinas. During the crisis-ridden 1980s migrating to the Chapare was one of the survival strategies of displaced highland miners and peasants, the latter who were also affected by the worst highland drought in over a hundred years.[3] These migrants brought with them to the tropics of Cochabamba their century-old traditions and decades of organizational experience, which soon became essential to their self-defense against the "war on drugs" sponsored and promoted by the United States.

Although COCAMTROP was not officially founded until 1997, for the previous decade the *cocaleras* were already demonstrating their mettle. The "war on drugs" in the Chapare officially started in 1988 with Law 1008, which made the growing of coca leaf eventually illegal, among other measures. In 1992 women *cocaleras* from Evo Morales's home Federation of the Tropics (Federación del Trópico) stormed a facility of the special national drug police where their detained male companions were awaiting transfer to the nearby military base in Chimoré. Later that year the men from the same federation blockaded the road from the Chapare to Cochabamba when the forced eradication forces tried to accomplish their nefarious task locally. Women armed with nothing more than sticks and stones and an occasional machete confronted the armed uniformed forces in defense of their coca and their men and drove them away.

Women linked to other nearby federations of coca growers (the Centrales Unidas, Chimoré, and Carrasco federations) also began organizing in this period. The March for Life and National Sovereignty from the Chapare to La Paz in 1995–96, led by women *cocaleras* linked to the Federation of the Tropics, helped solidify this movement. For the women who marched for thirty-one days from the Amazon Basin of the Chapare to the Andean highlands of La Paz, followed by a twelve-day hunger strike there, this experience was a great lesson in organizing and advocacy, one that included risking their own lives.[4] They returned to the Chapare ready to take the next steps.

The formation of an organization for women parallel to the men's *cocalero* federations in the Chapare was an initiative of Evo Morales. This process began in 1994 and despite some male resistance along the way, by 1999 such parallel female organizations had been formed in all of the then existing federations.[5] Leonida Zurita was elected the first president of the women's Federation of the Tropics and remained in that position until May 2006. She also became the first president of COCAMTROP when it was founded in 1997 to bring together all of the different women's federations, and she held that position until August 2006.

While each of the six parallel federations of *cocalera* women (Trópico, Yungas, Centrales Unidas, Chimoré, Carrasco, and Mamoré) remain independent at the local level, since its founding COCAMTROP has been important at the regional, national, and international levels. In 2003, COCAMTROP acquired its own legal personality, not only providing it legal protection, but also permitting it to receive international grants. The latter have strengthened the organization internally and vis-à-vis the male *cocalero* federations (and even with the Bartolinas).

As noted above, Leonida Zurita was the president of COCAMTROP from 1997 to 2006, and during 1998–2002 she was also the president of the national-level Bartolinas, moving these organizations closer together and bringing both of them into the international spotlight. Zurita was reelected as head of the Bartolinas in 2004 by a narrow margin, but in order to prevent a national split (as had already happened to the male-dominated CSUTCB) she withdrew her name to allow the woman with the second highest number of votes (who was from the Santa Cruz area) to take over the leadership.[6]

Zurita explains the objectives behind COCAMTROP's ongoing efforts:

There are many things for which we have to keep struggling. . . . First, women's rights; second, human rights because the violence violates our human rights; third, coca and natural resources; and fourth, the land. Land is our Mother; she gives life to the poor. The Ley INRA has resulted in land being given to private entrepreneurs. . . . Lately the land is not for those who work it, but for those who have money. There is now a land market for those who can afford to participate in it. . . . With respect to women's rights, women also have the right to be mayors, congresspeople, counselors. Before women did not have equal rights. That is why we organized into women's unions. . . . In government and other offices they used to not even acknowledge or respect those of us in traditional clothes. Now, thanks to COCAMTROP they can't treat us that way. Now we have mayors, congresswomen.

We, the current women leaders, want there to be many women leaders. . . . That is our challenge—to be many—to confront the neoliberal economic model designed to dominate the peasants and to have our rights recognized. (quoted in COCAMTROP with Zabalaga 2004, 63–4)[7]

And indeed this is what the COCAMTROP leadership is attempting to do. With the support of the Global Fund for Women, based in San Francisco, COCAMTROP is providing seminars and training courses to its forty-thousand members. In April 2006 a new five-month women's leadership course began that not only trains women to be leaders in their own right but also trains them in how to supervise local, municipal organizational structures that are still male-dominated. The need for this particular type of women's training became evident as members of Zurita's generation arduously worked their way into municipal, departmental, and national elected positions, confronting and changing the dominant cultural mores. The move of the original women leaders into electoral politics left vacancies for new leadership within COCAMTROP and its affiliated federations. The new generation of young women needs a more formal venue to learn the leadership skills they require to continue the struggle for peasant women's rights at the local level. The leadership course is one important way to achieve that. In 2008 the Global Fund for Women began supporting computer training for leaders of COCAMTROP; the computers were donated by the Venezuelan government.

Achieving adult female literacy has long been the number one priority expressed by the leaders and the rank and file of COCAMTROP alike, since the gender literacy gap is large.[8] Several years ago UNICEF offered U.S.$800,000 for such a project if the male-dominated Chapare municipalities would provide the counterpart financing of U.S.$100,000. Despite COCAMTROP's efforts, this project was never approved. This experience helped raise consciousnesses. Many of the women draw upon this example of the lack of support from male-dominated institutions to their advantage in negotiating support for other priorities from new and more sympathetic elected male officials. Now under the new Morales government, Cuba and Venezuela are carrying out a national adult literacy program that will hopefully close the gender literacy gap.

Zurita's own Federation of the Tropics benefited from the only productive project thus far undertaken with external financing, a sewing project funded by the United Methodist Women. What was originally perceived as an economic project (sewing clothes for one's family to save on expenditures and eventually producing clothes for sale to earn income) turned into an exhilarating experience in local women's empowerment. First, several men asked to participate in the project, and the women democratically decided to allow 10 percent of the students to be male. Second, the participants learned economically important skills. But it was the unanticipated psychological and sociological benefits that most amazed everyone. At the first graduation celebration, the women were asked what the most important thing they had learned was. Unanimously, these mostly monolingual Quechua indigenous women replied that previously they had thought they were incapable of doing anything outside the home. Now they felt confident in doing *anything* they set their minds to, including achieving literacy, going to school, and even learning how to use computers and other skills and trades. At the formal graduation ceremony, the graduates were dressed in their own creations and were accompanied by their sponsors (usually family members); they received diplomas as meaningful as that of any high school graduate. They were lauded not only by the presence of the local mayor (who had previously refused to support adult female literacy) but also by Evo Morales, who was a congressman at the time. The sewing classes continue to this day.

More than any other women's peasant group in Bolivia, COCAMTROP has learned to overcome tremendous adversity. It is important to keep in mind that the membership is made up mostly of an economically displaced migrant population from the highlands who has had to learn to survive in the tropics. In addition, they have been the victims of the U.S. "war on drugs." And as women, they have had to confront the ever-present machismo. There is little doubt that this adversity has helped to forge these women into the strong local, regional, national, and international leaders that they are today.

The Demands of the Rural Women's Movement

In this section we focus on the demands and concrete proposals that the Bartolinas and COCAMTROP have in common. Both organizations have been part of the broader struggle for social justice in rural Bolivia, and both share most of the demands and aspirations of the male-dominated organizations with which they are affiliated (Arnold and Spedding 2005). Nonetheless, as women, subject to the double or triple discrimination of being women and peasants and indigenous, they have tried to elaborate their own proposals in those areas that generally do not get sufficient attention among the main peasant and indigenous organizations. Their point of departure is the struggle against the violation of their basic human rights. But they must also struggle to guarantee their participation within the male-dominated organizations and especially to participate in decision making so that their views and visions as rural women are taken into account.

Among the main demands of the peasant women's movement has been for approval of a law that would facilitate women's access to birth certificates and identity cards. Without a birth certificate, it is impossible to get an identity card. And without an identity card it is nearly impossible for women to exercise their most basic human rights. For example, an identity card is needed to be a beneficiary of the national land titling program, to obtain credit, and to vote in and stand for elections. Indigenous and peasant women used to face tremendous obstacles in obtaining their birth certificates. They faced discrimination within their own communities when local officials required them to present proof that was impossible to obtain. In effect, they were prevented from acquiring a birth certificate and hence an identity card.

As a result of the lobbying, a group of peasant women in the Congress introduced a law that facilitated the granting of birth certificates and identity cards; it was finally passed in 2004. The law made the acquisition of these free for children under eighteen and for senior citizens. While this was an advance, it did not solve the problem of rural women, and the peasant women's organizations continued to lobby so that the acquisition of birth certificates and identity cards be facilitated and free to *all* those residing in rural areas, irrespective of age. Finally, in 2006, under the government of

Evo Morales, a more ample law was passed whose implementation is being financed by Venezuela. As a result, rural women and men throughout the country are now obtaining their identity documents free of charge.

For years the peasant women's movement has been struggling to make the male-dominated peasant organizations respect women's participation in these organizations and incorporate their demands and points of view. Changing age-old community customs and traditional organizational practices that do not take women's participation into account sometimes seems nearly impossible. The peasant women's organizations realize that change is not going to take place overnight. Nonetheless, they are affecting change. Some of the male-dominated organizations (from the local to the national level) are slowly opening up and there is greater respect for women's participation.

There are costs to ignoring the concerns and demands of organized rural women. For example, as a result of the involvement of both the Bartolinas and COCAMTROP in CLOC and La Vía Campesina, the women's organizations have incorporated the importance of food sovereignty and sustainable development among their demands. They consider these demands to be inextricably linked to their interests and rights as indigenous and peasant women. The male-dominated organizations give insufficient attention to these issues and argue that there are "more pressing" issues on the table.

The Bartolinas and COCAMTROP have tried to encourage the CSUTCB, the Syndical Confederation of Bolivian Colonists (CSCB), the Movement of Landless Peasant and Indigenous Workers of Bolivia (MST-Bolivia), and indigenous organizations to participate in these as actively as they do. They believe that if they were to do so, these organizations would realize that demands for food sovereignty and sustainable development are not just women's demands, but that these issues affect peasant and indigenous communities worldwide. Once the men's organizations understand this, they will surely be more receptive to the issues that the rural women raise. Some progress has been made on this front, at least at the rhetorical level.

The Bartolinas and COCAMTROP have also taken the leadership nationally in another campaign by La Vía Campesina, this one against the use of genetically modified seeds that are being utilized legally in *soya* production in the department of Santa Cruz. The campaign highlights how the right of indigenous peoples and peasants to own their own seeds must be protected. Women have been the ones protecting the seed supply for thousands of years and seeds cannot be allowed to become just another commodity. Moreover, genetically modified seeds will make peasants even more dependent on the market, will make the country even more dependent on imports, and will also harm consumers. The efforts of the rural women's organizations resulted in the defeat of a proposed congressional bill that would have legalized the use of genetically modified seeds in crops other than *soya*.

The peasant women's organizations are also using the new modes of work promoted by La Vía Campesina, such as the exchange of agricultural knowledge between and among peasants. They believe that men and women farmers are capable of solving their own problems, and that it is crucially important to share experiences about successful efforts to diversify agricultural production and make it more ecologically sustainable. They have organized groups of peasant women at the local level who use the peasant-to-peasant method to teach each other the principles of ecological production. With these experiences they hope to generate consciousness among their members as well as lessons that can be applied at the national level. Thus, an ecological, family-based agriculture and food sovereignty are essential elements of the platform of organized rural women in Bolivia. Another important demand that the rural women's organizations have championed has been for a thorough agrarian reform that guarantees women's land rights.[9]

The MAS Government: "The 54% Is Not a Blank Check; It Is a Loan"

The surprisingly strong showing of the MAS in the national elections of December 2005 belies the difficulties the party faces in governing with the very social movements that brought it to power.[10] Vice President Alvaro García Lineras, the MAS "link" to the social movements, ironically asks, "How can you govern through social movements? . . . Governments concentrate the decision-making process and social movements decentralize it. . . . Social movements cannot direct nor occupy the state" (cited in Zibechi 2005). This debate is crucial for a party that has essentially been forged from the movement of peasant coca leaf producers of the Chapare and support from other sectors.[11]

Among Morales's first actions, on May 1, 2006, was the announcement of a hydrocarbon nationalization plan. Supreme Decree 28701 builds upon the hydrocarbon law passed by the Congress in November 2005. With a dramatic show of force and resolve, Morales sent armed troops to all of the gas and oil fields, refineries, and distribution centers as he declared that from that day forward Bolivians once again were owners of their own natural resources. All foreign corporations operating in this sector must renegotiate and sign new contracts. These contracts must acknowledge that their previous investment is limited to the infrastructure (which, according to the Morales government, has already been fully amortized over the last decade of unethically high and illegal profits). Henceforth these companies are to be considered as simple service providers to the Bolivian state-owned national hydrocarbon industry, which will be the majority owner of all activities and facilities. The two largest foreign corporations, Brazil's state-owned PETROBRAS and Spain's REPSOL, are required to pay 82 percent of their profits to the Bolivian government while smaller companies must pay approximately 50 percent of their earnings to the Bolivian national company. This represents some $300 million in extra revenues for the Bolivian government per year and will be used to modernize the state-owned industry. It will be many years before such funds can be used for social purposes.

So far the only social movement to speak out openly against this announcement has been the Central Workers' Union of Bolivia (COB), which declared the move inadequate since it does not fully nationalize the sector or confiscate foreign investments outright, as was demanded in the October Agenda of 2003. The so-called October Agenda, which brought down the governments of Sánchez de Lozada and subsequently Mesa, called for 1) the nationalization of all hydrocarbons (and derogation of Law 21060); 2) the extradition and trial of Sánchez de Lozada for genocide; and 3) the convocation of a constitutional assembly. In its first one hundred days in office the MAS government partly accomplished the first point with DS 28701; sent a failed special commission to Washington regarding the second point; and implemented the third point.

The May Day "nationalization" declaration overshadowed other demands of the social movements, such as for an increase in the minimum wage[12] and an increase in the number of teachers and health-care workers. When Vice President García Lineras was asked why the "savings" from the debt relief that Bolivia has obtained could not be applied to social needs, his reply was that those savings have gone to reduce the debt and strengthen the macro-economic situation overall.[13] It remains to be seen how long the Morales government can continue to favor macro-economic fiscal constraint over legitimate poverty alleviation needs and the demands of the country's majority. Even the signing in Havana in April 2006 of the first

Trade Agreement of the Peoples (TCP) among Bolivia, Cuba, and Venezuela, while welcome as an alternative to the Free Trade Area of the Americas (FTAA) promoted by the United States, is more ideologically sound than economically profitable.[14] The economic development plan seems to be leaning strongly toward more state involvement in the economy, and a dramatically announced new land reform initiative is causing as much national debate as did the hydrocarbon "nationalization" plan.[15]

Peasant Women, the New MAS Government, and the Constitutional Assembly

One of the points of contention between the peasant women's movement and the MAS is in terms of women's formal participation in the party as well as the MAS government. Bolivia instituted a quota system in 1997 whereby women must represent 30 percent of the candidates for Congress in the list of each contending party.[16] A problem is that women are often so low on the party list that they stand no chance of winning or at best they are selected as alternates. Another is that while there have been some gains, the participation of women from the rural social movements in the formal electoral process is quite low. Moreover, while for a number of years the MAS party has endorsed the position that women should represent 50 percent of the party's electoral candidates, this has never been put into practice.

As a result of the national elections of December 2005, there are ten MAS congresswomen, representing 14 percent of the total MAS congressional delegation, and there is only one female MAS senator, representing 8 percent of the MAS senators. Women did slightly better as "runners-up," with MAS female *alternate* congresswomen and senators making up 14 percent of the total MAS alternate representatives (Corte Nacional 2006). One has to ask, what happened to the promised 50 percent?[17] Among the alternate senators are two historic leaders of the peasant women's movement, Leonida Zurita and Isabel Ortega, the latter a founder and former president of the Bartolinas and currently the president of the Indigenous American Parliament.

With respect to Morales's cabinet, there were initially four women: the ministers of justice, government, health, and productivity/micro-enterprise. Only the minister of justice was from a peasant and labor movement background. She is the former leader of the domestic workers' union, and as a *mujer de pollera*[18] she was seen by many as a "token" who was not up to the task of taking on a ministry that is the preserve of lawyers. She was removed from her post in January 2007 but was replaced by a more power-ful *mujer de pollera*.

Turning to the constituent assembly, the popular insurrection of Octo-ber 2003 brought to a head a cycle of increasing social conflict that shook the structures of the Bolivian state. One of the main demands of the social movements, including the Bartolinas, was the need to convoke a constitu-ent assembly to write a new national constitution. When Evo Morales was elected president, one of his first initiatives was the elaboration of the law convoking a constituent assembly.

It is worth highlighting that it is precisely the peasant and indigenous organizations that have been the most active proponents of a fundamen-tal change in the structure of the state since they have been the ones who have suffered most from social exclusion and discrimination. In Morales's presidential campaign, the MAS party had promised that indigenous and rural organizations would play a significant role in the proposed constituent assembly. But although the law convoking a constituent assembly was writ-ten and promulgated by the majority MAS Congress, it omitted guarantees for the specific participation of the various ethnic groups and indigenous and rural organizations. Instead, candidates to the assembly were to be elected from the normal voting districts. The MAS justified this procedure by pointing to its landslide electoral victory in December 2005.

Another issue has to do with women's participation in the proposed con-stituent assembly. As noted earlier, for a number of years the MAS party has officially endorsed the position that women should be 50 percent of the party's candidates in elections, one of the long-standing demands of the rural women's movement. During the presidential campaign the MAS promised that 50 percent of the candidates to the proposed constituent assembly would be women. In the law of 2006 that convoked the constitu-ent assembly, however, this requirement was watered down to 30 percent. Moreover, the demand that women be placed first or second on the voting lists was ignored; thus there was no guarantee that women would end up being 30 percent of those elected to the assembly.

According to the Coordinadora de la Mujer, a record 43 percent of the candidates nationally for the Constituent Assembly were women, but only one-third of these were peasant women in a country where the majority of the population is rural (Cortez Pérez 2006). Women ended up being 35 percent of the total elected delegates, and 48 percent of the 119 MAS del-egates to the Constituent Assembly.[19] Hence, for the first time MAS women achieved near gender parity in an election. Moreover, the MAS selected a peasant woman, Silvia Lazarte, as president of the assembly. However, the MAS women in the assembly have failed to organize on behalf of women or women's issues.

The MAS party dealt with the perceived disenfranchisement of the social movements and indigenous groups first by courting them and then encouraging them to take to the streets in protest over any disputes with the opposition in the Constituent Assembly. After more than six months of futile, hostile, and even violent differences between the MAS and the opposition over such questions as whether the new constitution would be approved by a simple majority or two-thirds vote, an apparent agreement was reached in early 2007. And even though the Constituent Assembly completed its work in December 2007, it would be premature to suggest that consensus has been reached on the framework for a new constitution.[20] The proposed draft still requires approval by a national referendum.

Conclusion: The Bartolinas and COCAMTROP in the New MAS Political Landscape

In their seminal book, *The Making of New Social Movements in Latin America*, Arturo Escobar and Sonia Alvarez (1992) sketch the outcome of most, if not all, Latin American social movements in the following terms:

1) They continue to exist until they win their single issue campaign and then disband. (The MST-Bolivia, for example, is fighting for land reform.)
2) They win their single issue campaign and transform themselves structurally, taking on new issues and forms of organization. This is what has happened with the Cochabamba-based water war movement of 2000, mostly identified with Oscar Olivera. It has since evolved into a well-funded foundation and can hardly be recognized as the original social movement that took to the streets and successfully fought back against the World Bank, the IMF, and Bechtel.[21]
3) They win their issue and get on with new concerns that complement their original work. This is the case with the El Alto Federation of Neighborhood Committees (FEJUVE).
4) They are "incorporated" by political parties. This is what we consider to have happened in the case of the Bartolinas.
5) The social movement becomes a political party in its own right. This is the case with the *cocaleros*, COCAMTROP, and the MAS.

In the case of the Bartolinas (number 4 above) this co-optation is not necessarily nefarious, but it is a political reality. It follows a path similar to that of Felipe Quispe's Katariska movement, which became the MIP political party and which gave way to the more successful MAS political machine. The current president of the Bartolinas, Isabel Dominguez, is also a MAS representative in the Constituent Assembly and her predecessor is now a MAS congresswoman. The COCAMTROP literally grew up in the hearth of the MAS, so its close (and nearly absolute) affiliation is only natural. One previous leader of COCAMTROP is now also a MAS congresswoman, and its past president Leonida Zurita is an MAS alternate senator and the third-ranking MAS party member.

In sum, MAS's strategic May Day "nationalization" of hydrocarbons followed by a popular new land reform decree is solidifying the support of the peasant movement behind Morales. However, there is not the same degree of enthusiasm for the process of constituent assembly or support for broader and deeper women's participation overall, although both the Bartolinas and COCAMTROP will defend approval of the new constitution. Zurita remains optimistic: "The men have changed and now the struggle is of both men and women—for the land, for coca, and for our rights." The role of the rural social movements in this landscape remains clear: vigilance regarding the promises made; a continual struggle for social control and oversight of the MAS; and if all else fails back to the streets to press for social change.

Notes

Authors' note: The primary author assumes responsibility for the interpretations offered herein.

1. On differing views of the impact of structural adjustment policies in Bolivia, see Potter 1988 and Morales and Sachs 1990. The neoliberal model is still partially in place today despite Evo Morales's campaign promise to dismantle it.

2. For example, Leonida Zurita completed this two-year program while serving as a MAS alternate senator, earning her high school equivalency in December 2007.

3. Many also migrated to El Alto (outside La Paz) and Santa Cruz in the eastern lowlands, making these the largest cities in the country.

4. See Agreda et al. 1996 for the early history of women's participation in the Chapare and on the march of 1995–96.

5. A few years later new male and female federations were organized in Mamoré.

6. In the 2006 bi-annual national elections of the Bartolinas, Zurita was once again a prime candidate for the presidency, but there was a backlash against further *cocalera* leadership at this time.

7. Also see COCAMTROP n.d.

8. Editors' note: The literacy rate for rural men in Bolivia is 86 percent, but it is only 62 percent for rural women (age fifteen and over) (UNICEF 2001).

9. For example, at the first congress of FECAMTROP in 1995 one of the main demands coming from the Women's Rights Commission was the right of women to own their own lands in their own names (Agreda et al. 1996). See FNMCB-BS 2003 on the more recent demands of the organizations affiliated with La Vía Campesina and the summary in http://www.fian.org/resources/documents/others/declaration-of-cochabamba/pdf, accessed February 23, 2008.

10. The MAS won these elections with 54 percent of the vote. The subtitle to this section quotes the Bolivian political analyst Helena Argirakis, as reported in Ortíz 2006.

11. García Lineras et al. 2004 defends the centrality of the state as essential even when the very social movements that brought it to power may resist this notion.

12. The minimum wage was increased by a paltry 60 Bolivian pesos, amounting to a mere U.S.$7 per month. This was considered an insult by Oscar Olivera, the coordinator of the water war movement in Cochabamba in 2000, and leaders of other social movements, such as of the Federation of Neighborhood Committees (FEJUVE) in El Alto.

13. The Morales government inherited a favorable macro-economy, boosted by high global energy prices, and appears to be committed to keeping this macro-economic boom alive and well. So strong is Bolivia's current macro-economic situation that it no longer needs or wants support from the IMF and will not sign a new stand-by agreement with the IMF.

14. The export of Bolivian soy (the main legal GMO in the country) is the cornerstone of this treaty.

15. See PASOC 2006 for a useful discussion of the challenges, opportunities, agenda, and image of the new MAS government and the demands of the social movements. On the new agrarian reform law, see chapter 6 in this volume.

16. Editors' note: As a result of this law, women's representation in the Congress has increased steadily, from less than 10 percent in the period from 1997 to 2002 to 17 percent in the period from 2002 to 2005 (COCAMTROP, 54).

17. Editors' note: In the MAS delegation of 2002 there was only one female senator and three congresswomen. The number of female members of MAS in the Congress increased only slightly even though the total number of MAS congresspeople more than doubled, increasing from twenty-seven to seventy-two. In the Senate, the share of women among MAS senators fell. http://www.cne.org.bo/proces_electoral/eg2002.aspx, accessed November 16, 2006.

18. Editors' note: A *mujer de pollera* is an indigenous woman who wears traditional dress.

19. Editors' note: MAS delegates represent 119 of the total 211 elected delegates. http://www.lostiempos.com/noticias/dossierbolivia/asamblea_constituyente/composicion, accessed November 16, 2006.

20. The Constitutional Assembly was to complete its work by August 2007 but did not, requiring a four month extension. During this period delegates of the opposition refused to participate in the work of the assembly, so the draft was completed and presented to the government in December without their participation.

21. Olivera's foundation dabbles in new and often seemingly extraneous issues (like saving the national airline), while maintaining its concern over water. It even (unsuccessfully) attempted to form a semi-political party to run in the elections to the Constitutional Assembly.

References

Arnold, Denise Y., and Alison Spedding. 2005. *Mujeres en los movimientos sociales en Bolivia 2000–2003*. La Paz: CIDEM/ILCA.

Agreda, Evelin, Norma Rodríguez, Alex Contreras, and Comité Coordinador de las Cinco Federaciones del Trópico de Cochabamba. 1996. *Mujeres Cocaleras: Marchando por una vida sin violencia*. Cochabamba: Comité Coordinador de las Cinco Federaciones del Trópico de Cochabamba.

COCAMTROP (Coordinadora Campesina de Mujeres del Trópico de Cochabamba). N.d. *Informes/Actas del Tercer y Cuarto Congresos Organicos/Ordinarios, 2001 y 2003*. Chapare, Bolivia: COCAMTROP.

COCAMTROP with Carmen Zabalaga. 2004. *Las Mujeres del Chapare: Su historia, su lucha por la dignidad y sus liderazgos*. Cochabamba, Bolivia: COCAMTROP.

Corte Nacional Electoral de Bolivia. 2006. *Lista de Mujeres en el Nuevo Congreso 2006*. La Paz: CNE.

Cortez Pérez, Leila. 2006. "Mujeres en la Asamblea Constituyente: Hacia donde vamos?, Editorial, *Los Tiempos* (Cochabamba), April 29. http://www.lostiempos.com/noticias/29–04–06/29_04_06_pv1.php, accessed January 27, 2007.

Escobar, Arturo, and Sonia Alvarez, eds. 1992. *The Making of New Social Movements in Latin America: Identity, Strategy, and Democracy*. Boulder, Colo.: Westview Press.

FNMCB-BS (Federación Nacional de Mujeres Campesinas de Bolivia "Bartolina Sisa"). 2003. *Seminario internacional sobre "reforma agraria y genero": Memoria general del evento*. La Paz: CESA.

García Lineras, Alvaro (coordinador) et al. 2004. *Sociología de los movimientos sociales en Bolivia: Estructuras de movilización, repertorio culturales y acción política*. La Paz: PLURAL and Diakonia/Oxfam.

Morales, Juan Antonio, and Jeffrey D. Sachs. 1990. "Bolivia's Economic Crisis." In *Developing Country Debt and Economic Performance: Country Case Studies—Argentina, Bolivia, Brazil, and Mexico*, edited by Jeffrey D. Sachs, 157–95. Chicago: University of Chicago Press and National Bureau of Economic Research.

Ortíz, Pablo. 2006. "Evo tiene mucha tarea pero muy poco tiempo." *Los Tiempos* (Cochabamba), January 3. http://www.lostiempos.com/noticias/03–01–06/nacional.php, accessed February 23, 2008.

PASOC, Equipo de Análisis de Coyuntura. 2006. *Los desafíos del gobierno de Evo Morales*. Santa Cruz: PASOC.

Potter, GeorgeAnn. 1988. *Dialogue on Debt: Alternative Analyses and Solutions*. Washington, D.C.: Center of Concern.

UNICEF. 2001. *Demographic, Economic, and Education Indicators*. http://www.unicef.org/bolivia/bo_child_indicators_eng.pdf, accessed November 19, 2006.

Zibechi, Raul. 2005. "Two Opposing Views of Social Change in Bolivia." Translated by Nick Henry. Americas Program, International Relations Center, December 14. http://americas.irc-online.org/am/2987, accessed February 23, 2008.

IV

Transnational Perspectives on Organizing
for Social Justice

14

Reflections on ICTs, Telecenters, and Social Movements

SCOTT S. ROBINSON

Throughout Latin America today social movements are connected through diffuse and overlapping networks of individuals exchanging e-mail and visiting Web sites. Over the past decade, commercial cybercafes, including mom-and-pop shops selling access to the Internet by the hour, have proliferated to the extent that any social movement organizer can remain in touch, with few exceptions, from small towns throughout the region. Social movement leaders and their NGO allies use information technology to spread their messages; refine policy goals; train staff; inform the press; lobby legislators, regulators, and politicians; link to donors and international agencies; plan events and mobilize their members; and generally enhance their legitimacy and impact.

Related to this activity is a less visible "movement" of "digital activists" who facilitate access to Internet communication technologies (ICT) yet transcend these networks. This complementary movement consists of those involved in telecenter and related information technology projects that provide points of public Internet access throughout Latin America. Largely shaped and led by national (and sometimes local) NGOs over the past two decades, this diffuse movement has gradually catalyzed awareness and skillful use of basic digital communication tools and stimulated demand for Internet access as well as for meaningful content. This parallel movement is directly confronting the challenge of "digital poverty," what Halperin and Mariscal (2005, 8) define as "a concept that grasps the multiple dimensions of inadequate levels of access to ICT services by people and organizations, as well as the barriers to their productive use."

This chapter addresses an apparent paradox. On the one hand, there has been a virtual explosion in access to the Internet, which has, in turn, facilitated social movement organizing. On the other hand, there are tremendous obstacles to fully democratizing access and assuring that social movements take advantage of the potential of Internet communication technologies. Those that struggle to confront digital poverty face indifference by elites, regulatory discrimination, and market concentration, among other problems.[1]

It is difficult to evaluate the impact of the ICTs that currently serve the diverse social movements and related NGOs throughout the region. Internet communication technologies clearly reduce the costs of information and transactions, which in the past represented a significant impediment to the effective use of the Internet by social movements. Access to ICTs enables enhanced networking, an increased voice in public debates, and potentially a direct impact on policy in arenas where traditionally only elites have tread. Even so, the access and use of existing ICTs by social movements falls far short of the use made of these technologies by business and government elites.

As table 14.1 shows, the share of Internet users in the total population varies considerably across Latin America. At the low end are Cuba (1.7 percent), Nicaragua (2.2), Paraguay (2.7), and Honduras (3.3). At the high end are Jamaica (27), Chile (35.7), and Argentina (42).

With broad sectors of the population still without access to ICTs, social movements and their allies need to engage elites and specifically the regulatory entities dealing with telecommunications, finance, and consumer protection. This requires that social movement leaders and NGOs train their cadres in the complex legal, social, and technical issues inherent in digital inclusion. Yet only a few NGOs have lobbied for regulatory reform that would expand connectivity in domestic venues or for broader reform.

Support for Telecenters

Within the context of rural development, a genuine digital inclusion policy must address the issues of low-cost connectivity, universal access, and content both relevant and culturally appropriate for low-income rural youth. In the absence of any such official policy in the 1990s, a small group of concerned academics and activists hoped that pilot community telecenters could demonstrate the power of the emerging tools, stimulate local private investment in cybercafes, and attract the attention of policymakers. This approach led to collaboration between foundations, NGOs, and government agencies in various Latin American countries.

Table 14.1. Recent Estimates of Regional Connectivity

Country/Total Population	Number of Internet Users	Share of Total Population Using Internet(%)	Share of Total Population with Cell Phones(%)
ARGENTINA			
38 m.	16 m.	42	77
BELIZE			
302,000	35,000	11.6	50
BOLIVIA			
9.3 m.	350,000	3.8	37
BRAZIL			
190 m.	40 m.	21	65
CHILE			
15.7 m.	5.6 m.	35.7	80
COLOMBIA			
42 m.	10 m.	24	80
COSTA RICA			
4.4 m.	1 m.	22.7	31
CUBA			
11.3 m.	190,000	1.7	7
DOMINICAN REPUBLIC			
9.8 m.	800,000	8.8	59
ECUADOR			
12 m.	1 m.	8	82
EL SALVADOR			
6.7 m.	588,000	8.9	35
GUATEMALA			
12.7 m.	756,000	5.9	36
GUYANA			
800,000	145,000	16.4	22
HAITI			
8.3 m.	500,000	6	6
HONDURAS			
7.4 m.	223,000	3.3	27
JAMAICA			
2.4 m.	648,000	27	62
MEXICO			
103 m.	23 m.	22	67
NICARAGUA			
5.6 m.	125,000	2.2	30
PANAMA			
3.1 m.	300,000	9.6	77
PARAGUAY			
5.6 m.	150,000	2.7	82
PERU			
28.5 m.	5.2 m.	16.4	55
SURINAME			
440,000	30,000	6.8	51
URUGUAY			
3.4 m.	630,000	19.3	100
VENEZUELA			
26.5 m.	3.3 m.	12.4	87

Source: http://www.funredes.org/mistica/english/cyberlibrary/participants/docuparti/
LAT_AMER_TABLA_MODES_Eng2.htm, accessed Aug 13, 2008.

During the 1990s, when Internet access was still ramping up, foundations and philanthropies based in the United States supported the use of IT and digital tools in small-scale projects. The Ford, Kellogg, and Rockefeller foundations all invested in social endeavors where the telecommunications component was a key ingredient, as did the government-financed Inter-American Foundation. However, the U.S. Agency for International Development sponsored very few major initiatives. European funders also stayed clear of strictly telecenter initiatives.[2]

Among the international funding agencies that have played a more positive role in providing digital tools to NGOs and social movements has been the Canadian International Development Research Centre (IDRC). Beginning in the late 1990s, the IDRC was the prime funder for pilot telecenter projects throughout Latin America and the Caribbean.[3] On balance, this represented a successful exercise in "stimulus diffusion" (Linton 1936, 324). Modest grants, usually less than U.S.$80,000, were made to established local and national NGOs, and sometimes to projects organized by public universities.[4] The resulting assortment of local telecenters, many of which remain functioning in a sustainable manner as of this writing, evolved into Telecentros.Org.

Among "digital activists," such as those who worked through the regional telecenter network, Somos@Telecentros,[5] these experiences generated an awareness of resistance to digital inclusion. Sometimes the source of the resistance was the leadership of social movements, who may have feared losing privileged control over information within their organizations. Regardless of the source, the resistance to digital inclusion resulted in uneven rates of diffusion of the digital tool kit. National elites, in contrast, have aggressively integrated emerging information technologies into their own lives and institutions, but they have shown great reluctance to direct public budgets toward universal access and connectivity programs. Thus under neoliberalism, public education budgets have been reduced while elite private schools everywhere embrace ICTs, broadening the gap between rich and poor.[6]

Nonetheless, the large number of successful projects proved to technology-oriented NGOs with social agendas that small investments in connectivity projects could have large effects. Demand was stimulated for IT hardware and software, pleasing the computer hardware and software industry. High-profile pilot projects demonstrated to skeptical policy makers and donors that connectivity and training for small, nonprofit institutions was feasible. More aggressive NGOs that already employed e-mail in their internal communications and lobbying tactics began to perceive telecenters as potential democratizing spaces in the struggle for communication rights.

For the first time, mass communication strategies using the Internet and public points of access became a frontline topic at the World Social Forum in Porto Alegre in 2002. The Information Network for the Third Sector (RITS), a Brazilian NGO supported by the IDRC, was responsible for setting up and maintaining the communications backbone for what was perhaps the first multi-thematic meeting of regional NGOs and social movements that was widely covered in the mainstream media.[7] The Information Network for the Third Sector remains influential in the government of Brazil's telecenter development program, and in the government's aggressive advocacy of free and open source software.

Telecenter Smorgasbord

"Telecenter" is an ambiguous term that generally refers to local institutions offering access to the Internet and its tools, usually for a small fee. Within this category there exists a range of institutions with varied objectives, connectivity technologies, levels of capitalization, and external partners (Roman 2003). Ideally, a community telecenter would occupy a convenient locale, and it would be sponsored and sustained by NGO or social movement personnel. The staff would train users in computing tools and skills, including information access, for both personal and community benefit. Unfortunately, the typical government telecenter (often called Infocentros, Centros Comunitarios Digitales, Centros Tecnológicos Comunitarios, among other names) does not meet these ideal criteria. They tend to be imposed by bureaucratic fiat and are located within a schoolroom, in the corner of a public library or a post office, or occasionally at a health center. Their hours of operation conform to those of the host institution, resulting in operation only during business hours, which is not convenient for their young clientele. In Mexico, for example, these government facilities are seldom open after school or on weekends, as originally planned and publicized. Attention to users is provided by host institution personnel, who receive cursory training and are expected to maintain the equipment and oversee its use. Training of users cannot be expected under these circumstances. Often there is neither local "buy in" nor a salary supplement for responsible personnel, and the facilities languish when connections fail, a virus is downloaded, and maintenance simply cannot keep up with the system's needs.

In contrast, a cybercafe or internet cafe,[8] is a small commercial enterprise selling Internet access by the hour to all comers. User training is not a priority, and organic links to local development projects are scarce. While it is difficult to estimate the number of such centers in each country, it is evident that cybercafe owners and operators have created a vast network of points of access, which far outnumber government projects and community telecenters.

Sufficient data are not yet available to estimate the distribution of the three forms of telecenters by country.[9] With respect to government telecenters, the available data suggest that these are most prevalent in Brazil (10,000 as of 2007), Mexico (9,200), and Chile.[10] In all three of these countries, the number of government telecenters dwarfs the number of community telecenters, whose financial sustainability remains problematic.

Rarely are there links among the three forms of public ICT access. In all three cases, however, users tend to be young people engaged in intensive patterns of infotainment, employing the "chat" function, looking for sports and media gossip, and downloading porn and content for homework assignments.[11] There are few attempts from official sponsors to offer learning incentives and culturally appropriate content for young clients over this hybrid range of telecenters.

The recent proliferation of commercial Internet access points in small towns almost everywhere in Latin America has produced challenges for community telecenters linked to project-specific NGOs. Participants in the current hybrid mix of public points of Internet access compete on price, not necessarily on loyalty to a given facility, creating problems for community telecenters that aspire to be more than simple Internet access points.

Contesting Cyberspace

According to Lovink and Zehle (2005): "We have become used to thinking of 'civil society organizations' and NGOs as 'natural' development actors. But their presence is itself indicative of a fundamental transformation of an originally state-centered development regime." This "regime" is increasingly in private hands, and the growing influence of private leadership and that of NGOs raises questions regarding these organizations as self-appointed representatives of grass-roots social movements. As aid donors and corporations look beyond centralized, top-down state or private development agents they turn to NGOs, in part attempting to neutralize radical social movements. This may help explain donors' and, more recently, governments' attention to the generic telecenter model of connectivity.

Non-governmental organizations are consciously adopting corporate models of professionalization in their operations and emphasizing compromise and dialog in their programs. This contrasts markedly with peasant-led, rural social movements that embrace direct action tactics to confront their corporate and government adversaries (Veltmeyer 2005). Under these circumstances, the dependence of social movements on NGOs for maintenance and expansion of rural and small town ICT infrastructure and training may become increasingly problematic.[12]

In the case of post-privatization telecommunications policy, elites in the region are shaping regulatory legislation and staffing the administrative agencies that determine how digital technologies are introduced and allowed to expand in national markets and spaces. Telecommunication policy today is often negotiated inside a triangle of interests formed by the regulatory agency, the ministry of communications, and the dominant market players: Internet carriers, telephony, wireless, television and radio consortia, and their technology suppliers. Independent "telecenter" and cybercafe lobbies, where they exist, and the vast network of NGOs and allied social movements whose communications lifelines and extensions into remote regions depend on licensed digital infrastructures, are not represented at these policy-formulating sessions. Their absence is a critical factor in policymaking as digital convergence arrives. The concentration of voice, data, and video availability over a single cable or wireless connection opens the possibility for an even smaller number of players to dominate regional and even global communications markets. Non-governmental organizations such as the Association of Progressive Communications,[13] which are committed to "digital inclusion" and its policy implications, have taken note and are increasingly mobilizing around these issues.

Business and government elites are highly motivated to invest in high-level information technology infrastructure to compete for foreign capital within a globalized marketplace. It is hardly surprising that they serve themselves with IT innovations first, since there is little or no corresponding incentive to invest in connectivity for the economically marginal population.[14] The lagging of affordable digital connectivity options, of "IT for the people," throughout the region represents a skewed pattern of technological diffusion and is clearly related to the control of regulatory agencies, and public expenditures, by elites or the "market dominant minority" (Chua 2003).

Of course, not only are the rules and technology choices set by elites, but ultimately the core issues of content development, distribution, and respect for cultural diversity are as well. With the high cost-to-market for independents and commercial newcomers, plus the observable consolidation of analog media consortia and their recent moves to create and expand digital services, the ideological power of media consortia (for example, Televisa in Mexico) also profoundly influences public awareness (or ignorance) of the issues.

That popular demand exists for ICT inclusion is shown both by the rapid spread of cybercafes, even to small towns and villages, and by the phenomenal expansion of prepaid cellular telephone services, especially among youth. As table 14.1 shows, in most countries, a much larger share of the population has cell phones than access to the Internet.

Info-Development Issues

Over the last decade, expanding Internet and communication access has spawned civil society concerns and commitments to ICT policy reform worldwide.[15] Communication rights are a key goal of this reform effort, as exemplified by the Communications Rights for the Information Society campaign,[16] which mobilized around the two World Summits for the Information Society (December 2003 and November 2005). For the first time NGOs were represented, or at least present, at such an international gathering. There they confronted uncomfortable and often intractable government, industry, and UN bureaucrats over a range of substantive, technical issues, including financing extended connectivity, domain registry management,[17] spam messages, cyber security, open source software, digital rights management, and intellectual property rights. Beyond these specific issues, the central policy question is Internet governance and its link to info-development.

Info-development (that is, overcoming digital poverty) implies a commitment to technical infrastructure as well as broad-based participation. The needs, remedies, and resources can all be identified and related to concrete policy design, intellectual rights, and content that respects cultural diversity. Yet, this is where negotiations inside the heterogeneous civil society space bog down. The activist academics and NGOs who counsel the leadership of social movements seldom engage in focused IT and info-development policy debates. Furthermore, many of the initiatives that arise are based on faith in reforms and systemic changes that are tenaciously resisted by the elites.

Info-development projects are often "expected to meet a host of often contradictory aims: alleviating info-poverty, catapulting peasants into the information age, promoting local ICT and knowledge based industries, or facilitating democratisation through increased participation and local empowerment" (Lovink and Zehle 2005). Such lofty expectations notwithstanding, grass-roots ICT efforts simultaneously raise expectations and collide with the tightening intellectual property regime that restricts access to information and tools for those unable to buy their way in. This frustration with and even rejection of the legal foundation of the commercial information industry contributes to the tendency for southern countries to embrace the "digital commons" (that is, open-source oriented) organizations. As this opposition develops, it could eventually challenge northern states on their self-serving commitment to intellectual property rights and their dominance of key info-political organizations such as the recent round of meetings of the World Summit for the Information Society.

Unlike more familiar agricultural or industrial economies, the information economy is defined by extremely low marginal costs of production. Therefore, the profitability of the largest information-based corporations, and by extension the amount of capital extracted from less developed countries depends on the ability of the info-developed countries, especially the United States, to elaborate and enforce increasingly strict intellectual property rules. Active promotion of information and communications technology for development by the digital corporations (Microsoft, Intel, Cisco, Hewlett Packard, Oracle, and others) in international forums is indicative of their expectations that their intellectual property regime is robust enough to assure the continued high profitability of their products in the global south.[18] Yet, free information sharing and open source software may threaten this U.S.-dominated information economy. To the extent that this economy requires a commodification of information and ideas, the privatization of knowledge and limits on access and learning, it is likely to stymie info-development beyond the elites who can afford to pay. In contrast, an open source regime would define development as expansion of the digital commons, that is, the public domain of information relevant for citizens and decision makers.

A palpable ahistorical techno-determinism is observable among emergent activist info-development NGOs. This heterogeneous community, which today tends to dominate among Latin American regional IT activists who negotiate with state actors, tends to ignore the hegemonic economic and social policies carried out in the name of development. Rather, it possesses an ingenuous faith in the power of information access and connectivity, which together with digital skills will lead to "progress" and poverty reduction. Yet the absence of any regional effort to provide connectivity and relevant services to diaspora communities reflects the incompleteness of this vision. The current discourse regarding "information and communications technology for development" bundles the issues of development with the politics of aid and security, and it risks confusing, rather than enhancing, critical thinking within NGOs. The risks of co-optation are high as the region's media and communication consortia lobby to sustain their dominance under terms they unilaterally define in order to assure profit from future digital convergence.[19]

These are issues that the communication rights activists enjoin, but awareness remains low of their long-term implications. Discussion about these issues in academic circles is rare or lopsided. Few social movements or NGOs are capable of effective lobbying since the required common regional agenda for the needed technical, regulatory, and intellectual reforms is missing. Thus negotiating strategies remain fragmented, with NGOs inevitably encapsulated by state boundaries and national political cultures. Info-development appears to be a lurching process with incremental advances, linked to market expansion, telecenter presence, donor initiatives, elite resistance, and an uneven technology and information usage learning curve among young social movement militants and their older leadership.

What then are the appropriate learning strategies for social movements with access to the emerging digital tools? While the distribution of Internet access points is now widespread, the fragmentation of civil society organizations, the absence of credible NGOs with an overarching digital learning focus, and distrust among social movement leaderships make fashioning any comprehensive "learning program" a tall order.

Public universities appear both unable to meet the challenge of delivering the "modern core competencies" required by citizens and unwilling to adapt their facilities and offer the content to meet this need. Moreover, the lack of employment opportunities in the formal labor market make a public university education less attractive for students from poor families. Distance education programs abound, but often they are expensive and culturally inappropriate for those who might demand their services and "certifications." The leadership of NGOs and social movements is charged de facto with the challenge of harnessing ICT-based learning tools and their content in their efforts to train and equip their constituencies.

Telecenters, Digital Convergence, Mobile Telephony

The traditional state radio and television "licensed concessions" have become outmoded in the face of the IT digital convergence process now underway. The delivery of voice, data, and video via a single cable or wireless connection threatens to rewrite the business plans for many legacy players in the telecommunications sector. Combined broadband, mobile telephony, and wireless technologies could vastly expand the range of local, including rural, connectivity available via telecenters and cybercafes if current broadcast restrictions by regulatory agencies were revised. Yet, recasting rules that currently benefit powerful telecom networks into forms that favor the digital rights of a broader public will require a more concerted effort than currently exists.

Mobile telephones, however, already connect almost everyone, with the vast majority using prepaid services.[20] Compared to older forms of telecommunications, the mobile services have no glaring disadvantages and already have proven superior in personal convenience, as well as for a variety of economic transactions.[21] For example, mobile phones as credit terminals are now available and are becoming a potential component of public and private transfer payments, even including transfer of remittances from overseas (Aguilar 2006). Pilot projects have extended this activity to micro-credit loans for poor people without access to bank branch offices. Although mobile phone technology is unlikely by itself to effect poverty substantially, the use of mobile telephony will continue to expand linkages to and between the rural poor.[22] Creating innovative interfaces between mobile phones and telecenters of different kinds will therefore be an important challenge for rural development NGOs and micro-banks, particularly in remittance-receiving economies.

Conclusion

Throughout Latin America, expanding communication and connectivity networks link fragmented civil society organizations and social movement leaderships within and between nations. Internet communication technology will continue to facilitate alliances among those at the bottom of the social pyramid, while paradoxically highlighting the tensions between social movements, NGOs, and government agencies. Indeed, this tension may continue to impede the unity of purpose necessary to leverage public policy reforms, which would increase access to digital tools and knowledge. Social movement activists now employ simple digital tools on a regular basis. However, these are underused as learning devices, while more complex tools, well known to corporate or academic users, are seldom adopted. For example, the spatially enabled database, with geographically tagged data layers of particular interest to rural constituents, remains a technical and planning innovation that NGOs and social movements have largely ignored.

A combination of technical and economic barriers have prevented these political actors from moving beyond e-mail and Web site retrievals to employ the decision support tools that their corporate and elite adversaries routinely rely upon for strategic planning and action. Digital activists are partly at fault since they are often unable to transcend technological fetishism and demonstrate the practical value of such tools. Conservative regimes are pleased with this apparent disarray, and their intransigence is predictable on questions of digital inclusion and convergence, the expansion of the digital commons, more transparency in government procurement and procedures, or obligatory open source software for public agencies. The negotiation process on this range of issues, however, has only just begun.

Notes

1. Halperin and Mariscal (2005, 7) note: "In the rush to attract private investments, privatize inefficient operators and establish new industry regulators, the adequate supply of ICT services to the more vulnerable sectors of the population and the more isolated communities was, for much of the 1990s, relegated to the policy backburner."

2. The European–Latin America Cooperation portal on the Information Society is exemplary (www.alis-online.org). A few expensive, high-profile "multipurpose community telecenters" were sponsored by UNESCO, but most were given failing marks by post-mortem evaluators of NGOs.

3. See http://www.idrc.ca/es/ev-115372–201–1–DO_TOPIC.html, accessed February 17, 2008. A video documentary featuring short clips on some of these projects is available online for free downloads: "Telecentros en America Latina" at http://www.bcnet.cc/baax/, accessed February 17, 2008.

4. In 1999 the author received such a grant through his public university affiliation, the Universidad Autónoma Metropolitana, Iztapalapa campus, Mexico, D.F. http://www.uam-antropologia.info, accessed June 4, 2007.

5. See www.tele-centros.org.

6. Almanza and Chacón 2006. The greatest challenge confronting Mexico is the scarcity of computers in schools, especially in public schools. http://www.reforma.com/negocios/articulo/612653/, accessed November 2007.

7. Consult http://www.idrc.ca/es/ev-47029–201–1–DO_TOPIC.html, accessed February 17, 2008. The previous World Social Forum in Porto Alegre in 2001 did not have the same wide spectrum of themes nor the impressive number of attendees.

8. These are also called *cabinas públicas* in Peru, *locutorios* in Argentina, even *tele-centros* in some places.

9. Francisco Proenza at the FAO has made an important effort in this direction. See table 5 of the following document: http://www.e-forall.org/pdf/Wireless&VoIP_5October2005.pdf, accessed February 17, 2008.

10. See http://www.infocentros.gov.cl and http://www.infocentros.gov.ve, both accessed February 17, 2008.

11. See the short video available online: "Los Piratas de la Antigua Escritura." http://uam-antropologia.info/web/content/view/273/77/, accessed June 1, 2007.

12. There is a pressing need for an in-depth analysis of the role of NGOs in civil society and the degree to which they have become estranged from the social movements that many claim to service.

13. Consult www.apc.org.

14. Gholami et al. 2005 report that in developed countries, existing ICT infrastructure attracts foreign direct investment; a higher level of ICT investment leads to a higher level of inflows. This suggests that ICT contributes to productivity and economic growth indirectly by attracting more foreign direct investment. But in developing countries the direction of causality goes the other way.

15. See, for example, the World Bank's Knowledge for Development Programme. http://web.worldbank.org/WBSITE/EXTERNAL/WBI/WBIPROGRAMS/KFDLP/0,menuPK:461238~pagePK:64156143~piPK:64154155~theSitePK:461198,00.html, accessed February 6, 2008.

16. See http://www.crisinfo.org/, accessed February 6, 2008.

17. Consult http://www.icann.org and http://www.icannwatch.org, accessed February 17, 2008.

18. The consultation process prior to the second World Summit, held in Rio de Janeiro in June 2005, provided an example of how state actors and corporations set the agenda while legitimizing their efforts with NGO allies, who, absent a regional agenda, were thrilled to be innocent minor partners in a "participatory consultation."

19. The post–WSIS II review is summarized in http://lac.derechos.apc.org/boletin.shtml, accessed February 6, 2008.

20. Today there are 82 million cell phone subscriptions in Brazil and 43 million in Mexico while nearly 80 percent of people live in range of a mobile network. See "Hoy en Telecomunicaciones," January 23, 2006, an on-line Mexican commercial bulletin, http://www.lda.bz/xportal/xportal.php?cve=Te071116, and "Loose Talk Saves Lives," http://www.developments.org.uk/articles/loose-talk-saves-lives-1/, accessed February 6, 2008.

21. See "Hoy en Telecomunicaciones," January 11, 2006, http://www.lda.bz/xportal/xportal.php?cve=Te071116, accessed February 6, 2008.

22. See "Low-Cost Mobile Phones Planned for One Billion Users." http://www.tech-web.com/wire/networking/180205406, accessed June 5, 2007.

References

Aguilar, Alberto. 2006. "Juntos bancos y telefónicas empujarán 43 millones de celu-lares como medio de pago en este año." *Reforma* (Mexico City), February 13. http://www.reforma.com/editoriales/negocios/618881, accessed June 5, 2007.

Almanza, Lucero, and Lilia Chacón. 2006. "Tienen Jóvenes Poco Acceso a La Red." *Reforma* (Mexico City), January 24.

Chua, Amy. 2003. *World on Fire: How Exporting Free Market Democracy Breeds Ethnic Hatred and Global Instability*. New York: Doubleday.

Gholami, Raghieh, Sang-Yong Tom Lee, and Almas Helmati. 2005. "The Causal Re-lationship between ICT and FDI." Research Paper No. 2005/26. Helsinki: United Nations University-World Institute for Development Economics Research (UNU-WIDER). http://www.wider.unu.edu/publications/working-papers/research-pa-pers/2005/en_GB/rp2005–26/, accessed February 17, 2008.

Halperin, Hernán, and Judith Mariscal. 2005. "Digital Poverty." *Latin American and Caribbean Perspectives*. http://www.idrc.ca/en/ev-112564–201–1–DO_TOPIC.html, accessed February 17, 2008.

Linton, Ralph. 1936. *The Study of Man*. New York: Appleton Century Crofts.

Lovink, Geert, and Soenke Zehle. 2005. "Incommunicado Glossary." Institute for Distributed Creativity. http://distributedcreativity.typepad.com/idc/2005/10/incommunicado_g.html, accessed April 16, 2007.

Roman, Raúl. 2003. "Diffusion of Innovations as a Theoretical Framework for Telecen-ters." *Information Technologies and International Development* 1 (2): 55–68.

Veltmeyer, Henry. 2005. "The Dynamics of Land Occupations in Latin America." In *Reclaiming the Land: The Resurgence of Rural Movements in Africa, Asia, and Latin America*, edited by Sam Moyo and Paris Yeros, 285–316. London: Zed Books.

15

Exit Followed by Voice

Mapping Mexico's Emerging Migrant Civil Society

JONATHAN FOX

More and more of Mexico's rural youth imagine their futures far from home, and those with the necessary social networks increasingly go to the United States. Will the broadening and deepening of migration seal the fate of future rural social movements? The objective of this chapter is to contribute to a rethinking of the relationship between rural out-migration and collective action. Is migration necessarily *instead of* collective action, or can it lead to *new forms* of collective action? Diverse forms of Mexican migrant collective action suggest that while exit might substitute for voice in the short term, exit can also be followed by voice.

Migration to Mexico's cities and to the United States has long been a pathway to escape the landlessness and the weakening of smallholder agriculture, often as part of diversified family survival strategies. While out-migration to the United States was historically concentrated in Mexico's center-west, since the 1980s and 1990s migration has spread throughout the nation's countryside, as well as into cities and across a broader mix of social classes. For rural Mexico, consider the implications of the fact that the one million Mexican farmworkers who gained permanent residency in the United States under the immigration reform of 1986 were equivalent to one-sixth of the adult men in rural Mexico at that time (Martin 2005, 6). For increasing numbers of Mexicans, what previously was circular migration has become a one-way trip.

Since NAFTA, estimated annual Mexican migration levels to the United States have risen by 63 percent, from 329,000 people in 1992 to over 530,000 in 2000.[1] Given this context, analysts need to go beyond merely referring in passing to the social and political relevance of cross-border migration as an "escape valve" and begin to explore more systematically how migration influences the future of public life in Mexico.

According to the Mexican census of 2000, 25 percent of the population continued to live in localities with less than 2,500 inhabitants. According to the most recent National Employment Survey, the share of agricultural employment fell from 24 percent in 1991 to under 15 percent at the end of 2005.[2] Another similar survey found a loss of 1.3 million agricultural jobs between 1993 and 2002. These data indicate a growing gap between the population that lives *in* the countryside and the population that lives *from* the countryside. The growth in the share of the rural population that does not live off agriculture has major implications for the future of public life in the countryside.

Exit and Voice: Dichotomous or Interactive?

This exodus of working-age adults must affect the prospects for future social and political change in the countryside, but the patterns of this impact remain unclear. It is no coincidence that analysts in Mexico often refer to this issue as the "migration problem," yet for the migrants themselves, access to the U.S. labor market represents a solution. What are the possible effects of this massive exercise of the "exit option" on the prospects for addressing the problem of the underrepresentation of the concerns of the rural poor in the national policy process?

It is worth recalling that during the post-NAFTA decade, with the notable exception of the regionally bounded Zapatista movement, Mexico experienced no sustained protest movement of the rural poor of national scope.[3] The broad-based but brief "Countryside Won't Take Any More" march on Mexico City in 2003 was the decade's only peasant protest of national significance that focused on making family farming economically sustainable. Though the mobilization was much larger than even sympathetic observers expected, it ended up having virtually no impact on national agricultural trade and investment policies, which continued to be extremely biased in favor of better-off producers.[4]

Does the "exit option" offer an alternative to "voice," potentially undermining the capacity for collective action among those left behind? As one of Mexico's most incisive political analysts put it, migration, along with the lack of formal sector employment, "stimulates the disintegration of the communities and the social fabric that sustain popular movements. They severely erode traditional forms of political and social mediation" (Hernández Navarro 2006, 27). Meanwhile, in spite of the change after 2000 in official Mexican rhetoric toward greater public recognition of migrants' contributions to the homeland, many still refer to those who moved to work in the United States as having "abandoned" their country. At least until recently, migrants were widely considered in Mexico as second-class citizens, too subject to U.S. influence to be worthy of the right to vote. In Mexico, the "exit" option is still widely associated with a lack of loyalty.

These concepts of exit, voice, and loyalty draw from the classic approach developed by the heterodox economist Albert Hirschman (1970). In this view, exit and voice are two alternative responses to decline (in firms, organizations, states). Exit refers to opting out, voting with one's feet—whether as a consumer changing brands or as an emigrant leaving one's homeland. Voice refers to more direct expressions of dissent, whether through protest, electoral contestation, or suasion. Loyalty cuts across both options, affecting decisions about whether to use exit or voice by making voice more likely. One of Hirschman's main points was that easy availability of exit is inimical to voice, because voice is generally more costly than exit. "The more pressure escapes through exit, the less is available to foment voice" (Hirschman 1993, 176). If this hypothesis holds for rural Mexico, then the implications are dramatic.

Yet the relationship between exit and voice may not be predetermined. This is the context for asking, along with one of Hirschman's critics, "whether in some cases the same factors make for exit *and* for lack of voice among those remaining" (Barry 1974, 85). Hirschman later recognized that under certain conditions, exit and voice can be mutually reinforcing, and the East German revolution of 1989–90 offered a vivid example. It remains to be seen under what conditions exit and voice are complementary versus contradictory.

Looking back at the dramatic increase in levels of out-migration from Mexico during the 1990s, it might be useful to rethink the importance of Mexico's national elections of 1994. The public policies that are now widely associated with the increase in out-migration—notably the end of crop support prices, cuts in input subsidies, and NAFTA—date primarily from the Salinas presidency (1988–94). In this sense, the elections of 1994, had they been fully democratic for rural voters, might have served as a referendum on this package of public policies.

Reports from the citizens' movement for independent election monitoring in 1994, led by the Civic Alliance, show that at least half of the polling places in the countryside lacked guaranteed ballot secrecy (Fox 1996). The Civic Alliance also found vote-buying pressures in 35 percent of rural polling places, which means that a significant fraction of the rural electorate was denied free and fair electoral choices about the country's national future. To put this in Hirschman's terms, given the lack of political voice for most of the rural poor, many turned to exit. While this was certainly not the only migratory push factor, out-migration rates did rise substantially over the rest of the decade, perhaps suggesting some relationship between lack of voice and the exit option—at least at that political turning point.

The clearest expression of rural political voice during this period came from Mexico's indigenous peoples, whose numerous local and regional organizations began to come together nationally for the first time during the 1990s and influence the national political agenda. Yet during the same decade, cross-border migration processes began to extend for the first time to almost all of Mexico's indigenous regions (Fox and Rivera-Salgado 2004). Looking back over the past decade and a half, Mexico's indigenous peoples have been exercising *both* voice *and* exit more than during the previous decades. Both decisions involve agency, though with very different implications for the balance of power in the countryside.

In Hirschman's approach, loyalty is an "intervening variable" that influences the choice between collective action in communities of origin versus the individual or family-based strategy of migration. Yet a growing body of research on migrant collective action based on shared communities of origin suggests that many migrants bring their sense of community with them and re-create it with their *paisanos* in the United States. Migrants' sense of shared collective identity is broadened when hometown associations form statewide federations, constructing a regional civic identity that the migrants may not have shared before they left. Similarly, the experience of collective identity formation of Oaxacan indigenous migrants suggests that they developed shared ethnic and pan-ethnic identities through and because of the migration process, leaving behind more traditional, highly localized identities (Fox 2006).

At the same time as one recognizes the emergence and consolidation of transnational communities, to be discussed below, one must also recognize that many who migrate do abandon their communities. Some do not return. Not all send resources to support their families. Plus, when organizers migrate, their organizations suffer a loss—especially if the organizations have invested in their training, as in the case of coffee cooperative certifiers of organic production (Mutersbaugh 2002).

These patterns suggest that while exit may sometimes weaken voice, and at other times exit and voice may reinforce each other, perhaps exit can also

Table 15.1. Locating Migrant Civil Society in Terms of Exit and Voice

Exit options:		
Leave	Unorganized migrants	Migrant civil society
Stay	Compliance, clientelism	Mass protest, electoral opposition
Voice options:	Silence	Voice

Source: This approach draws on ideas presented in Barry 1974, in response to Hirschman 1970.

reflect the prior weakness of voice. Many people point to regions of long-term out-migration and see a very thin civil society, yet the cause and effect relationship is not so clear-cut. Many migrants leave regions where rural civil society was already thin. In addition, even in regions that had experienced autonomous collective action, few campaigns had produced lasting change, and even fewer could offer viable future options from the point of view of young people. But if we extend the temporal and geographic frame for considering the interaction between exit and voice and take the binational arena into account, new ways of considering the relationship between exit and voice emerge, as well as the role of loyalty as a mediating factor.

Several steps are involved in broadening the frame. The first is to recognize that at least some migrants engage in collective action, along a range of possible pathways to be discussed further below. Second, for many migration has a collective dimension, insofar as it is only possible thanks to extended networks of social capital in which loyalty and trust can make the difference between life and death, between economic success and disaster, and between deep alienation and cultural survival. Third, when migrants send a significant fraction of their wages to their relatives and communities, they are also expressing loyalty. As suggested schematically in table 15.1, when migrants come together in hometown associations to send collective remittances, they are expressing not only loyalty, but also voice—as they participate in debates over what social investments are most important. For those migrants who did not have access to autonomous, dense civil society alternatives back home, their exit can permit the exercise of their voice, whose costs are born out of loyalty.[5]

In other words, one could argue that many of the diverse and growing patterns of social, civic, and political engagement among Mexican migrants in the United States reflect the exercise of voice by a (formerly) rural population that had exercised the exit option. In this view, exit was a step toward voice rather than a substitute.

Mapping Migrant Civil Society

Possibly hundreds of thousands of Mexican migrants work together with their *paisanos* to promote "philanthropy from below," funding hundreds of community development initiatives in their hometowns. More than forty thousand exercised their newly won right to cast absentee ballots in Mexico's presidential election of 2006. Others are more engaged with their communities in the United States—as organized workers, parents, members of religious congregations, and naturalized voters. In addition, some Mexican migrants are working to become full members of both U.S. and Mexican societies at the same time, constructing practices of "civic binationality" that have a great deal to teach us about new forms of immigrant integration into the United States.

Increasingly, to account for both migrant collective action and patterns of continued engagement with their home countries, many scholars have worked with the concept of "transnational communities." Transnational communities are groups of migrants whose daily lives, work, and social relationships extend across national borders. This idea helps to reveal relationships that are not visible when migrants are seen only through the lens of their engagements in the United States, yet the concept also risks tilting too far in the other direction, leaving out migrants' engagements in the United States.

The idea of "migrant civil society" offers an alternative frame for understanding Mexican migrant collective action in the United States. Transnational communities provide a social foundation for, but are not the same as, an emerging migrant civil society, which also involves the construction of public spaces and representative social and civic organizations. Just as only some migrants are members of transnational communities, only some transnational communities become the building blocks for representative social and civic organizations of migrants themselves. This idea is the point of departure for a comparative approach to analyzing Mexican migrants in the United States, which involves recognizing the diverse and sometimes overlapping patterns of migrant collective action in the United States.

Most often, in migration studies comparative analysis refers to one specific approach, the comparison of different national origin groups. This approach, most often used in survey research, has generated rich findings. Yet the Mexican migrant population in the United States is so large and so diverse that national-origin averages can mask key variables, such as ethnicity, region of origin, or region of settlement. For example, migrants from different Mexican states organize hometown associations at widely varying rates. Mexicans from the same states organize at different rates in different regions of the United States. Among indigenous Mexican migrants, members of some ethnic groups organize much more than others, in some regions more than others. Sectoral differences may also matter, insofar as we have not yet compared participation trends across hometown associations, workers' organizations, neighborhood associations, or religious communities. In the literature on naturalization and voting patterns of new citizens, it turns out that national samples can hide significant regional differences. Migrants in California have followed a much more highly politicized path than those in Texas and Florida, in terms of their rates of naturalization and voting (Pantoja et al. 2001). These differences only become visible once one takes a comparative approach—across regions, sectors, and patterns of participation.

Simply put, migrant civil society refers to migrant-led membership organizations and public institutions. Specifically, this includes four very tangible arenas of collective action. Each arena is constituted by actors, while each set of actors also constitutes an arena.

Migrant-led Membership Organizations

Membership organizations composed primarily of migrants can range from hometown associations (HTAs) to workers' organizations and religious congregations. The Mexican consulates have registered well over six hundred such clubs (Rivera-Salgado et al. 2005). Each has a core membership of perhaps an average of two dozen families, some with hundreds more. They are primarily concentrated in metropolitan areas. Many members of HTAs are relatively established, and many leaders of HTAs have relative economic stability and are either legal residents or U.S. citizens. Hometown associations have in turn federated into associations that bring people from one state in Mexico together in another state in the United States.

Today's Mexican HTAs have a long history, with the first Zacatecan club in California dating back to 1962 (Moctezuma 2005). But their numbers and membership have boomed in the past fifteen years as the result of several converging factors. Within the United States, the massive regularization of undocumented workers that followed the immigration reform of 1986 facilitated both economic improvement and increased cross-border freedom of movement for millions of migrants. On the Mexican side, the government deployed the convening power of its extensive consular apparatus, bringing together people from the same communities of origin and offering matching funds for community development to encourage collective social remittances, through the Three-for-One program. Though this policy began as a response to pressures from organized Zacatecan migrants, it also served as a powerful inducement for other migrants to come together in formal organizations for the first time. After all, many transnational social and civic relationships unfold outside of the clubs and federations. In addition, the Mexican state changed the tone of its relationship with the diaspora by formally permitting dual nationality for the first time (Castañeda 2006). While many clubs emerged from below, many of the state-level federations were formed through engagement with the Mexican state (Goldring 2002).[6]

At least until recently, many Mexican migrant organizations were disengaged from U.S. civil society. For example, back in 1994, Mexican HTAs participated little in the broad campaign against California's notorious anti-immigrant Proposition 187 (Escala Rabadán and Zabin 2002). In contrast, a decade later, when the main state-level immigrants' rights advocacy campaign involved the right to drivers' licenses for the undocumented, members of HTAs were actively involved, working the phone banks at the headquarters of Los Angeles's trade union movement.[7] The leadership of the Southern California Council of Presidents of Mexican Federations has now joined the fray of state politics (Rivera-Salgado et al. 2005). Some Mexican federations have also joined the National Alliance of Latin American and Caribbean Communities, especially in the Midwest. These kinds of alliances would have been hard to imagine a decade ago.

While HTAs are one of the main forms of expression of Mexican migrant civil society, they are but one among many. The broad category of migrant membership organizations also includes workers,' religious, community-based, and indigenous organizations. Some include migrants of diverse nationalities, while others are primarily or exclusively Mexican—as in the case of a growing number of trade union locals (discussed further below).

Migrant-led Communications Media

Migrant-led communications media can range from local and binational newspapers to radio programs, independent video, and now numerous Internet discussions oriented to hometowns or regions. For example, the Oaxacan community in Los Angeles is now sufficiently large and established to support *two* serious newspapers, *El Oaxaqueño* and *Impulso de Oaxaca*. The first publishes more than thirty thousand copies bi-weekly and circulates both in California and Oaxaca. The migrant-run Spanish-language public radio network, Radio Bilingüe, is broadcast on approximately fifty stations in the United States and twenty more in Mexico. In addition, for many years it broadcast the only regular programming in indigenous Mexican languages. For many migrant farmworker communities, Radio Bilingüe is their principal news source.

Beyond the nonprofit media is the huge world of commercial Spanish-language media. Though for-profit enterprises fall outside of most definitions of civil society, these media nevertheless play key civic roles, not only informing their publics, but also encouraging public service. Spanish-language media have actively encouraged both U.S. citizenship and voter turnout (Rodríguez 1999). Such practices contrast sharply with critics' assumptions that the persistence of Spanish is associated with an unwillingness to join U.S. civil society (for example, Huntington 2004). At the same time, migrant-oriented media is not necessarily the same as migrant-owned, so Spanish-language media institutions therefore only overlap partially with a strict definition of migrant civil society. In many cases, however, key media decision makers, such as editors and reporters, are most often migrants.[8]

Migrant-led NGOs

While many NGOs, or nonprofits, serve migrant communities, in this approach only those that are migrant-led would be considered part of migrant civil society. Here one must keep in mind the clear distinction between NGOs and membership organizations—a distinction that is side-stepped by the fuzzy U.S. term "community-based organization." In some cases migrant membership organizations have spun off their own NGOs, as in the case of the Indigenous Front of Binational Organizations (FIOB), which has set up its own NGOs in California and in Oaxaca to provide support services and to invest in community development and public education projects.[9]

To continue recognizing gray areas of overlap, this category within migrant civil society can also include those migrants who, as individuals, have gained positions of leadership within established U.S. nonprofits, including foundations. They are strategically located to make major contributions to the capacity building of other migrant civil society institutions.

Autonomous Migrant-led Public Spaces

This term refers to large public gatherings where migrants can come together to interact and to express themselves with relative freedom and autonomy. Here culture, religion, sports, and recreation are key. For example, in California, indigenous Oaxacan migrants now organize huge annual music, dance, and food festivals known as Guelaguetzas. They are the embodiment of the imagined cultural and civic space known as "Oaxacalifornia."[10] Specifically Oaxacan migrant civil society in California is now sufficiently dense that migrants put on six different Guelaguetza festivals each year. They are held in parks, high school auditoriums, and college campuses, and the largest is held in the Los Angeles Sports Arena—the former home of the Los Angeles Lakers basketball team. In each one, hundreds volunteer their time so that thousands can come together, so that parents can share their culture with their children. Indeed, probably few had had the opportunity to see such a festival when they were living in Oaxaca. With so much activity, California's multigenerational Oaxacan migrant dance groups are in high demand, and they represent yet another network of membership organizations. Each of the six annual festivals reveals an x-ray of the social networks and organizational styles of different strands of the web of Oaxacan civil society in California. For example, some work with local Latino politicians and organizations, others collaborate with the Oaxacan state government, which is controlled by the Institutional Revolutionary Party (PRI), while others keep their distance.

Having reviewed these four different arenas of migrant civil society, how might we think about their relationships with U.S. civil society? Is migrant civil society the U.S. branch of Mexico's civil society? Or is it the Mexican branch of U.S. civil society? The concept of migrant civil society proposed here would include both, because it is defined by the migrants themselves rather than by the national arena within which they are active. The hometown associations would be the clearest example of a branch of Mexican civil society that is *in*, but not necessarily *of* the United States. They have created a public sphere that is clearly Mexican, not only because of its participants' national origin, but also because of its culture, organizational style, symbolic references, and principal counterparts. In contrast, for examples of Mexican branches of U.S. civil society, we could look at the trade union locals that have become majority-migrant and migrant-led, as in the case of several major agro-industrial, service, and construction unions in California, or the probably hundreds of religious congregations that have become Mexican spaces within U.S. churches.[11]

When Organized Migrants Go Public—As Immigrants, as Workers, and as Mexicans

A key part of forging civil society involves migrants "coming out" as public, collective actors, representing themselves rather than relying on advocates. To illustrate this process, here follows a brief comparison of two different ways in which migrants have entered the U.S. public sphere. In the first one, organized migrants came together through the cross-country Immigrant Worker Freedom Ride in 2003. This initiative was led in part by the broadest multiracial set of U.S. civil society organizations—the trade union movement. This convergence was made possible, in turn, by the growing voice and clout of Latino leaders within the mainstream labor movement— most notably in California.[12]

By highlighting the historic legacy of freedom rides, migrants of many nationalities explicitly reached out to diverse U.S. constituencies by framing immigrants' rights under the historical mantle of the African American civil rights movement. Migrant organizations, including California's Oaxacan Federation, were officially represented on the ride.[13] In several areas of recent Mexican settlement in the United States, such as Nashville, the Freedom Ride permitted migrant organizations to become public actors for the first time.[14] Old habits die hard, though, and some Mexican migrant bus riders were frustrated with what they described as their trade union handlers' "mania for control." This cross-cultural disconnect erupted at one point into a brief, behind-the-scenes "rebellion" by migrant riders against the coordinators of one of the buses.[15] This small but revealing incident is emblematic of how much more work is needed to build and sustain cross-cultural coalitions. Overall, the Immigrant Worker Freedom Ride made unprecedented inroads in terms of projecting humanizing images of migrants in the mainstream media.

In contrast to what could be called the Immigrant Worker Freedom Ride's "integration strategy," Mexican migrant-led organizations also construct and deploy their own collective identities as their primary basis for claiming a space in the public sphere. For example, not long after the freedom ride, the Tepeyac Association—a Mexican faith-based membership organization in New York—led its own mass traveling collective action for immigrants' rights. Tepeyac's second annual relay Torch Run traveled through several of Mexico's "sending" regions and arrived in Saint Patrick's Cathedral in New York City on December 12. Along the way, the runners, called "Messengers for the Dignity of a People Divided by the Border" prayed to the Virgin for the right to permanent legal residency. Their repertoire resonates widely, though Mexicans in New York also form hometown associations and workers' organizations.

The Tepeyac Association pursues a distinctive strategy for forging the collective identity of its members, based around the combined ethno-national and spiritual symbolism of the Virgin of Guadalupe, together with an explicit effort to build a shared collective identity as undocumented workers (Rivera Sánchez 2004). Founded by Jesuits, its New York City social base is organized in forty different neighborhood Guadalupano communities. This is very different from the hometown-based approach to migrant organizing. Tepeyac's original U.S. partner was the New York Diocese of the Catholic Church, whose leadership took the initiative that led Tepeyac to form in the first place, by reaching out to Mexican church counterparts.

Both the Immigrant Worker Freedom Ride and Tepeyac's Torch Run brought organized migrants into the public sphere, both crossed vast territories in the process, and both were organized from below but counted on institutional allies in the United States. Yet they followed different strategies to broaden their bases—one ventured from west to east, while the other traveled from south to north. The Immigrant Worker Freedom Ride framed migrants as the most recent wave in the long history of struggle against social exclusion in the United States, building a multiracial class identity as immigrant workers, while Tepeyac looked across the border to build a shared identity as Mexicans fighting for dignity and recognition as Mexicans. Each strategy has its own strengths and limitations.

As one considers the idea of migrant civil society, then, migrants are represented through two main pathways. The first is the most straightforward: organizations that are led by and made up of migrants themselves. The second is less straightforward because the boundaries are more blurred, and it takes the form of U.S. civil society organizations that have effectively been transformed by migrant participation. This would describe many Catholic parishes, trade union locals, workers' centers, and parent teacher associations—or Chicago's 170 elected School Councils that are primarily Mexican (IME 2005).

Mexican workers are an increasingly important part of the trade union movement in those regions and sectors where unions are dynamic and organizing new members. By 2004, Mexican-born workers represented 2.3 percent of all union members, over 360,000, with unionization rates much higher for long-term residents (Milkman 2006, 5). In regions of high union density, Mexican migrants are well-represented in the membership of

unions that represent primarily low-wage workers, such as UNITE-HERE
(a merger of the Union of Needletrades, Industrial and Textile Employees
and the Hotel Employees and Restaurant Employees International Union),
the Service Employees International Union (services, including health-care
workers and the legendary Justice for Janitors campaign), the United Food
and Commercial Workers (food processing), and the Teamsters (agro-
industry). Further research would be needed to map Mexican workers' presence across sectors and regions with precision, and to determine how many
of those union locals are migrant-led and therefore part of migrant civil
society as defined here. Clearly, however, in terms of both sheer numbers
and the impact on members' daily lives, unions are by far one of the most
important institutions for the representation of Mexicans in the United
States.

Nevertheless, trade unions face many structural, institutional, and cultural constraints in their efforts to organize immigrant workers. In response, a new set of institutions has emerged to try to fill the gap between
traditional workplace-based unions and low-wage immigrant workers.
Workers' centers include a wide range of grass-roots organizing initiatives
that operate separately from trade unions. Sometimes they coordinate,
and sometimes they are in tension. A comprehensive recent survey found
137 workers' centers across the United States, 122 of which work closely
with immigrant workers (Fine 2006). Of the 40 studied in depth, about 17
have a significant Mexican constituency, and 13 of them are predominantly
Mexican.[16] Central Americans have played a key leadership role in workers' centers, in part because of their experiences organizing in their home
countries before escaping the repression of the late 1970s and 1980s. Some
workers' centers operate more like NGOs, while others are membership-
led. The National Network of Day Laborers brings together 29 workers'
centers from 11 states, with half in New York and California.[17]

Workers' centers that are migrant-led could be seen as institutions of
migrant civil society. If the first approach to unpacking migrant civil society
involves distinguishing between organizations in terms of whether they are
U.S. institutions transformed by migrants or are "migrant institutions," a
second approach would involve unpacking the participation of migrants as
individuals. The same people may participate in both arenas of migrant civil
society, though sometimes separately, a form of double militancy. Note the
case of Oregon's farmworkers' organization, the Northwest Treeplanters
and Farmworkers United (PCUN), whose membership combines Mexican
Americans, mestizo Mexican migrants, and indigenous Mixteco migrants

from Mexico's state of Oaxaca. While the PCUN is very much a U.S. organization, some of its Mexican members are also active in their own hometown associations. In the case of some of the Oaxacan HTAs, they have as many as a dozen branches spread across the United States, each raising funds to support community development projects back home.[18]

The PCUN is one of several regional U.S. farmworkers' organizations, each one with thousands of members. Some have won tangible victories, which are especially notable in the overall national context of eroding union bargaining power—including the Farm Labor Organizing Committee (FLOC), a trade union based in the Midwest and North Carolina, and Florida's Coalition of Immokalee Workers (CIW). Majority-migrant workers' organizations, like so many trade union locals in California, the United Farm Workers (UFW), the PCUN, FLOC, the CIW, and day laborer organizations, are all U.S. organizations whose goals are to defend their members' rights, both as workers and as migrants in the United States. In some of these regional organizations the vast majority of members are Mexican, while others include workers of multiple nationalities, as in the case of the CIW. Few have binational or cross-border priorities, with the exception of FLOC. Yet their members may also have other affiliations, often invisible to outsiders, as in the case of the PCUN, or the representation of leadership of the UFW on the Mexican government's migrant Advisory Council. Further research would be necessary to see whether their members are also organized binationally around their communities of origin.

While most civic binationality takes the form of individuals who do double duty, some migrant organizations are following what we could call "fully binational" paths as well. This means being engaged with social, civic, or political agendas in both countries. The leading example in the United States is the Indigenous Front of Binational Organizations, formerly known as the Oaxacan Indigenous Binational Front (FIOB). The FIOB is one of the very few mass membership organizations that include organized bases in both the United States and in Mexico, with thousands of affiliated members organized in branches in California, Baja California, and in their home state of Oaxaca.[19]

The FIOB is not a federation of hometown associations, though its members have a strong sense of shared homeland, in the sense of being *paisanos*. Their sense of being *oaxaqueño* is a shared identity that comes out of a struggle against the intense racism they face in northern Mexico and in California, where they face ethnic slurs, like "*oaxaquito*," or "*oaxaco*," from other Mexicans. In this context, *oaxaqueño* is not just a geographic reference, but rather a term of both respect and self-respect. In the process, regional identity becomes socially constructed as a pan-ethnic umbrella identity, since Oaxaca includes at least sixteen distinct ethnic groups. In this context, the FIOB's recent decision to change its name is especially notable. The change in the wording from "Oaxacan" to "Organizations," while keeping the FIOB acronym, reflected the new realities of its mass bases in California and Baja California, where indigenous migrants from states other than Oaxaca are increasingly involved. Among the new binational leadership commission elected in March 2005, five Mexican languages are spoken (Mixtec, Zapotec, Mixe, Purépecha, and Spanish).

The FIOB actively pursues a wide-ranging rights agenda on issues that range from family and community-level public interest advocacy, environmental justice, public health education, and PTA training to national immigrants' and indigenous people's rights in both countries (Domínguez Santos 2004; Martínez Saldaña 2004). The FIOB works closely with a wide range of public interest groups in both countries, its leaders run for local and state offices in Oaxaca, and it does public interest advocacy at local, state, and federal levels in both countries. This raises a conceptual issue. Does the FIOB represent the migrant wing of Mexico's national indigenous movement? Does the FIOB represent the indigenous wing of a broader cross-border migrant movement? Clearly the FIOB plays both roles.

Puzzles for Future Research

Based on this review of the contours of the landscape of Mexican migrant civil society, here follow three of the many possible analytical puzzles that emerge. In some sectors, significant additional research is needed even to formulate the analytical questions—most notably in the areas of Mexican migrant civic-religious participation, women's participation, workers' organization, and community organization. These are all areas where a binational perspective would shed light on "where Mexicans are coming from" in arenas that have so far been analyzed through exclusively U.S. lenses.

What Are the Social, Civic, and Political Effects of Migrant Associations in Their Hometowns?

The discussion of the impact of migration on sending communities has shifted from an earlier focus on the loss of human capital to a debate over whether family remittances contribute to more than survival for the relatives who stay behind, and whether remittances can become a lever for job creation (for example, Goldring 2004). In terms of the dichotomy often posed between the use of remittances for consumption versus investment, documented experiences with sustainable job-creating enterprises beyond a very small scale are very limited, at least so far. Family investment of re-mittances in education appears to be much more substantial, though often miscategorized as consumption. There are many powerful reasons why the results of job-creating investment of remittances have been limited, includ-ing a less-than-hospitable policy environment, the greater attraction of public versus private goods (in the case of collective remittances), and very limited investment opportunities in many sending communities.

In the discussion of the effects on sending communities, one could ar-gue that the focus on economic flows has "crowded out" recognition of *non*-economic effects, which can be described as social and cultural remit-tances (Levitt 2001). How do migrant hometown clubs affect public life in their communities of origin? Do they encourage local democratization? Do they affect women's opportunities for participation and representation?[20] Many participants and observers expect that HTAs do have democratizing effects, though the evidence is not yet clear. Clearly, returned migrants play key roles in public life, as individuals. According to a survey carried out by the migrant support agency of the Michoacan state government, 37 percent of the 113 mayors who governed in the state from 2002 to 2004 were for-mer migrants (Bada 2004b).[21]

But the fact that some migrants return to fill local leadership roles does not answer the question about the civic and political effects of HTAs. To what degree do the hometown associations reproduce the political culture that dominated Mexico in the twentieth century? Optimists often suggest that organized civil society generates democratic values and practices, and this is sometimes the case. But civil society also carries the weight of history and is cross-cut by hierarchies and inequality between genders, classes, and ethnic groups, as well as the legacy of less-than-democratic political ideolo-gies. After all, many of the federations, as well as some of the HTAs, came together in response to initiatives of the Mexican government. If one inter-prets this relationship through the lens of state-society relations in Mexico, then this government strategy represents a response to real demands from below, while also serving as an institutional channel to regulate relation-ships with migrant civil society.[22] In principle, in contrast to similar govern-ment efforts *in* Mexico, one might expect that migrants in the United States would be less vulnerable to clientelistic manipulation.

The broad question of home community impact needs to be unpacked in at least two ways. First, to what degree do the HTAs themselves generate democratic values and practices? So far, research that compares the internal practices of different state federations finds a wide range of practices, from more to less democratic (Rivera-Salgado and Escala Rabadán 2004). The second question would focus on their effects in home communities. These questions are distinct because, in principle, hometown clubs could be highly representative of their constituencies, but not necessarily of the non-migrant population.

Some studies argue that HTAs tend to hold local governments accountable (for example, Burgess 2006). Even if most clubs are internally democratic, and even if they hold local governments accountable, this does not necessarily generate democratization within the home community. Accountability refers to a power relationship, checks and balances, in this case between a specific constituency and the local government—but not necessarily vis-à-vis the majority of the community (whether defined in local or translocal terms). Do the non-migrants play any role in determining how to invest collective remittances? How are choices weighed between infrastructure projects that the migrants use on their annual visits home and those that may have a greater impact on the daily lives of non-migrants (for example, rodeo rings versus water systems)? It should be no surprise that relationships between migrants and mayors are not always easy, especially now that local elections are more democratic in many regions of Mexico.

How Can Disenfranchised Migrants Gain Political Representation?

The issue of how migrants can gain political representation poses a puzzle. If they lack voting rights in their host country, then host country politicians have little electoral incentive to make the political investment necessary to enfranchise them. If they also lack voting rights in their home country, then their home country politicians will lack political incentives to enfranchise them. This presents a "chicken and egg" problem—migrants need to gain electoral clout for politicians to pay attention, yet they need politicians to pay attention to get electoral clout.

In Mexico, the recent approval of the absentee ballot represents a first step toward overcoming this problem, though the voting procedures discouraged participation. The complex mail-in balloting, combined with the impossibility of registering abroad, was approved by a near-total consensus in the Mexican Congress. This allowed congressional representatives to show their recognition of Mexican migrants' citizenship rights without actually risking a significant change in the composition of the electorate.

In the United States, the unrepresented population is huge and growing. In California, for example, 20 percent of the adult population lacks
the right to vote. The discursive frame of "non-citizen enfranchisement"
challenges the systemic political exclusion of immigrants but also blurs the
distinction between undocumented immigrants and permanent residents.
The respective reasons for their exclusion are different, as are their possible pathways to inclusion. In the first case, the enfranchisement of undocumented immigrants would require a comprehensive policy reform that
included a pathway to citizenship, which in turn would require a dramatic
shift in U.S. politics at the national level—an issue too complex to address
adequately here. In contrast, in the second case, more active support for
the enfranchisement of legal permanent residents would not require major
legal changes and could be pursued by a wide range of actors at all levels of
government and civil society.

The size of the immigrant population that is already eligible for citizenship is huge. In 2003, eligible permanent U.S. residents of Mexican origin
numbered 2.4 million people, or 30.2 percent of the total (Rytina 2005,
4–5). Yet the federal government lacks a policy to encourage immigrant
integration. As Murguia and Muñoz (2005) suggest, a serious new effort
to encourage naturalization would require substantial changes in the priorities of a wide range of U.S. institutions, though civil society actors and
local governments do not need to wait for new federal laws to make a difference.

Why the Persistent Disconnect Between Analysis and Action Involving
Migration and Development?

In light of the clear overlap between the challenges of migration and rural
development, one might expect high levels of dialogue and convergence between the analysts and social actors involved.[23] After all, the growth in migrant workers' remittances, combined with the spread of organized hometown associations, has provoked widespread optimism about prospects for
investing in cross-border community development. Yet analyses of Mexican migration and development continue to engage at most sporadically,
for reasons that are not well understood. Each agenda tends to treat the
other as a residual category, while fully integrated approaches have yet to
be developed. One factor may be that specifying the nature of the linkages
between migration and development turns out to be easier said than done.
For example, does organic and fair-trade coffee production and marketing

provide an alternative to migration, does it serve as a source of funding for marketing, or do remittances end up subsidizing coffee production because demand at fair-trade prices is insufficient?[24]

So far, the huge volumes of remittances have attracted most of the public and policy attention. The framing of migration and development issues through the lens of remittances draws attention to questions of how financial institutions can capture the funds. While "banking the unbanked" is certainly important to those sending remittances, the connection to broader development remains uncertain. For migrants and their families, the most tangible impact of the widespread public discussion has been the significant recent reduction in transaction costs, driven in part by increased competition from the private sector. The focus on remittances also draws attention to the efforts of organized migrants to generate collective investment funds, primarily for social infrastructure rather than economic development. As a result, neither the financial nor the social emphasis on remittances directly engages with the challenge of making rural communities economically sustainable.

From a development point of view, most of the policy discussion involving remittances has focused on the Mexican government's cutting-edge efforts to support collective social remittances through its Three-for-One matching fund program. The program now has a significant track record that analysts are carefully examining, but its high public profile contrasts remarkably with its practical application. In 2004, the Mexican Social Development Ministry budget marked about $18 million, less than 1 percent of its budget, for matching migrant-generated funds for social development projects in migrants' home communities. Almost none of these funds supported productive projects.

Indeed, in spite of almost a decade of public discussion about the potential of remittance investments to create development alternatives, in Mexico there is still little tangible evidence of remittance investments that generate sustainable jobs beyond a few micro-level cases. This should not be surprising given the dearth of investment opportunities in so many sending communities, as well as the critical need for on-the-ground entrepreneurial and technical capacity. The issues of economic viability are compounded by the structure of the decision-making process. When migrants pool their hard-earned money for hometown projects, they place a premium on those investments that provide benefits to the community as whole. Most job-creating investments, in contrast, directly affect only a small subset of the community. In addition, their benefits may be perceived as at risk of being captured by local elites—in a context in which long-distance accountability is difficult. This dilemma suggests the importance of identifying those productive investments that can also have "public goods" effects, such as improved coffee-processing infrastructure in those communities where most people depend on coffee and already have years of experience working together in a marketing cooperative whose leadership is publicly accountable. Yet this category of potential investment projects has yet to be linked to migrant collective action.

Creative practitioners and analysts are beginning to address this long-standing disconnect between migration and development agendas. Yet efforts to bring migrant organizations into the broader development policy debate are still incipient, as their Mexican policy agenda continues to be dominated by the traditionally bounded "migration policy" framework, limited to the Three-for-One program, the Institute for Mexicans Abroad, and Mexico's approach to U.S. immigration and border policies. Even at the level of local and translocal policy agendas, few cross- border membership organizations support grass-roots development agendas both in communities of origin and of settlement. The FIOB is a notable exception, as it consolidates a participatory grass-roots micro-credit network back home to build a locally accountable institutional base that could effectively receive and invest remittances.

In an effort to craft a new way of framing the relationship between migration and development, the Mexican rural development strategist Armando Bartra (2003) bridges the migration, development, and rights agendas with the call for respect for "the right to not [have to] migrate." After all, Article 123 of the Mexican Constitution still speaks of citizens' right to "dignified and socially useful work." The "right to not migrate" can be a useful bridging concept for promoting reflection and discussion between diverse and sometimes disparate actors who see the process differently. This principle recognizes that while migration is an option, it is a choice made within a context imposed by public policies that enable some development strategies over others. The idea also shows how the term "migration policy" is deceptive insofar as it is often limited to those policies that deal with migrants, such as matching funds for projects or protection from police abuse on the way home for the holidays. The idea of "migration policy" should also take into account how the full range of public policies, such as the withdrawal of support for family farming, affects the decision to migrate. Yet the apparently limited impact of the concept of the "right to not migrate" suggests that translating an evocative frame into practical strategies for grass-roots organizations turns out to be a serious challenge.

What might explain this persistent disconnect between migration and development? Migration is increasingly recognized as spreading throughout Mexico, remittances are widely seen as a development resource, and those practitioners and analysts working on migration increasingly acknowledge the need to take into account dynamics in communities of origin. Perhaps the roots go deeper and one needs to look at the basic frameworks used to define strategies for change. For almost all of Mexico's rural development practitioners and analysts, migration is still seen as occurring *outside* the framework. Migration is treated as an external process happening "around" the grass-roots development process, whereas for peasant families, migration is inside the box, a central component of a diversified survival strategy. For most practitioners and analysts who are working on migration, in contrast, the development dimension of the relationship between receiving and sending community focuses on the "philanthropy from below" process, including the challenges of raising and sending the funds, and finding high-profile projects that offer "something for everyone." But who decides how to invest the funds, who ends up managing the projects, how sustainable are they? How do longer-term development effects figure into the decision-making process?[25] Where do the rest of the government's social, economic, and environmental policies fit in?

To contribute more directly to grass-roots development strategies on the ground, a next stage of mapping is necessary. Perhaps at the level of a state or a region, it would be very useful to take a map of those communities whose migrants have generated hometown associations and lay it over a map of those communities of origin that have also generated the social, civic, and economic development organizations that could serve as counterparts with the organized migrants. Some "sending" communities in the state of Oaxaca have very limited economic development prospects, but others have significant, scaled-up community-based enterprises, such as organic coffee and timber cooperatives. Imagining alternatives with those organized migrants who come from hometowns with community-based economic development track records could go a long way toward addressing the issues that make productive investments of remittances difficult. Those issues include the need for viable investment prospects, for entrepreneurial experience and reliable technical support, for public accountability to the communities of origin, and for positive social spillover effects beyond the local interested parties. Yet matching organized migrants to grass-roots initiatives has yet to be done.

Conclusions

The emergence of Mexican migrant civil society suggests that exit can be followed by voice. For many Mexican migrants, autonomous collective action begins as they look homeward. For those who were active before they left, civic life back home may be undermined, at least in the short term—though some return to provide community service later in life. Untold numbers of activist Mexican migrants had track records of collective action before leaving, suggesting that many find new pathways for expressing their commitments, following Hirschman's (1984) principle of the "transformation and mutation of social energy."

When compared to the vast size and diversity of Mexican society in the United States, clearly the vast majority of migrants remain unrepresented by formal organizations of any kind. Nevertheless, the idea of migrant civil society recognizes that Mexicans in the United States are creating their own institutions, as well as joining existing ones. Some are building multi-national and multi-ethnic workers' organizations. Others are joining community and faith-based organizations. Some also participate in cross-border Mexican civil society, joining with their *paisanos* in hometown associations and voting rights campaigns, while at the same time campaigning for immigration policy reform in the United States. Meanwhile, much of Mexican migrant social and civic participation unfolds within the U.S. categories of Mexican American, Hispanic, and Latino.

Mexican migrant civil society in the United States is just beginning to emerge. Organized migrants are just beginning to construct points of convergence—across social sectors, regions of origin, and regions of settlement in the United States. With the exception of the voting rights campaign, organized Mexican migrants also lack consolidated partnerships with potential counterparts in Mexican civil society. The debates needed to identify shared agendas and to agree on shared goals have yet to happen. The future of rural Mexico has yet to be imagined jointly, between those who left and those who stayed. While the whole may be greater than the sum of the parts, it is not yet clear how these parts will come together.

Notes

Author's note: This is an abridged version of a chapter in Fox 2008. An earlier version was presented as the keynote address to the fifth congress of the Mexican Association of Rural Studies, Oaxaca, May, 2005, http://www.amer.org.mx, accessed February 25, 2008. The research was made possible by grants from the Rockefeller and Ford foundations, as well a 2004–5 fellowship from the Woodrow Wilson Center. The ideas presented here were informed by ongoing conversations with colleagues too numerous to thank here, but I would like to express my special appreciation for input from Xóchitl Bada and Gaspar Rivera-Salgado.

1. See the dramatic chart in Passel and Suro 2005, table 5a. Their estimate of Mexican migration rates later fell to 460,000 in 2004, apparently in response to rising unemployment levels in the United States after September 11, 2001.

2. "Población ocupada según sector económica (nacional)," Encuesta Nacional de Ocupación y Empleo, http://www.inegi.gob.mx, accessed January 23, 2008.

3. The well-known Barzón movement for debt relief reached national scope but represented primarily small-to-medium-sized commercial producers. Only a minority of Mexican farmers were sufficiently well-off to have received bank credit in the first place.

4. On the distribution of the Mexican government's agricultural spending across social classes, see the little known but nominally public social incidence analysis by the World Bank (2004). For background on the "El campo no aguanta más" movement, see, among others, Schwentesius et al. 2004; a thematic issue of *El Cotidiano* (no. 124, March-April 2004); and the extended debate in 2003 between Luis Hernández Navarro and Armando Bartra in the pages of *La Jornada*.

5. This proposition leaves aside the question of whether exit undermines the voice option for those who remain, a major dilemma that is beyond the scope of this discussion.

6. For more on Mexican HTAs, see also, among others, Bada 2004a, 2004b; Goldring 2002; Lanly and Valenzuela 2004; Moctezuma 2005; Rivera-Salgado and Escala Rabadán 2004; and Smith 2005.

7. On the role of trade unions in Los Angeles as channels for political participation by noncitizens, see Varsanyi 2005. On subnational immigration politics more generally, see Wells 2004.

8. Consider an effervescent immigrants' rights march in Chicago that predated the mobilization of spring 2006, led by a Spanish-language radio host and inspired by a local Mexican priest's call-in to denounce the claims of the "Minutemen" (Martínez and Piña 2005).

9. See http://www.fiob.org, accessed February 25, 2008; Domínguez Santos 2004; Rivera-Salgado 2002; Fox 2006; and Fox and Rivera-Salgado 2004.

10. For background on this concept, see Nagengast and Kearney 1990.

11. More research is needed to determine the degree of specifically Mexican presence within the U.S. Catholic Church with greater precision, including comparison across regions, dioceses, and religious orders.

12. On U.S. workers' organizations and Mexican migrants, see Bacon 2004, 2005, 2006; Fine 2006; Gordon 2005; Johnston 2003, 2004a, 2004b; and Milkman 2006.

13. The two returning Oaxacan migrant federation representatives on the ride were honored with a photo on the front page of the *El Oaxaqueño* newspaper, which is based in Los Angeles (October 18, 2003, 4 [116]).

14. See, for example, Miller 2004 and Reyes 2003a, 2003b. On the broader processes of new Mexican settlement in the South and the Midwest, see Hernández-León and Zuñiga 2005.

15. See Ehrenreich 2003 and Jamison 2005 for detailed accounts.

16. Janice Fine, personal communication, June 2005.

17. See http://www.ndlon.org, accessed January 23, 2008.

18. See http://www.pcun.org, accessed February 25, 2008; and Stephen 2004 2007.

19. The campaign of the ex-*bracero* workers for the restitution of government wage deductions is one of the few others that is both cross-border and binational.

20. For a case study of the relationship between migration and women's empowerment in a home community in Oaxaca, see Maldonado and Artía Rodríguez 2004.

21. Such roles are also very common in Oaxacan towns and villages, many of which retain high expectations in terms of their expatriate citizens' duties and responsibilities (Kearney and Besserer 2004; Mutersbaugh 2002; Robles 2004).

22. The government's role in inducing the formation of HTA federations recalls and parallels Mexico's experience with the National Solidarity Program, which induced the formation of only nominally participatory committees from above in some areas, while in others bolstering representative social organizations that took advantage of this partial opening to consolidate.

23. This section draws on Fox 2006.

24. For one of the few studies to directly address the relationship between coffee and migration, see Lewis and Runsten 2005.

25. For a heterodox critique of the conventional discussion of remittances and development, see the Declaración de Cuernavaca from the Migration and Development Network, *Enlaces News* 10 (August 2005), http://www.enlacesamerica.org, accessed January 23, 2008. It is worth noting that researchers have yet to agree on the validity of the official data, the share of the Mexican population that receives remittances, or the degree to which they reach the poorest communities.

References

Bacon, David. 2004. *The Children of NAFTA: Labor Wars on the Mexico-U.S. Border.* Berkeley: University of California.

———. 2006. *Communities without Borders.* Ithaca, N.Y.: Cornell University Press.

Bada, Xóchitl. 2004a. "Reconstrucción de identidades regionales a través de proyectos de remesas colectivos: La participación ciudadana extraterritorial de comunidades migrantes michoacanas en el área metropolitana de Chicago." In *Organizaciones de Mexicanos en Estados Unidos: La política transnacional de la nueva sociedad civil migrante,* edited by Guillaume Lanly and M. Basilia Valenzuela, 175–224. Guadala-jara: Universidad de Guadalajara.

———. 2004b. "Las remesas colectivas de las organizaciones de migrantes mexicanos: Participación cívica transnacional y estrategias comunitarias de desarrollo." Paper presented at the fourth Congreso sobre la Inmigración en España, Ciudadanía y Participación, Girona, November 10–13.

Barry, Brian. 1974. "Review: Exit, Voice, and Royalty; Responses to Decline in Firms, Organizations, and States." *British Journal of Political Science* 4 (1): 79–107.

Bartra, Armando. 2003. *Cosechas de ira: Economía política de la contrareforma agrarian.* México: Ed. Ithaca/Instituto Maya.

Burgess, Katrina. 2006. "Migrant Philanthropy and Local Governance in Mexico." In *New Patterns for Mexico: Remittances, Philanthropic Living, and Equitable Development,* edited by Barbara Merz, 99–125. Cambridge, Mass.: Harvard University Press

Castañeda, Alejandra. 2006. *The Politics of Citizenship of Mexican Migrants.* New York: LFB Scholarly Publishing.

Domínguez Santos, Rufino. 2004. "The FIOB Experience: Internal Crisis and Future Challenges." In *Indigenous Mexican Migrants in the United States,* edited by Jonathan Fox and Gaspar Rivera-Salgado, 69–80. La Jolla: University of California, San Diego, Center for Comparative Immigration Studies and Center for U.S.-Mexican Studies.

Ehrenreich, Ben. 2003. "Si, Se Puede! L.A.'s New Freedom Riders Take Their Quest for Immigrant Equality on the Road." *LA Weekly* (October), 24–30.

Escala Rabadán, Luis, and Carol Zabin. 2002. "Mexican Hometown Associations and Mexican Immigrant Political Empowerment in Los Angeles." *Frontera Norte* 27.

Fine, Janice. 2006. *Worker Centers: Organizing Communities at the Edge of the Dream.* Ithaca, N.Y.: Cornell University Press.

Fox, Jonathan. 1996. "National Electoral Choices in Rural Mexico." In *The Reform of the Mexican Agrarian Reform,* edited by Laura Randall, 185–209. Armonk, N.Y.: M. E. Sharpe.

———. 2006. "Reframing Mexican Migration as a Multi-Ethnic Process." *Latino Studies* 4 (1–2): 39.

———. 2008. *Accountability Politics: Power and Voice in Rural Mexico.* Oxford: Oxford University Press.

Fox, Jonathan, and Gaspar Rivera-Salgado, eds. 2004. *Indigenous Mexican Migrants in the United States.* La Jolla: University of California, San Diego, Center for Comparative Immigration Studies and Center for U.S.-Mexican Studies.

Goldring, Luin. 2002. "The Mexican State and Transmigrant Organizations: Negotiating the Boundaries of Membership and Participation." *Latin American Research Review* 37 (3): 55–99.

———. 2004. "Family and Collective Remittances to Mexico: A Multidimensional Typology." *Development and Change* 35 (4): 799–840.

Gordon, Jennifer. 2005. *Suburban Sweatshops: The Fight for Immigrant Rights.* Cambridge, Mass.: Harvard University.

Hernández Navarro, Luis. 2006. "Optimismo y cambio en América Latina." *La Jornada*, January 31, p. 27.

Hirschman, Albert. 1970. *Exit, Voice, and Royalty: Responses to Decline in Firms, Organizations, and States*. Cambridge, Mass.: Harvard University.

———. 1984. *Getting Ahead Collectively*. New York: Pergamon.

———. 1993. "Exit, Voice, and the Fate of the German Democratic Republic: An Essay in Conceptual History." *World Politics* 45 (2): 173–202.

Huntington, Samuel. 2004. *Who Are We? The Challenges to America's National Identity*. New York: Simon and Schuster.

IME (Instituto de los Mexicanos en el Exterior). 2005. "Organizaciones Comunitarias Mexicanas en Chicago." *Lazos*, Boletín Especial 255 (April 21).

Jamison, Angela. 2005. "Embedded on the Left: Aggressive Media Strategies and Their Organizational Impact on the Immigrant Worker Freedom Ride." *Theory and Research in Comparative Social Analysis* (University of California, Department of Sociology) 24 (February).http://repositories.cdlib.org/escholarship/, accessed January 23, 2008.

Johnston, Paul. 2003. "Transnational Citizenries: Reflections from the Field in California." *Citizenship Studies* 7 (2): 199–217.

———. 2004. "Outflanking Power, Reframing Unionism: The Basic Strike of 1999–2001." *Labor Studies Journal* 28 (4): 1–24.

Kearney, Michael, and Federico Besserer. 2004. "Oaxacan Municipal Governance in Transnational Context." In *Indigenous Mexican Migrants in the United States*, edited by Jonathan Fox and Gaspar Rivera-Salgado, 449–68. La Jolla: University of California, San Diego, Center for Comparative Immigration Studies and Center for U.S.-Mexican Studies.

Lanly, Guillaume, and M. Basilia Valenzuela, eds. 2004. *Clubes de migrantes oriundos mexicanos en los Estados Unidos: La política transnacional de la nueva sociedad civil migrante*. Guadalajara: Universidad de Guadalajara.

Lewis, Jessa, and David Runsten. 2005. "Does Fair Trade Coffee Have a Future in Mexico? The Impact of Migration in a Oaxacan Community." Paper presented at Trading Morsels Conference, Princeton University, February.

Maldonado, Centolia, and Patricia Artia Rodríguez. 2004. "'Now We Are Awake': Women's Participation in the Oaxacan Indigenous Binacional Front." In *Indigenous Mexican Migrants in the United States*, edited by Jonathan Fox and Gaspar Rivera-Salgado, 495–510. La Jolla: University of California, San Diego, Center for Comparative Immigration Studies and Center for U.S.-Mexican Studies.

Martin, Philip. 2005. "NAFTA and Mexico-U.S. Migration." Paper presented at Consejo Nacional de Población, Mexico City, December 16.

Martínez, Cindy, and Francisco Piña. 2005. "Chicago en marcha por reforma migratoria." *MX Sin Fronteras* 20, August.

Martínez Saldaña, Jesús. 2004. "Building the Future: The FIOB and Civic Participation of Mexican Immigrants in Fresno, California." In *Indigenous Mexican Migrants in the United States*, edited by Jonathan Fox and Gaspar Rivera-Salgado, 125–44.

La Jolla: University of California, San Diego, Center for Comparative Immigration Studies and Center for U.S.-Mexican Studies.

Milkman, Ruth. 2006. *L.A. Story: Immigrant Workers and the Future of the U.S. Labor Movement.* New York: Russell Sage.

Miller, Spring. 2004. "A Report from Nashville on the Immigrant Worker Freedom Ride." *Enlaces News,* January. http://www.enlacesamerica.org/articles0303/FreedomRide.htm, accessed January 23, 2008.

Moctezuma Longoria, Miguel. 2005. "Transnacionalismo, agentes y sujetos migrantes: Estructura y niveles de las asociaciones de mexicanos en Estados Unidos." Paper presented at the conference entitled Problemas y Desafíos de la Migración y Desarrollo en América, Red Internacional de Migración y Desarrollo. Centro Regional de Investigaciones Multidisciplinarias de la UNAM y CERLAC, Cuernavaca, April 7–9.

Murguia, Janet, and Cecilia Muñoz. 2005. "From Immigrant to Citizen: Most Still Want to Become Americans." *The American Prospect* 16 (11): A22–24.

Mutersbaugh, Tad. 2002. "Migration, Common Property, and Communal Labor: Cultural Politics and Agency in a Mexican Village." *Political Geography* 21 (4): 473–94.

Nagengast, Carole, and Michael Kearney. 1990. "Mixtec Ethnicity: Social Identity, Political Consciousness, and Political Activism." *Latin American Research Review* 25 (2): 61–91.

Pantoja, Adrian D., Ricardo Ramirez, and Gary M. Segura. 2001. "Citizens by Choice, Voters by Necessity: Patterns in Political Mobilization by Naturalized Latinos." *Political Research Quarterly* 54 (4): 729–50.

Reyes, Teofilo. 2003a. "Chicago Immigrant Workers 'Get on the Bus' for Freedom Rides." *Labor Notes,* October. http://www.labornotes.org, accessed January 23, 2008.

———. 2003b. "Rallies Across the Country Greet Immigrant Worker Freedom Riders." *Labor Notes,* November. http://www.labornotes.org, accessed January 23, 2008.

Rivera-Salgado, Gaspar. 2002. "Binational Grass-Roots Organizations and the Experience of Indigenous Migrants." In *Cross-Border Dialogues: U.S.-Mexico Social Movement Networking,* edited by David Brooks and Jonathan Fox, 259–74. La Jolla: University of California, San Diego, Center for U.S.-Mexican Studies.

Rivera-Salgado, Gaspar, and Luis Escala Rabadán. 2004. "Collective Identity and Organizational Strategies among Indigenous and Mestizo Mexican Migrants." In *Indigenous Mexican Migrants in the United States,* edited by Jonathan Fox and Gaspar Rivera-Salgado, 145–78. La Jolla: University of California, San Diego, Center for Comparative Immigration Studies and Center for U.S.-Mexican Studies.

Rivera-Salgado, Gaspar, Xochitl Bada, and Luis Escala-Rabadán. 2005. "Mexican Migrant Civic and Political Participation in the U.S.: The Case of Hometown Associations in Los Angeles and Chicago." Paper presented at the conference entitled Mexican Migrant Civic and Political Participation, Woodrow Wilson Center and Latin American and Latino Studies Department, University of California, Santa Cruz, Washington, D.C., November.

Rivera Sánchez, Liliana. 2004. "Expressions of Identity and Belonging: Mexican Immigrants in New York." In *Indigenous Mexican Migrants in the United States*, edited by Jonathan Fox and Gaspar Rivera-Salgado, 417–48. La Jolla: University of California, San Diego, Center for Comparative Immigration Studies and Center for U.S.-Mexican Studies.

Robles, Sergio. 2004. "Migration and Return in the *Sierra Juárez*." In *Indigenous Mexican Migrants in the United States*, edited by Jonathan Fox and Gaspar Rivera-Salgado, 467–82. La Jolla: University of California, San Diego, Center for Comparative Immigration Studies and Center for U.S.-Mexican Studies.

Rodríguez, América. 1999. *Making Latino News: Race, Language, Class*. Thousand Oaks, Calif.: Sage.

Rytina, Nancy. 2005. "Estimates of the Legal Permanent Resident Population and Population Eligible to Naturalize in 2003." *Population Estimates* (Homeland Security, Office of Immigration Statistics), January.

Schwentesius, Rita, Miguel Angel Gomez, José Luis Calva Tellez, and Luis Hernández Navarro, eds. 2004. *¿El campo no aguanta mas?* 2nd ed. Chapingo: Universidad Autónoma de Chapingo, CIESTAAM.

Smith, Robert. 2005. *Mexican New York*. Berkeley: University of California.

Stephen, Lynn. 2004. "Mixtec Farmworkers in Oregon: Linking Labor and Ethnicity through Farmworker Unions and Hometown Associations." In *Indigenous Mexican Migrants in the United States*, edited by Jonathan Fox and Gaspar Rivera-Salgado, 179–204. La Jolla: University of California, San Diego, Center for Comparative Immigration Studies and Center for U.S.-Mexican Studies.

———. 2007. *Transborder Lives: Indigenous Oaxacans in Mexico, California, and Oregon*, Durham, N.C.: Duke University Press.

Varsanyi, Monica Weiler. 2005. "The Paradox of Contemporary Political Mobilization: Organized Labor, Undocumented Migrants, and Electoral Participation in Los Angeles." *Antipode* 37 (4): 775–95.

Wells, Miriam. 2004. "The Grassroots Reconfiguration of U.S. Immigration Policy." *International Migration Review* 38 (4): 1308–47.

World Bank. 2004. *Mexico: Public Expenditure Review*. 2 vols. Report no. 27894–MX, August 10. http://www.worldbank.org, accessed January 23, 2008.

16

Women and Social Movements in Transborder Communities

Mexico and the United States

LYNN STEPHEN

It is impossible to talk about women and social movements in Latin America without considering the role of both internal and cross-border migration. In this chapter I focus on the ways that women from rural transborder migrant and immigrant communities are using bifocal vision—seeing what is going on close to home as well as in their communities spread out over borders—to guide their participation in local, regional, and cross-border organizations. This exploration requires that we reconceptualize our ideas about communities in terms of how they function in relation to multiple sites, in relation to multiple nation-states and legal statuses, and in terms of the networks and resources they have to work with in the context of significant levels of transborder movement. I will highlight the case of women from the Mixtec region of Oaxaca and their organizing efforts there and in the state of Oregon.

The two organizations I focus on are the Women's Regional Council of the Indigenous Front of Binational Organizations (FIOB) of Juxtlahuaca, Oaxaca, Mexico and Women Fighting for Progress (MLP) based in Woodburn, Oregon. The Women's Regional Council integrates women's groups from Mixtec and Triqui communities in Juxtlahuaca who have organized themselves around income-generating projects. The council is part of the FIOB, which has a total of more than twenty thousand members and offices in Juxtlahuaca, Tijuana, Los Angeles, and Fresno (California).

The MLP brings together Mixtec, Zapotec, Triqui, Mam, and Kanjobal indigenous immigrants living in Oregon along with some mestiza immigrant workers in an organization focused on income-generating activities and in developing technical, business, and leadership skills among its members. The organization grew out of Oregon's only farmworkers' union, Northwest Treeplanters and Farmworkers United (PCUN), which now has more than five thousand members, almost all of them immigrants.

In both cases, while the women's organizations are based on productive projects that are providing alternative sources of income for women and their families, their larger purposes include providing women with a space to exchange experiences, to develop political and organizational skills, and to deal with the burdens they experience as part of transborder families and marriages. They also serve to build skills and confidence among women that allow some to assume leadership roles in larger mixed organizations of men and women. Because both of these organizations are based in what I call transborder communities, the nature of women's participation in them involves a double consciousness about life in two or more locations. In addition, while both organizations have initially organized women around income-producing and productive projects, the ultimate outcome for both groups not only has been to reinforce alternative development visions in the context of broader rural movements, but also to produce a new source of political "voice" and "presence" for Mexican women from immigrant-sending communities. This chapter, like that of Fox (this volume), suggests that exit and voice can exist simultaneously and that exit can also be followed by voice—not only in sending communities but also in reterritorialized communities throughout Mexico and in the United States.

Putting Movements and Communities in a Transborder Context

Basic immigration statistics for Mexico, El Salvador, and Guatemala alert us to the necessity of rethinking our models of communities and people's participation in them. According to the U.S. Census of 2000, 480,665 people who were born in Guatemala, 817,335 people who were born in El Salvador, and 9.2 million people who were born in Mexico now live in the United States (U.S. Census Bureau 2000a, 2000b, 2000c). These figures do not include, of course, those people who are the children of Mexican, Salvadoran, and Guatemalan immigrants who are U.S. citizens by virtue of being born in the United States. They also do not include migrants from these countries who live in places other than the United States. Roughly 25 percent of the population of El Salvador is living abroad (Baker-Cristales 2004); between 10 and 11 percent of Mexico's population and between 9 and 10 percent of Guatemala's population is living abroad. In 2005 Mexicans living abroad sent home about U.S.$18.3 billion in economic remittances (Estrada

2006) while Guatemalans and Salvadorans living abroad each sent home about $3 billion (Organization for International Immigration 2005; Sánchez 2005). From 2001 and 2003, Mexicans living in the United States, for example, sent home about 22 percent of their incomes or about $400 per month (Orozco 2004, 4). On the receiving end, in 2003 in Mexico, about 70 percent of remittances were spent on living expenses (food, rent, utilities, mortgages); in El Salvador, 80 percent; and in Guatemala, 68 percent (Orozco 2004, 5). These figures illustrate the strength and importance of the economic links between Mexican and Central American communities spread out over borders.

Of equal importance to these structural links are the social, cultural, political, kinship, and interpersonal links between people spread out in interconnected locations. Research on transnational communities has encouraged scholars to work outside the container of the nation-state and the kinds of binary divisions that have permeated so much of social analysis, such as global versus local and national versus transnational. Levitt and Glick-Schiller (2004, 5) analyze local, national, transnational, and global connections in the following terms: "In one sense, all are local in that near and distant connections permeate the daily lives of individuals lived within a locale. But within this locale, a person may participate in personal networks, or receive ideas and information that connect them to others in a nation-state, across the borders of a nation-state, or globally, without ever having migrated. . . . individuals within these fields are through their everyday activities and relationships, influenced by multiple sets of laws and institutions."

It is certainly important to consider the "national" in the "trans" part of migrant and immigrant histories and experience—particularly when it comes to the recognition or lack thereof of basic human and labor rights often connected to their positions in relation to the legal frameworks of the nations they are moving between. I want to suggest, however, that we have to look beyond "the national" as De Genova (2005), Fox (2005a, 2005b), Kearney (1995, 1998, 2000), and other recent theorists do in order to understand the complete nature of what people are moving or "transing" between. In the cases of the indigenous Mixtec and Zapotec migrants I study, the borders they have crossed and continue to cross are much more than national.

In many communities where migration to and from other places has become a norm that spans three, four, and now five generations, the borders people cross are ethnic, cultural, colonial, and state borders within Mexico as well as between Mexico and the United States. When Mixtecos and Zapotecos come into the United States, they are crossing a new set of regional borders that are often different from those in Mexico but may also overlap with those of Mexico (for example the racial and ethnic hierarchy of Mexico, which lives on in Mexican communities in the United States). For these reasons, it makes more sense to speak of "transborder" migration rather than simply "transnational." The transnational becomes a subset of the "transborder" experience. The concept of transborder can be applied elsewhere in the Americas as well to processes of immigration and migration and is of growing importance in understanding the dynamics underlying many rural social movements in the Americas.

What Are the Gendered Implications of Belonging to a Transborder Community for Women?

Women, like men, have varied positions in Mexican transborder communities. During the 1980s and early 1990s, women were more likely to remain in their home communities while men migrated to other parts of Mexico and the United States in search of work. Male absence from households, in community systems of governance, and in the economy strongly affected those who remained behind. It is important to note, however, that the "staying behind" is not a permanent category. Many women who currently live in their natal communities have migrated either to other parts of Mexico and/or to the United States at another point in their lives. Immigration status (documented versus undocumented), stage in the life cycle, number of children, and other factors are all important in structuring the migration experiences of both men and women. Finally, as pointed out by Jennifer Hirsh (2003, 181), "The lives of even those women who have never left Mexico have been profoundly affected by migration."

The most frequent outcome for women left behind whose husbands, fathers, brothers, or sons have migrated elsewhere to work is the challenge of finding a steady source of household income until men can begin to send remittances (if and when they do), and to maintain this through difficult periods. For this reason, rural social movements' organizing strategies that offer women the possibility of access to additional cash through rotating savings clubs and/or through small productive projects that generate extra income have often been initially successful in recruiting women. The test for these organizing projects comes when women assume the risks and challenges of the project and begin to invest their time in these projects versus other possible income-generating activities.

An additional challenge for women left behind is that they often are expected to take over their husbands' participation in the local system of governance. Rural communities—particularly indigenous communities—in Mexico are governed by systems of volunteer governance in which all local residents who want to receive rights of access to communal land, access to community forests, water, sand, minerals, plants, and wild game, the right to burial in the community cemetery, and the right to express opinions and vote in the decision-making process that takes place in community assemblies have corresponding responsibilities. These responsibilities include participation of primary adult men, but increasingly also women, in the local system of civil *cargos*, in which community members perform governmental duties without pay. Tasks are divided into dozens of positions that may range from mayor, judge, and police officer to school board or irrigation committee member. Work performed through *cargos* includes fighting fires, service on committees regulating the use of communal land, and caring for the local Catholic church. In communities where political parties are a part of local systems of governance, some of these jobs, such as mayor and the equivalent of city councilors, are elected as part of party slates (see Stephen 2005b, 140–43).

In addition, many communities also have religious *cargo* systems in which community members sponsor the celebrations of feast days of saints venerated in the local Catholic church. Sponsorship is often rotating between pairs of male and female heads of households or may be the responsibility of *cofradías*. A *cofradía* refers to a religious corporate organization that is responsible for financing and carrying out the cult activities celebrated for the saints represented in the local church. Responsibilities might include paying for a mass, providing music, paying for dancers, preparing and serving food, and coordinating the elements of the celebration. Participation in the religious *cargo* system gives both women and men an association with the holy entities of the community.

A final arena of civic participation required of men and increasingly of women in rural communities is in performing *tequio* or collective community work. Most public works projects, such as the construction of roads, the construction of new municipal buildings or markets, the introduction of drainage systems, the building of basketball courts, the restoration of buildings, and more, is done in large part through voluntary labor contributions of each community member. Women may be called on to provide food, drinks, and other services as *tequio*. Men tend to provide the kind of physical labor associated with day laborers.

When men migrate, women often take their place both in community assemblies related to local governance and communal land governance. In addition, they take on the labor associated with religious or civil *cargos* assigned to them and their husbands, often as couples. Finally, women often have to coordinate substitutes or payments for men's *tequio*. While some men pay someone to take on their civil *cargo* responsibilities, the cost of paying for a substitute can be as high as U.S.$200 per month. For many women this is a large amount of money and they may attempt try to take on the tasks themselves. Aurora, a participant in the Regional Women's Council of the FIOB, observed: "I was paying 1,500 pesos per month (roughly U.S.$150) in order to have someone substitute for my husband. But now I have been doing that *cargo* because I can't afford that amount. Now I am doing the work of the president of the school committee as well as serving on the health committee. Because my husband is gone I am doing two *cargos* at once—one that is mine and one that is his. I am really busy."[1]

When women take on some of men's civic responsibilities it increases their workloads significantly, but it also exposes them to local political processes and gives them experience and skills in public speaking, participating in collective decision making, and an understanding of how local governments relate to state and national politics. In this case, the "exit" of men pushes women into formal local political spheres—sometimes willingly, sometimes unwillingly. There, they may begin to establish a presence and a voice in local assemblies related to local town governance and the governance of collective landholdings—either as communal lands or *ejidos*.[2]

The absence of large numbers of men in rural communities can also affect the ways in which women participate in the organizations and events of independent social movements. For example, although the FIOB was founded in 1991, women did not begin to participate in earnest until 1994, when they began to participate in protest marches and demonstrations that called on the Oaxacan state government to better serve the needs of indigenous communities and to engage in direct conversation with the leadership of the FIOB. Some women had already had the experience of attending community assemblies. It was through their participation in demonstrations and marches that women were first told by male leaders that they had the same rights as men (Maldonado and Artía Rodríguez 2004). After that they began to go to community assemblies as a group and also to attend the local and regional meetings of the FIOB and eventually to organize their own projects and regional women's group. Here, men's exit and the subsequent existence of a binational social movement that mobilized women in Mexico led directly to their "voice" within an independent rural social movement and in some cases in local governance assemblies where they had been previously excluded (see Maldonado and Artía Rodríguez 2004).

Women left behind in their communities also confront emotional stress and insecurity. Many women face uncertainly about the stability of their marriages if they do not hear from their husbands for extended periods of time. If women have no personal experience with what life is like for their husbands and others in the United States, their pictures of what goes on in the lives of their men is strongly informed by what return migrants tell them and by gossip. This discourse often focuses on the likelihood that men who have gone to the United States have other female partners or have started other families. This is often the ongoing assumption until proven otherwise. Thus in their home communities women who stay behind may be placed into a new social category of "abandoned women," which socially erases their ties to their husbands. Having a support network to share these feelings as well as the stress of constantly having to look for sources of income is one of the other benefits women often derive from participating in productive projects linked to rural social movements.

Once women are living in the United States, often united with their husbands, they face a whole new set of challenges. Some may have brought their children with them. Others leave their children behind temporarily or permanently in the care of a mother or mother-in-law. For indigenous immigrant women, issues of language can be paramount as they rarely speak English and often may have limited Spanish-speaking ability. Depending on where they live, recently arrived immigrant women may live in isolated locations where transportation is costly and/or they are dependent on men for their mobility. In cases where they are not working outside of the home, they may face high levels of isolation as they cope with small children and have little contact with others.

Most frequently both men and women are in the wage labor force, usually working for a minimum wage or less. It is very difficult for either a single parent or a two-parent household with children to survive economically on just one minimum wage. If dependent children are U.S. citizens, they have the right to Medicaid, food stamps, the Special Supplemental Nutrition Program for Women, Infants, and Children, and other programs. In many cases I have encountered, however, undocumented women are afraid to access the government services to which their children have a right as U.S. citizens. In some cases women are reluctant to ask for these services for fear that they will be disqualified for U.S. residency in the future. In November 2004, voters of Arizona approved Proposition 200, which requires state and local employees to verify the immigration status of those applying for public benefits and to report undocumented immigrants or face possible criminal prosecution. This kind of anti-immigrant measure discourages women from applying for benefits for their children born in the United States. Thus for many women who come to live with their husbands and children in the United States it is considered completely normal that both parents work outside of the home, often on opposite shifts so that domestic chores and child-care can be shared.

While working full-time and managing a family is challenging for migrant women in the United States, the challenge is even greater when their children are in Mexico. In my discussions with dozens of families about their migration histories, a majority have experienced at least some period of time where children born in Mexico were separated from their parents because one or both parents were in the United States while the children remained in Mexico. For both women and men, being away from their children is emotionally difficult and trying as children get older and are no longer emotionally connected to parents who have long been absent.

There have been a number of approaches to understanding the gendered implications of transnational families and transnational mothering. Beginning at a structural level, authors such as Salazar Parreñas (2001) and Chang (2000) analyze transnational households as ways that receiving societies can retain low-wage immigrant workers without paying for the costs of social reproduction of workers and their children. When women are working in the United States with their children in Mexico being cared for by relatives, the costs of social reproduction are assumed by the kin in Mexico. At the same time, the wages of workers in the United States can be kept to a minimum. If these workers are undocumented as well, then they are not likely to pressure for higher wages.

With the implementation of increased border barriers and patrolling, and sky-rocketing costs for traveling back and forth to the United States for undocumented workers, fewer people return to Mexico. Since the events of September 11, 2001, Mexican men are more likely to stay in the United States, having the effect of probably increasing the number of Mexican women and children crossing the border (Shorey 2005). In deciding whether or not to come to the United States in the first place, the thought of leaving children behind is quite distressing for many women. As pointed out by Hondagneu-Sotelo and Alavez (1999, 325) in their study of trans-national mothering among immigrant Latinas in Los Angeles, "Being a transnational mother means more than being the mother to children raised in another country. It means forsaking deeply-felt beliefs that biological mothers should raise their own children and replacing that belief with new definitions of motherhood." While a variety of mothering arrangements can be found both in the United States and Mexico, most discussions assume that mothers reside with their children—one mother, one place. Being apart from children places an additional stress on immigrant women who are in the United States.

Bifocal Vision and Its Implication for Organizing Women in Trans-border Communities

By necessity, women in transborder communities have developed what I call "bifocal" vision, which allows them to see both near and far at the same time. Put another way, bifocal vision is a socially and experientially devel-oped pair of glasses that transborder migrant women wear that permits them to imagine and think through the implications of daily occurrences and their subsequent actions in a multi-sited context. I came upon this model after reading Patricia Zavella's (2000) insightful discussion about "peripheral vision" as a way to envision how young women in the United States and in Mexico keep track of norms and family expectations in simul-taneous locations. As Castañeda and Zavalla (2003, 131) state, "Whether they reside in Mexico or in the United States, migrants imagine their own situation and family lives in terms of how they compare with *el otro lado* (on the other side of the border)." I find that women use this kind of vision not only to keep track of norms and family expectations in multiple places, but also in relation to a wide range of other issues. Men from transborder com-munities also have bifocal vision as well. Because of the gendered nature of transborder social relations, however, I believe that women are more likely to invoke bifocal vision than men because of their broader arena of concern. Because women are so often the social glue of extended families, they tend to the emotional work of maintaining these connections—as in the case of transborder mothering—in a more sustained and intense way than men do. The fact that women from transborder communities have developed bifocal vision with regard to their daily lives and concerns has important implica-tions for how women engage with social movements.

Bifocal Vision in the Women's Regional Council of the FIOB, Juxtlahuaca

The Mixtec-Zapotec Binational Front (FM-ZB, precursor to the FIOB) was formed in October 1991 in Los Angeles as a coalition of organizations, communities, and individuals of indigenous origin. At the time it was formed, a majority of the members of the FM-ZB resided in the Mixtec, Zapotec, and Triqui regions of the state of Oaxaca as well as in the northwest of Mexico, Baja California, and California. As other indigenous groups from Oaxaca and, later, other parts of Mexico joined it changed its name twice, settling on the Indigenous Front of Binational Organizations (FIOB) in 2005. The organization formed a sister NGO, the Binational Center for the Development of Oaxacan Indigenous Communities as a 501(c)(3) entity in the United States in order to apply for funding to support the communities with development and educational programs. The FIOB has focused on the promotion, training, and organization of the indigenous communities of origin of its membership as well as programs and organizing activities focused on the well-being of indigenous migrants outside of their home communities. In 2006 the mission statement of the FIOB indicated that the group's mission was to "contribute in the development and self-determination of the migrant and non-migrant indigenous communities, as well as struggle for the defense of human rights with justice and gender equity at the binational level" (FIOB 2006).

The FIOB emerged in Mexico in the early 1990s at the same time that other indigenous organizations were consolidating at the regional level and later at the national level. One of the FIOB's key leaders, Rufino Domínguez Santos, began working on a local struggle in his Mixtec community of San Miguel Cuevas, went on to work with the regional indigenous peasant organization, the Coalition of Workers, Peasants, and Students of the Isthmus (COCEI), formed in the 1970s in the Isthmus of Tehuantepec, and then began organizing indigenous migrants in Baja California and later California—all before helping to found the FM-ZB. The COCEI is a city-based organization in Juchitan that defended claims to land, credit, wages, benefits, and municipal services while also embarking on an ambitious cultural program centered on the Zapotec languages (see Rubin 1997; Campbell 1993). In 1981 the COCEI won municipal elections, ushering in Mexico's first leftist and indigenous city government.

In the 1980s other important indigenous organizations were created in Oaxaca as well, including the Assembly of Mixe Producers (ASAPROM), which was established to address the economic concerns of the Mixe people as producers. Other indigenous organizations created in the 1980s in Oaxaca based their claims on the rights of indigenous people to maintain themselves as culturally distinct populations. Many indigenous organizations also participated in a wide range of activities protesting five hundred years of colonialism in 1992, which was what spurred the formation of the precursor to the FIOB, the FM-ZB. According to Domínguez Santos, "[The] FM-ZB was intended to coordinate with other indigenous organizations in opposition to official celebrations marking the quincentenary of Christopher Columbus's arrival in the Americas" (2004, 71). The Independent National Peasant Alliance "Emiliano Zapata," the regional and then national indigenous peasant group of Chiapas that served as the aboveground organizing front for what became the Zapatista National Liberation Army (EZLN), was also active in 1992 and then went underground. From 1992 to 1994 representatives from the FIOB attended many national and international meetings on indigenous rights in Latin America.

As a binational indigenous organization already networked throughout Latin America and the United States, the FM-ZB became one of many support links for the EZLN in the campaign to stop the Mexican government from going to war in early 1994 and in subsequent solidarity and organizing efforts. In 1994 after the Zapatista rebellion, the FM-ZB mounted actions to pressure the Mexican government not to use military force and joined in hunger strikes and demonstrations in front of the offices of Mexican consulates and other government offices in California (Bacon 2002). The use of e-mail lists and faxes was crucial in these efforts, both in the United States and in Mexico. The FM-ZB also became active in the National Indigenous Congress (CNI), which was formed in 1996 in support of the implementation of the San Andrés Accords on Indigenous Rights and Culture signed by the EZLN and the Mexican government. The FIOB did not participate in the founding of what became the Plural National Indigenous Assembly for Autonomy (ANIPA). By October 1996 when the CNI was formed, ANIPA had parted ways with the EZLN and groups that continued to work with the Zapatistas (see Stephen 1997b, 29–31).

In September 1994, the FM-ZB held its second binational assembly in Tijuana, Baja California, where the assembly changed the organization's name to the Oaxacan Indigenous Binational Front (FIOB), reflecting the integration of a wide range of Oaxacan indigenous ethnic groups into the organization and marking the articulation of a pan-Oaxacan indigenous identity. The period following this congress is when women became more active in the FIOB. After their experiences in the mid-1990s in marches, demonstrations, and attending local community assemblies as a group, women whose husbands had left as migrants began to participate in FIOB workshops, where they reflected on their experiences. One of the key issues that they focused on was how they were often forced to borrow money at very high interest rates from local money lenders. Out of these conversations the women decided to form savings clubs. At the same time they also began to participate in a more systematic way in their communities on local health committees, school committees, and other forms of local governance (Maldonado and Artía Rodríguez 2004, 500–506).

The savings clubs began in 1999 and were run completely by volunteer labor out of the FIOB office in Juxtlahuaca and in seven Mixtec and Triqui communities. This number later expanded to ten. The savings clubs were formed in each community with a group of *socias* or members who elected a president, secretary, and treasurer to administer the funds. Each woman put in a set amount from as little as 10 pesos (U.S.$1) to 100 pesos (U.S.$10) and sometimes more. The funds were then loaned out to savings club members at a lower interest rate than to non-members. After a set period of time (one to six months), the interest was paid out to group members and the principal was reinvested. For women whose husbands were away, borrowing from the savings club gave them a source of cash during difficult periods—for example, after the household had borrowed money elsewhere to pay the $3,000 it costs to pay a *coyote* (smuggler) to cross the U.S. border. They could also use the loan to begin a small business of some kind, such as selling tamales or *pozoles* or crafts or to begin a small store or simply to meet temporary expenses such as buying school uniforms, books, and shoes for children in September.

While some of the savings clubs worked well, not all did. Reasons for failure were often due to a lack of systematic monitoring and training, and the interpersonal dynamics of the women involved in the effort and their past histories together. While some women were learning how to produce official documents and gained the skills to manage and administer their accounts, not all did and women who were leaders sometimes left. In addition, sometimes the small businesses that women tried to set up were unable to flourish due to too much competition or a lack of marketing channels. As a result, local women leaders and the FIOB decided to rethink their approach to the savings clubs.

In 2003, led by women leaders in Juxtlahuaca and aided by advisors, the FIOB submitted a proposal for funding to the Inter-American Foundation through the FIOB's affiliated NGO. The proposal suggested strengthening the savings clubs by creating a regional women's association and pairing the saving clubs with other productive projects. These included artisan production and distribution, commercialization of food products, production and marketing of horticulture and poultry, and a project to help women better control and harness remittances from their husbands and others. In 2004–5 new projects involving first mushroom production and then chicken production for local markets were begun, all based on the logic of providing women with additional income sources and outlets for commercialization. The production of artisan goods by Triqui women was also connected to a distribution network in Baja California and the United States.

The local groups were also merged into the Women's Regional Council, which holds periodic meetings, workshops, and events. The Women's Regional Council gives women a chance to exchange experiences with FIOB members from other communities, to see how others have worked out internal conflicts in their groups, and to envision alternatives to their local daily experiences. The council meetings also allow FIOB organizers to see what their own strengths and weaknesses are in relation to the projects as a group.

According to Centolia Maldonado, the FIOB organizer for the productive projects: "The productive projects really helped women to work as a group. Before they would say that they were organized and they had to work together, for example, to improve their houses with materials, but what happens when that project is done? And with the savings clubs, they only meet once a month. But taking care of a chicken hatchery or mushroom planting and harvesting requires a daily commitment and daily interaction. This provides a higher level of organizational interaction and experience for women."

By 2005 the Women's Regional Council was holding regular monthly meetings. In addition to attending council meetings and activities, the women involved in chicken hatcheries and mushroom production projects have to organize a system of daily labor rotation for their projects. They also often have weekly local meetings. In August 2005 I visited the productive projects of three communities: San Pedro Chayuco, San Fransisco Paxtlahuaca, and San Agustín Atenango. While all were functioning, they all had the typical problems associated with group enterprises—some women were doing more work than others, some did not show up for their assigned tasks, and people complained that the projects were not producing maximum results. In one community all of the baby chicks had died and one woman brought in a dead chick to the monthly meeting of the Women's Regional Council as evidence of how difficult it was to keep the birds healthy. Local groups and FIOB organizers were experimenting with the best chicken coop design and disinfection procedures in conjunction with local veterinarians.

The kinds of problems encountered in these projects are typical of women's productive projects all over Latin America. In a useful comparative analysis of many decades of women's productive projects, Butler Flora (1987) found that in order to function effectively, productive projects must not only function internally, but must also produce an economic surplus and have clear organizational goals. When such productive projects are trying to compete with other economic activities of the informal sector, which is the case for all of the projects of the Women's Regional Council, then a problem of self-exploitation emerges. To compete with other projects in the informal sector, collective projects have to "follow the informal sector pattern of cost savings through self-exploitation or exploitation of labor" (Butler Flora 1987, 217). This would be contrary to the goals of empowering the women involved. Butler Flora suggests, however, that organizations created as mobilizers for production can become mobilizers in the social and political arena as well.

The history of the Women's Regional Council of the FIOB is the reverse of that trend. The productive projects grew out of and continue to be connected to a strong binational rural social movement that is constantly pushing for economic and social change. Thus while the productive projects may still be lacking in their economic outcome, they continue to build women's political experience, skills, and leadership. These projects serve as a medium for women to continue developing their political voice.

The reason why the productive projects and savings clubs resonate so strongly for the Women's Regional Council of the FIOB is related to dramatic changes in the regional economy in the Mixtec and Triqui regions of Oaxaca. Out-migration has been a regular feature of many communities since the 1940s (and probably before), beginning with trips to other parts of Oaxaca and Veracruz. In the late 1950s, entire families began migrating to the state of Sinaloa and later further north in Mexico to work as agricultural laborers and then returning to work for part of the year in subsistence agriculture. Beginning in the late 1970s, when increasing numbers of men began to migrate to the United States over the northern Mexican border, this pattern began to change. Men stayed away longer and women were left to try to cope with planting corn, beans, and squash. As more men failed to return, the conditions for small-scale corn production also deteriorated in rural Mexico.

In the early 1990s, there were about 3 million corn producers in Mexico, equivalent to about 40 percent of all rural Mexicans working in agriculture (Woodall et. al 2001, 23). "The real price farmers received for corn declined by 26 percent between 1993 and 1995" (White et al. 2003, 14). By 2001, real corn prices had fallen more than 70 percent, meaning that corn farmers and their families had to live on less than one-third of the income that they had earned in 1995 (Fanjul and Fraser 2003, 17).

Between 1991 and 2000, the total number of corn producers for household consumption declined by 670,000 and the number of producers cultivating corn for sale declined by 343,000. Thus a little over 1 million corn producers have stopped producing corn and have had to find another source of income (White et al. 2003, 18). These trends are strongly related to increased levels of out-migration from 1995 to the present in many of the communities the FIOB works in. While some women have tried to maintain subsistence farming, others have given up and more land is lying fallow. What subsistence farming has continued relies heavily on women to recruit men to work the land, on remittances from men to pay for this, and when there is no money—as is often the case—on women's labor. There is only so much of women's labor to go around and in times of emergencies and political mobilization, their labor is even further stretched as the following examples show.

In San Agustín Atenango, where women had begun a rotating savings club and were preparing to start a mushroom-raising project, their focus was quickly interrupted by an emergency situation that illustrates the concept of bifocal vision. On July 16, 2005, seven people left Atenango on a bus to go to the border town of Sonoyta, where they expected to cross over to the United States. Sonoyta is located across the border from Lukeville, Arizona and crossings take migrants into the most desolate areas of the western Arizona desert where temperatures in July often go well above 110 degrees Fahrenheit on a daily basis. The group of seven that left San Agustín Atenango included five men between the ages of twenty-six and forty-nine and two boys ages fifteen and sixteen. A month after they had left, there was still no word from any of them. The mothers of the two boys, one of whom was active in the FIOB, became very disconcerted and began talking to everyone they met about the disappearances.

Quickly, the disappearances on the border became the focus of the women in the FIOB project as well as the entire community. For the mothers of the two boys and the female relatives of the others, trying to find and get news of the disappeared became a full-time job; unable to sleep, they circulated endlessly around San Agustín, Juxtlahuaca, and elsewhere seeking help in locating their children. The two mothers appealed to Centolia in the FIOB office in Juxtlahuaca and to others from the Regional Women's Council for help.

One of the women active in the council from San Pedro Chayuco, Paula Angela Galinda Flores, who provides the land for the women's projects in this community, was all too familiar with what had happened. In May 2000 her oldest daughter, Yolanda, who was nineteen at the time, perished in the Arizona desert along with ten others. Her last act, reportedly, was to save the life of her eighteen-month-old daughter by giving her the remaining drinking water. Paula has now adopted this granddaughter and is raising her along with her other children. Paula—who has a husband and nephews in Gresham, Oregon and a niece who is an organizer for Oregon's only farmworkers' union, the PCUN, in Woodburn, Oregon—was very sympathetic to what the women from San Agustín with missing relatives were experiencing.

Aided by local officials, the women from San Agustín and their families created flyers with photographs of the missing migrants to circulate. They called and faxed family members in California, Oregon, Arizona, and elsewhere and began to phone and fax the various Mexican consulates. The offices of the FIOB in Juxtlahuaca, Tijuana, Los Angeles, and Fresno were alerted, and other NGOs and government organizations such as the Oaxacan Institute for Attention to the Migrant (IOAM) were notified of the details of the seven *desaparecidos*. Their female relatives are still looking for them today and continue to devote much energy to this cause. While this is an extreme example of the power of bifocal vision to influence and determine the ways that women are able to engage with local and regional social movements such as the FIOB, it does suggest the importance of an awareness of how this perspective functions in women's daily lives. Because the FIOB is structured as a binational U.S.-Mexican organization with regional focuses in four locations and was built by people from transborder communities, it tends to have a high level of awareness of the importance of bifocal vision for its members.

In October 2006, many of the women active in the Women's Regional Council helped to found a regional branch of the Popular Assembly of the Peoples of Oaxaca (APPO) in Juxtlahuaca. Created in June 2006 following an attempt to violently evict thousands of teachers from the center of

Oaxaca, the APPO is a coalition of more than 350 different communities and organizations—urban, indigenous, peasant, women's, and others— that called for the destitution of Oaxaca's governor, who was a member of the PRI, and efforts to deal with a whole host of issues related to poverty and social justice in the state. In September and October 2006, regional branches of the APPO began forming, taking over local city halls, and organizing marches. In Juxtlahuaca, women from the Women's Regional Council were members of groups that built and manned barricades, occupied the city hall, and marched around the city defiantly demanding the end of local and state governments controlled by the PRI. According to the FIOB organizer Centolia Maldonado, "The women from the indigenous communities were the bravest. They were not afraid of people shouting at them or of confrontation like some of the women from the town of Juxtlahuaca. They held their ground and were very brave." For women with bifocal vision in the Women's Regional Council, the act of men walking over the border to El Norte and their own walking in the streets of Juxtlahuaca or Oaxaca City to demand justice and a change in how the majority of Oaxaca's poor, working, and indigenous people are treated are connected. Every person who has joined the APPO and is marching for justice in Oaxaca has an extended family member, neighbor, or friend who is in the United States now or once was. The conditions in Oaxaca that push people to risk their lives and become one of the potential dead or disappeared on the border are part of the protest message of the APPO and of the FIOB.

The challenge for the FIOB and other similar organizations has been to anticipate and work with the gendered version of this bifocal vision in structuring projects and organizational strategies. In Mixtec communities more men than women migrate. More women are left behind for longer periods of time, and women are in charge of the emotional and social work of maintaining family connections. They are also increasingly participating in local systems of governance and managing family economies. The structure of the Women's Regional Council and of the local productive projects and savings clubs has provided some important avenues for income generation, but more importantly women are utilizing these structures to establish their voice and presence, not only within the FIOB but in the larger state and national political scene. As a deliberately constructed binational organization, the FIOB has certainly connected exit to voice. And it has self-consciously cultivated the participation of women in its membership and to a limited degree in its leadership. As more women gain experience and skills in the economic, political, and cultural arenas of their local communities, in the Women's Regional Council, in the FIOB, and in other kinds of organizational spaces such as the APPO, their impact on the FIOB will surely continue to increase. In 2006 the FIOB began a deliberate process of self-reflection about how to build new and better leadership among youth and women. Surely the experiences of the Women's Regional Council will provide important insights for that effort.

Bifocal Vision in Women Fighting for Progress in Woodburn, Oregon

The organizing of largely indigenous immigrant Mexican women workers began within the structure of the PCUN in 1992 in Woodburn, Oregon (see Stephen 2001a, 2001b, 2003, 2004). Oregon's farmworkers' union—the PCUN—had its origins in the 1970s, when several organizations, inspired by the work of César Chávez, envisioned a social movement of Mexican immigrants and farmworkers in Oregon. Their initial organizing strategies were influenced by the climate of harassment and fear faced by Mexican immigrant farmworkers in the Willamette Valley. In May 1977, the Willamette Valley Immigration Project (WVIP) opened its doors to provide legal representation for undocumented workers, first in Portland and then in 1978 in Woodburn. The staff and organizers of the WVIP went on to facilitate the creation of the PCUN in 1985. The initial goal of the PCUN was to change working conditions for treeplanters and farmworkers. The eight-year track record of the WVIP was crucial to building trust in the farmworker and treeplanter community so that open discussion of a farmworkers' union could begin. During the 1990s, the union engaged in a series of actions aimed at opening up political and cultural space for immigrant Mexican farmworkers, raising farmworkers' wages, and achieved its first contracts with small organic growers. From the late 1990s to the present the PCUN has also been a major organizer for immigrants' rights in the state of Oregon and nationally. (See Stephen 2001b and 2007 for a general history.)

In the early 1990s, the PCUN's service center staff noticed a marked increase in women members who were reporting spousal abuse, sexual harassment in the workplace, and other gender-specific problems. There was also a low level of women's participation in leadership positions in the union. In 1995, a precursor organization to the MLP called the Farmworker Women's Leadership Project was begun by the PCUN and was supported by a three-year grant from A Territorial Resource, an NGO.

In the early days of the group, women were polled by the PCUN's staff about what kinds of classes or services would be most helpful to them. Many stated that they wanted to learn to drive. Without the ability to drive, women's mobility was often very limited, particularly if they were living in labor camps, in workers' housing on farms, or on the outskirts of Woodburn or other surrounding towns. Some initial driving classes were offered but were difficult to maintain due to resistance from some men and other factors. Two other economic projects were tried before the production of Christmas wreaths became a successful income-generating project.[3] With the Christmas wreath project in 1997, however, the group hit its stride. Participants acquired most of their raw materials for free (pine branches gathered in the national forests) and were able to earn a reasonable return on their labor—usually $.50 to $1.25 above the minimum wage—for the time they invested in making the wreaths. They assembled the wreaths in the union hall on long tables and decorated them with red velvet ribbons and pine cones. In 1997 the group took the name Women Fighting for Progress (MLP).

Like the Women's Regional Council of the FIOB in Juxtlahuaca, women were first motivated to participate in the project by their need to augment their incomes and by the opportunity to socialize and learn from each other; once they were participants they were motivated to gain business skills and leadership experience. The need for additional income while in the United States results from the periods of unemployment that they or their husbands or children face as seasonal agricultural workers. They also feel pressure to send money home to their communities in Mexico. Many members of the MLP send home monthly remittances to parents or other relatives. Thus like the women of the FIOB in the Juxtlahuaca region, their bifocal vision begins with their multi-sited economic relations and moves out from there. In addition, women who were arriving in Oregon from Oaxaca or from Baja, California may have had some limited exposure to grass-roots organizing, but many came from communities where women's political participation has been limited in some regard. Many Mixtec and other indigenous and rural women who arrive in Oregon have not participated in organizing projects of any kind. Their social world is centered on their extended family and their daily routines. A few of the women's husbands were involved in independent rural and peasant organization in Mexico before coming to the United States, but most were not.

Organizationally, the MLP focused on expanding its sales of Christmas wreaths through a network of churches, student organizations, independent community markets, and local fair-trade organizations. The women of the MLP also began to circulate as speakers not only about their own project, but also as advocates for immigrants' rights. In 2002 the MLP sold twelve hundred Christmas wreaths and had worked its way up to fifteen hundred by 2004. This cooperative business venture has permitted the women involved to learn how to balance a checkbook, give financial reports, and plan projects. In addition to providing a small source of income and financial management experience, the MLP also provides farmworker women with an opportunity to gain a sense of satisfaction and pride in their endeavors, to provide each other with mutual support, and to learn new skills in public speaking and leadership. In monthly meetings during the off-season and intense interactions during the wreath-making season (October to December) the group provides a refuge for women.

The importance of organizational spaces that are female-only has proven to be important throughout Latin America in fostering basic confidence and skills among women as well as preparing them for public leadership roles (see Stephen 1997a). While many members of the MLP come from communities in Mexico and Guatemala where they spent long blocks of time in the company of female relatives and other women in their communities on a daily basis, once they were living in Oregon many experienced social isolation and a lack of female support networks.

Fidelia Domínguez, a Mixteca from Ixpantepec Nieves, first came to the Service Center at the PCUN in 1997 in order to straighten out an auto insurance claim. She joined the women's project and eventually was elected president. She recalled how much the group means to the women who arrive and are socially isolated, lonely, and miss their extended families in Mexico. The kind of space created by a group of women provides many who arrive with a special haven for sharing their feelings and working with others to resolve common issues. Having a female-only space also gives women the confidence to speak up. Once they have gained self-confidence within the women's group and are comfortable taking positions and speaking up in public, they can translate these skills to other arenas, including union leadership, participation in local political forums such as PTA meetings and city council meetings, and in renegotiating domestic roles. Fidelia explained to me how she had come into the group, how women grow in the group, and why it is important that the group be female-only: "Most of [the women] come because they are poor and don't know what to do. There are also families where they don't have work. Or the husband may be working, but he doesn't earn enough money to support the kids. There are women who can't pay the rent and single mothers who also come. They are all women who feel there is no one to help them." Positive changes begin to occur once the women join. "The first thing that happens is that it helps women to cope with all that they have been through. When someone comes to meet with us they start to talk. It is like family if you don't have a family. Women start to feel confident and then they talk. They have a good time and start to forget all of their problems." When I asked Fidelia what she had learned in the group, she replied, "I learned so much. I learned how to speak. Not that I literally couldn't speak before, but I learned how to speak up. I lost my fear. I learned how to speak in front of a lot of other people in public. I am not afraid to do that anymore. Before, I was a very fearful person. I used to tremble if I had to speak in front of people. But now I have the courage to speak . . . In Oaxaca a lot of women are afraid to speak in front of people."

In Fidelia's narrative, she talks about the importance of "learning how to speak" in public and feeling like one has the right to hold an opinion and voice it. She notes how in Oaxaca women are very afraid to speak in front of anyone, particularly in front of men. Over its ten-year history, perhaps one of the most important functions of the MLP has been to serve as a training ground for upcoming women leaders in the PCUN, in the community of Woodburn, and elsewhere. While the Christmas wreath project has continued to be a financial success and is an important underpinning of the group, the development of self-confidence and female leadership has been a major outcome of the women's organization.

In 2002, the MLP became independent of the PCUN as a self-standing nonprofit organization. By that time there were several seasoned women leaders in the MLP as well as many long-time members who knew how to run the wreath project and others. Both union activists and the women in the group viewed this break as a measure of their success, as an indication of the capacity of the women to be self-supporting and run their own organization. The breaking away of the MLP as an autonomous organization from the PCUN is consistent with a pattern found in women's rural organizing throughout Latin America, where many rural women's organizations grew out of the women's secretariats and commissions of mixed-sex peasant organizations (Deere and León 2001, 129). While many of these women's organizations became autonomous in order to pursue their own practical and strategic gender interests, which is also the case for the MLP, many of the women in the MLP continue to participate in the PCUN and others have gone on to be leaders in other organizations, such as the CAUSA, Oregon's state-wide immigrants' rights coalition, or projects combating domestic violence against farmworker women.

The year it became autonomous, the MLP received a grant from the Peace Development Fund to "develop an organized and collective response to the racism, sexism, and economic oppression faced by Latina farmworkers" (Peace Development Fund 2002 Grantees). In February 2005, the board of directors of the MLP announced an initiative to improve members' management and business skills by integrating the use of technology into their work. In cooperation with the Cirpirano Ferrell Education Center (named for the first president of the PCUN), members of the MLP enrolled in computer classes. They hope to be able to directly market their Christmas wreathes on-line and to communicate by e-mail with their customers throughout the state. Being able to function on the Internet and through e-mail can be seen as an extension of "learning to speak." In November 2006, the MLP began a weekly radio program as a part of KPCN-LP, the PCUN's new low-powered FM station broadcasting from Woodburn, Oregon.

Increasingly for women in the MLP and others like them, access to the Internet and telephones allows them to maintain better communications with relatives in both the United States and Mexico. E-mail is much cheaper than the telephone and it is particularly the younger members of the MLP who use e-mail to communicate with relatives in Mexico (see chapter 14, this volume). While some members of the MLP have returned home for visits, most who do are those with legal residency. Increased militarization of the border and the prohibitive costs of returning to the United States inhibit many undocumented members of the MLP from going back to their hometowns.

The aspiration of the MLP's members, besides marketing their wreaths, is to use the Internet to communicate with other social movements working on similar issues. Here, the Internet functions as a way to bypass more expensive modes of communication and potentially to link together social movements with similar concerns. Internet and telephone contact were important in disseminating information about the large-scale immigrants' rights marches that took place from March through May 2006 as well as more localized news of the PCUN, the MLP, and other organizational events. It is difficult to assess whether or not the political activities of the MLP and the PCUN are directly affecting social movements in Mexico, but both groups have had ongoing contact and exchanges with a range of social movements, such as the FIOB and other peasant and indigenous rights organizations participating in the anti-globalization movement.

Conclusions

An analysis of how women from transborder communities are participating in rural social movements in Mexico and in the United States permits us to see new alternatives to neoliberalism (or at least surviving neoliberalism), how local and regional movements are linked across borders and within them, and the importance of creating gender-specific and ethnically specific spaces for movement participation. I have argued here that people from transborder communities function in daily life with bifocal vision that permits them to imagine and think through the implications of daily occurrences and their subsequent actions in a multi-sited context. Additionally, I have suggested, following Fox's chapter, that exit—in the form of migration and immigration—can indeed lead to voice through the formation of both binational rural organizations and farmworkers' unions and immigrants' rights organizations in the United States.

I have focused on the gendered dimensions of this bifocal vision for women and how this can affect their participation and the emergence of their voice in rural social movements in Mexico and in the United States. As illustrated through the examples of the Women's Regional Council of the FIOB in Juxtlahuaca, Oaxaca and the MLP in Woodburn, Oregon we see that a significant dimension of women's bifocal vision is their awareness of economic relationships within their home-base communities as well as in the locations where men and others have migrated. Like most rural women in Latin America, they are concerned with generating sources of income. Thus, productive projects and savings clubs that help them to secure extra cash are usually a successful initial organizing strategy for movement organizations such as the FIOB and MLP. Because of their specific awareness of the experience of migrant laborers and how this work may fluctuate seasonally and from place to place, women automatically keep track of fluctuating income sources in multiple sites.

Additionally, these women's organizations that are linked to wider rural social movement organizations have focused simultaneously on generating alternative forms of economic development and in developing organizational skills and leadership. In both cases, women's productive projects grew out of an already existing organizational context in which women were explicitly included and encouraged within mixed-sex organizations. In one case, the women's organization became independent and in the other case it is still attached to a larger binational, mixed-sex indigenous rights organization.

In Oaxaca, women such as Paula Angela Galinda Flores were aware that chicken and mushroom production were small-scale projects but ones that could make a difference at critical times in small ways. Nonetheless, such projects did not compensate for a lack of long-term income security. Her dilemma was how to convince her own children not to take on the risks of crossing into the United States as undocumented workers but rather to stay home to try to make a living there. While the productive projects of the FIOB are not an alternative in and of themselves to the high levels of migration that have resulted from the economic integration of the U.S. and Mexican labor markets, they do represent an alternative source of public discourse and have recently served as training grounds for serious mobilizations in Juxtlahuaca and Oaxaca that are demanding structural change in the ways that resources are allocated and political decision making takes place. The productive projects taken on by members of the Women's Regional Council offer a collective model for coping with economic difficulty, unlike the individual model of migrating to the north for work. In addition, the skills and experiences gained by women who have worked in the Women's Regional Council and in their own communities have strengthened the presence of the FIOB regionally and in the state of Oaxaca. Since many of the FIOB's male members are in the United States, female members are the core of the organization's political presence and bargaining power to push for structural change at the state level in Oaxaca. In significant marches, occupations of buildings, and maintenance of barricades in the city of Juxtlahuaca and elsewhere in 2006 it was the women members of the FIOB who were most visible in support of the APPO, demanding the resignation of unresponsive elected officials and calling attention to poverty and social injustice through the physical occupation of public space.

In Woodburn, Oregon, where women in the MLP are often working in seasonal agriculture or produce-processing work, the wreath project has functioned in a similar way. While not a full-time job that offers an alternative to the temporary, low-paying jobs without benefits that women have, the collective production of wreathes offers a group strategy for confronting economic difficulty. In addition, both projects offer a different social philosophy than the social Darwinism that is often implied by neoliberal economic models—that those who succeed do so through hard work, individual initiative, and better economic fitness (see George 1999). The kind of discussions that permeate both the meetings of the MLP and the Women's Regional Counsel focus on the structural conditions that lead to migration—the ways in which unequal economic relations between Mexico and the United States have resulted in the loss of jobs in Mexico and the growth of low-paying jobs for immigrants in the United States—and suggest a collective means of working to improve the economic and social situations of families from transborder communities. This is consistent with discussions of indigenous women in collective projects in other parts of Mexico as well, such as artisan cooperatives (see Stephen 2005a).

This bifocal vision of women in social movements from transborder communities also provides them with a natural basis for linking their local and regional movements with other similar movements. While the Women's Regional Council of the FIOB in Juxtlahuaca is the only structure of its kind within the FIOB, recent discussions suggest that it may be a model for the forming of similar councils elsewhere. While women from the Juxtlahuaca Regional Women's Council have participated in broader movement events and activities (including traveling outside of their own region to Oaxaca City to regional meetings or to binational assemblies in Tijuana), they have not yet networked in a systematic manner with female members of the FIOB in other regions of Mexico and the United States. Again, this process appears to be slowly beginning. Their awareness of the female-gendered side of life on both sides of the border between the United States and Mexico is a resource that could be mobilized to connect their regional movement to others, such as the MLP in Oregon. At the same time, women in the MLP sitting on the U.S. side of the border have the same kind of vision and share many of the direct or indirect concerns of the Mixtec and Triqui women in the regional council in Juxtlahuaca.

Both the MLP in Oregon and the Women's Regional Council of the FIOB in Juxtlahuaca suggest the importance of creating gender-specific and ethnically specific spaces for organizing women from transborder communities. A majority of women in both groups are indigenous and from rural backgrounds, although there are some differences between them. But the female-only space in which they participate provides some common ground for mediating ethnic differences and for addressing the particular burdens that women bear in transborder families. In addition, the fact that most of the women in both groups are indigenous also creates common ground for discussing experiences of discrimination and racism in Mexico and within larger Mexicano and Latino communities in the United States. In a broad sense, both groups provide women with the space to discuss and confront the multiple oppressions and possibilities they face in relation to their rural, indigenous, and female identities and experiences. This similarity also suggests fertile ground for connecting these two kinds of groups.

Transborder communities offer unique possibilities for organizing that can suggest alternatives to neoliberal economic models and promote local participatory democracy that encourages regular interaction between group members in relation to their multi-sited existence. Transborder men and women have a high level of awareness of a wide range of political, economic, and social issues on a binational level and their bifocal vision is a special resource that can be harnessed. As transborder communities and networks develop and thicken with time in specific locations within Mexico and the United States, these networks and the people and resources attached to them have come to be able to compete with and in many cases outsmart state-controlled legal systems, labor markets, political systems, and border patrolling institutions and technologies. These communities are both beyond and within the control of nation-states. All too often women have had low profiles in binational civil society organizing, but they have much to offer. The models of the FIOB Women's Regional Council and Women Fighting for Progress (MLP) suggest ways that women's energy and insights can be further harnessed to organizing efforts in transborder communities to create new and better possibilities for rural peoples in the Americas.

Notes

Author's note: The fieldwork for this chapter was carried out in Oregon from 1998 through 2003 primarily through interviews, group conversations, and participant observation in Woodburn and Salem with members of the MLP and of the PCUN. Information on the Women's Regional Council of the FIOB was collected during the summers of 2004, 2005, and 2006 in the Juxtlahuaca region of Oaxaca. Data collection involved more than twenty individual interviews, participant observation of meetings, and collective discussions with members of the Women's Regional Council. Grants that supported the research reflected in this chapter include two research grants from the Wayne Morse Center for Law and Politics at the University of Oregon, two research grants from the Center for the Study of Women in Society at the University of Oregon, and two Summer Research Awards for Faculty from the University of Oregon. A sabbatical leave during 2004–5, research funds from the Radcliffe Institute for Advanced Studies at Harvard University, and funds from my award as a distinguished professor of arts and sciences at the University of Oregon have also supported the research.

1. Author's interview, San Pedro Chayuco, Oaxaca, Mexico, August 14, 2006.

2. Because these meetings have to be scheduled around community ritual calendars where whole weeks are knocked out by the celebrations for local patron saints and virgins (often accompanied by the return of some transborder migrants from the United States for a few weeks), there are some parts of the year when council activities are less frequent.

3. In 1995 and 1996, the Women's Project produced crocheted items and piñatas and sold them through a bazaar. Although both of these products found a market, they were very labor intensive and the financial returns were low.

References

Bacon, David. 2002. "Binational Oaxacan Indigenous Migrant Organizers Face New Century." *Americas Program*. International Relations Program. Silver City, New Mexico, August 21. http://americas.irc-online.org/articles/2002/0208oaxaca.html, accessed June 7, 2005.

Baker-Cristales, Beth. 2004. "Magical Pursuits: Legitimacy and Representation in a Transnational Political Field." *Latin American Perspectives* 31 (5): 15–33.

Butler Flora, Cornelia. 1987. "Income Generation Projects for Rural Women." In *Rural Women and State Policy*, edited by Carmen Diana Deere and Magdalena León, 212–38. Boulder:, Colo. Westview Press.

Campbell, Howard. 1993. "Class Struggle, Ethnic Politics, and Cultural Revivalism in Juchitán." In *Zapotec Struggles: Histories, Politics, and Representations from Juchitán, Mexico*, edited by Howard Campbell and Leigh Binford, 213–44. Washington, D.C.: Smithsonian Institute.

Castañeda, Xóchitl, and Patricia Zavella. 2003. "Changing Constructions of Sexuality and Risk: Migrant Mexican Women Farmworkers in California." *Journal of Latin American Anthropology* 8 (2): 126–50.

Chang, Grace. 2000. *Disposable Domestics: Immigrant Women Workers in the Global Economy*. Boston: South End Press.

Deere, Carmen Diana, and Magdalena León. 2001. *Empowering Women: Land and Property Rights in Latin America*. Pittsburgh, Pa.: University of Pittsburgh Press.

De Genova, Nicholas. 2005. *Working the Boundaries: Race, Space, and "Illegality" in Mexican Chicago*. Durham, N.C.: Duke University Press.

Domínguez Santos, Rufino. 2004. "The FIOB Experience: Internal Crisis and Future Challenges." In *Indigenous Mexican Migrants in the United States*, edited by Jonathan Fox and Gaspar Rivera-Salgado, 69–80. La Jolla: University of California, San Diego, Center for Comparative Immigration Studies and Center for U.S.-Mexican Studies.

Estrada, Patricia. 2006. "Mexicans Send Record Amount to Homeland." *Dallas Morning News*, January 20. http://www.dallasnews.com/cgi-bin/bi/gold_print.cgi, accessed January 26, 2006.

Fanjul, Gonzalo, and Arabella Fraser. 2002. *Dumping without Borders: How U.S. Agricultural Policies Are Destroying the Livelihoods of Mexican Corn Farmers*. Oxfam Briefing Paper 50. Washington, D.C.: Oxfam International. http://www.oxfam.org/eng/pdfs/pp030827_corn_dumping.pdf, accessed April 3, 2004.

FIOB. 2006. "Frente Indígena de Organizaciones Binacionales." http://www.fiob.org/english/ours.html, accessed February 18, 2008.

Fox, Jonathan. 2005a. "Unpacking Transnational Citizenship." *Annual Reviews in Political Science* 8: 171–201.

———. 2005b. "Mapping Mexican Migrant Civil Society." Paper presented at the Conference on Mexican Migrant Civic and Political Participation, Mexico Institute and Division of United States Studies, Woodrow Wilson International Center for Scholars, Washington, D.C., November.

George, Susan. 1999. "A Short History of Neoliberalism." Paper presented at the Conference on Economic Sovereignty in a Globalizing World, Bangkok, March 24–26. Published on line by the Global Policy Forum. http://www.globalpolicy.org/globaliz/econ/histneol.htm, accessed January 16, 2006.

Hirsch, Jennifer. 2003. *A Courtship after Marriage: Sexuality and Love in Mexican Transnational Families*. Berkeley: University of California Press.

Hondagneu-Sotelo, Pierrette, and Ernestine Alavez. 1999. "I'm Here, but I'm There: The Meanings of Latina Transnational Motherhood." In *Gender and U.S. Immigration: Contemporary Trends*, edited by Pierrette Hondagneu-Sotelo, 317–40. Berkeley: University of California Press.

Kearney, Michael. 1995. "The Local and the Global: The Anthropology of Globalization and Transnationalism." *Annual Review of Anthropology* 24: 547–65.

———. 1998. "Transnationalism in California and Mexico at the End of Empire." In *Border Identities: Nation and State at International Frontiers*, edited by Thomas W. Wilson and Hastings Connan, 117–41. Cambridge: Cambridge University Press.

———. 2000. "Transnational Oaxaca Indigenous Identity: The Case of Mixtecs and Zapotecs." *Identities* 7 (2): 173–95.

Levitt, Peggy, and Nina Glick Schiller. 2004. "Conceptualizing Simultaneity: A Transnational Social Field Perspective on Society." *International Migration Review*. http://www.findarticles.com/p/articles/mi_qa3668/is_200410/ai_n9471690, accessed June 15, 2005.

Maldonado, Centolia, and Patricia Artías Rodríguez. 2004. "Now We Are Awake: Women's Political Participation in the Oaxacan Indigenous Binational Front." In *Indigenous Mexican Migrants in the United States*, edited by Jonathan Fox and Gaspar Rivera-Salgado, 495–511. La Jolla: University of California, San Diego, Center for Comparative Immigration Studies and Center for U.S.-Mexican Studies.

Organization for International Immigration. 2005. "Guatemala Survey on Remittances and Microenterprises." http://www.iom.int/en/news/PBN041105.shtml#item3, accessed January 25, 2006.

Orozco, Manuel. 2004. "Remittances to Latin America and the Caribbean: Issues and Perspectives on Development." Washington, D.C.: Organization of the American States. http://www.frbatlanta.org/news/CONFEREN/payments04/orozco.pdf, accessed January 26, 2006.

Peace Development Fund 2002 Grantees. http://www.peacefund.org/what/wtgrlist_02.htm, accessed February 18, 2008.

Rubin, Jeffrey. 1997. *Decentering the Regime: Ethnicity, Radicalism, and Democracy in Juchitán, Mexico*. Durham, N.C.: Duke University Press.

Salazar Parreñas, Rhacel. 2001. *Servants of Globalization: Women, Migration, and Domestic Work*. Stanford, Calif.: Stanford University Press.

Sanchez, Marcela. 2005. "The Trouble with Sending Money Home: El Salvador's Dependence on U.S. Dollars." *Washington Post*, December 8. http://www.washingtonpost.com/wpdyn/content/article/2005/12/08/AR2005120801309_pf.html, accessed April 13, 2007.

Shorey, Amanda. 2005. "Migrant Smugglers Getting Creative." *Associated Press*, April 4. http://www.saveourstate.org/vforums/showthread.php?t=1087, accessed April 13, 2007.

Stephen, Lynn. 1997a. *Women and Social Movements in Latin America: Power from Below*. Austin: University of Texas Press.

———. 1997b. "The Zapatista Opening: The Movement for Indigenous Autonomy and State Discourses on Indigenous Rights in Mexico: 1970–1996." *Journal of Latin American Anthropology* 2 (2): 2–41.

———. 2001a. "Globalization, the State, and the Creation of Flexible Indigenous Workers: Mixtec Farmworkers in Oregon." *Urban Anthropology and Studies of Cultural Systems and World Economic Development* 30 (2–3): 189–214.

———. 2001b. *The Story of PCUN and the Farmworkers Movement in Oregon*. Eugene: University of Oregon, University Publications.

———. 2002. *Zapata Lives! Histories and Cultural Politics in Southern Mexico*. Berkeley: University of California Press.

———. 2003. "Cultural Citizenship and Labor Rights for Oregon Farmworkers: The Case of Pineros y Campesinos Unidos del Nordoeste (PCUN)." *Human Organization* 62 (1): 27–38.

———. 2004. "Mixtec Farmworkers in Oregon: Linking Labor and Ethnicity through Farmworkers Unions and Hometown Associations." In *Indigenous Mexican Migrants in the United States*, edited by Jonathan Fox and Gaspar Rivera-Salgado, 179–204. La Jolla: University of California, San Diego, Center for Comparative Immigration Studies and Center for U.S.-Mexican Studies.

———. 2005a. *Zapotec Women: Gender, Class, and Ethnicity in Globalized Oaxaca*. Durham, N.C.: Duke University Press.

———. 2005b. "Negotiating Global, National, and Local 'Rights' in a Zapotec Community." *Political and Legal Anthropology Review* 28 (1): 133–50.

———. 2007. *Transborder Lives: Indigenous Oaxacans in Mexico, California, and Oregon*. Durham, N.C.: Duke University Press.

U.S. Census Bureau. 2000a. *Profile of Selected Demographic and Social Characteristics—People Born in Guatemala*. U.S. Census. Washington, D.C.: U.S. Census Bureau. http://www.census.gov/population/cen2000/stp-159/stp159–guatemala.pdf, accessed February 11, 2007.

———. 2000b. *Profile of Selected Demographic and Social Characteristics—People Born in El Salvador*. U.S. Census. Washington, D.C.: U.S. Census Bureau. http://www.census.gov/population/cen2000/stp-159/stp159–el_salvador.pdf, accessed February 11, 2007.

———. 2000c. *Profile of Selected Demographic and Social Characteristics—People Born in Mexico*. U.S. Census. Washington, D.C.: U.S. Census Bureau. http://www.census.gov/population/cen2000/stp-159/STP-159–Mexico.pdf, accessed February 11, 2007.

White, Marceline, Carlos Salas, and Sarah Gammage. 2003. *Trade Impact Review: Mexico Case Study; NAFTA and the FTAA, a Gender Analysis of Employment and Poverty Impacts in Agriculture*. Washington, D.C.: Women's Edge Coalition.

Woodall, Patrick, Lori Wallach, Jessica Prach, and Darshana Patel. 2001. *Down on the Farm: NAFTA's Seven Years War on Farmers and Ranchers in the U.S., Canada and Mexico.* Washington, D.C.: Public Citizen's Global Trade Watch.

Zavella, Patricia. 2000. "Engendering Transnationalism in Food Processing: Peripheral Vision on Both Sides of the U.S.-Mexico Border." In *Las nuevas fronteras del siglo XXI: Dimensiones culturales, políticas y socioeconómicas de las relaciones México-Estados* Unidos, edited by Norma Klahn, Pedro Castillo, Alejandro Alvarez, and Federico Manchon, 397–424. Mexico, D.F.: La Jornada Ediciones: Centro de Investigaciones Colección: La Democracia en México.

17

Transnational Social Movements
Linking North and South
The Struggle for Fair Trade

MICHAEL E. CONROY

The concept of fair trade carries many meanings in contemporary usage. President George W. Bush used the term in an address to the Chicago Economic Club on January 6, 2006, when he argued that the United States will continue to push for "free and fair trade" ("President Discusses Strong and Growing Economy" 2006). Governor Jennifer Granholm of Michigan, in the Democrat's radio response to President Bush's State of the Union address in 2006, in which he emphasized technical training and tax breaks for corporate research as the best approach for increasing U.S. competitiveness, said the president should, instead, focus his attention on protecting automakers such as Ford Motor Co. and General Motors Corp. from "unfair foreign competition" and by helping them provide health care and pensions for their workers. "Fight for fair trade," Granholm said. "Fight for our manufacturers. Fight for our automakers. Fight for our American workers" ("Bush Calls on Congress to Boost U.S. Competitiveness" 2006).

Reflecting another use, *Mother Jones* magazine identifies Chris Martin, the lead singer in the rock band Coldplay, as "Fair Trade's front man." Martin had gathered more than 30,000 signatures for Oxfam's "Fair Trade petition" at Coldplay's concerts, and then he had presented the full Oxfam collection of more than 4 million signatures to the head of the WTO at the ministerial meeting in Cancún in 2003 (Turman 2004). That petition, signed by nearly 18 million people by the end of 2005, calls for broad changes in the rules affecting international trade, including dramatic reductions in the agricultural subsidies that northern countries offer their own farmers, increased access to northern markets for the products of the global south, and less pressure to force open the markets of developing countries under conditions favorable to exports from the north.[1]

However, the Fair Trade movement has a separate history that emerged in the years after World War II when organizations such as SERRV International (Sales Exchange for Refugee Rehabilitation Vocation), a faith-based organization, began their work among European refugees with the mission to "promote the social and economic progress of people in developing regions of the world by marketing their handcrafts and foods in a just and direct manner" (SERRV n.d.).[2] At approximately the same time, Ten Thousand Villages was created by the Mennonite Central Committee, and it has grown to encompass more than 160 nonprofit retail stores across the United States and Canada. The organization seeks to provide "vital, fair income to Third World people by marketing their handicrafts and telling their stories in North America" ("Vision, Mission, and Principles" 2006). Its guiding principles are common among these and comparable organizations.

In the 1990s Oxfam America and Oxfam Canada developed jointly a large and relatively successful catalogue-sales operation for handicrafts sourced directly from village-level producers around the world. And other stand-alone efforts, such as "Pueblo to People" (now defunct), attempted to expand the market and build direct-sale supply chains from impoverished handicraft producers to ethically motivated final consumers. The definitions of fair trade varied, although in most cases producers received higher prices than they would have received through normal commercial handicraft channels.

As efforts proliferated worldwide to create alternative marketing channels for products from less-developed countries, the International Federation for Alternative Trade (IFAT) was established in 1989. IFAT's mission is "to improve the livelihoods and well-being of disadvantaged producers by linking and promoting Fair Trade Organizations, and speaking out for greater justice in world trade" ("Mission Statement" 2006). Ten Thousand Villages and SERRV were among the founding members.

In the United States the work of these and other "alternative trading organizations" led to the creation of the Fair Trade Federation (FTF) in 1994, which was set up as "an association of fair trade wholesalers, retailers, and producers whose members are committed to providing fair wages and good employment opportunities to economically disadvantaged artisans and farmers worldwide" (Fair Trade Federation n.d.). The FTF also sees its role as educational and policy-oriented, fostering "a more equitable and sustainable system of production and trade that benefits people and their communities."

In Europe, Oxfam developed a multi-national network of shops, initially identified as "Oxfam Shops" and ultimately spun-off and branded as "World Shops," whose purpose was to provide direct marketing access to products from developing countries, sold to ethical consumers and used as a basis for promoting discussion of the conditions under which they were produced. By the end of 2006 there were more than 2,500 World Shops across 13 European countries, run by more than 100,000 volunteers. Its work is consolidated in the Network of European World Shops, also created in 1994.[3]

In retrospect, most of this early Fair Trade movement was unified by the following characteristics:

- Most, if not all, of the vendors were nonprofit organizations that depended heavily on volunteer staffing. This reflected their specific interest in providing a higher price to producers while not seeking profits for themselves. It also provided a basis for selling products in final markets at relatively competitive prices when compared with the equivalent commercial for-profit products. There were few, if any, formal guidelines for what constituted Fair Trade.
- Virtually all of the vendors were associated with well-known non-profit organizations, such as religious groups, social advocacy groups, or other NGOs whose name recognition conveyed legitimacy to their claims that the products represented some form of Fair Trade.
- Most of the Fair Trade vendors sold nothing but Fair Trade products, whatever the implicit definition. This gave them a unity of selling points and reduced the likelihood that final consumers would question or challenge the legitimacy of the claims made for the products.
- And, as it happens, most of these organizations were concerned by the mid-1990s that their sales were stagnating, that they had difficulty reaching larger, "mainstream" markets, and that the extent of the benefits that they could deliver to producers was, therefore, severely constrained. This theme was reflected in the content of many discussions at conferences of the FTF and the IFAT.

Certified Fair Trade

The challenge of creating an identifiable Fair Trade product that could be sold in mainstream shops and grocery stores was first taken up by the Dutch development organization Solidaridad. In 1988 Solidaridad began importing Mexican coffee into European markets and selling it with a whimsical "Max Havelaar" seal as an indication that it had been obtained under specified Fair Trade conditions.[4] As seals of this sort proliferated in Europe, Fairtrade Labelling Organizations International (FLO) was created in 1997 to harmonize the efforts of the emerging certified Fair Trade movement. By the end of 2006 FLO had twenty-one member organizations, each a "national labeling initiative" responsible for promoting Fair Trade products in its respective country.[5] FLO had developed or endorsed Fair Trade producer standards for twelve categories of products.[6] FLO initially focused solely on agricultural products produced in the global south and sold in markets of the global north; it has subsequently explored broadening its reach to include Fair Trade apparel and composite products such as brownies, ice cream, and similar products. In general the standards at the production end of the supply chain are of two types: 1) those that apply to small-scale producers organized in democratically functioning cooperatives, and 2) those that apply to larger farms that focus specifically on the conditions faced by hired labor, where workers must be represented by some form of democratic bargaining representation.

For both of these types of producers, FLO's trading standards stipulate that importers must

- pay a predetermined floor price to producers of most products that covers the costs of sustainable production at the local cost of living; these prices are negotiated, product by product and region by region with the producers;
- pay a small "social premium" above that price (or over the market price, whichever is higher) so that producers can invest in development; the use of the premium is determined by producers' or workers' representatives in an audited transparent manner;
- pay partially for products in advance at the time of the sale, when producers ask for it, rather than waiting until all of the product is sold by importers to retailers (as is common in coffee and other markets); and
- sign contracts that allow for long-term planning and sustainable production practices, rather than leaving producers at the whim of "spot markets" from year to year.

There are also additional, product-specific standards that determine minimum quality, environmental conditions, and processing requirements that must be met ("Standards" 2006). FLO has developed and promoted a unified Fair Trade seal, now used all over Europe but not yet adopted in the United States and Canada.

FLO and its national labeling initiatives also require that importers, processors, and other traders be certified with respect to their pricing practices, payment of the social premium, and administrative controls to keep certified products separate from conventional products; participants must meet all requirements in order to use FLO's Fair Tradelogos on their final consumer-facing products. FLO's independent certifying and auditing organization, FLO-Cert, is responsible for determining whether producer groups meet its Fair Trade requirements, for the annual monitoring of the certified producer organizations, and for the annual auditing of certified and licensed traders.[7] Producers and traders share the actual costs of on-site initial certification and subsequent monitoring. The rest of the system (standard-setting, dispute resolution, marketing, promotion, and administrative overhead) is financed primarily through a labeling fee on licensed products, which ranges from approximately five cents to ten cents per pound in coffee, one cent per pound in bananas, and comparable prices in other products. In some countries, including the United States, the licensing fee also varies with the total volume and percent of total sales that are Fair Trade Certified™, encouraging companies to increase both volumes and proportions that are certified. The fees are collected by the national Labeling Initiatives, and a prorated share is sent to FLO and FLO-Cert to cover their standard-setting costs, as well as the administrative part of certifying, monitoring, and auditing functions.

As of December 2007, FLO has worked with more than 800 certified producer organizations; they represent over 1.4 million farmers and workers in 50 countries of Africa, Asia, and Latin America. Including their dependents, more than 7 million people are affected by the certified Fair Trade program managed by FLO ("Impact" 2007). On the business side, FLO works with more than 900 registered traders, including exporters, importers, processors, and manufacturers, again in more than 50 countries around the world. The distribution of the Fair Trade producers varies by commodity (Raynolds and Long 2007). As of 2005, 80 percent of the certified coffee producer groups were in Latin America, spread more or less evenly across Mexico, Peru, Guatemala, Bolivia, and Honduras, with smaller numbers across most of the other coffee-producing countries. Virtually all of the Fair Trade bananas came from Ecuador and the Dominican Republic and almost all of the Fair Trade tea came from India, Sri Lanka, Kenya, and Thailand.

Any qualifying producer group can become certified, and scores of new groups are added each year, especially as new product categories enter into the Fair Trade system. It is a continuing challenge for FLO-Cert to meet the needs of all new groups that want to become certified. Requests for initial certification inspections are (generally) dealt with on a first-come, first-served basis.

Fair Trade prices for coffee were set in 2007, after lengthy negotiations with representatives of producer groups, at U.S.$1.31 per pound of dry green coffee FOB at the point of export, and U.S.$1.51 per pound for coffee that is also certified organic. There are slight variations from country to country on the basis of transportation costs and local conditions. Producers in South America, for example, do not want to be disadvantaged vis-à-vis producers in Mexico and Central America because of the latter's lower shipping costs to the United States and Europe, so their minimum price may be a few cents less per pound of coffee.[8] Those prices have been consistently well above the Commodity C prices offered by brokers in the New York Coffee Exchange for all but a couple of years out of the last fifteen years. Comparable prices have been set for bananas, cocoa, tea, and other commodities: they were negotiated with producer groups on the basis of cost of production and cost of living, and they are generally well above the spot market prices for those products.

While extensively "transnational" in its rapid evolution in consuming countries, the certified Fair Trade movement has tended to be less inclusive of producers and producer organizations until fairly recently. Fair Trade producers in Latin America have been organized since 2002 in the Latin American and Caribbean Network of Small Fair Trade Producers (CLAC). The association seeks to represent all certified Fair Trade producer groups in Latin America and the Caribbean. It meets every other year, and it has begun to exercise growing influence over the policies of FLO through its membership on FLO's board of directors. The strongest level of engagement by the CLAC has been concerted advocacy for reserving Fair Trade certification in coffee to small-scale producers rather than providing coverage for the workers on larger estates, an important tension in the movement to which we will turn shortly. Asian producers of Fair Trade tea and spices began to organize the Association of National Producers in 2005 with a similar intention: advocacy within FLO for the interests of tea and spice producers, many of whom work on estates. And a similar producer organization for Africa emerged in 2006. Each of these three producer organizations elects one or more voting representatives to FLO's board of directors.

There have also emerged a small number of domestically oriented Fair Trade programs in Latin America that are informally associated with FLO. Comercio Justo de México may be the best developed. It uses its own proprietary seal to identify Fair Trade coffee products in the Mexican market.[9] FLO also maintains offices in San Salvador and Quito, as *puntos de enlace* with producers.[10]

The Scale and Effects of Fair Trade

There were no reliable estimates of the overall size or impact of the Fair Trade movement prior to 2007. There are several reasons for this. First, there was no central registry for all of the various components of the movement: handicrafts and other artisanal products, as well as the certified Fair Trade commodities. Second, different components measured sales at different points in the supply chain. The 100 percent Fair Trade handicrafts and food products shops maintain relatively clear records on their final sales. FLO and Transfair USA, in contrast, produced voluminous statistics on pounds of coffee, bananas, oranges, cocoa, tea, and other products whose licensed sales they have recorded and verified at the wholesale level, in many cases before final processing. But the conversion of those pounds into dollar values, either at retail or wholesale, was much more difficult.

The movement-level scale of Fair Trade is increasingly apparent in Europe. As of 2005, the following statistics characterize the magnitude of fair trade in Europe:

- Fair Trade products were available in an estimated total of 79,000 points of sale;
- annual estimated net retail value of Fair Trade products sold in Europe reached €660 million (U.S.$800 million);
- nearly €597 million were attributable to FLO's certified Fair Trade products ("Fair Trade labeled products," in European terminology);
- market shares were growing: in Switzerland, Fair Trade bananas accounted for 47 percent of total banana sales while Fair Trade flowers accounted for 28 percent of total flower sales; and in the United Kingdom, Fair Trade coffee reached 20 percent of ground coffee sales (Krier 2005).

Total estimated sales in the United States, Canada, and the Pacific Rim (mostly Japan) in 2002 reached U.S.$180 million, up 41 percent from 2001. Figure 17.1 shows the dramatic increase in Transfair USA sales over those years and beyond. The estimated retail value of all Fair Trade Certified™ products in the United States alone rose from $131 million in 2002 to more than $1 billion in 2006.

A second measure, shown in figure 17.2, is available from Transfair USA

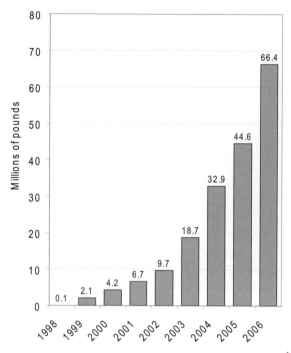

Figure 17.1 Green coffee imports to the United States certified by TransFair USA. Data from Transfair USA (2006 estimated).

for estimates of the impact of Fair Trade coffee sales: the additional coffee income generated for producers by Fair Trade sales in the United States was nearly $100 million from 1998 to 2005. This calculation comes from comparing the Fair Trade price received with the Commodity C price for all coffee on the New York Coffee Exchange over those same years.[11] Preliminary estimates indicated that U.S. sales in 2005 were nearly half the total worldwide sales of Fair Trade coffee; that would imply total global retail sales of Fair Trade coffee in the range of $2 billion.

Benefits to farmers and other producers are not limited to the higher prices and the social premium. An analysis by the Fair Trade Research Group at Colorado State University has documented a wide array of social benefits perceived by Mexican participants in the certified Fair Trade system. They include

1. greater access to credit for the expansion of production, given the relative stability of the Fair Trade financial relationships;
2. greater economic and social stability for Fair Trade farmers because of the Fair Trade financial relationships;

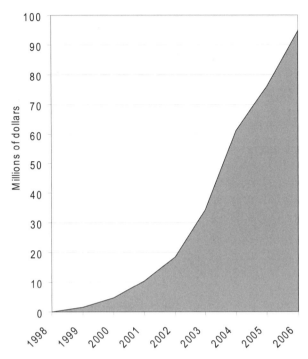

Figure 17.2 Estimated cumulative additional income for farmers from Fair Trade exports to the United States (coffee, tea, cocoa, and fruit). Data from Transfair USA.

3. greater access to training and enhanced ability to improve the quality of their coffee;
4. development of new and beneficial networks of contacts among producers participating in the Fair Trade network;
5. increased welfare through projects developed by their cooperatives with the social premium;
6. training and marketing opportunities for family members to develop alternative income sources;
7. enhanced family stability;
8. contributions to cultural revival;
9. increased organizational credibility; and
10. access to a broader range of government support programs (Murray et al. 2003).

Market Dynamics in the United States

The rapid growth of certified Fair Trade product sales in the United States can be attributed to three principal factors: 1) the organization of successful "market campaigns" by advocacy NGOs designed to put pressure on companies to adopt lines of Fair Trade coffee and other products; 2) the adoption of Fair Trade products by a number of coffee roasters and retailers as a distinguishing characteristic of their coffee offerings, for marketing purposes; and 3) the creation of a sophisticated business-oriented service structure by Transfair USA for its Fair Trade licensees. Each of these dimensions, however, has its limitations; and, in the end, each has contributed to the struggles within the Fair Trade movement, in the United States and elsewhere.

Uncertified "fair trade" coffee has been available in the United States since 1986 through Equal Exchange, a for-profit worker-owned firm based in Philadelphia that began selling "fairly priced" coffees through cooperative and solidarity networks throughout the United States. Equal Exchange built its name, and its practice, on the theoretical notion of "unequal exchange" as faced by countries in the global "periphery." From its perspective, the Fair Trade standards, as first articulated by Max Havelaar and other European traders, provided a more equitable distribution of the production risk across farmers, intermediate traders, and roasters and retailers (Berman and Rozyne 1997). Today Equal Exchange views its mission as "building long-term trade partnerships that are economically just and environmentally sound, to foster mutually beneficial relations between farmers and consumers and to demonstrate . . . the viability of worker cooperatives and Fair Trade" ("Our Co-Op" 2007). When Transfair USA was founded in 1998, Equal Exchange was one of the first licensees; and through growth in recent years, especially in partnership with the Interfaith Fair Trade Initiative, which engages thousands of churches, temples, mosques, and other congregations, it has become one of the largest vendors of Fair Trade products in the United States.

The "breakthrough" moment for certified Fair Trade in "mainstream" markets came on April 13, 2000, when Starbucks, the largest chain of specialty coffee houses in the world, responded to a yearlong campaign by Global Exchange, the social activist organization in Oakland, California, and signed a letter of intent with Transfair USA to offer certified coffee in all 2,700 Starbucks coffee shops that it then owned in the United States. On October 4, 2000, certified Fair Trade coffee began to be sold in all Starbucks coffee shops nationwide. Prior to the signing, Global Exchange had threatened to organize simultaneous demonstrations against Starbucks coffee shops in thirty U.S. cities. In response to the signing, it turned the demonstrations into high-profile celebrations of Starbucks's commitment to purchase Fair Trade coffee and to introduce it in its shops nationwide.

Commitments followed quickly on the part of Peet's Coffee, Tully's Coffee, and a host of other competing coffee companies in the Pacific Northwest. None of these major vendors was willing to commit to selling solely Fair Trade coffees, but the dramatic increase in sales of Fair Trade coffee in 2001 and 2002 was fueled by these companies, which began to sell increasing amounts of it, motivated more by the pressure from Global Exchange, national media, and other organizations than by either internal corporate culture or consumer demand. But this would change.

One major contemporary vendor of Fair Trade coffees that never faced pressures from NGOs was Green Mountain Coffee Roasters (GMCR), based in Vermont. Green Mountain, founded in 1981, had been built on a corporate culture that emphasized long-term, sustainable, and equitable relationships with producers. Well before the arrival of certified Fair Trade in the United States, GMCR had established strong ties to cooperatives in Mexico, Peru, and the Aceh region of Sumatra; and its corporate advertising emphasized its commitment to equitable relationships with the coffee farmers. This was, however, just a "first party" claim, that is, GMCR's own assertion of its trading relationships, without independent verification or validation.

Green Mountain's business model is in many ways the opposite of the Starbucks model. From a company that had a few coffee shops in its early days, GMCR evolved into a wholesale and direct-mail coffee business with no shops of its own. In 2000, the company signed a contract with Exxon-Mobil to supply coffee to 900 convenience stores and nearly 13,000 dealer and franchise stores throughout the northeastern United States. It continued to expand its sales in supermarkets, on Jet Blue Airlines, and to natural foods supermarkets. It is one of the fastest growing coffee roasters in the United States, and its dual-certified Fair Trade and organic coffees are the leading edge of that growth.

Green Mountain first became interested in organic coffees in 1998 and quickly expanded its line of organic coffees to include nearly a dozen by 2001. In 2002 GMCR was approached by Transfair USA to integrate Fair Trade Certified™ coffees into its lines, and it began, somewhat hesitatingly, because the higher price and the labeling fee seemed to risk making the coffee uncompetitive in national markets. By 2003 GMCR began a series of strategic partnerships that have served to expand its Fair Trade and organic sales at a very rapid pace. Green Mountain established a co-branding relationship with Newman's Own Organics to introduce a line of coffees associated with the actor, Paul Newman, who had already established a series of socially responsible food product lines in other products. Then it expanded into a cross-branded line of Fair Trade and organic teas with Hain Celestials, a leading organic foods manufacturer. The crowning arrangement came in late 2005 when GMCR contracted with McDonald's to provide Fair Trade Certified™ coffee for *all* of the coffee that would be sold in McDonald's stores in New England and upstate New York (Grodnik and Conroy 2007).

By 2007 all of the espresso coffee sold in the more than 3,000 Dunkin Donuts stores across the United States was Fair Trade Certified™; the Costco warehouse chain had converted all of its private label Kirkland coffee brand to Fair Trade Certified™; and Sam's Club began to offer several lines of Fair Trade Certified™ coffee as well as chocolate. Of even greater importance, Tully's Coffee, with more than 140 shops in the western United States, began co-branding with Fair Trade Certified™, announcing throughout its coffee shops that all of the coffee sold in them was both certified organic and Fair Trade Certified™. It placed banners in all of its shops' windows displaying the Fair Trade logo and claiming this commitment. This was the first time that a major coffee company with highly prominent shops had formally associated its brand with Fair Trade Certified™.

The principal actors in the market campaigns on behalf of Fair Trade products in the United States have evolved. Building on the work of Global Exchange with students on campuses, Oxfam America has been actively involved, especially in training student leaders, to develop campus campaigns to persuade colleges and universities to serve Fair Trade coffee in their institutions. Much of this has been accomplished, as well, through assisting with the launch of the United Students for Fair Trade organization. In addition, Lutheran World Relief created the Interfaith Fair Trade Initiative to encourage congregations of many faiths to purchase and serve Fair Trade Certified™ coffee and tea in their institutions, and to encourage their members to purchase Fair Trade products for their homes. Much of the benefit of this campaign has been channeled through Equal Exchange, which has doubled its sales in the past three years. And Co-op America has focused much of its efforts on a successful campaign to convince other mainstream coffee companies, such as Procter and Gamble, to introduce a line of Fair Trade Certified™ coffees.

The producers of certified Fair Trade products are often closely associated with social movements in both their countries of origin and across the north-south divide. Rapid recent growth of certified Fair Trade in Brazil has led to the creation of the Brazilian Association for Fair Trade, which is closely linked with the Landless Rural Workers' Movement (MST) and is focused on building markets for fairly traded products within Brazil. In Mexico, Comércio Justo México has close ties to organized worker and farmer groups such as UNORCA (National Union of Regional Autonomous Peasant Organizations). And many of the second-level organizations within the Fair Trade movement, such as CEPCO (Coordinadora Estatal de Productores de Café Orgánico; Oaxaca State Coordinating Committee for Organic Coffee Producers) in Oaxaca and "Café de la Selva" in Chiapas, have had close links with European and U.S. solidarity organizations that have helped them with technical assistance and financial support.

Bananas became the next big market for Fair Trade products. Fair Trade Certified™ bananas from the Dominican Republic and Ecuador began to edge out conventional bananas in European markets in 2003. The Wild Oats supermarket chain (with some one hundred stores, mostly in the western United States) led the introduction of fair trade and organic bananas into the United States. But their introduction of Fair Trade bananas was troubled by delivery problems from producers who have not had access to the fast, refrigerated banana boats of the major *bananeras*. The relatively small-scale shipments sent by those producers take considerably longer to reach market than the bananas shipped by the five global *bananeras*; and the result is serious problems of quality in the delivered bananas. Chiquita and Dole have had discussions with Transfair USA for the introduction of a Fair Trade line of bananas and other fruits. Their motivation appears to be the search for a distinguishing characteristic for some of their bananas that would allow them to sell the bananas at a price-point well above the brutally competitive basic conventional banana price. However, the very discussion of the possibility of Fair Trade products from these commercial giants has led to a major polemic within the Fair Trade movement, to which we will now turn.

The Evolving Struggle within the Movement

The certified Fair Trade movement faces a number of critical issues worldwide that have caused great concern. The principal issues fall into three categories: 1) tensions between traders committed 100 percent to Fair Trade products and those that sell both Fair Trade and non-Fair Trade products; 2) tensions over the future growth of the movement with respect to the extension of Fair Trade certification to cover the workers on larger estates, rather than restricting it to small-scale producers organized in cooperatives; and 3) tensions around the licensing of giant multi-national corporations with dubious historical records, which some are beginning to refer to as "Darth Vader companies."

In the early days of the Fair Trade movement, all sales of Fair Trade products were handled by organizations committed to selling nothing but Fair Trade products. This was also true in the early days of the certified Fair Trade portion of the movement, when Equal Exchange and a number of other "100 percenters" formed the nucleus of the movement. Yet total Fair Trade sales were heavily constrained, in those days, by the smallness of many of those organizations and by their limited market penetration.

The boom in sales—and, therefore, in benefits to farmers—has come primarily as mainstream companies have introduced lines of certified Fair Trade products alongside their ordinary commercial grade (and often less expensive) products. Some of the small 100-percenter companies began seeking a competitive edge by publicly criticizing their larger competitors, whose commitment to Fair Trade, they argued, was suspect. However, this was ruled a violation of their Transfair USA licensing agreements, which barred attacks upon other licensees. When warned of that violation, a small number of the 100 percenters cancelled their links to Transfair USA and began a variety of practices to become independently identified as "Fair Trade" without certification by Transfair USA.[12]

These companies continue to claim that their products are at least as worthy as those that carry the Transfair USA label. And some of them use an IFAT label as evidence of certification, even though IFAT has no mechanism for verifying or certifying compliance with its own code of conduct for members. Dean's Beans provided a good example of the "Fair Trade Plus" approaches of a small number of companies in the United States ("Fair Trade Roadmap" 2007).

Dean's Beans advertises that it adheres to FLO's minimum prices, that is, $1.51 per pound for the Fair Trade and organic coffees it sells. It suggests that it purchases only from organizations that are on FLO's registry "or who have become members of IFAT." The company then publishes the list of cooperatives from which it purchases, provides documentation on the extra six-cents per pound social premium it pays, and has its transactions audited independently by Quality Assurance International.

The Dean's Beans Web site contains a passionate and personal critique of the practices of its competitors that do not commit fully to selling only Fair Trade products. Although these 100 percenters appear to represent a very small proportion of total Fair Trade sales in the United States, they represent the leading edge of the push for higher levels of commitment.

The issue of small-scale producers versus plantations is another serious threat to the future expansion of Fair Trade, and this issue seemed fundamentally intractable as recently as late 2006. Worldwide, most certified Fair Trade producers sell only a relatively small proportion of their production on Fair Trade terms. At the same time, some major potential roasters and retailers are offering to convert much larger proportions of their coffee lines to Fair Trade if FLO is willing to create and implement a set of Fair Trade standards for estate-grown coffees. The application of FLO's hired labor standards to coffee estates would give those companies an opportunity to encourage their current preferred vendors to qualify for Fair Trade certification within a reasonable amount of time, or lose their access to that buyer.

The certified Fair Trade movement has standards developed for estate-grown tea and for plantation-grown bananas. The key difference between standards for producers themselves (and for their cooperatives) and standards for estates is that the latter involves a focus on the workers on the estates, rather than on the small-scale producer who, presumably, uses mostly family labor. Hired-labor standards require that workers have access to some type of formal worker representation in the setting of wages and working conditions, sometimes a labor union, sometimes a "workers committee" on the farm. In places like Sri Lanka, from which a significant share of Fair Trade tea is sourced, the worker representation question is relatively simple. Sri Lankan national legislation requires that every tea estate have union representation for its workers. On many estates there is competition among several unions to represent the workers, both tea pluckers and tea factory workers.

The critical problem is that the well-organized representatives of small-scale producers believe that the incorporation of estates or plantations will destroy the fundamental global image of Fair Trade as a movement that favors small and often impoverished producers. Secondly, they are concerned that the alleged growth of the market for Fair Trade products that estate certification is expected to produce will not benefit them because it will not increase the proportion of the products that they can sell into Fair Trade markets, and, on the contrary, that it could reduce their access by increasing the share covered by estate-based products. They recognize that there is an unfortunate class-war dimension to these concerns, for incorporating estates and plantations into the Fair Trade movement extends the umbrella of Fair Trade so that it benefits farmworkers as well as small-scale farm owners.

The problem became more acute, in late 2005, as the prospects for licensing plantation-based bananas for a Chiquita Brands International farm in Honduras roiled through the movement. The Honduras branch of COLSIBA, the regional banana workers' union, was strongly in favor of Fair Trade certification of farmworkers, as was the labor solidarity organization,

USLEAP (the U.S. Labor Education and Action Project).[13] Chiquita Brands was the only major banana company that had accepted union organization on some of its farms, and that had resulted in significantly higher wages and improved working conditions for Chiquita's farmworkers. But most of the Fair Trade banana market was being served by cooperatives in the Dominican Republic and Ecuador at that time, and their representatives were skeptical about the impact upon their efforts of allowing Chiquita to enter the market with a Fair Trade banana. Chiquita had undertaken a preliminary assessment of the conditions on the Honduran farm with respect to FLO's standards, and it was prepared to implement whatever corrective actions might be needed. Unfortunately, the issue was resolved tragically. In late 2005, Hurricane Wilma destroyed the farm that had sought certification, the third time in ten years that it had been hit by a weather disaster, and Chiquita decided to close it down.

Chiquita Brands International is also emblematic of the problem that the Fair Trade movement faces as it decides how to deal with major transnational corporations that are increasingly interested in selling, or at least experimenting with, certified Fair Trade products. Chiquita is the renamed successor to United Fruit International, the company whose checkered history in Central America is closely associated with neocolonial takeover of large tracts of land and the intervention of the CIA in Guatemala when the democratically elected government of Jacobo Arbenz attempted to renationalize those lands in the 1950s. Much of the subsequent fifty years of right-wing dictatorships in Central America, insurgencies, and civil war is laid at the feet of United Fruit, whether accurately or not. For some members of the Fair Trade movement, it is inconceivable that the historical heir to that history could be considered a reasonable partner within the movement. Similar reactions have arisen when the Sam's Club branch of the Wal-Mart empire announced that it was going to begin to sell a line of Fair Trade certified Brazilian coffee; when McDonald's announced that it was going to serve *only* Fair Trade certified coffee in its restaurants in New England; and when Nestlé launched a line of Fair Trade instant coffee in the United Kingdom—all within four months at the end of 2005.

The essence of the critique of this expansion of the Fair Trade movement is epitomized in a recent (widely redistributed) e-mail from Rodney North, the co-founder of Equal Exchange, to the organizers of the 2006 United Students for Fair Trade "convergence," their annual conference:

> Something odd, and possibly very disturbing, happened recently in the United Kingdom that should interest everyone who believes that Fair

Trade can help create a more just, morally grounded global economy. Nestlé—the world's largest food conglomerate and most boycotted company—recently introduced to the UK market its first ever Fair Trade Certified™ product, an instant coffee called "Partners Blend™." But so what? Large US corporations have already jumped (or been pushed) onto the Fair Trade bandwagon. "What's the problem? Don't we want corporations to move in this direction?" Good point. We do. But what we're learning from the Nestlé example is that even a tiny bit of Fair Trade can go a long way to polishing even the worst corporate image, and all at the expense of real reform.

The challenge to the movement is to decide whether it wants to permit the Fair Trade label to be utilized by major transnational companies when only a small proportion of their total sales will come from Fair Trade sources. The trade-off is seen as increased medium-term benefits to some farmers versus the long-run integrity of the Fair Trade brand. The ongoing debate within the movement ranges from complete rejection of the idea of dealing with "Darth Vader companies," these representatives of iconic evil to members of different parts of the movement, to arguments about how they might be incorporated, under what special conditions, and with what levels of commitment to increasing the share of Fair Trade products in their entire product lines.

The Evolving Struggle Outside the Movement

At the same time, numerous new external challenges to the movement have arisen. As has happened in many other certification systems, an industry under pressure to improve its social and environmental practices responds by attempting to create alternative, well-funded, and less-demanding competitive certification processes.[14] The challenges to the Fair Trade movement take many forms. For example, the Rainforest Alliance and its sustainable agriculture certification program remains the greatest competitor, at present, to certified Fair Trade. Although Transfair USA and the Rainforest Alliance have attempted to create a commonly agreed upon language to describe the benefits of each certification system, producers, processors, and retailers certified by the Rainforest Alliance often make claims of wage and price fairness that infringe on Fair Trade claims. And some Transfair USA licensees have made claims of environmental sustainability that go beyond what can be documented. The biggest success for the Rainforest Alliance was the launch in all European markets in 2005 of Chiquita bananas with the Rainforest Alliance certificate of sustainable agricultural practices.

The Dutch coffee industry has helped to launch Utz Kapeh, a rival to FLO's certified Fair Trade brand, which claims to offer "a worldwide certification program that sets the standard for responsible coffee production and sourcing." Utz Kapeh, which is supposed to mean "good coffee" in a Mayan language, gives the assurance of "social and environmental quality in coffee production that coffee drinkers expect."[15] Its standards of 2006 represent a combination of weakened Rainforest Alliance sustainability standards and broad ILO-based workers' rights and safety standards. Farmers must seek, and pay for, independent verification of their compliance with the standards; and the standards provide no rules on wages (other than payment of local minimum wages) or prices for the finished product.

The German aid agency GTZ and the Swiss aid agency SECO have also helped to create and launch the Common Code for the Coffee Community (4C). This is claimed to be "a joint initiative of coffee producers, trade and industry, trade unions and social as well as environmental NGOs to develop a global code of conduct aiming at overall sustainability in the production, post-harvest processing and trading of mainstream green coffee" ("The 4C Association" n.d.). This system, which underwent preliminary testing at the start of 2006, asserts that FLO's Fair Trade system is a "niche system, inappropriate to the mainstream market." It also provides an extensive set of conditions that farmers must meet, is ambiguous about how those costs will be met, and rejects the notion that a fixed minimum price can be consistent with a market economy.[16]

The combined threat to the Fair Trade movement from these competing initiatives cannot be overstated. None of them shows promise of incorporating the fundamental characteristics of the movement, that is, an ability to deliver significantly higher prices to commodity producers so that more equitable trading relations are achieved, together with greater development opportunities and real empowerment for poor and disadvantaged producers and workers in developing countries.

The struggles within the movement have absorbed enormous amounts of time and energy on the part of its principal advocates. There is danger that it has served to distract them from the greater external threats mentioned above. Without immediate attention to that threat, it is increasingly likely that the Fair Trade movement will collapse and decline, becoming the niche market, as irrelevant to mainstream commodity trade as its opponents claim that it is.

The strength and resilience of the Fair Trade movement itself, however, seems to grow each day. In 2006 and early 2007 the level of public commitment to certified Fair Trade in the United Kingdom grew enormously, with duels among the leading retail giants, Tesco, Sainsbury, and Marks and Spencer, to see who could offer the largest amount and the widest array of Fair Trade products. The growth in the number of producer organizations seeking Fair Trade certification, and the access it brings to Fair Trade markets, exceeded the capacity of FLO's independent certification body, FLO-Cert, to meet it, with significant backlogs that were building. And the improvements in FLO's governance, with additional representatives for producers from the global south, the growth of Fair Trade consuming communities in Mexico, Brazil, and South Africa, and the explorations around expansion of Fair Trade to cover a range of other products, from tourism and ecotourism to artisanally mined gold and diamonds, as well as a much wider array of fresh fruits, suggest that the opportunities to strengthen this unusual north-south social movement remain very encouraging.

Resolution of the Tensions?

The Fair Trade movement, worldwide, took very large steps in 2007 to resolve many of these internal tensions. It undertook a global "strategic review" to identify and address the major challenges that it faces across movements and within markets. Recognizing that FLO would complete ten years of activities in 2008, the strategic review process consisted of several distinct and cumulative steps. There was first a round of consultation meetings among all stakeholders in the system, beginning in April 2007, for the purpose of reaching consensus on the "fundamental trends which are most likely to impact on [Fair Trade certification] and influence its strategy in the coming years" (Fair Trade Labelling Strategic Review White Paper 2008). The second stage then consisted of a set of consultations "to identify a coherent set of strategic options based on the context analysis, issues and dilemmas" identified in the first stage, which were laid out in a draft White Paper (p. 18). The consultations that followed stretched from "from Kampala to Managua, from Colombo to Lima, from Paris to New York" (p. 3).

The resulting final "White Paper," approved by FLO's board of directors in November 2007, represents a significant series of steps forward to resolve many, if not most, of the contentious issues discussed above. On the question of who the "market partners" for Fair Trade would be, for example, the White Paper asserts a new consensus that Fair Trade "is a non-exclusive system which is ready to engage with any market partner that demonstrates genuine commitment to [certified Fair Trade] (including globalized companies)." But it also affirms: "In particular, ATOs (Alternative Trade Organizations) are core market partners."

On the issues of scale of production, the phrase "plantations" appears nowhere in the White Paper. Through a long process of negotiation, it was agreed that the polarization around "small farmers" versus "plantations" was no longer relevant to the debate. Production units of many different sizes are already part of certified Fair Trade, and the need for recognition of implicit and explicit competition among them was embodied directly in the discussion of the future (using the European language of Fairtrade Labelling [FTL] in lieu of the term "certified Fair Trade" that we have used in this chapter):

- "A key concern of FTL is to ensure fair competition within its system among a wide range of producers' organizations and market operators that differ in size, level of capacities, level of vertical integration, financial resources, etc.
- "To achieve it, producers who are more disadvantaged, producers who are already part of the system and situations with proven impact are specifically supported/promoted so that they can participate on fair terms in the growth of the FTL market."

On questions dividing producers on small farms and workers on larger production units, the agreed wording and the basis for moving forward was unambiguous: "All disadvantaged producers who fit into the Fairtrade Labelling development approach, are fully entitled to benefit from it. Smallholders, who are at the heart of FTL, and workers both enjoy the right to access it."

Throughout the White Paper the full partnership around the needs and voices of producers and workers is clear, indicating a major representational improvement for the movement as a whole:

[The] FTL intends to move from its actual organization to a system where:
- Labelling Initiatives are responsible for growing the demand and generate commitment of the industry through negotiation and support.
- Producer Networks are responsible for growing the [supply] and generate capacity building and support for producers' organizations.
- An umbrella/central body provides economies of scale, consistency and coordination.

In addition, Labelling Initiatives and Producer Networks take joint responsibility in implementing an efficient integrated management of supply chains.

Finally, the question of potentially controversial companies was resolved in the direction preferred by the producer organizations: "disloyal" competition by vertically integrated companies will be actively discouraged. However, unless sales by a global corporation with severe reputational risk endangers the whole Fair Trade brand, no constraints will be placed on such companies. And, at the same time, it was agreed that the system will actively seek to provide "preferential market access for more disadvantaged producers."

The final stage of this strategic review process is the building of a new, enhanced certified Fair Trade business model. This task has been given to a task force whose results will be presented to FLO's board, consulted worldwide in the months that follow, and adopted before the end of 2008.

The ability of the multiplicity of northern and southern producer organizations, advocacy groups, and the Fair Trade labeling national initiatives to reach agreement on these broad principles augurs very well for the future of Fair Trade, in general, and of certified Fair Trade in particular. Crude ideological positions, long-held beliefs, and adamant criticisms have yielded to north-south consultations on the best way to hone further this development tool for the benefit of disadvantaged producers and workers worldwide.

Epilogue

The Fair Trade movement has continued to grow rapidly since the conclusion of the last revision of this chapter. Total estimated retail sales of certified Fair Trade products are expected to exceed U.S.$5 billion in 2008, up another 30 percent over the 2007 figures. By the end of 2007, both the U.S. and the U.K. markets reached U.S.$1.1 billion, with the former growing at 26 percent (year over year) and the latter at 72 percent. The next largest markets were France at $336 million (and growing at 27 percent), Switzerland at $252 million (11 percent), and Germany at $226 million (29 percent). But new markets were growing even more rapidly: Sweden at 166 percent, Norway at 110 percent, and Ireland at 101 percent (Fairtrade Labelling Organizations 2008: 12–13).

Most of the growth in U.S. and U.K. markets is coming from the competitive introduction of Fair Trade products in major chains, including Whole Foods Markets, Costco, Sam's Clubs, and Wal-Mart in the United States, and the COOP, Marks and Spencer, Sainsbury, and Waitrose in the United Kingdom. The drive for expansion in both markets shows little NGO pressure behind it, at this point. Rather, major grocery chains are finding that consumers are willing to pay a slightly higher price for a certified Fair Trade product than they do for conventional products, whose sources and supply conditions are unknown, or for products with other certifications. One exception to that is at Wal-Mart, where the introduction of Fair Trade Certified™ coffee in the United States has come as part of its overall shift in practices toward greater environmental and social accountability, prompted significantly by a unified campaign of more than 80 NGOs in the United States (Conroy 2007).

IFAT has begun moving toward creating new standards and auditing for its member organizations, leading toward a more robust certification system for the handicrafts and other artisanal products that are the core sales items of its members.

And even Dean Cycon, owner of the Dean's Beans coffee company and a leader in the breakaway of several small 100-percenter Fair Trade licensees, has returned to Transfair USA certification after nearly four years, apparently responding to market pressures for a credible global label on his products. He now competes on the basis of that certification, as well as on his own claims of the ways in which his products surpass the minimum requirements for global certification under Fair Trade Certified™.

Notes

Editors' note: By convention, the Fair Trade movement, since its inception, has capitalized "fair trade" to distinguish it from other uses of the phrase, while using "Fairtrade" in Europe; scholars have followed suit. For a recent example, see Laura T. Raynolds, Douglas L. Murray, and John Wilkinson, eds., *Fair Trade: The Challenges of Transforming Globalization,* London: Routledge, 2007. This chapter follows that practice. Also see http://books.google.com/books?id=0gQymQ7nbTIC.

1. The petition adheres closely to the ideas articulated in Watkins 2002.

2. Created by the evangelical Church of the Brethren in 1949, SERRV International continues to function as an independent nonprofit that in 2004 sold about $6 million of handicrafts from some thirty countries, mostly through Internet sales. See SERRV n.d.

3. See www.worldshops.org, accessed March 1, 2008.

4. Max Havelaar was a fictional character in a Dutch novel of 1860 that focused on the colonial trade policies of the Netherlands in the Dutch East Indies. The book illustrated the ways in which Dutch consumer wealth was built upon the suffering of the residents of the East Indies. The book ultimately led the Dutch government to implement a somewhat more ethical set of development policies.

5. The members are TransFair Austria, Max Havelaar Belgium, Transfair Canada, Max Havelaar France, Max Havelaar Denmark, TransFair Germany, Fairtrade Foun-

dation U.K., Fairtrade TransFair Italy, FairTrade Mark Ireland, Fairtrade Label Japan, TransFair Minka Luxemburg, Stichting Max Havelaar Netherlands, Stichting Max Havelaar Norway, Reilun kaupan edistämisyhdistys ry. Finland, Asociación para el Sello de Comércio Justo Spain, Föreningen för Rättvisemärkt Sweden, Max Havelaar Stiftung Switzerland, Fairtrade Labelling Australia and New Zealand, and TransFair USA. Comércio Justo México is an associate member.

6. The products are coffee, tea, rice, fresh fruit, wine, juices, cocoa, sugar, honey, sports balls, cotton, and flowers.

7. In some countries, the local labeling initiative, such as TransFair USA and the Fair Trade Foundation in the United Kingdom, conducts the trade certification of importers and licensees.

8. There is also an issue of the depreciations of the dollar in recent years with respect to the euro and other currencies. This has meant a de facto decrease in the price received by farmers; but FLO system has not dealt with that issue yet.

9. See http://www.comerciojusto.com.mx, accessed February 22, 2008.

10. See http://www.comerciojustoecuadorperu.net, and http://www.flocentroamerica.net, accessed February 22, 2008.

11. Transfair USA, personal communication. This price may overstate the benefits to some extent, for it implicitly assumes that all of the Fair Trade producers who shipped coffee to the United States would have received no more than the Commodity C price for the coffee sold through the Fair Trade system. Since most of that coffee is also certified organic, it is likely that the alternative price would have been somewhat higher.

12. The group included Dean's Beans, Café Campesino, Larry's Beans, and several others.

13. Personal communication with Stephen Coates, the executive director of USLEAP.

14. See Conroy 2007.

15. See http://www.utzcertified.org/, accessed February 22, 2008.

16. See http://www.glifood.org/commodities, accessed February 6, 2006.

References

Berman, Virginia, and Michael Rozyne. 1997. "Never Underestimate Hope: The Impact of Fair Trade on Coffee Farmers." *Equal Exchange Research Report.*

"Bush Calls on Congress to Boost U.S. Competitiveness." 2006. Bloomberg. http://www.bloomberg.com/apps/news?pid=10000087&sid=a7mmW4HiXGKM&refer=top_world_news, accessed June 21, 2007.

Conroy, Michael E. 2007. *Branded! How the "Certification Revolution" Is Transforming Global Corporations.* Vancouver: New Society Publishers.

"Fair Trade Federation." N.d. http://www.fairtradefederation.org/index.html, accessed June 21, 2007.

"Fair Trade Labelling Strategic Review White Paper." 2008. FLO e.V., Reference: doc STF 26—23/01/2008.

"Fair Trade Roadmap." 2007. Dean's Beans. http://www.deansbeans.com/coffee/fair_trade_roadmap.html?id=Nhue3W2f, accessed June 21, 2007.

Fairtrade Labelling Organizations. 2008. *An Inspiration for Change: Fairtrade Labelling Organizations International Annual Report 2007*. Bonn, Germany: Fairtrade Labelling Organizations.

"The 4C Association." N.d. Common Code for the Coffee Community Association. http://www.sustainable-coffee.net/index.html, accessed June 21, 2007.

Grodnik, Ann, and Michael E. Conroy. 2007. "Fair Trade Certification in the U.S.: Why Companies Join the Movement." In *Fair Trade: The Challenges of Transforming Globalization*, edited by Laura T. Raynolds, Douglas L. Murray, and John Wilkinson, 83–102. London: Routledge.

"Impact." 2006. Fairtrade Labelling Organizations International. http://www.fairtrade.net/impact.html, accessed June 21, 2007.

Krier, Jean-Marie. 2005. "Fair Trade in Europe 2005: Facts and Figures on Fair Trade in 25 European Countries." Fairtrade Labelling Organizations. http://www.fairtrade.net/fileadmin/user_upload/content/FairTradeinEurope2005.pdf, accessed June 21, 2007.

"Mission Statement." 2006. International Federation for Alternative Trade. http://www.ifat.org/index.php?option=com_content&task=view&id=9&Itemid=4, accessed June 21, 2007.

"Mission Statement." 2007. Sustainable Food Laboratory. http://www.sustainablefood-lab.org/, accessed June 21, 2007.

Murray, Douglas et al. 2003. "One Cup at a Time: Poverty Alleviation and Fair Trade Coffee in Latin America." Boulder, Colo.: Colorado State University Fair Trade Research Group. http://www.colostate.edu/Depts/Sociology/FairTradeResearchGroup/, accessed June 21, 2007.

"Our Co-Op." 2007. Equal Exchange. http://www.equalexchange.com/our-co-op, accessed June 21, 2007.

"President Discusses Strong and Growing Economy." 2006. Speech given by President George W. Bush to the Economic Club of Chicago on January 6. http://www.whitehouse.gov/news/releases/2006/01/20060106–7.html, accessed on June 21, 2007.

Raynolds, Laura T., and Michael A. Long. 2007. "Fair/Alternative Trade: Historical and Empirical Dimensions." In *Fair Trade: The Challenges of Transforming Globalization*, edited by Laura T. Raynolds, Douglas L. Murray, and John Wilkerson, 15–47. London: Routledge.

"SERRV." N.d. Church of the Brethern Network. http://www.cob-net.org/serrv.htm, accessed June 21, 2007.

"Standards." 2006. Fairtrade Labelling Organizations International. http://www.fairtrade.net/standards.html, accessed June 21, 2007.

Turman, Katherine. 2004. "Chris Martin." *Mother Jones* 29 (1): 78–79.

"Vision, Mission, and Principles." 2006. Ten Thousand Villages. http://www.tenthousandvillages.com/php/about.us/mission.principles.php, accessed June 21, 2007.

Watkins, Kevin. 2002. "Rigged Rules and Double Standards: Trade, Globalization, and the Fight against Poverty." Oxfam. http://www.maketradefair.com/assets/english/report_english.pdf, accessed June 21, 2007.

Contributors

Mary Allegretti is a Brazilian anthropologist and an independent researcher and consultant. She is the former secretary for the Amazon at the Ministry of the Environment, Brazil. In the fall of 2005 she was the Bacardi Family Eminent Scholar in Latin American Studies at the Center for Latin American Studies, University of Florida. She has also been a visiting scholar at Yale University, the University of Chicago, and the University of Wisconsin.

Miguel Carter is an assistant professor of International Development at the School of International Service, American University, Washington, D.C. He is the editor of the forthcoming volume, *Challenging Social Inequality: The Landless Rural Workers' Movement (MST) and Agrarian Reform in Brazil* (Durham: Duke University Press, 2009).

Michael E. Conroy is a co-founder of Colibri Consulting—Certification for Sustainable Development. He has been a professor of Economics at the University of Texas, Austin, a senior research scholar and senior lecturer at the Yale School of Forestry and Environmental Studies, and a program officer at the Ford Foundation and the Rockefeller Brothers Fund. He is a member of the board of directors of Transfair USA, the U.S. certifier of fair trade products. He is the author of *Branded! How the "Certification Revolution" Is Transforming Global Corporations* (Vancouver: New Society Publishers, 2007).

Daniel Corrêa has been a member of the Landless Rural Workers Movement (MST) in Brazil since 1993. He worked in the training section for many years and is currently part of the International Relations Department of the National Coordination of the MST. He is studying to complete his bachelor's degree in economics at the National Federal University of Espiritu Santo.

Carmen Diana Deere is the director of the Center for Latin American Studies and a professor of food and resource economics and Latin American studies at the University of Florida. She is the co-author of *Empowering Women: Land and Property Rights in Latin America* (Pittsburgh: University of Pittsburgh Press, 2001), which received the 2003 Bryce Wood Book Award of the Latin American Studies Association.

Annette Aurélie Desmarais is an associate professor of justice studies at the University of Regina, Canada, and she is an associate member of the National Farmers Union of Canada. She is the author of *La Vía Campesina: Globalization and the Power of Peasants* (Black Point, Nova Scotia: Fernwood Publishing; London: Pluto Press, 2007).

Andréia Borges Ferreira represents the state of Santa Catarina on the MST National Directorate in Brazil. She is a member of the agrarian reform settlement of Assentamento Conquista no Litoral in Santa Catarina.

Jonathan Fox is a professor of Latin American and Latino studies at the University of California, Santa Cruz. He is the author of *Accountability Politics: Power and Voice in Rural Mexico* (Oxford: Oxford University Press, 2008) and the co-editor of *Mexico's Right-to-Know Reforms: Civil Society Perspectives* (Mexico City: Fundar, 2007). He serves as an advisor to the Binational Front of Indigenous Organizations (FIOB).

Miguel Palacín is the president of the National Confederation of Communities Affected by Mining (CONACAMI), as well as of the Permanent Conference of Indigenous Peoples of Peru (COPPIP). He also serves as the president of the Andean Coordinator of Indigenous Organizations (CAOI). A Quechua from the community of Vicco in central Peru, he studied animal husbandry at the National University Daniel Aviles Carrión in Pasco, Peru.

George Ann Potter is an anthropologist residing in Bolivia who has served as an advisor to the Coordinator of Peasant Women of the Tropics (COCAMTROP).

Scott S. Robinson teaches social anthropology at the Universidad Metropolitana, Iztapalapa campus in Mexico City. In 1994 he created the Rural Information Network-Mexico Web site www.laneta.apc.org/rir. With his students, he tracks hydropower dam resettlement projects, writes about diasporas and information technology, and most recently, shares the coordination of a project designed to provide binational health insurance for Mexican immigrants in the United States.

Peter Rosset resides in Chiapas, Mexico, and is a researcher with the Center for the Study of Change in the Mexican Countryside (CECCAM), in Oaxaca, Mexico. He is also the co-coordinator of the Land Research and Action Network and a visiting scholar at the University of California, Berkeley. He is a former director of Food First/The Institute for Food and Development Policy in Oakland, Calif., and the co-editor of *Promised Land: Competing Visions of Agrarian Reform* (Oakland, Calif.: Food First Books, 2006).

Frederick S. Royce is an assistant scientist in the Department of Agricultural and Biological Engineering at the Institute of Food and Agricultural Sciences, University of Florida, and has carried out research in Nicaragua and Cuba.

Silvestre Saisari is national coordinator of the Indigenous, Peasant and Landless Workers Movement of Bolivia (MST-Bolivia). He was formerly president of the MST in Santa Cruz, Bolivia, and also served as the secretary of the MST-Bolivia National Land Commission.

Marianne Schmink is the director of the Tropical Conservation and Development Program at the Center for Latin American Studies and a professor of anthropology and Latin American studies at the University of Florida. She is the co-author of *Contested Frontiers in Amazonia* (New York: Columbia University Press, 1992).

Cecilio Solís Librado, a Nahua from the Northern Sierra of Puebla, was a founder of the Plural National Indigenous Assembly for Autonomy (ANIPA) in Mexico. He also founded and is president of the Indigenous Tourism Network of Mexico (RITA).

Lynn Stephen is a professor of anthropology at the University of Oregon, Eugene. She is the author of *Women and Social Movements in Latin America: Power from Below* (Austin: University of Texas Press, 1997) and *Transborder Lives: Indigenous Oaxacans in Mexico, California, and Oregon* (Durham, N.C.: Duke University Press, 2007).

Juan Tiney is the executive secretary of the Latin American Coordinator of Rural Organizations (CLOC). A Tz'utujil Maya from Santiago Atitlan, Solalá, Guatemala, he is also the secretary general of the National Indigenous and Peasant Coordinator of Guatemala (CONIC-Guatemala) and served on the planning commission for the Third Continental Summit of Indigenous Peoples and Nationalities held in Guatemala in 2007.

Carlos B. Vainer, an economist and sociologist, is a professor at the Institute of Urban and Regional Planning and Research at the Federal University of Rio de Janeiro in Brazil. He chairs the laboratory on state, labor, territory, and nature, where he advises students on a broad range of research topics. He serves as the international coordinator for the Research and Cooperation Program on Social Movements in the South, which includes Brazil, South Africa, India, and Thailand. He is also an advisor to the Movement of People Affected by Dams (MAB).

Martha Heriberta Valle is the founding president of the Federation of Agricultural Cooperatives of Rural Women Producers of Nicaragua (FEMU-PROCAN). She is also a former deputy of the Sandinista National Liberation Front, representing the National Union of Farmers and Ranches (UNAG) in the Nicaraguan Congress, and was a leader of the Women's Secretariat of the UNAG for many years.

Alvaro Velasco Álvarez is a researcher with Fundaminga, a nongovernmental organization in Bogotá, Colombia. In 2005–6 he was a Moore Visiting Fellow in the Tropical Conservation and Development Program at the Center for Latin American Studies, University of Florida.

Leonida Zurita is an alternate senator for the Movement Toward Socialism (MAS) party in Bolivia and serves as the party's international liaison. She was recently re-elected as the national executive secretary of the Bartolina Sisa National Federation of Bolivian Peasant Women. She was formerly the executive secretary of the Coordinator of Peasant Women of the Tropics (COCAMTROP).

Index

The letter *t* following a page number denotes a table.